ORNAMENTAL SHRUBS

Books by C. E. Lucas Phillips and Peter N. Barber

The Rothschild Rhododendrons
The Trees Around Us
Ornamental Shrubs

ORNAMENTAL SHRUBS

HARDY IN TEMPERATE CLIMATES

C. E. Lucas Phillips & Peter N. Barber

in association with
William Flemer III
of Princeton, N.J.

VNR VAN NOSTRAND REINHOLD COMPANY
NEW YORK CINCINNATI TORONTO LONDON MELBOURNE

Printed in Great Britain

Published by Van Nostrand Reinhold Company
135 West 50th Street, New York, NY 10020, USA

Van Nostrand Reinhold Limited
1410 Birchmount Road
Scarborough, Ontario M1P 2E7, Canada

CONTENTS

PART TWO

ILLUSTRATIONS

Photographs marked with an asterisk are by Valerie Finnis. Rose 'Golden Chernonese' is by courtesy of Mr E. F. Allen. The remainder are from the Harry Smith Horticultural Photographs Collection, except those marked with a dagger, which are from the author's collection. The line drawings are by J. A. Clary.

Colour Plates

following page 32

Photographs

Part I

Part II

Drawings

Other drawings will be found in or close to their appropriate texts in the Register

AUTHORITIES CONSULTED

This book is the outcome of our own experiences, observations and opinions, augmented and sometimes modified by leading authorities in various fields.

The chief published Authorities consulted have been:

Trees and Shrubs Hardy in the British Isles, by W. J. Bean, 8th edition (4 vols)
Manual of Trees and Shrubs, by Alfred Rehder (USA)
Manual of Trees and Shrubs, by Hillier and Sons
Shrubs and Vines for American Gardens, by Donald Wyman
Encyclopedia of Gardening, Royal Horticultural Society
The Pruning of Trees, Shrubs and Conifers, by George Brown (of Kew)
Pruning, by Christopher Brickell (RHS)
Shrubs for the Milder Counties, by W. Arnold-Forster

We are particularly indebted also to Mr William Flemer III, of Princeton, and Mr C. D. Brickell, BSc, VMH, Director of the Royal Horticultural Society's Garden, who have read nearly the whole of our manuscript, and to the following specialists in their subjects:

Mr Michael Haworth-Booth, hydrangeas
Major-General P. G. Turpin, CB, OBE, MA, heathers
Mr Douglas Chalk, NDH, hebes
Mr E. F. Allen, MA, shrub roses

We are further indebted to Mr Brickell for his kindness in having read the proofs of the book and making several valuable suggestions.

Other hands have also contributed by their knowledge of diverse climates and conditions.

Last, but very far from least, we jointly acknowledge our indebtedness to my dear wife, Barbara, for her painstaking typing of a long and difficult manuscript.

C. E. LUCAS PHILLIPS

PART ONE

I
SHRUBS AND PEOPLE

A S LIONS ASSEMBLE in prides, starlings in murmurations and geese in gaggles, so may we say that shrubs assemble in splendours; for, of all the works of nature, there are no greater congregations of splendour than these that are assembled in these pages.

Apart from the South Pole, thousands of feet deep in ice, there is virtually no land mass in which shrubs of one sort or another do not prosper. The deserts have their cacti and their thorny bushes, the lands of the Arctic Circle here and there break out in a froth of leaf and flower for a few brief weeks. Large expanses of the earth, however, still lie in an uneasy sleep, in expectation of an awakening by some far-seeing husbandman. So also do the material deserts of many a town and city hope that their municipal governors will rouse themselves from their thraldom to bricks and concrete. A harsher picture still is painted across all those countrysides where the merciless engineer has cut great swathes of concrete for new roads and airfields, with no regard to the amelioration of their "gross handiwork" by means of trees and shrubs.

Fortunately there are signs of an awakening and here and there men are beginning to rub the sleep and apathy from their eyes. In *The Trees Around Us* we have written at length on the value to the environment of the larger works of nature and here we enter a wider and more colourful field to pick its treasures for the same purpose. For the environment — by which we mean all those factors that affect the ecology of man and bestow upon him some alleviation from the cares or emptiness of life — is influenced not only by the plants of the countryside, but also by what is grown in private gardens, in the streets and squares of our towns and in the parks and concourses to which people daily resort. For such alleviations shrubs provide the most reposeful and heartening of tonics, whether in the splendour of a flowering camellia "startling the sloth of February" or in the Persian carpet of an expanse of heathers, or in the fragrance of a rose or a philadelphus.

The majority of public authorities are extremely laggard in this matter. Nearly all large industrial undertakings are worse, exposing their harsh artefacts naked to the world. When shrubs and trees do occur to them their choices are absurdly limited. Unlike the great landowners of old, who were far-seeing and open-handed, your municipal councillor and your lord of industry think only in terms of "instant gardening". How often in public places do you see a magnolia, a camellia, a crinodendron or a bed of heathers? Such shrubs as are planted are commonplace, quickly forgotten, left unpruned, unwatered and unprotected from vandals.

Thus it is usually the private gardener, on scales both large and small, who probably makes the best contribution to our environmental fund. Much of what he plants is seen and enjoyed by his neighbours and by the passer-by. Today gardeners are becoming more and more aware of the advantages of shrubs and their use is increasing widely. Undoubtedly they are the chief garden plants of the future. Apart from their intrinsic beauty, shrubs, with very few exceptions, need far less care than herbaceous and rock plants, not to speak of all those specialist plants that hold so many men and women in thrall — the bedding roses, delphiniums, sweet peas, dahlias, chrysanthemums and so on. These people will continue in their happy thraldom, but gardeners of wider horizons, whether in baronial acres or in cottage plots, are remodelling their Edens more and more to accommodate shrubs, which can, of course, consort happily with other plants, giving them a fresh force and purpose.

A prime reason for this is the expense and scarcity of paid labour. Today, many a man must be to a large extent his own gardener, and he finds that, once they are properly planted, shrubs in general need very little pruning or cossetting and are attacked by very few maladies. The garden hybrid roses, unfortunately, are the main exception to this generalization, but those with which we shall be concerned here are less trouble than the popular bedding varieties.

In addition to reduced maintenance — indeed, very often none at all — shrubs are designed by nature and man's art to bestow all kinds of favours. Together with trees, they form the background or matrix to the whole scene and are, indeed, essential for this purpose everywhere except in the tiniest plot. They form magnificent hedges and screens, whether on a boundary or between one part of a garden and another. They make splendid roadside plantings, both for the adornment of the scene and for baffling car headlights. Many serve as ideal windbreaks or filters, acting as nurses to plants that shiver under a cold blast or shrivel up in a hot one or are mutilated by the salt of ocean gales. The branches of many, sweeping down to the ground, overwhelm nearly all weeds, a function for which the creepy-crawly shrublets are also specifically designed.

To these varieties of purpose, shrubs add an enormous versatility of character, both practical and aesthetic. In their almost limitless range of form, colour, deportment and texture they satisfy even what Samuel Johnson called "the wild vicissitudes of taste". They may be evergreen or deciduous. They may be very small or very big. They may be light and dainty or clothed in a dense luxuriance of leaf and flower. They may display their splendours amid "winter's icy rages", as do the witch hazel, the winter-sweet, the mahonia and many heathers, or in the equatorial breath of high summer, as do the roses, the hibiscus, and the hypericum, as well as those born in warmer homelands. Their flowers may be sumptuous and borne in profusion, as in the azalea and the camellia, or dainty and charming, as in the sweet-scented daphne and the kolkwitzia.

In addition to flowers they may add sparkling and jewel-like fruits, as in the pernettya, the cotoneaster, the barberry and the holly. Some have no noticeable flowers but a tumbling abundance of beautiful foliage, as in the dwarf Japanese maple. Others have a strong architectural structure which is valuable in design, as in Maries' viburnum, David's buddleia, the sumach and the yucca. They may prosper in bogs, in hot sands, in stiff clay, in stony ground, the soft leaf-soil of woodlands, in acid peat or in lime. We have but to match the plant to the soil and the elements, avoiding the temptation of planting something we may covet in conditions which are hostile to it and bearing in mind always Alexander Pope's exhortation to consult "the genius of the place" in all.

In foliage alone shrubs come very near rivalling all the hues of the painter's palette, so much so that a garden could be marvellously colourful with no flowers at all. Green is evident in all its wide range of tints. Gold, silver, blue, purple and even pink are there. Scarlet and orange appear in many of the heathers when "icicles hang by the wall". Parti-coloured leaves abound, either splashed or margined gold or silver, or suffused with blue or pewter, or even, as in the fuchsia 'Versicolor' and the hypericum 'Tricolor', charmingly composed of pink, gold and pale green. One may say, indeed, that in the composition of the garden picture, foliage is the first consideration.

Because of these wide variations, very often within one genus (viburnums, for example, differ largely from each other), you should take every opportunity to see plants in growth, and preferably in their prime. Descriptions in books do not always tell you the full story; those in catalogues almost never do. Pictures can be misleading. So haunt the big botanic gardens, where plants are usually well labelled. Haunt the gardens that are "open to the public" (where labels are often lacking). Haunt the best tree and shrub nurseries, pick your own plant and put a label on it. Subscribe to the leading societies, especially the Royal Horticultural Society and the American Horticultural Society.

On the debit side arguments against the use of shrubs are few. Compared with the general run of herbaceous plants, bedding roses, the small pearls of the rock garden, annuals and bulbs, they are relatively dear and many are rather slow of growth, so that large gaps yawn between them when first planted, giving a warm invitation to eager weeds. Various defensive stratagems are open to us, which we shall discuss in Chapter 5.

In this book we shall attempt, as far as we can within our restricted acreage of words, to provide for all situations except extreme abnormalities, and shall have always before us the purpose of creating pictures that will give balm to the spirit and some repose from the fevers of the world. In a special section we shall consider the reclamation of desolate places. Our vision extends to the embellishment of a whole countryside and to the public park, but will be focused chiefly on the private garden.

Our net will be spread widely, but it cannot possibly cover the whole vast array of shrubs that nature and man have provided. Obviously, we shall omit anything that assumes the proportions of a "tree", a term that is not without ambiguity, for a holly or an eucryphia may be a shrub in some gardens but become trees in others. So, also, one genus may embrace both shrub-like and tree-like species, as in the magnolia, which in *M.stellata* seldom grows more than 9ft high, but in *campbellii* and *grandiflora* become towering specimens, higher than many a house. By horticultural definition a "shrub" is a perennial plant with several permanent woody stems above ground; there are also "sub-shrubs", in which the lower part of the stem is woody but the upper part soft or herbaceous, as in rue, cotton-lavender and the Russian sage (Perovskia).

Against some candidates for inclusion, we have had regretfully to harden our hearts. Thus there will be very little about conifers and there will be no climbers. There will be none of the pygmy darlings that enchant the heart of the rock gardener, nor any prostrate crawlers, but, where they are useful to our purpose, we shall include some of the dwarf species of the larger shrubs, as in barberries and hypericums. Some of these come within the compass of Chapter 5. We have not, however, excluded all things that are small, because it is impossible to write about shrubs without considering the impressive value of heathers.

GARDENERS' JARGON

In our splendour of shrubs, as set out in the Register, we shall be addressing a mixed multitude. We have assumed that you, Reader, are not a complete novice and have a basic acquaintance with the chief precepts of garden husbandry and its commoner terms. We shall expect you to know the chief constituents of soils, how to dig and hoe and prune and to propagate simple things and to have ceased to be frightened by the so-called "Latin" names of plants. You will know the difference between a growth bud and a flower bud and you must certainly know what is meant by a "species". A lady, now dead, who won considerable eminence as a gardener, thought that it was the plural of "specie".

On the other hand we have thought it a mistake to go to the opposite extreme and to suppose that we are addressing persons of profound experience. Our purpose is to encourage the knowledge and love of shrubs among gardeners generally and we shall avoid botanical terms that are not generally understood, such as rachis, peduncle, imbricate, ciliate, tomentum and so on; but some are unavoidable and their meanings are given in the glossary at the end of the book. To save a lot of explanation, it is quite important to know what is meant by such words as inflorescence, panicle, bract and clone (very important), but of less importance to distinguish between a spike (as in

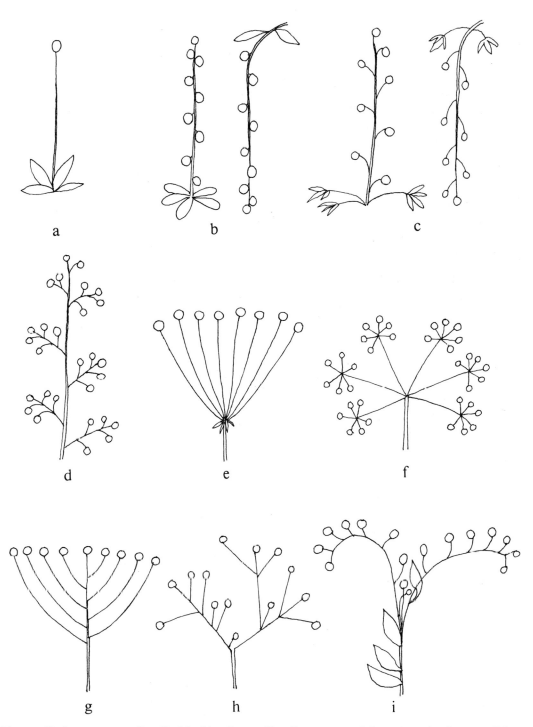

1.   Types of inflorescence or floral habit. (*a*) solitary; (*b*) spikes, erect and drooping, the florets stalkless; (*c*) racemes, erect and drooping, the florets shortly stalked; (*d*) panicle, being a branched raceme; (*e*) umbel; (*f*) compound umbel; (*g*) corymb; (*h*) dichotomous cyme; (*i*) scorpoid cyme, *see further in* Glossary

lavender) and a raceme (as in lupins), or between an umbel, a corymb and a cyme, which are just bunches of differing constructions. As Dr W. T. Stearn has said in his book *Botanical Latin*, "it is more important to be understood than to conform to botanical standards".

Thus we shall often use informal terms of everyday speech, but the value of botanical terms does sometimes appear in such names as Hydrangea paniculata or Rhododendron racemosum, which describe how they differ from others of their kinds. On the other hand the earnest gardener who seeks to be "correct" can easily become bemused by the controversies of botanists themselves, as we shall find here, for example, in the names of certain lilacs and junipers. In all such cases what really matters is not the botanical name but the clonal, varietal or cultivar one. Thus you will be on safe ground if, among camellias, for example, you say simply 'Donation', without going through the whole rigmarole.

In leaves one should recognise what is meant by pinnate, but whether a leaf is serrate, serrulate, incised or dentate concerns mainly the expert and the botanist; to most of us it is sufficient to say that they are saw-edged or toothed. When the fruit of a plant has the outward appearance of a berry, we shall use that term, though it may be technically a drupe or a pome.

Likewise we shall not always use the term "cultivar" where a strict botanist would, but shall often instead say "variety", as expressly permitted by the *International Code* governing these matters. Even botanists have their differences!

We have been much exercised in our minds whether our pages should be "plagued with an itching leprosy" of italics. Many readers find them irritating and smacking of technological cultism, and so skip them. Italics are merely a botanist's convention, and a recent one, and they trip up one's reading. We think them silly and pretentious, possibly having some validity in a botanical treatise, but none in horticultural use. We do not write people's name in italics and even botanical works list the names of plants in thick Roman type. As Somerset Maugham said, one should write as one speaks in polite society.

However, fearing schoolmasterly wrath, we have been rather cowardly about this and have in great part submitted to the new orthodoxy in our Register, especially when we think that italics serve a useful purpose, as for example, to distinguish between a natural "variety" of the wild (in italics) and a variety (or "cultivar") arising in cultivation (in Roman). But we make no excuses for our inconsistency and shall go as we please. See more in Appendix B.

In the Register of Shrubs we shall employ the latest orthodox names of plants as far as we know them, but cannot promise that we shall always submissively swallow the new concoctions that certain botanists are always trying to pour down our throats. Indeed, botanical names are changing as we write. A name that is generally recognisable is what is important. See, for example, what is said under the syringa (lilac) popularly known as "Palibiniana".

We shall also use the vernacular names of shrubs that are of long standing and well known by all, such as maple, lilac, dogwood and so on; but we shall eschew most of those new and fancy names that have usually been invented by journalists (chiefly American) who underestimate the intelligence of their readers and that are not generally accepted and are often of only local use. "Rock rose" and "sun rose" mean different things to different people. In Britain the "rose-of-Sharon" is Hypericum calycinum, but in America it is sometimes Hibiscus syriacus. Vernacular names that are fairly generally accepted are listed in the Register and such of the fancy ones as we have been able to catch in our net are in the Index.

As a final note to these preliminaries, we should warn you, Reader, that not all of the plants in this book are readily obtainable, certainly not from your little local nursery, which may be very good but whose stock is necessarily limited. Always go to the top-class nurseries and even among these you will have to "shop around". For some genera, notably rhododendrons and roses, the specialist nurseries are usually the best hunting-grounds. Get in plenty of catalogues, but beware of their plant naming. Quite understandably, many nurseries do not use what the botanist considers to be the latest "correct" names; we shall often give acceptable synonyms best known to gardeners, but cannot possibly record all.

To American readers we should point out that in Britain and many other countries the term "evergreen" is not confined to conifers but includes any shrub or tree that retains its foliage, that "vine" means only the grape-vine and that "secateurs" are one-handed shears.

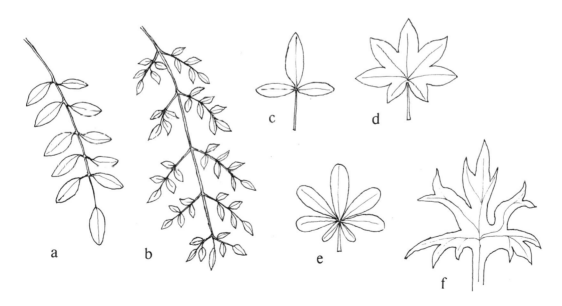

2. Compound leaves. (*a*) pinnate; (*b*) bi-pinnate or doubly pinnate; (*c*) trifoliate; (*d*) palmate; (*e*) digitate or compound palmate; (*f*) pedate

2
DESIGN AND DISPLAY

THE CHIEF FACTORS that we have to consider at the very beginning are:

> Personal predilections
> Climate (see next chapter)
> Aspect
> Soil (Chapter 4)

Of personal predilections we can say very little. If your heart is engaged to roses, dahlias, alpines or other specialities, your conception of your Eden is likely to be dominated by their particular needs. Every man should have the kind of garden that he likes, but a little analysis of what has made other gardens beautiful may perhaps persuade him that his first ideas may not be the best. We think, with William Shenstone, the gardener-poet, that our prime purpose should be "to stimulate the imagination", however small the scale. We must think also of shrubs not as things apart, but also holding converse with trees, herbaceous perennials and annuals in all their gaiety and grace.

We shall assume that the plot is a new one and unencumbered. Even if it is an existing garden, experience shows that its design and its contents are best mentally ignored and the garden redesigned according to one's desire, retaining only those features that fit one's own ideas. Be not enslaved by those of your predecessor in tenure. Paths, for example, are often all wrong. On the other hand, some noble tree, a charming pool or a sumptuous magnolia may so captivate your eye that it will sway your whole outlook. Apart from such overriding influences, however, it is best to stride out into the new territory ruthlessly, axe in hand. "Woodman spare that tree" is a nice philosophy, but it is equally important that the tree should not dominate your conception of the whole tableau. From the very beginning you must be master of the garden, not its slave.

ASPECT

The aspect of the ground or garden in relation to the points of the compass may dictate one's initial assessment of the lay-out. Though there are plenty of shrubs that enjoy some shade, the majority display their attractions best in the sun. Thus in the northern hemisphere that side of the house, or other viewpoint, that faces north gives the best view of the plants, since in whole or in part they will face the sun. Conversely a room facing south may show the plants at their least colourful, but this is not always so, especially for plants that like some shade. Think also of the relationship of one plant to another, since a sun-loving plant may not do its best if it is itself in the shade of a plant on its south side.

LAY-OUT

Design may also be governed at the start by the shape of the garden or ground. A simple square presents no difficulties, but other forms of rectangle, especially the broad, short garden, make one think hard, so also, of course, may the garden that is of an odd shape. The desires and ambitions of most people will usually be best satisfied by making the vista as long as possible. If the garden itself has no great length, the object can be achieved by what I call the "swung axis", diverting it, for example, from the south-west to the north-east, as shown in the sketch in Fig. 3.

Another highly effective stratagem, especially in short, broad gardens, is the "bent axis", as in Fig. 4. This is a very telling method for the use of evergreen shrubs, for it is one of the best means of creating that most desirable element in all gardens, whether private or public — the element of surprise, as valuable in the garden as on the battlefield. You see before you a curving path, its extremity hidden, and you are

3.   Outline idea of the swung axis

4.   Outline of the general idea of the "bent axis" for a short, broad garden

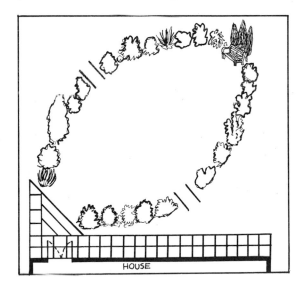

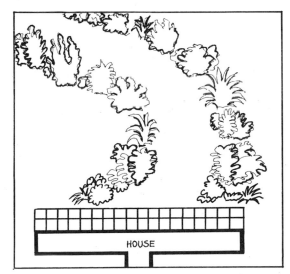

enticed to walk round it to discover what lies beyond. These are the kinds of lay-out that "stimulate the imagination".

With these few initial governing or limiting factors, the lay-out can be devised in any number of ways, but one should think first of keeping it simple. No fuss. No wriggles. No confusion to the eye. Let all the curves be gentle and flowing, such as will be as easy to the mower as to the eye. Straight lines are often appropriate, but as a rule the lines of the geometrician are less satisfying than those of the artist; this is especially valid in a small garden, in which gentle curves create the illusion of increasing its size. They also create a sense of rhythm and an illusion of movement. The mile-long vista, however, is quite certainly the thing for a straight line, so also is any setting, large or small, which is fortunate enough to have a glimpse of the sea or the open countryside or a noble building in the distance. None of these should be obscured by shrubs or trees. Nor should that other delectable situation which is occasionally offered in a larger panorama — the brow of a hill, ridge or slope. Here shrubs and trees should flank an avenue, broad or narrow, with nothing beyond but the open sky. Happy is the gardener who is given such an opportunity, for he may then claim the whole landscape as his own. For a like reason, do not, for heaven's sake, shut off the view of a pastoral scene.

All this is not intended to gainsay entirely the merits of a formal garden composed on a matrix of straight lines. One loses rhythm and acquires rigidity, but sometimes this suits the house and the situation. Much depends, not only on one's taste, but also what is to be grown. A strict formality agrees well with bedding roses, dahlias, delphiniums and so on, but it is ill-suited to the character of most shrubs. In large and fairly large grounds there is a lot to be said for what the French call a "goose-foot" (Fig. 5) design, in which, emerging from the house, you see a semi-circle of grass (forming a small "open centre"), wherefrom a number of avenues branch off like the toes of a goose or the rays of the sun. This is quite an entertaining plan, very suitable indeed to shrubs and trees, but it calls for some focal point of the main alley at least. The goose-foot, of course, needs rather more than an acre. To emphasize the perspective put the largest shrubs nearest the house and the smaller at the distant end.

We have thought so far of integrated gardens (or large expanses) that are all in one piece. Very often, however, all sorts of delights can be created by dividing the garden into two or more kingdoms or satraps, as did the emperors and Caesars of old. This was charmingly done, for example, by Major Lawrence Johnson, the American who settled in England near the end of the last century (and served in the British Army) and who later devised that beautiful and much-visited garden at Hidcote, not far from Stratford-upon-Avon. Many such examples can now be seen in the great gardens of the world. Sometimes even quite small gardens can be divided with very good effect.

Shrubs are the natural material for such divisions. The usual and most obvious example is where the pleasure garden is separated from the orchard or the kitchen garden, but the flower garden itself can be enchantingly divided into separate little

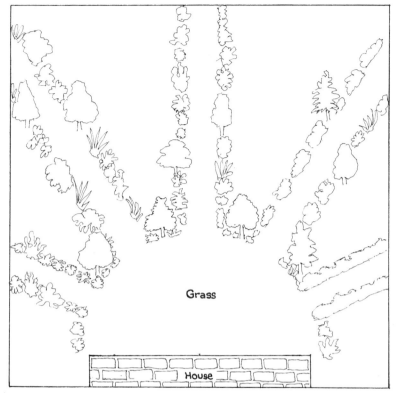

5.   Outline of the "goosefoot", a French design for a larger garden

The garden of repose, "exempt from public haunt". Sternfield House

realms, again satisfying the tactical doctrine of surprise. One realm may be given to roses, another to a lily pool, a third to a rock garden, a fourth to a sitting-out place in which "to weave the garlands of repose" or "make sweet solace to oneself alone", paved with stone and furnished with an arbour embowered with honeysuckle or roses. All will be embraced and garlanded by shrubs, of size and character conformable to the scale of the whole prospect and preferably scented.

THE GARDEN PICTURE

Returning to the more intimate scene, the aim must be to paint a "garden picture", as prescribed for us by so many of the best practitioners ever since gardens ceased to be merely utilitarian and began to wear an aesthetic dress, nearly four hundred years ago. Alexander Pope, William Shenstone and the architect Sir John Vanbrugh were united in declaring that the best man to design a garden was a landscape painter. To paint a picture satisfactorily demands obedience to some disciplines which may be inborn in a heaven-sent genius but which in others means a little thought. Only occasionally, because the gardener is endowed with a natural instinct, does one see a haphazard garden of genuine charm.

By an analysis of the most beautiful gardens, large and small, we may deduce certain simple precepts that will start us on the right path. The first is to keep the centre open. Do not clutter up the middle distance. The centre is usually of grass, but it may be of water and in tiny town gardens it may be of paving or gravel. Beyond and around this open centre you build up what William Chambers called "rich, harmonious masses" of green foliage; and this is where nothing but shrubs will serve.

The rich, harmonious masses need not, of course, provide merely a clothing of the periphery. Shrubs may encroach towards the interior to form clusters or headlands or strong-points or hedges. They may stretch in bank upon bank around the open centre, separated by paths or be grouped as colonies in those parts of the garden that lie away from the centre.

A third precept for painting the picture is that of mass or concentration of force. The circumstances of gardens vary considerably, but it may be said, by way of example, that, if you have but three hydrangeas, plant them all together, not dotted about separately. If you have a hundred, deploy them in platoons of 25 or 50. Heathers in particular must be massed if you are to get the best value out of their special charms, whether the mass be of ten or of a thousand. But the doctrine of mass is modified by that of scale. Only in the largest expanses would you plant a quantity of Rhododendron arboreum, or Cotoneaster 'Cornubia' or magnolias or elaeagnus. These are best used singly as accent notes among shrubs of lesser stature or in other special situations where they will stimulate the imagination or emphasize a feature or conceal some undesired object. Certain small shrubs also expect to be placed as solitary specimens, especially the dwarf Japanese maples, whose delicate, filigree leaves must have their companions chosen with as much care as a solicitous mother would bestow on her only darling.

More obviously, scale means also that the chosen plants should bear some relationship to the size of the property. A mass of midgets in a five-acre garden would be as ridiculous as a dozen giants in a garden of a few square yards. The whole picture should have balance, good proportions and unity.

All this designing of the lay-out needs planning on squared paper, proceeding from a first rough idea to a scale drawing. If there is a lot of work to be done, make first a simple, basic plan, which must be very firm and final but to which you can add minor modifications, refinements and additions in the future. Bear in mind that there may be some failures and that your own ideas are liable to change. When converting the plan from paper to earth, your gently flowing curves are easily marked out in the first instance by a reel of twine, preferably white or otherwise pale of hue for better visibility, or by a long, flexible garden hose. You will often find that the paper curves have to be slightly modified on the ground, as the view in perspective is likely to differ from the view in plan. Indeed, the best place from which to plan the lay-out is from a bedroom window, but remember that the garden picture is multi-dimensional and that, as you walk about, the back of a garden bed may be as important as its front. So also, as you look athwart the scene.

MATCHING PLANTS TO THE SOIL

Our detailed choice of shrubs will normally be delayed until after we have sketched the lay-out, but very often we shall have a pretty firm idea from the very beginning of what we most wish to grow. Your rhododendron fancier, for example, will certainly decide that these shall dominate the garden, if there is a suitable soil for them. Apart from such special partialities, our choice of shrubs is likely to be strongly influenced right at the start by local factors. It is too early in our appreciation to go into details, which we do in Chapter 3 and 4, but at the outset we must be careful that, whatever the other conditions, the shrub and the soil suit each other. The shrub must match whatever soil there is. As Pope tells us: "If vain our toil we ought to blame the culture not the soil." It is useless, for example, to plant rhododendrons in a very limy soil, brooms in a watery hollow or hydrangeas in a parched and over-heated sand.

WOODLANDS

One of the most enchanting types of garden, where it can be contrived, is a woodland one, a little removed from the house. The larger the better, of course, but even in quite small plots the thing can be done. When a boy, I (the senior author), lived in a house with scarcely a quarter of an acre, but even there a little belt of woodland flourished, peacefully enjoyed by the parents and an adventurous playground for the young. In cordial alliance with a few trees, large or small according to the scale, shrubs of many kinds, especially those that enjoy some shade from the sun and others that find

A woodland glade in a garden at Eastcote

comfort from overhead protection from frost, find the most congenial of homes and about their feet you can adorn the scene still further with primroses, violets, woodland anemones, hellebores, trilliums and all manner of herbaceous delights and bulbs of every hue. Here will melodious birds sing madrigals, the leaves whisper their roundelays and, when all is established and the fleet-footed groundlings have woven their thick carpets over the earth, the gardener can throw away his hoe. In woodland that is large enough you may leave some open glades, into which the sun will pour as into an open casement.

THE WINTER TEST
It has been said by some authority that the test of a well-designed garden is how it looks in winter. There is some truth in this, if we disregard the aspirations of the specialist under the thraldom of some particular fancy of his own, notably roses, irises,

delphiniums, sweet-peas and similar delights. All such specialist gardens are apt to be rather dreary spectacles out of their due seasons, in which the plants have "nothing but their nudity", unless moderated by some other influence. Faults in design are certainly shown up in winter. In the blaze of summer's wealth, when our gardens "gay wardrobes wear", the eye may well be bewitched by a Joseph's coat of flowers, but when the Zodiac wanes and "milk comes frozen home in pail" the plants are reduced to mere sticks or have disappeared entirely below ground, so that the picture will be unbecoming if the plantings have been haphazard or chancy.

We insist upon "the picture" and the picture must have a design. Shrubs (with some trees) are the best of all materials for such a purpose. Even if only deciduous shrubs are used we can enjoy, not only the beauty of the flowers in their seasons, but also the architecture of skeletal shapes in their diverse forms, as in the conjunction of the erect and the horizontal. Such an effect is created, for example, with the erect stems of the red-barked dogwoods or the slim varieties of some barberries, with the wide-spreading tabulation of Maries' viburnum. The arching, ostrich plumes of the rose 'Nevada' look lovely when frosted and their elegance is emphasized when they are accompanied by the dwarfer forms of barberry, daphne or broom. There must always be a tree or two, however small, according to the scale of the garden. The tracery of the naked branches and twigs against the sky, or even among bricks and mortar, is often delightful to the discerning eye.

Better still, of course, is to include some evergreen shrubs of rich foliage to form a backdrop of the floral drama. In the harsher climates, such as the prairie states of North America, conifers may be the only answer, but elsewhere the broad-leaved evergreens provide a rich treasury on which to build up a garden fortune.

In addition to these mere outlines, many charming shrubs come into full bloom in winter. The witch hazel becomes thronged with its golden tassels, the mahonias throw out their golden sprays, several viburnums open pink-tinted snowballs, the shrubby species of honeysuckle distil their perfume from cream florets, and several varieties of Williams' hybrid camellia and Camellia sasanqua also richly "warm the cold bosom of the hoary year". Above all, however, there are the winter heaths — Erica carnea in its many varieties, the hybrid darleyensis and the taller E. mediterranea (now labelled erigena). These bloom in prodigal profusion more or less all winter and early spring, flooding the garden in various shades of red and pink or in white; many of them are dressed also in golden foliage, illuminating the garden as with pools of sunshine.

Try to plan all these and other winter-flowering shrubs where you can see them from the house or where you habitually walk in your comings and goings. Few people, other than the gardener himself, will make a special expedition in the chill of the year to see a witch hazel or a patch of heather far away. The winter scene becomes more enchanting still if the feet of the taller shrubs stand among plantations of the winter hellebores or Christmas roses or are studded with snowdrops, winter crocuses and the little, gleaming winter aconite, while, standing guard above them all is the winter-flowering cherry, Prunus subhirtella autumnalis, in its robes of white or pink.

SLOPES, BANKS AND HUMMOCKS

Happy the man whose plot is not entirely level, provided that it is not rude, mountain-goat country. Gentle or moderately steep slopes have marvellous "capabilities", as the immortal Lancelot Brown would have said, though transverse slopes, athwart the plot, demand some designing skill and artful scheming. Hummocks and tumbling banks open the way to dwarf and creeping shrubs and to others that will swoop down them. The matter, with its almost infinite variations, is outside our scope here, beyond observing that the terrain may be artificially terraced, with little walls and ironed-out levels, or it may be left in its natural form (where mowing will be a problem). In both such situations and in mountain-goat places the tumbling shrubs are good answers to the gardener's prayer, particularly Forsythia suspensa, the winter jasmine (Jasminum nudiflorum) and the various prostrate junipers and roses, as well as shrubs that have a pendulous, broadly arching

Small shrubs to soften outline of steps

deportment, such as the unique Genista lydia, the camellia 'Lady Clare' and that splendour in blue, Ceanothus thyrsiflorus repens, unsatisfactorily known by some as the "creeping blue blossom".

On steep and difficult banks in danger of erosion shrubs that extend themselves by suckers or by stolons serve well to stabilise and clothe the soil. Some are decorative as well as useful, such as Rosa virginiana, the Rugosa roses (especially in sandy places), bamboos, some barberries, amelanchiers, dogwood, several spiraeas, the big sorbarias or false spiraeas and brambles of the choicer sorts. Plenty more will be found in these pages, some of them merely utilitarian.

In large gardens, parks and the open landscape the prime ordinance is to follow the natural rhythm of the terrain and not to run counter to it. At all costs avoid solid rectangles splayed across ridges or spurs. Contrasts between high ground and low can be most impressive, as by planting the spurs or ribs or knobs with evergreen shrubs and the lower ground with deciduous ones, or the other way round. In each differing elevation keep to plants that are sympathetic to one another, or even to a single genus, as you can very happily do with rhododendrons, pieris, heathers, pernettyas and their like; indeed, one may say that this is ideal designing. In flat places mixed plantings are entirely acceptable.

PLANT PARTNERSHIPS

When we come to "plant associations" we tread on difficult ground. There is a terrible risk of becoming "arty" or affected or pretentious. We are on fairly safe ground if we keep plants of the same family together, as in the *Ericaceae*, which includes rhododendrons (and azaleas), heathers, the berried pernettyas, kalmias, the sumptuous pieris, gaultherias and many more, but such a practice savours of the botanical purist and is seldom possible or even one to our liking, although it is worth bearing in mind that birds of similar feathers like to flock together. So we shall issue no commandments but merely make suggestions. What is perhaps most important of all is to think first of diverse shapes and foliage before deciding on flowers; for many shrubs, especially among the evergreens, have foliage quite as colourful as flowers. Make your garden picture one in which, "though all things differ, all agree".

Where there is room put some engaging shrub in front of those which, however enchanting when in flower, are of no distinction in the garden picture at other times. Such plants include the larger hybrid lilacs (though the smaller ones are never dowdy), forsythias, Rosa moyesii and other roses of somewhat gaunt bearing, the winter-sweet (Chimonanthus fragrans or praecox), Viburnum carlesii, the clerodendrums and the witch hazels. In some opinions the same would be said of "hardy hybrid" rhododendrons when *en masse*, but there are plenty of rhododendrons with distinguished and elegant foliage.

If the garden is large enough, try to cover the whole cycle of the Zodiac, which is not at all difficult, for there are plenty of shrubs that, whether in flower or in beautiful foliage, will span the months from January to December. In smaller plots an almost continuous display from March to September can be contrived with camellias, flowering (or Japanese) quinces, evergreen and deciduous azaleas, roses and hydrangeas. Where the climate allows what could be better? Nor is September the end, for in October some of the heathers will still be in bloom and then come the berry-bearing shrubs, mahonias, more camellias where the weather is mild, and finally, just about Christmas, the witch hazels.

Since personal tastes differ so profoundly, and since there is an even greater danger of becoming arty, we shall have little to say about colour associations. What woman would combine scarlet and purple in her dress? Yet in the fuchsia nature combines them convincingly. We decline to lay down any rules and to say that this colour does not go with that. We find no objection whatever to planting the rhododendron 'Purple Splendour' next to the scarlet 'Britannia'. Green unifies all and each man must please himself.

There are, however, a few guiding lights that may help us in our choices. The first is not to overpower some delicate tint with a violent one that flowers at the same time. Use fierce colours as occasional accent notes. Exclude bright reds, orange and purple from the more distant scene and plant them rather nearer to the house. As Mr Sheaphard, the distinguished architect, has said, they "burn holes" in the background of the garden picture. If you possibly can, contrive a partnership of blues and yellows, whether in flowers or foliage. This is a classic and always charming partnership, as you will find by putting the blue-rinsed rue, the steely blue conifer 'Boulevard', the silvery-blue Euryops among golden heathers, or, where "the genius of the place" is a genial one, the sumptuous fremontodendron 'California Glory' with a blue abutilon or a purple sumach.

Try always to include some shrubs with silvery or pearly-grey foliage, such as the artemisias, the cotton-lavender, Senecio 'Sunshine', Euryops acraeus, or, in the larger scene, the oleaster (Elaeagnus angustifolia) and Buddleia fallowiana. Place these silver plants (for preference) where they will abate the exuberance of fierce colours. They make the happiest of consorts also for shrubs of coloured foliage, such as the plum-leaved varieties of the Venetian sumach (Cotinus coggygria), the purple of the Ottawa barberry or the bronze of Thunberg's barberry and its prettily variegated offspring.

Golden-leaved shrubs are also of great value, as in the gilded forms of elderberry, philadelphus, elaeagnus, heathers, usually more beautiful than their flowers, as well as the golden conifers. Nearly all, however (the golden forms of elaeagnus being notable exceptions), must be planted in full sun, which seems, as it were, to drain out some of the chlorophyll without doing any harm other than diminishing the size of the plant. Plant them in shade and they become green, with a full flow of chlorophyll.

Do not, however, over-plant the scene with gold, and be especially cautious in excessively hot places and in "continental" climates, such as the mid and east zones of

PLATE I: *opposite*, The winter picture. Early February in the garden of co-author Brigadier Lucas Phillips. In the foreground is the procumbent form of the blue spruce, Picea pungens. Beyond are mainly heathers and small conifers

PLATE 2: *opposite*: Abutilon × suntense

PLATE 3: *above*, Buddleia fallowiana 'Lochinch';
right, Ceanothus 'Gloire de Versailles'

PLATE 4: *opposite*, Pieris japonica 'Variegata'

PLATE 5: *right*, Dipelta floribunda; *below*,
Coronilla emerus

PLATE 6: Camellias: *above left*, 'Tricolor'; *above right*, C × w. 'Barbara Lucas Phillips' in January; *left*, 'Donation'; *above*, C. saluenenis

PLATE 7: *opposite*, Chamaecyparis obtusa 'Crippsii' watches over a bed of mixed heathers and the silver-blue of Euryops acraeus in the garden of Brigadier Lucas Phillips. *See also* PLATE 10

PLATE 8: *opposite above*, Ceanothus thyrsiflorus
'Repens'; *opposite below*, Bupleurum fruticosum

PLATE 9: *right*, Cantua buxifolia (a bit larger than
life); *below*, Hibiscus syriacus 'Blue Bird'

PLATE II: Close-up of Embothrium 'Norquinco'

PLATE IO: *opposite above left*, Caryopteris
clandonensis; *below left*, Cornus alba
'Elegantissima'; *above right*, Perovskia atriplicifolia;
below right, Euryops acraeus

PLATE 12: Some daphnes. *above left*, D. retusa; *centre*, D. 'Somerset'; *left*, D. collina; *above*, D. cneorum 'Eximia'

PLATE 13: *opposite*, Fremontodendron 'California Glory'

PLATE 14: *above*, 'Thalia', an example of the triphylla style of fuchsias; *left*, Mahonia 'Lionel Fortescue'

PLATE 15: *opposite*, summer in the garden of author Lucas Phillips. Mainly heathers, conifers, silver-rimmed holly and a young tree of the golden Robinia pseudoacacia 'Frisia'

North America, where the gleaming tints so beautiful in the equable summers of Western Europe and the Pacific north-west of America are apt to be dried out to a dirty brown by the fierce heat of summer. The golden hybrid privet, Ligustrum 'Vicaryi', is an exception, defying the sun, and so, among conifers, are the elegant Chamaecyparis obtusa 'Crippsii' and C.pisifera 'Aurea' and a few others. But the beautiful gilded yews and the like-coloured "needled" conifers that look so well in Britain and in western North America lose their golden touch.

HOUSES AND WALLS

Since the house is the dominant feature of most gardens, we must certainly embrace it in our design. The nature of the house — whether cottage, mansion, Victorian villa or modern — may well influence the design and the choice of plants. We may question, for example, whether the sophisticated rhododendrons are suited to the native simplicity of an antique cottage, which generally looks best with an apparently haphazard mingling of soft colours, but the hideosity of many sham Italian Victorian villas needs livening up with bright colours and luxuriant foliage. Houses of particular architectural distinction are best left entirely naked, that they may be admired in their pure forms. Who would clothe the Parthenon with Virginia creeper? In general, however, we are sure that the garden should march forward to embrace the house, giving unity to the whole home, for the home is house-and-garden together. Avoid, therefore, "too sudden a translation from architecture to horticulture".

Our first consideration is usually for climbing plants such as ivies, roses, wisterias, vines and so on, but we are not concerned with them in this book. The house and other garden walls and structures, however, provide a splendid background for many a shrub and may indeed clamour for concealment. Garages, sheds and other outbuildings need to be decently clothed. In the north temperate zones walls that face south or west are ideally suited for the less hardy shrubs, of which we shall see a good many of great beauty. Shrubs that need a climate of Zone 8, for example, will prosper against a warm wall in Zone 7 or even Zone 6. Abutilons, the gorgeous fremontia 'California Glory', crinodendrons, several ceanothus, Carpenteria californica, Daphne odora, the holly-like desfontainia, myrtles, the lemon-scented verbena and the pretty New Zealand "tea tree" (Leptospermum scoparium) are a few random examples. Camellias are quite safe on a wall in Zone 7 at least.

Many shrubs, both hardy and not-hardy, when planted near a wall, will lean towards it and extend their stature, as do, for example, the pyracantha and the cotoneaster. It is amusing also to see how the handsomely coloured varieties of Euonymus fortunei will quickly turn towards a nearby wall and, having touched it, behave like an ivy and cling to it.

In all wall plantings be careful about windows. Only the smaller shrubs should go immediately below them. Others must be planted in between pairs of windows and

PLATE 16: *opposite*, Genista aethnensis, the Mount Etna broom, at Cranborne Manor

33

one of the disadvantages of the modern over-fenestrated house is that only the most slender plants can be fitted in, the most suitable being such slender roses as 'Golden Showers', 'Aloha', 'Mme Pierre Oger' and some other Bourbons.

ISOLATION

So far we have been talking about agglomerations of shrubs. Very often, however, we shall feel the need of some shrub in splendid isolation in a lawn or elsewhere. Almost any shrub, of course, can be so used, but we shall normally prefer one that has some special beauty of outline or of foliage, with or without floral adornment. As we have seen earlier, the dwarf Japanese maples, with their delicate foliage and elegant deportment, are outstanding for this purpose.

Other very good choices (although small trees are usually to be preferred) are the dazzling embothriums, cornus, sumachs, any of the pieris according to scale (especially the beautifully tinted P. japonica 'Variegata'), the wide-spreading Maries and Lanarth viburnums, Buddleia alternifolia when trained as a small tree, magnolias, the brilliantly golden-leaved forms of elaeagnus for a distant view and the choicer sorts of conifers. Of these the embothriums, pieris, elaeagnus and most conifers are evergreen and the golden varieties of elaeagnus are superlative in winter, seeming to illuminate the scene with sunshine. Of conifers, smaller varieties of the blue spruce (Picea pungens), the small thuja 'Rheingold' and the slim Irish yew (Taxus baccata 'Fastigiata', particularly the gilded form) are perhaps the first choices, apart from larger sorts. The steely-blue cypress 'Boulevard' is a great temptation, but becomes ragged when more than 3ft high.

3
THE ELEMENTS

Our ideas and choices are likely to be strongly influenced by natural elements beyond our control, though we may be able to moderate them. These elements include the climate, the altitude and the degree of exposure, apart from the different elements of the soil. This chapter, we fear, may well read like a catalogue of imminent calamities, but, like a good general, we must assess the hazards before planning our battle. Sometimes one element cancels out or modifies another, but we must not challenge the genius of the place with excessive audacity.

"Fear no more the heat o' the sun, Nor the furious winter's rages". Nothing is more beautiful than an almond blossom enclosed in a capsule of ice or the silvery filigree of twigs sheathed in hoar frost. Winds, whether gentle lullabies or angry hymns of hate, bring movement and music to the garden and are "not so unkind as man's ingratitude". The sun gives heart to men and plants. Shade mitigates its excesses and gives a quiet charm to the whole garden picture.

COLD-HARDINESS

This is the most critical of all the elements affecting the garden, though it may be moderated by other factors. The cold-hardiness of the shrubs which we shall be considering in the Register varies enormously, from the sub-arctic to the sub-tropic. Their degrees of susceptibility to frost have been classified by a zonal system originally evolved by the Arnold Arboretum for North America, which we have previously adapted to Europe also. These temperature zones range from Zone 1, in which plants will stand temperatures as low as −50°F, to Zone 10, which embraces plants that will barely stand any degree below freezing-point. Maps displaying these zones are on pp 58–59.

Generally speaking, a plant that will survive in a very low temperature will survive and even greatly improve in a higher one, but this is not always so, for they may languish and expire in heat, especially heat untempered by rain, as do some of the far-north American conifers, the sugar maple and the white canoe-bark birch; these, indeed, are seldom happy in any climate warmer than Zone 7, though in Britain and adjacent parts of Europe they do well in Zone 8.

It may be platitudinous to say that (in the northern hemisphere) the south is warm and the north cold, but this is not always so, for altitudes and local air currents exert strong influences. The higher the altitude the lower the temperature, the later the spring and the earlier the autumn. A plant that is hardy at sea-level may succumb at 1,000ft. On the west coast of Scotland and even in York (which is well inland but almost at sea-level) they grow such superlative shrubs as the desfontainia and the crinodendron that no one would dare to grow at high altitudes. On the other hand, temperatures in large towns and beside the sea tend to be a little higher than in the country and inland. The British Isles as a whole and slices of western Europe are greatly blessed by the warm Gulf Stream from Mexico that caresses its shores and pervades its atmosphere inland. An extreme example of variations within a particular zone is provided by the Grand Canyon of North America, in the abyss of which tropical plants are to be found, with sub-arctic ones at the top. A somewhat similar situation occurs in the Great Rift of East Africa.

Even in the milder zones we have to beware of the frost-pocket, which is a low-lying area from which cold air cannot escape, for what in summer looks like a warm and cosy dell may act as a trap for the waves of frost that flow down into it. Town gardens on the flat, enclosed by buildings and trees, can be terrible frost-pockets. A hill-top may be blasted by winds, and very cold ones too, but will be free of stagnant frost, which flows downhill like water. In England peaches (such as 'Peregrine') flourish on a hill-top on Zone 7. On any kind of slope one can do a lot by avoiding solid obstructions and by providing instead a filter, drain or by-pass for the frost waves by leaving gaps in hedges, of tough species of shrubs, such as pyracantha, or planting them in staggered sections. This is the same sort of notion as outlined in the section below on wind.

A few other factors also influence a plant's resistance to cold. One is its age, a young one being more susceptible than an old one with well-ripened wood. Another is the "microclimate". Shielded from biting winds by tough companions, a sensitive shrub is better off than it would be in the open. A warm south-facing wall gives life to many a shrub that would otherwise give up the ghost.

The origin of a plant, whether native or cultivated, is another factor. An eucalypt from seed collected at sea-level is less hardy than one of the same species collected at 3,000ft. It has been found that seed collected from a species (wild) rhododendron established in England produced plants hardier than those collected from its native Asia. Likewise clonal variations occur in hybrids. If Mr Smith in Britain, Herr Schmidt in Germany and Mr Brown in America effect matings between Abelia chinensis and A. uniflora, they will all get the hybrid A. × grandiflora, but one of them may be hardier than the others. This particular example is of special interest because it may explain why, very curiously, this hybrid is hardier in America than in Britain generally.

Striking differences in hardiness are also to be observed in maritime climates and "continental" or far inland ones. By and large, your maritime climate exerts a benign influence, giving comfort to a very large range of plants of all sorts, except those that cannot stand being ravaged by salty gales. Britain and the western fringes of Europe down as far as the Pyrenees are richly blessed by this factor, combined with the warm breath of the Gulf Stream. Nowhere will you find a more benign climate for plants generally than on the west coast of Scotland, Wales, Cornwall and Ireland. London is much nearer the North Pole than New York, but gives a good home to many plants that will die across the Atlantic. Japan, New Zealand and, of course, many other islands enjoy a maritime climate, but are not touched by the magic of the Gulf Stream.

On the other hand many plants that are native to a continental climate, which will survive winter freezes far more rigorous than those of Britain and similar localities, expect very hot summers, especially late summers. This late heat hardens their wood, which not only prepares them for a tough winter but which also stimulates the development of flower buds. To such "continental" plants the weaker summer sun and less extreme seasonal changes in temperature of equable maritime climates is discouraging. Thus, as examples, the "pink siris" (Albizia julibrissin, of Bean), the American redbud (Cercis canadensis) and most of the flowering dogwoods, especially Cornus florida, though resistant to icy temperatures of $-10°$ Fahrenheit, do not get a late-summer roasting in Britain and do not often blossom in their full splendour; whereas Cornus mas, the Cornelian cherry, being native to Britain and Europe generally, does not cry aloud for a summer roasting and (for what it is worth) flowers well.

Sometimes, when a winter is harsher than is usual for its zone, you will find, in spring, plants that are normally hardy in that zone now appear to be dead. This occurred in the nasty winter of 1978/9 in England, when very cold spells alternated with very wet ones, with the wind always from the North Pole. Evergreen azaleas, nearly all hebes, clerodendrums, crinodendrons (admittedly not very hardy), the pretty tri-coloured form of the hybrid Hypericum moseranum and others appeared to be quite dead. Be not unduly alarmed in such cases, for the top may be dead but life remain in the crown and the roots. By June many of these had begun to put on new growth, even the crinodendron.

We have found the same behaviour in most ceanothus, many daisy-bushes (Olearia), pomegranate (Punica granatum), myrtles (especially Myrtus communis) and lemon-scented verbena (Lippia citriodora). So do not entirely give up hope until midsummer.

Plants known as sub-shrubs, such as fuchsia, perovskia and cotton-lavender, nearly all behave in this way. In the colder zones of North America, however, many shrubs far more hardy than these have to be heavily protected by one means or another, even to covering them completely.

A particular peril is encountered if an unseasonably warm spell occurs in late winter while the soil is still frozen, a situation that we shall consider when we discuss mulching.

WATER

The need of all plants for water at their roots, preferably rain water, needs no emphasis, beyond remarking that some need a great deal more than others. Plants that are susceptible to drought will often stand up to it to some extent if planted in shady places, where there will be less transpiration from the leaves. Shrubs whose roots delve deep are also better equipped, but, whenever the heavens fail us, we must studiously and copiously water all shrubs when they are young and all that are transplanted when no longer so. In addition, when transplanting an evergreen broad-leaved shrub we must prune back some of the branches, again to restrict transpiration.

What is less obvious, and usually impossible to provide artifically, is the craving that some shrubs have for a moist atmosphere. This is felt particularly by those evergreens that originate from regions of high rainfall and from the moisture-laden proximity of sea, lake or river. These need a moist breath on their leaves as well as a bathing of their feet. The luxuriance of many plants on the west coast of Britain, California, British Columbia, Ireland and similar places testifies eloquently to this law. We can see this most remarkably in magnolias, rhododendrons, camellias, myrtles, hydrangeas and some others.

"Continental" territories, in addition to their relative extremes of heat and cold, tend to be much drier than maritime or riverine ones, except where mountain ranges induce ample rainfall. Of equal importance is the odd fact that, in the territories in which we are interested, the Eastern flank is drier than the Western but, even in a fairly small island like Britain, the damp, warm west coast is much luckier than the dry, colder east coast and the Midlands. The conditions on the eastern and western coasts of North America also differ sharply, the west being the milder.

The effects of humidity are very well seen in parts of North America. For example, although both Florida and Southern California are in similar warm-climate zones, the similarity from the horticultural view is misleading. Southern California is very dry in summer and Florida very humid, so that shrubs that originate from dry Australian regions flourish in California but fall prey to leaf diseases in Florida. Similar differences occur in Rhode Island and southern Illinois, which are both of Zone 6, but rhododendrons and other broad-leaf evergreens thrive in Rhode Island and languish in the winter dryness of Illinois.

On the other hand there can be too much water. As we shall see, plenty of our shrubs appreciate or tolerate a dry soil, such as brooms, barberries, cistus, yuccas, carpenterias and cotoneasters. Plenty of others like a really moist soil, but, if their toes are permanently immersed in standing water underground, they are likely to die as surely as they would from drought, except for a few bog plants. Water-logging of the soil is therefore a condition that we must at all costs prevent by some system of drainage if excess water does not drain away naturally.

Wind

Beautiful in our eyes is the fluid movement of foliage under the impulse of wind. The slender arms of the weeping willow stream out like a girl's hair, the silvery leaves of the poplars flutter like little white doves at play, the filigree of the Japanese maple tosses and frolics, the statuesque forms of erect trees bend and sway. The whole garden is alive with movement and with the lisp of leaves. Almost inevitably one is reminded that

> *Where e'er you walk cool gales shall fan the glade,*
> *Trees where you sit shall crowd into a shade.*

This is a sweet enough thought in the Mediterranean, in Florida or "where the remote Bermudas ride", yet even in such benign climates, as well as in harsher ones, wind can be the gardener's worst elemental enemy. Under the desiccating breath of a fierce gale the leaves of shrubs and trees shiver and shrivel. It breaks branches, beheads roses, strews the ground with litter, may permanently damage "the beauteous shapes of things" and rip whole plants completely out of their anchorages. Young shrubs and trees are in particular peril unless securely staked. The higher the altitude and the nearer the sea the greater are the perils from wind. Less obviously, where buildings are close together, wind tunnels may be created, through which fierce air currents rush with sudden gusts. When wind is accompanied by rain, however, leaves are sufficiently protected against dehydration, whatever other damage may be done.

We must, therefore, provide protection of one sort or another wherever gardens and parks are very dangerously exposed. All-round protection is seldom practical and we must accordingly find out the direction from which the prevailing winds blow. In the northern hemisphere this usually means the north or east (north of west in parts of North America), but in towns winds may be confusedly tunnelled in any direction.

Walls and fences seem to be obviously the best methods of protection, but this is an illusion. Their value is very limited, for the wind leaps over them and swoops down on the further side with a swirling turbulence over an area some ten to twelve times the height of the barrier and then reasserts its full force. This area of turbulence is even more damaging than the wind's direct blast, for it shakes plants to and fro, as a terrier shakes a rat, loosening their footholds and tearing their leaves. Only very close up to the barrier is a susceptible plant safe.

What is better than a solid obstacle is one that will *filter* the wind and so break its velocity. This means a semi-permeable barrier, which should be approximately only 50 per cent solid. Such a barrier reduces a 50 m.p.h. wind to 10 m.p.h. up to a distance of four times the height of the barrier and the full velocity is not reasserted until 30 to

40 times that height, free of turbulence. Thus a 6ft permeable barrier gives some protection (gradually decreasing) for some 200ft or more.

The semi-permeable barrier can be an artificial one such as wooded palings, vertical or horizontal, but not wider than 2 inches, with similar spacing. More aesthetic are natural filters provided by hedges which, in given circumstances, will filter frost also. Excellent for this particular purpose (and included in our Register) are:

> sea-buckthorn, tamarisks, the sloe (Prunus spinosa), pyracanthas, hawthorns, cotoneasters, elder, gorse, tree-purslane (Atriplex halimus), the elegant griselinia (for milder districts), the Japanese spindle (Euonymus japonicus), the mountain pine (Pinus mugo) and the more hardy of the New Zealand daisy-bushes (olearias).

Where space allows, add a few trees suited to these conditions, such as the alders (Alnus rubra and A. incana) which are very tough and good filters. The sycamore (Acer pseudoplatanus), the evergreen ilex or holm-oak, and the "black" Italian poplar.

Beside the Sea

In maritime climates winds can be particularly vicious and their destructive force enormously multiplied by the salt spray that they carry in from the ocean. Salt is extremely damaging to most shrubs and other plants, scalding or blistering their leaves, and it may be carried quite a long way inland by high-velocity gales. Close to the shore (up to 400 yards) wind-driven sand abrades the bark of shrubs and trees as well as reducing their leaves to tatters.

Fortunately, nature herself has given us some means of overcoming even these hazardous conditions and has evolved shrubs, trees and other plants that have conditioned themselves to them or are capable of resisting them. All those that we have just mentioned have this resilient quality and others are given in Appendix A. Extreme conditions, however, call for a deep shelter belt where space allows. On the seaward side there will be such tough shrubs as tamarisk, sea-buckthorn and elder to act as shock-absorbers and to leeward of them will be a belt of equally tough trees to provide "defence in depth". Two of the best are Corsican pine (Pinus nigra maritima) and the black pine (P. thunbergii). The result, when the plants have grown beyond juvenility, will be to carry the wind and salt high up and over the danger zones. Plant the young trees and shrubs close together and thin them out when they begin to touch one another. (Fig. 6).

Sun and Shade

From tempests, drought, floods and frost (good Lord, deliver us!) we move to softer elements; though the sun is by no means always gentle, for its hot breath is cruel to those shrubs that are accustomed by nature to shade or to a moist atmosphere.

Shade, whether permanent or fleeting, is an important element in the garden

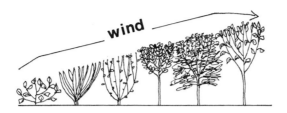

6.   Coastal shelter-belt for larger gardens

picture. Slim shadows creeping and extending across the lawn in late afternoon, are beautiful. Alternating or contrasting light and shade, which artists call *chiaroscuro*, is the touchstone of the landscape painting as of the garden one. Yet shade bothers many a gardener and we are often asked what can be grown in it. The answer is: "Plenty, but it depends on the nature of the shade."

There is the dense umbrage immediately below a big beech, horse-chestnut, plane or linden. There is the dappled shade cast by small trees of light foliage. There is the oblique shade thrown by buildings and trees at certain times of the day and there are the awkward, dark corners which seem to defy the gardener's ingenuity. The majority of plants certainly flower more abundantly in the direct rays of the sun, which harden their stems and encourage the development of flower buds, but may, as noticeably in roses, cause premature petal-fall. For some plants the full power of the sun is essential, but generally what is more important is light, for it is through light (and there is nearly always some in daytime) that the leaves manufacture the elements essential to the plant's growth and health, besides the chemical salts in solution that it absorbs from the soil by its roots.

Some plants, however, both shrubby and herbaceous, are by their leaf structure conditioned in their native pastures to slow absorption of carbon dioxide and are happiest in a light of low intensity. Others again, are able to adapt themselves to almost any conditions; ivies and lily-of-the-valley, for example, will scamper away happily in either full light or deep shade.

Precious little, it is generally supposed, will prosper directly beneath big, leafy trees, but those conditioned to a light of low intensity and slow absorption of CO_2 are quite happy, though they are the least ornamental. Shrubby examples are the butcher's broom (Ruscus aculeatus), the Alexandrian laurel (Danaë racemosa), and several sarcococcas ("Christmas Box"). We can also call upon the herbaceous plants, such as Solomon's-seal, which waves its arching wands in the most Stygian gloom, the lily-of-the-valley, violets, the green-flowered hellebore (Helleborus foetidus) and the little sweet-woodruff (Asperula odoratus).

All these are able to compete with the roots of big trees. The opportunities are greatly increased by removing the lower branches of the trees flush with the trunk and by heavy watering by rain or hose to replace the moisture which the roots of such

"Lighten our darkness". Hypericum 'Hidcote' and other plants in the dense shade of a big cherry (Lucas Phillips's garden)

trees suck up thirstily from the soil. Peonies, both shrubby and herbaceous, and skimmias will prosper. Under smaller trees and those lightly clad with leafage, such as the silver birch, gleditsia and the eucalypt, many shrubs behave splendidly, enjoying the filtered sunlight and presenting one of the most charming of garden pictures. Some of the shrubs that enjoy this kind of diapered light are rhododendrons, pieris,

42

camellias, hypericums, mahonias, spiraeas, hydrangeas, cornus, together with plenty of herbaceous plants and such climbers as the clematis and the honeysuckle. Trees whose roots go straight down and deep, such as the great Atlas cedar (Cedrus atlantica and its blue-washed form) also surprisingly allow quite big bushes to grow almost right up to their boles, as I have proved with Spiraea thunbergii, Hypericum patulum and Viburnum tomentosum. Likewise, *pace* what others say, we find that plenty of plants prosper beneath birches, despite its allegedly voracious roots. Of course, to all these shrubs shade is not essential, but they are examples of what can be done.

The shade of a north-facing wall perplexes many gardeners, but (as artists will tell you) there is plenty of light there, and a soft light, too, provided the wall itself is not occluded by buildings or plants further to its own north. The problem is less one of shade than of cold wind. Apart from the various climbers available, plenty of shrubs will grow in such a situation, provided it is not directly assaulted by searing winds. Hypericums, mahonias, camellias, Japanese quinces (Chaenomeles species), Choisya ternata, eucryphias and many hollies are the first that come to mind, though, for sheer hardiness, all give place to the pyracanthas, the hardiest of which will withstand cruel winds down to −5°F.

One of the first things to be done, therefore, in any garden, large or small, is to take note of the points of the compass. Observe where there is permanent shade or oblique, moving shade, in which most plants are quite happy. We shall often use the terms "part-shade" or "semi-shade", which may mean shade for part of the day, or dappled shade or oblique shade.

In addition to unavoidable shade, we often need to create some degree of shade deliberately, especially in the warmer climes, whether to provide a light canopy for the sorts of shrubs we have just mentioned or as a relief from an over-mighty sun, beneath which we ourselves can seek repose in reveries or the more lively repose of gin and tonic. For these purposes some trees rather than shrubs are needed. Too strong a sun can usually be corrected by ample moisture either at the roots or overhead. If rain does not do the job for you, water the ground thoroughly and damp down the foliage in the evening by either a sprayer or watering can. Damping down can be very important for evergreen shrubs in industrial towns, where deposits from the air settle on the leaves and choke the stomata, which are, one may say, their lungs. The same is true of any shrub close to a much-used road, where they face the greater danger of exhaust fumes from motors.

Very gloomy corners, especially in town gardens, of the sort that Milton calls "shagged with horrid shade", often tax our ingenuity, but there is a surprisingly large parade of various plants at our command. Of shrubs, the outstanding ones are hypericums, mahonias, the gold-splashed species of elaeagnus, hollies (especially those with silvered or gilded leaves), the winter-flowering jasmine, the low-growing Viburnum davidii and skimmias. A great many herbaceous plants also do very well. In addition to those that we have already noted are the white or pale blue sorts of small campanulas, foxgloves and the white bergenia 'Silberlicht' ('Silver Light'). If you do not mind an invasive plant Polygonum campanulatum is a conspicuous success, even in poor soils, making a low mound of nice foliage topped by small pink bells.

And there are always the ivies, which will densely cover the ground as well as climbing walls. Many are beautifully coloured, as in the pewter-tinted Canary ivy, Hedera canariensis 'Gloire de Marengo' and the brilliant 'Goldheart' which is a cultivar of the English ivy, Hedera helix.

4
CULTIVATION

SOILS

E HAVE ALREADY ASSUMED, Reader, that you know something about the qualities of soils, whether of sand, clay or loam. Besides these physical properties there are many chemical ones, but what concerns us most here is that some soils are acid and others alkaline or limy. Chalk, which is found mostly in Britain and France and may be unfamiliar to many readers, is very alkaline indeed as well as being difficult to work.

Nearly all shrubs are happy in an acid soil, but a good many become sickly and may die in an alkaline one, which, in a way that only a chemist can explain, does not allow the roots to absorb iron, one of the many needs of plants. This results in the condition known as "lime-induced chlorosis", in which the leaves turn yellow and then drop. The plants most commonly affected are rhododendrons, the summer heathers, witch hazels, camellias, pieris, pernettya and kalmia. The shrubs that prosper in more or less limy soils, however, are legion and it is surprising how many take easily to chalk, such as barberries, forsythias, cistuses, fuchsias and many more. Starved, stony, gravelly or rocky soils give a welcome to quite a lot of shrubs, such as artemisias, the little helianthemum, the beautiful Carpenteria californica, brooms, cistus, yuccas and many others that we shall note.

The acidity of soils is measured by what is called the pH scale, a purely arbitrary one in which pH7 represents neutrality. Figures above 7 represent ascending degrees of alkalinity, those below an increasing degree of acidity. Almost everything will grow in a neutral soil. You can have your soil tested by your local horticultural officer or by some horticultural institute, but remember that it may vary in different parts of the garden. As we have said earlier, you must choose plants that are appropriate to your soil.

For derelict and waste soils, see Appendix A, at end.

PLANTING
We shall assume that the ground has been properly prepared all over or in individual

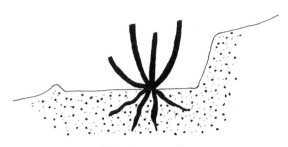

7. Planting on a slope

sites. If in individual sites, prepare it a good four feet square, especially in lawns, though very small shrubs can do with less.

Except for container-grown ones, shrubs, as a broad general rule, are best planted in autumn, while the soil is still open and warm. Winter is suitable if the ground is not frozen or sodden. Early spring is preferred in some cases and we shall note a few in the Register.

Make the planting hole rather larger than seems necessary. To very stiff soil work in a generous helping of peat or ancient leaf-mould (up to one-third of the volume of the soil), together with a sprinkling of an all-round fertilizer. If the soil is very dry, soak it. Offer up the young plant, making sure that it is at the right depth, which usually means the nurseryman's soil-mark at the crown. If the plant is on naked roots, spread them out well, throw in some fine soil about half-way, give a drink of water, firm the soil *lightly*, then complete filling up the hole and again firm lightly.

Plants in pots or other containers are often found to be pot-bound, the roots crowded at the bottom and curling round. Loosen all such roots and spread them out, cutting back any that are excessively long. One is often advised to tread the roots down firmly with the foot. This is a mistake, for it serves merely to compact the soil and damage its structure, especially if it is wet. Better to give a thorough watering, which will bring the soil into intimate contact with the roots and firm it sufficiently. Wait several hours before giving it a final light firming with the foot. A counsel of perfection is to add a dollop of well-rotted manure before the final topping up of the hole, but do not let the manure actually touch the roots.

If the stems of the shrub are more than about 3ft high, or if the site is a windy one, plant at least one stake, and tie the plant to it, a trifle loosely. In all cases make sure that the plant presents itself to the world most effectively — not lopsidedly, not with a bare patch facing the front, not where its best limbs are pointing in the least favourable direction.

Most shrubs can be transplanted to new positions quite easily, such as rhododendrons and maples, but others, such as daphnes, brooms and fremontias, quickly give up the ghost.

PRUNING

As one of us has said in a book that has been much quoted (*The Small Garden*, by C. E. Lucas Phillips), the golden rule is: when in doubt, don't. A corollary to this is: when in doubt how hard to prune, prune lightly. Beware of becoming Milton's "blind Fury with th'abhorred shears and slits the thin-spun life". A second golden rule, applicable always and one which we shall not repeat in our notes on pruning throughout the book, is always to get rid of all dead, decadent and diseased stems and shorten damaged ones.

In our splendour of shrubs there are plenty that need no systematic pruning. Indeed, a few live in terror of the knife and to daphnes it is often fatal. No evergreen shrubs need systematic pruning, though they may have to be subjected to some discipline to be kept in good shape. In the general run of deciduous shrubs, the first need is to establish a good basal framework while the plant is still very young. This we do as soon as the plant arrives by cutting out any stem that is growing inwards or crossing another and any that is feeble and lacking substance. We do it for the first two years of the life of all deciduous plants, except those that need exceedingly hard amputation (Fig. 8). THIS INITIAL SHAPING YOU MUST ASSUME TO APPLY EVEN WHEN THERE IS NO MENTION OF PRUNING IN OUR REGISTER AND EVEN WHEN WE SAY "NO PRUNING". It is of special importance to all those shrubs that do not normally throw up new shoots, but develop by simply extending their main limbs, on which lateral branches form. The chief of these are:

rhododendrons
camellias
lilacs
hibiscus
deciduous magnolias
Buddlcia globosa (the one with orange balls)
dogwoods (Cornus), the shrubby sorts
clethras (sweet pepper *et al*)
witch hazels
potentillas
deciduous viburnums

This does not mean that all pruning is positively forbidden. All can be "tailored" if they become over-mighty.

Culturally similar to them is a cluster of shrubs that likewise develop by extension, but which do sometimes throw out new shoots, though not always where you want them. If suitably placed, these new shoots can be used to replace old ones. This group is headed, we may say, by the chokeberry (Aronia) and includes the stachyurus, which dangles its streamers in winter, the staphylea or bladder-nut, deciduous azaleas, the caragana or pea-tree and clerodendrums.

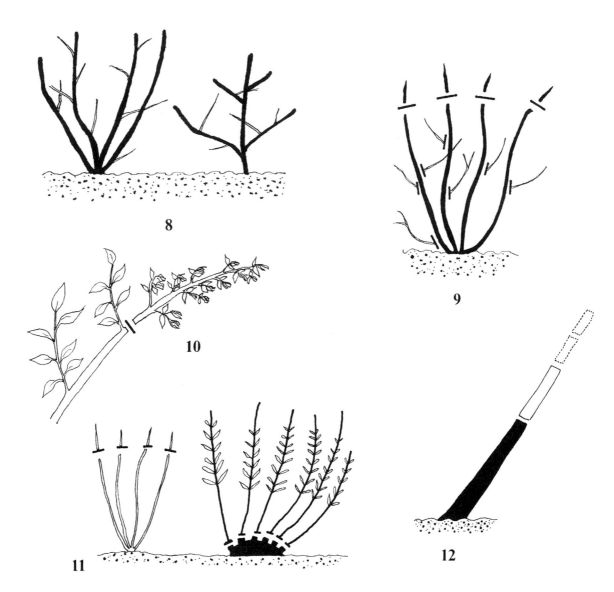

8–12 (8) Initial trimming of deciduous shrubs that develop by prolonging their main stems and do not respond to cutting back and producing replacement shoots. Remove all weak, crossing and inward-growing shoots, e.g., witch hazel, Buddleia globosa, lilac, deciduous cotoneasters, potentillas, shrubby dogwoods and deciduous magnolias; (9) Initial training of the bushier, early-flowering, deciduous shrubs. Start as in Fig. 8, but also shorten tips, e.g. philadelphus, deutzia, forsythia, kolkwitzia, weigela, spring spiraeas and Buddleia alternifolia. After blossom-fall, cut flowered stems hard as in Fig. 10; (10) Renewal pruning of deciduous shrubs that flower before July, as exemplified in Fig. 9; (11) Pruning deciduous shrubs that flower late. *Left*, in the first year merely shorten tips. Subsequently, in early spring, prune very hard, almost to the ground, e.g. hardy fuchsias, perovskia, indigofera, ceratostigma and leycesteria. See also separately under Buddleia davidii, ceanothus, spiraea, caryopteris and Cornus alba; (12) Late-flowering deciduous shrubs that need not be cut back so hard. In the first year treat as in Fig. 9. In the second spring cut back halfway. In subsequent years cut last season's growth to about 2in from its starting-point. The sketch (one stem only) shows the successive stages, e.g., deciduous ceanothus, Spartium junceum and caryopteris

Thus the pruning of shrubs is governed by one's knowledge of each plant's habit of growth. This applies particularly to the floral habits of deciduous shrubs, but fortunately nature makes it fairly easy to understand these in general terms.

Apart from particular exceptions, the disciplining of deciduous shrubs is governed by their seasons of flowering. This may be of critical importance. As someone has aptly said, the time is "when one cycle of growth has been completed and another is about to begin". This means that, as a general rule, you prune deciduous shrubs that flower before July immediately after they have finished their display. This display has been on "old wood" that had developed last year. This old wood is what you attack, cutting off that section of it that has borne blossoms, allowing young growths from below the flowered section to progress vigorously, so that you will get a good display next year. After the third year, if the shrub is one that forms a "stool" and throws up new stems from the ground, you amputate at about ground level about one in four of the old stems. Familiar examples are philadelphus, deutzias, weigelas, forsythias, the flowering currants and the early-flowering species of spiraea.

Shrubs that flower later, however, do so on growth that has developed during the spring ("new wood" or wood "of the current season's growth") and these are normally pruned during winter dormancy or early spring, and pruned very severely indeed, often almost to the ground. Familiar examples are David's buddleia, the deciduous species of ceanothus, Hydrangea paniculata and the late-flowering species of spiraea.

To this group also belong the sub-shrubs, which (you will remember) are soft-wooded in their upper parts, such as fuchsias, cotton-lavenders, perovskia, the connoisseur's desmodium and a few more.

Inevitably there are exceptions to these main classifications, as in the flowering cherries, heathers and Hydrangea × macrophylla, and these exceptions we shall note as we go along; but we shall not go far wrong if we bear in mind that the main purpose of pruning in deciduous shrubs is replacement of the old by the new, usually called "renewal pruning". As he was wont to do so often, Shakespeare put it neatly in the mouth of Richard II's gardener, when he said

Superfluous branches
We lop away that bearing boughs may live.

Quite a lot of shrubs obligingly form "stools", having a number of dormant growth buds just below ground level, waiting to be stimulated into emergence once the shrub has been rid of its old growths. These include the sub-shrubs and those that are grown for the beauty of their coloured stems, such as Cornus alba and the white-stemmed brambles and, more surprisingly, they include also the golden-leaved elder (Sambucus racemosa 'Plumosa Aurea'), the little blue ceratostigma and the leycesteria. All these we cut right down to the ground, or near it, in earliest spring,

49

though very often we give them only a light trim in their first year, as in the last two just mentioned and in the perovskia.

Stools are formed also by some shrubs which normally get only renewal pruning (the deutzia *et al*) and we have noted that we amputate to the ground some of the old stems after the third year, to stimulate new basal limbs. Always give a hearty feed of some sort to any shrub that you cut back extra hard.

Berrying shrubs are pruned after fruiting.

Wall shrubs need a little special attention. As we have said, we are not concerning ourselves with climbers, but a good many shrubs can with advantage be grown against a wall, either to adorn it or because the shrub is on the tender side for its zone. In whatever circumstances, never plant a shrub closer to a wall than 9in. Many that are given wall protection merely on the grounds of tenderness can be planted 3ft or so away and these we prune normally according to their kind. Other shrubs, whether hardy or not, are pinned back, as it were, against a wall and disciplined to face the world with a tight, flat face. Typical examples among the hardier shrubs suitable for this treatment are the flowering quince (Chaenomeles), the pyracantha and some cotoneasters. Among the more tender the evergreen species of ceanothus and Vitex agnus-castus (the "pure lamb") are typical.

For this sort of treatment you need a framework of horizontal wires and a few canes to which the main limbs of the shrub are tied, either fan-wise or as espaliers. Lateral growths from this main framework are tied in as they develop, but you must stop the development of outward-growing shoots ("breastwood") (Fig. 13). The quinces and pyracanthas are treated in just the same way as espaliered apples, summer-pruning the young shoots at the fifth leaf and cutting back further to about two buds in winter, to form flowering "spurs" or clusters.

Other shrubs will happily lean against a wall and hug it without support, such as the "herring-bone" cotoneaster, the crinodendron, Coronilla glauca, garrya and, very often, the ceanothus too. The various forms of Euonymus fortunei will lean towards a wall and begin to clamber up it, and of these nothing is better than 'Emerald Gaiety'. For the limited wall space beneath a south-facing window few shrubs are more delightful than the variegated form of Daphne odora and the caryopteris.

All these are good precepts for the gardener's guidance generally. A definite commandment applies, however, to all shrubs with variegated leaves, whether evergreen or deciduous. If an all-green branch or twig occurs, you must feel back to its point of origin with its parent stem and amputate it there.

Another form of pruning is the removal of suckers from below ground. A good many shrubs, particularly roses, rhododendrons and lilacs, are propagated by the nurseryman by grafting or budding a cultivated variety (the scion) on to a wild stock, either because the stock has more vigorous roots or because of difficulty or expense in propagating otherwise. Such suckers are usually recognisable by their leaves (and perhaps thorns) being noticeably different from those of the scion and they should be

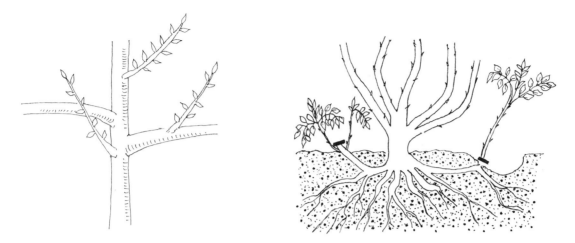

13.   Breastwood or fore-right shoots growing outward from the main framework of a well-trained shrub, e.g. pyracantha and flowering quince

14.   Suckers. *Left*, wrong; cut at ground level the sucker is merely pruned and breaks again. *Right*, correct; the sucker wrenched off at its point of origin. Typical of roses, as here

pulled or wrenched out or bashed off by spade or hoe at their points of origin, not cut by knife or secateurs, which, like pruning, merely stimulates the growth of more suckers. Sometimes, as in roses, the point of origin is not easy to find and you are liable "to unsphere the stars with oaths" (Fig. 14).

Other shrubs sucker naturally on their own roots. In bamboos, some barberries and amelanchiers you may possibly wish this to occur, in ground-cover shrublets you certainly do, in aralias you certainly do not. Suckering may be very useful when one needs to stabilize a bank of loose soil or clothe some patch of degenerate soil, but it is usually objectionable in the ornamental garden.

Veteran shrubs inherited from one's predecessor in title can usually be given new life without much trouble. Having got rid of the basal weaklings, amputate all the main stems with a saw to within a foot of the ground. Pare the saw-cut smooth with a sharp knife and coat it with a wound dressing made for the purpose. Do deciduous shrubs in winter dormancy, evergreens in late spring, and give the shrub a hearty feed. A forest of new shoots will result. Keep the strongest ones and scrap the rest.

NURSING

Make sure that the shrubs have all the water that they need, especially in their first year.

When practicable, pluck or cut off all flowers as they fade, unless, as in barberries, holly, pernettyas and cotoneasters, they give you later on a present of jewelry in their brilliant berries. Otherwise, do not allow any seeds to set, lest the vitality of the plant should diminish. Some shrubs, as in rhododendrons, hebes, olearias ("daisy bushes") and tree-lupins, bear enormous quantities of seeds. Even in berrying shrubs, quick growth is stimulated if the flowers are beheaded in the first year. This dead-heading becomes impossible in plants that so smother themselves with small flowers that the foliage cannot be seen, as in the dwarf rhododendrons and evergreen azaleas, but in the larger ones dead-heading is very important. On very large shrubs it is impracticable.

Feeding is of high importance for shrubs that do want a rich diet. We have assumed that you have fed the soil well in your first preparation. What you put underneath is much more valuable than what you may put on top later. However, once the plants are in, you can feed only from the top. Nothing is so good as a mulch of well-decayed manure, though you may get weed-seeds from it. Garden compost, if you have made it really well and it is free from weed-seeds, serves the same purpose. Alternatively, of course, you can apply an all-purpose chemical fertiliser to the top-soil, preferably one formulated specially for shrubs, containing magnesium. Better still, if the shrub is not a dwarf one, is to spread a thick quilt of oak or beech leaves over the ground in the fall, underspread with a sprinkling of nitrogenous fertiliser. Without the fertiliser the top-soil will become de-nitrified until the leaves rot. This leaf mulch keeps the shrub roots warm in winter, moist and cool in summer, rots down to provide excellent humus and deters the germination of weed-seeds. Other useful mulches (always with fertiliser) are coarse peat, shredded tree-bark and cocoa-bean hulls.

Foliar-feeding is another good method of providing nourishment. On thick-leaved shrubs it is best sprayed on to the under-surface of the leaf.

Look out for diseases and pests. We have not the space here to go into this difficult and disagreeable topic, especially as some maladies are localised and others affect particular shrubs, such as bud-blast on rhododendrons and black spot on roses. Aphids (greenfly, blackfly, etc.) suck away at many kinds of plants but are easily held at bay by a systemic insecticide. Mildews also affect many plants and there are several proprietary concoctions to counter-attack them. Pray remember that, as in human medicines, prevention is better than cure whenever possible. Soil fungi are the very devil, with awful long names, such as the *Phytophthora cinnamomi* that now attacks a lot of plants. Whenever a shrub displays death's pale flag for no apparent reason, consult a specialist institution.

Sexual Vagaries

Curiously, the marital habits of plants differ enormously and many an amateur gardener remains unaware of them after some years of experience. This is therefore a convenient place to disclose the secrets of one group of shrubs, some of which are grown mainly or partly for the jewelry of their coloured berries. This group bears male (or "staminate") flowers on one bush and female (or "pistillate") ones on another. The female is, of course, the one that wears the jewels, but cannot do so unless wooed by a male, the act of union being performed by the bee or other insect or sometimes by wind. Such plants are called dioecious, but we shall use some simpler term, such as single-sexed. The most familiar example is the holly (though not all are so discriminating). Others are the beautiful pernettya, whose berries are like porcelain beads, the skimmias (except one species), the aucuba or false laurel, the sea-buckthorn (Hippophae rhamnoides) and the yew. You must therefore instruct your nurseryman accordingly, for the differences are by no means always apparent. The usual allotment is one male to about five females (one more than Mahomet allowed). They need not be closely contiguous when planted, though it is better so. Another group of unisexual shrubs, known as monoecious, also has separate male and female flowers, but bears them on the same plant, so the gardener has no problem. All sorts of other sexual proclivities occur, but into their technical secrets we shall not pry.

5
CLOTHING THE GROUND

HAVING PLANTED THE YOUNG shrubs, you will find yourself staring at dolorous stretches of bare earth between them. Before deciding on any other course consider the merits of certain herbaceous plants, which will give immediate results and at least partially fill the gaps before the shrubs have filled out. The Michaelmas daisies and the purple loosestrife (Lythrum salicaria) are perhaps ideal, having themselves the appearance of shrubs.

Others that are very good for various seasons of the year are the bristly, metal-tinted sea-hollies or eryngiums, the feathery plumes of astilbes, the blue orbs of the agapanthus or African lily if the zone is no colder than 8, the elegant columbines, the wistful bleeding-heart (Dicentra spectabilis), the day lily or hemerocallis and the hellebores of Christmas and Lent. There are plenty more, but we must not begin a catalogue. Of course, hardy annuals and biennials are also readily at our command, especially chosen varieties of the annual "mallow", Lavatera trimestris, such as 'Loveliness' and 'Aurora', themselves much like shrubs.

In recent years a great deal has been written about "ground cover", much of it ill-informed. The plants used for this purpose should not only be of attractive appearance themselves, but also they should not throttle the roots of the superior shrubs to which they are intended to be mere handmaidens. Not long ago there was a great vogue for the variegated dead nettle now called Galeobdolon, which races and "leaps all civil bounds", but it is suitable only for large and wild places under trees. This was the "archangel" of our forefathers. The best of all weed inhibitors are those larger shrubs that, when well-established, provide their own ground-cover by sweeping the soil with their own lower branches and building up a rich mass of foliage. Camellias, many rhododendrons, pieris, heathers, pernettyas, evergreen barberries, the grey-leaved senecios and low hummocks of David's viburnum excel in this function.

Plants intended more specifically for covering the ground may be either prostrate, evergreen shrublets or they may be herbaceous plants that spread out into wide, dense mats. Both sorts extend themselves either by underground roots or, like ivies, by making fresh roots where their branches touch the ground.

The groundling shrubs make the most attractive of floorings throughout the year, rolling out gradually like green rugs. When developed they prevent you, however, from applying a top-dressing to the larger shrubs and foliar feeding remains the only means of nourishment. Herbaceous plants, dying down in winter, leave you free to mulch or top-dress otherwise. We must be brief in this topic, picking out only a few of the best. Readers who would like to delve more deeply into it should get Mr Graham Thomas's first-class book *Plants for Ground Cover* published by Dent, London, or Donald Wyman's *Ground Cover Plants* (Macmillan).

CARPETING SHRUBS

We consider that the best of all are the dwarf species of the gaultheria (the wintergreen or partridge-berry or, in the USA, the tea-berry), the arctostaphylos or bear-berry and the vacciniums. All are intolerant of lime. All have tiny, white or pale pink flowers, followed by little berries, usually red. Gaultheria procumbens, 4in high, is essentially a shade plant, shrinking back when it reaches the sun. Plant 18in apart. G. miqueliana is more refined but temperamental. Arctostaphylos uva-ursi is an inch or so taller, likes the sun or dappled shade and thrives in sandy seashore gardens. Plant 2ft apart. A. nevadensis is much the same but of larger spread.

The vaccinium gives us at least three good carpeters, for sun or shade. V. oxycoccus, the cranberry of Britain, and V. macrocarpum, the American cranberry, are tiny-leaved "sisters under the skin", 3 to 4in high, needing very moist, acid homes. V. vitis-idaea, the cow-berry, goes to 10in with box-like leaves, is easy and its best in its dwarf form 'Minus' or 'Minor', but does not like excessively hot summers.

Several others are more tolerant all round and are not scared of lime. Hypericum calycinum, the rose-of-Sharon, or St John's wort, is an everyman's plant with large, golden saucers, colonising rapidly in sun or shade by underground runners and splendid on a steep bank.

Lithospermum diffusum has a close foliage effect in sun or shade and acid soil, spreading fast. In 'Grace Ward' and 'Heavenly Blue' delightful blue flowers throng the plant in early summer. Not for colder counties.

Pachysandra terminalis is considered another lime-hater, but is less touchy. For sun or shade, even dense shade. Fresh, apple-green leaves and spikes of tiny, white flowers in spring. Spreads by underground runners. Usually considered to be a plant for leaf-mould soil, but grows for us in stiff clay.

Less well-known are the tough, leathery, evergreen pachistimas, which make thick rings about a foot deep, in light, sandy or peaty, acid soils in some shade. P. canbyi has small narrow leaves and comes from the dry eastern side of North America. P. myrtifolia has larger leaves, is more robust and comes from the wetter west.

Several cotoneasters, with their small, white flowers and red berries are at our service. Perhaps the best is the little evergreen C. dammeri, which moulds itself to the shape of the ground as it spreads. C. adpressus, deciduous, is also reckoned as prostrate, but it builds up to a depth of a foot and is thus less convenient as a mere undergrowth. Plant these two feet apart. Unexpectedly, the big, evergreen C. salicifolius, with its long, willow-like leaves, also gives us some very good groundlings, raised in Germany. Of these, 'Herbstfeuer' ('Autumn Fire') is exceptionally good, shooting out fast and flat upon the ground, then, as it ages, building into a dense mound of arching branches. Plant 4ft apart. 'Gnome' is also very good indeed and densely clothed. The recent 'Skogholm' builds up to 18in.

A few evergreen dwarf barberries can be used, such as the prostrate form of the hybrid Berberis × stenophylla, which builds up in time to 18in high. Easier, and much fleeter of foot, is our old friend the blue periwinkle (Vinca), which grows eagerly in shade or part-shade and in almost any kind of soil, rooting as it spreads. The most generally used is V. minor, 8in, of which there are several varieties, the most favoured being 'Bowles Variety'. In 'Caerulea Plena' the flowers are double, in 'Punicea' red-purple and in 'Multiplex' the same colour and double. 'Gertrude Jekyll' is white and there are a few with varicoloured leaves. V. major, is less hardy (Zone 7 in USA) has larger leaves and builds up to 15in and has a very pretty form with cream-splashed leaves, called 'Elegantissima'.

To all these, the prostrate conifers offer alternatives where they suit. They spread themselves very expansively and no weed has a chance against them. Junipers take first place and there are plenty of them, but they are more than mere space-fillers and may have to be rooted out in time if intended only for that purpose. They are fine shrubs in their own right and, like the prostrate cotoneasters, are splendid for clothing banks. The junipers we like best are the apple-green, prickly J. conferta and the rich, uncommon 'Bonin Isles', which is a variety of J. procumbens. The "common" juniper, J. communis, gives us the excellent *depressa* from Canada and the grey-green 'Hornibrookii' from Ireland. J. horizontalis abounds in good offspring, as in the grey-green 'Bar Harbor', 'Douglasii', the Waukangan juniper, and 'Emerson' the Black Hills Creeper.

Very like a juniper, but very rare, comes "from Russia with love". This is Microbiota decussata; its very small, scale-like leaves make a dense rug, tinted with bronze.

Herbaceous Carpeters

Many of these are far too invasive, penetrating into the root-balls of important shrubs and, as it were, strangling them. The lily-of-the-valley, otherwise so desirable and a good suppressor of weeds, is an offender; keep it well away from all other plants. The bugle, or *Ajuga*, is also a throttler, invading at great speed; keep it for the wilder places. The polygonums, or knot-weeds, are just as bad and there are others worse still.

In our experience the most satisfactory of all is the Labrador violet, Viola labradorica. Only 3in or so high, the little leaves are very decorative, being flushed with purple, more brightly so in sun than in shade. It will grow almost anywhere, colonising at a moderate speed with shallow roots that seem to do no harm to shrubs, but keep it away from heathers.

Dwarf campanulas also colonise quickly. Where fairly large places have to be filled, the Serbian campanula C. portenschlagiana, with its pale blue bells and dense, toothed leaves, is nice to look at and easily arrested if it threatens to break bounds. Several of the wild, hardy, true geraniums are very good indeed, luxuriant and beautiful in leaf and flower, our favourite being the blue G. grandiflorum alpinum. Other good ones include 'Johnson's Blue' and endressii. All are happy in sun or shade to a height of about a foot. For complete shade there is the tough macrorhizum and for hot, dry spots the vivid magnificum.

The dicentra, called of old Dutchman's breeches and Lucy Locket, provides pretty ground-cover in its species D. formosa. Dainty, ferny leaves, lightly touched with silver and ornamented with drooping, heart-shaped blossoms, spread rapidly and quite densely, sometimes excessively. In *alba* the flowers are, of course, white, and in the rather taller (12in) hybrid 'Bountiful' they are a rich, deep pink, very attractive. These creeping dicentras are not to be confused with the bleeding-heart, mentioned earlier, which is not a spreader.

There are lots more: the dainty little Maianthemum bifolium, invading slowly and harmlessly, the highly invasive spurge, Euphorbia robbiae, for deep shade, the creeping-Jenny, especially in its golden form, also luxuriating and fleet of foot in some shade, and the very decorative Waldsteinia ternata, with strawberry-like leaves and buttercup blossoms, colonising rapidly without much harm to strong shrubs.

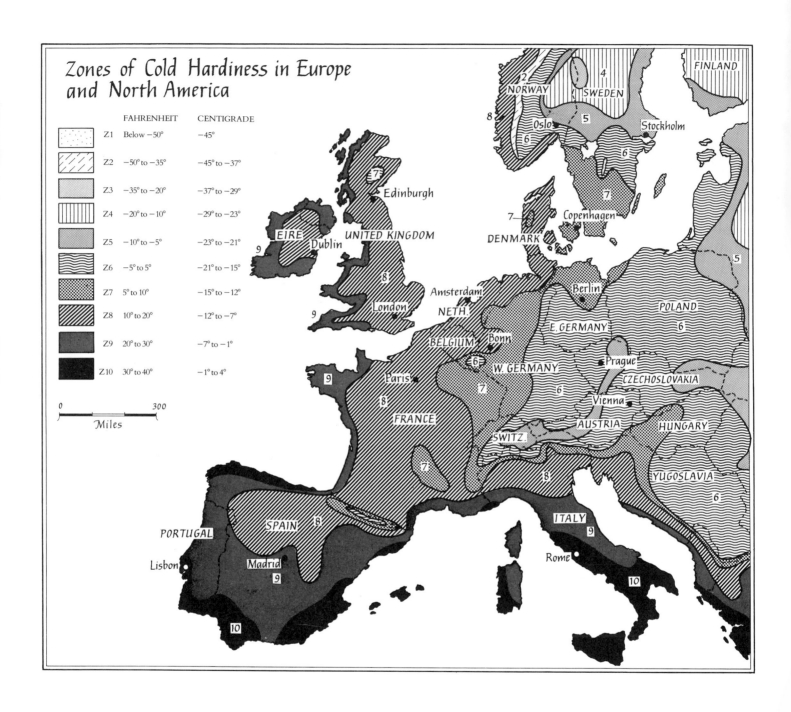

Zones of Cold Hardiness in Europe and North America

		FAHRENHEIT	CENTIGRADE
	Z1	Below −50°	−45°
	Z2	−50° to −35°	−45° to −37°
	Z3	−35° to −20°	−37° to −29°
	Z4	−20° to −10°	−29° to −23°
	Z5	−10° to −5°	−23° to −21°
	Z6	−5° to 5°	−21° to −15°
	Z7	5° to 10°	−15° to −12°
	Z8	10° to 20°	−12° to −7°
	Z9	20° to 30°	−7° to −1°
	Z10	30° to 40°	−1° to 4°

0   300
Miles

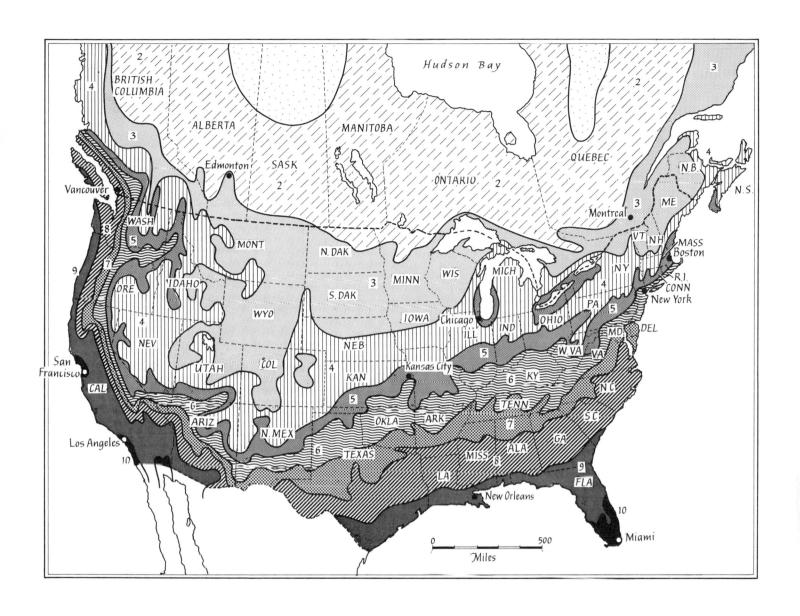

PART TWO

A REGISTER OF SHRUBS

O<small>UR ORIGINAL HOPE</small> W<small>AS</small> to produce as complete a list of shrubs as the botanist or specialist could expect within the limits of one volume, but our publishers have naturally been obliged to impose some limit. However, we have been able to draw up, if not a complete "collection", at least a "comprehensive" one within our restricted acreage of words.

As we have said in the preliminary chapters, we have adopted, with slight modifications, Rehder's "zone" system for indicating a plant's cold-hardiness; these are applicable to its northern limitation in the northern hemisphere. They are represented by the letter z. Most shrubs classified for, say, z7, will flourish also in the warmer zones of 8 to 10, but, as we have seen in Chapter 3, humidity, altitude and other factors may modify these expectations. On a warm wall many Zone 8 plants will succeed in Zone 7.

The heights that we give are those that a shrub might be expected to reach in reasonably good conditions of cultivation and in its appropriate environment. In very favourable circumstances it may grow much bigger and in less favourable ones much smaller. Likewise the flowering seasons are the normal ones for the appropriate zones in the open in the northern hemisphere; in the shelter of a warm wall they are likely to be earlier. Unless we say otherwise, assume that the plant will be happy in any reasonable fertile soil, acid or alkaline.

Pray remember the general pruning precepts of Chapter 4; particular cases will be noted as we go along.

We shall occasionally mention the location of particular examples of shrubs. To avoid frequent repetition we give here their identities.

Kew. The Royal Botanic Gardens, Kew, Surrey, most famous of all botanical institutions.

Arnold Arboretum. The celebrated establishment of that name, of Harvard University, Massachusetts.

Wisley. The Royal Horticultural Society's Garden at Wisley, Surrey.

Exbury. The garden of Major Edmund de Rothschild near Southampton.
Others are specified in the text.

ABELIA

Not absolutely in the front rank of hardiness, the abelias are usually small shrubs of gentle charm and graceful deportment, with small, bell-formed flowers of quiet hues, hanging from slender stems that have a slightly pendulous habit. They flower for a long time, revel in sun and are usually evergreen in warm climates. Though pretty at close quarters, they make little impact on the garden picture. We take schumannii as generally the most desirable all round, but the hybrid grandiflora is of more general use. Oddly, it is less hardy in Britain than in America and continental Europe and more susceptible when young. Probably there are differences in the clones of this hybrid.

No systematic pruning is needed, but, when established, occasionally cut out old stems right to the ground, the late-flowering species about 1st March. Propagate from summer cuttings under mist.

A. chinensis. A 4ft deciduous plant with sweetly scented, white flowers, tinted rose, freely produced in July and August. Not very hardy. z9.

A. 'Edward Goucher'. A first-class small shrub, with flowers of pale lilac-rose, exuberantly borne amid glossy foliage. The breeding is grandiflora × schumannii. Precariously z6.

A. floribunda. A rather tender beauty of about 8ft, with cherry-red, jasmine-like flowers in June. Good for a warm wall. z8.

A. × grandiflora (chinensis × uniflora), nearly evergreen, is a 5ft shrub much to be recommended. Its slender, arching branches are densely set with small, pointed, gleaming leaves and sprays of small, blush-pink bells from July till the fall. *Note* what we have said above. Rated z6 in America but is only z8 in Britain. 'Frances Mason' is an attractive newcomer with bright yellow leaves.

A. schumannii, deciduous, is of similar deportment, bearing flowers of a deeper pink in great abundance, for about the same period. z8.

A. serrata. A deciduous dwarf of slow growth, with orange-tinted flowers in May and June. For acid soil.

15.　Abelia schumannii

A. triflora. A big, handsome, deciduous shrub of 10ft, producing a thick mass of erect growth and blush, richly scented blossoms in threes in terminal clusters in June. The decorative calyces persist after flowering. Probably the hardiest of the abelias.

A. umbellata. A 6ft, wide-spreading shrub with white flowers in June.

ABELIOPHYLLUM

A. distichum is a little, deciduous bush, densely strung all along its branches and twigs with very small, white, four-pointed stars, scented of almonds, bursting forth for a short time on leafless branches. In nature it is used to cold winters but hot summers. Of slow growth, it reaches about 4ft in the open, but maybe 7ft against a warm wall. In genial climes the flowers delight the beholder in February, but in colder ones they wait until April. Rather a "plain Jane" in summer. Cut back by a quarter or a third after flowering. The pendulous lower branches often touch the ground, take root and make new plants. Remove them early.

PLATE 17: *above left*, Erica mediterranea 'Superba' in the main author's garden; *above right*, Cytisus × praecox 'Allgold'; *below right*, Hebe 'Andersonii Variegata'; *above*, Hebe 'Gauntlettii'

PLATE 18: *opposite*, the golden cut-leaf elder,
Sambucus racemosa 'Plumosa Aurea'

PLATE 19: Kalmia latifolia 'Brilliant'

PLATE 20: *above left*, Paeonia lutea ludlowii; *above*, Callicarpa giraldiana in berry; *left*, Exochorda racemosa

PLATE 21: Some rhododendrons. *above*, 'Jalisco Jubilant'; *above right*, Rhododendron yakushimanum; *below right*, Azalea 'George Reynolds'; *below*, R. 'Crest'

PLATE 23: *opposite*, azaleas in the Home Wood at Major Edmund de Rothschild's garden at Exbury

PLATE 22: *left*, Pieris formosa 'Wakehurst'; *below*, Photinia × fraseri 'Red Robin' serves as a stand–in for the pieris in limy soils

PLATE 24: *opposite*, shrub rose 'Canary Bird'

PLATE 25: more shrub roses: *right*, R. primula; *below right*, 'Golden Chernonese'; *below*, 'Frühlingsmorgen'

PLATE 26: *opposite*, Cornus alba 'Sibirica' in winter

PLATE 27: *right*, Staphylea colchica; *below*, Petteria ramentacea

PLATE 28: Some lilacs. *left*, Syringa × josiflexa
'Bellicent'; *below*, S. microphylla

PLATE 29: More lilacs. *opposite above*, S. persica;
below, S. vulgaris 'Diplomat' and 'Primrose'

PLATE 30: *opposite*, Viburnums. *above left*,
V. opulus 'Xanthocarpum' in fruit; *above right*,
V. × bodnantense 'Dawn'; *below*, V. sargentii

PLATE 31: Nice designing at Wakehurst, Sussex.
A brightly hued Acer palmatum 'Dissectum'
stands over a carpet of Polygonum vaccinifolium,
with Ellwood's cypress and other conifers

PLATE 32: *above*, Lavatera oblia; *left*, Halimiocistus wintonensis

ABUTILON

Fortunate is the gardener who lives in a climate genial enough to grow abutilons in the open, for they are shrubs of great beauty in leaf and in flower; but they will not survive in any climate colder than Zone 8 and even there must be grown against a warm wall. They are soft-wooded shrubs of variable character, some bearing open-faced flowers that resemble those of the mallow, to which they are related; others hanging down like tiny dolls' petticoats on a washing line. The ones most often grown are vitifolium and megapotamicum, but we are much attracted by the recent hybrid suntense.

Tie the shoots fairly close in to the wall, when so grown. Do not put the knife to them unless essential and then do so in spring, not autumn. All are deciduous. They flower for a very long spell in summer, but the plants themselves are usually short-lived. The following short descriptions must suffice.

A. megapotamicum. A delightful, lax shrub that may reach 6ft, from the branches of which hang tiny dolls with red blouses (the calyx), yellow skirts (the corolla) and purple shoes (the anthers). Though the branches may be killed in any icy winter, the rootstock usually survives. The clone 'Variegatum' has leaves prettily tessellated in yellow, but is perhaps less hardy.

A. × milleri. Orange bells, with crimson stamens, continuously opening. About 6ft or more.

A. ochsenii A fairly recent introduction, resembling its sister vitifolium but with small, violet flowers becoming in time a gaunt 8ft shrub. z8.

A. × suntense. A delightful new hybrid group, having ochsenii and vitifolium as its parents and displaying huge flowers in various hues of mauve, purple or blue. They grow very fast, reaching 10ft in three years. The lavender 'Jermyns' and 'White Charm' are good clones, z8 on a warm wall, otherwise z9.

A. vitifolium. A superb, fast-growing shrub that has been known to reach 25ft, but, is usually half that size, with grey-green vine-like

16.   Abutilon megapotanicum

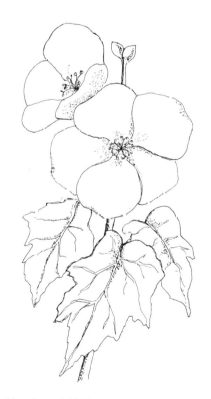

Abutilon vitifolium

65

leaves drawn out to a point and adorned with beautiful, mallow-form saucers of pale blue or mauve. Easy from seed. The finest of its manifestations is 'Veronica Tennant', with very large flowers of rich mauve. The white 'Alba' is less impressive.

Besides these there are several hybrid clones of rare beauty and excellence, including 'Ashford Red', 'Golden Fleece' and 'Kentish Belle'.

ACACIA
Wattle

We mean here, of course, the true acacia, not the tree falsely so-called, which is a robinia. Some species of acacia are even more ridiculously called 'mimosa'', a totally different genus.

Acacias are known by their very delicately cut, "doubly pinnate", leaves, like those of the common bracken or brake fern, from which they thrust out clusters of very small, fluffy florets, usually yellow. In many species the leaves become reduced to spikes, known as phyllodes. They are mainly Australian, flowering in the northern winter or early spring, and can rarely endure any climate colder than Zone 10, but have the virtue of being drought-hardy.

The finest become trees, which we have discussed in *The Trees Around Us*. Those that are of shrub habit are mainly the following, all having yellow flowers. Do any pruning that may be needed in late spring.

A. armata. The Kangaroo thorn, is a 10ft shrub of dense and bushy behaviour flowering profusely but fiercely armed.

Relatively hardy and very distinctive is **A. diffusa**. This is a low, lax, wide-spreading shrub, with sulphur flowers and needle-like phyllodes.

'Exeter Hybrid' is a beautiful specimen of garden origin, about 10ft high.

ACANTHOPANAX

Rather bristly, deciduous, hardy shrubs of no floral attraction but handsome in their compound foliage and their inky-black, ivy-like fruits. The best is *A. sieboldianus* 'Variegatus', an 8ft shrub, of slender, arching stems, its leaflets, which are usually in fives, broadly marginated in cream. It is sometimes fallaciously called the "five-leaved aralia". Excellent in shade and in towns. z4.

Less attractive are the large, sturdy *A. henryi*, which produce trusses of fruits like giant blackberries, and the spiny *simonii*, with downward-pointing thorns.

ACER
Maple

Most maples are trees, many of them very big trees. Very few can rank as shrubs, though there are plenty of border-line examples, which catalogues call "large shrub or small tree". In fact they usually begin as the one and develop into the other. Of such is the glorious 'Brilliantissimum', a small, very slow-growing sycamore, which begins the season in a pink dress, changes it to gold and finally to palest green. These we have considered in *The Trees Around Us*.

The smaller maples are grown essentially for the beauty of their leaves, the elegance of their deportment and often the splendour of their autumn clothing. We think of their leaves as being usually patterned in lobes drawn out to fine points, but they are not always so. In most examples their flowers are very inconspicuous, but the twin-winged seeds that follow, known as samarae (or samaras) are a familiar sight, some being in the shape of a horseshoe, others forming a straight line, others again something in between.

Maples prosper in any reasonable, well-prepared soil in sun or a little light shade. Avoid pruning them, but if you must, do so between August and Christmas, or else they will bleed.

The following are the species that we may specifically consider as shrubs and even some of these are big, the most popular being the various forms of *palmatum* and *japonicum*.

A. buergerianum, the trident maple, is a leafy, scented 20ft shrub of rounded habit, of which there are several leaf variants. In the rare 'Nusitoryama' they are pink. z6.

A. circinatum, the so-called "vine maple", ultimately needs a great deal of room, being a very big, wide-spreading shrub, with its lowest branches stretched out at ground level and its stems twisting in an engaging manner. The large leaves are round in general outline but scissor-snipped on the margin, and in the fall they become brilliantly dyed in crimson and orange. The flowers are quite conspicuous when, in April, they break out into clusters of small florets with claret sepals and ivory petals, followed by samarae that are nearly horizontal. z5.

Another large, spreading, shrubby, very hardy maple of attractive design is **A. ginnala**, the Amur maple. The leaves are of a bright dark green, formed in only three lobes and toothed along the rim. The white, scented flowers in May are followed by samarae in the

19.   Acer japonicum (life-size)

shape of an arch. Very good in towns. The variety *semenowii* has smaller leaves and 'Durond Dwarf' explains itself. z2.

When we come to **A. japonicum** (z5) we find a handful of choice, elegant shrubs which can on occasions become quite big, but which are usually well suited to small gardens. They prefer a moist soil. The cultivar favoured by most people is 'Aureum', which, when grown in partial or dappled shade, illuminates the scene with leaves of pale gold, rounded in general outline but toothed around the rim as though trimmed with pinking shears. Slow-growing and taking many years to exceed 10ft. Other desirable japonicums (the samarae of which are nearly horizontal) are:

'Aconitifolium'. A rounded bush, rather smaller than its brother, with the rims of the leaf much more deeply cut; also known as 'Laciniatum', etc.

'Vitifolium'. A big, fast-growing shrub with large, broad, lobed leaves that blaze magnificently in the fall.

Closely allied to *japonicum* are two species, *A.*

18.   Acer ginnala

20–21   (a) Acer palmatum; (b) Acer palmatum 'Dissectum', (c) Acer palmatum 'Heptalobum' group. Note smaller leaf and relatively broader lobes than in A. palmatum *sieboldianum*, a large shrub, with fine-cut leaves, and *A. pseudosieboldianum*, with elongated lobes to the leaves, which blazes as brilliantly as those of 'Vitifolium'.

In what is certainly the most popular of all the dwarf maples, **A. palmatum** (z5), we are confronted by a whole squadron dressed in slightly different uniforms and of slightly different postures. These are what are usually meant by the term "Japanese maples". Essentially, they have leaves that resemble a woman's hand, with finely pointed fingers extending from a small palm, or sometimes no "palm" at all. Many variations creep in and, unfortunately, there is some confusion about names, which are often burdensome. The palmatums, we are often told, need a certain amount of shade, but in fact they do best in full light, provided that the situation is not one "where the wind's like a whetted knife". The wings of the samarae are distinctly incurved. The most popular are those classified as the Dissectum group, airy and lacy, and the larger, stately Heptalobum group.

The best of the palmatums parade in the following order:

'Atropurpureum'. A great favourite, forming an elegant, wide-spreading dome and having fingers varnished in a blend of crimson and orange all summer.

'Burgundy Lace'. Explains itself.

'Corallinum'. A rare beauty, growing slowly to some 6ft. In spring the young shoots are painted in delicate coral and its leaves a shrimp-pink, turning pale green later.

'Crippsii' resembles 'Atropurpureum', but the fingers are very finely cut and pointed.

DISSECTUM GROUP. Admired by all for their airy grace, despite their dense, compact build. The twigs drop smoothly to the ground, so that the plant imitates the outline of a mushroom. Though rarely reaching 6ft in height, it spreads much more in breadth, the leaves dancing prettily to the impulses of the wind. It makes a beautiful specimen standing on its own. Each slender finger in the leaf is snipped along its edge as though with nail scissors, giving it

the appearance of having been shredded. The most popular form is the bronzy-crimson 'Dissectum Atropurpureum' (this is not to be confused with the previous unshredded 'Atropurpureum'). From this elegant shrub several distinctive clones of special merit have emerged. 'Garnet' is of the highest standing. 'Red Burgundy Lace' is a spectacular introduction from Oregon. 'Roseo-marginata' explains itself, 'Ornatum', the "spiderleaf" of the American vernacular, belongs here also in spirit if not botanically. In our view, however, the soft, fresh green form sometimes called 'Dissectum Viridis', is just as beautiful as these "coloured" ones and very refreshing to the eye.

The HEPTALOBUM (or SEPTEMLOBUM) Group of *A. palmatum* has much broader leaves, with usually seven-pointed lobes or fingers. They build up into stately shrubs, a good deal taller than the dissectums and with a more erect and open bearing. 'Osakazuki' is the favourite among the following:

'Elegans'. Green, 5in, toothed leaves; there is also a purple form.

'Linearilobum'. Long green fingers with little serrations; again there is a bronze form.

'Bloodgood'. Rich red-purple of spectacular quality. Samares red.

'Osakazuki'. Green leaves brilliantly ensanguined in the fall.

'Reticulatum'. Yellow leaves with dark veins and green margins.

'Ribesifolium'. Stiffly erect bearing, but opening to a spreading crown. Leaves dark green, deeply cut. Slow.

'Senkaki', the "coral-bark maple". Another great favourite, the young shoots being coral-pink, with small leaves of usually six fingers. Erect attitude. To maintain a succession of the pink stems, prune fairly hard in late August. In exceptional circumstances 'Senkaki' can grow very large indeed. Known also as 'Sango-kaku'.

A. sempervirens, the Cretan maple. A slow mover that rarely exceeds 15ft. The bright green leaves are of various shapes and often hang on until Christmas. Samarae widely angled. z8.

ACRADENIA

A. frankliniae is a tender evergreen Tasmanian of rounded outline, dressed in trifoliate leaves, the leaflets stalkless, and flowering in 2in clusters (corymbs) of small, white blossoms at the ends of the branches in May. Reaches 11ft on a wall in Northern Ireland. Interesting for the collector, but competition is strong in May. z9 on a warm wall.

ADAM'S NEEDLE. See *Yucca*

AESCULUS

Horse-chestnut or Buckeye

The big horse-chestnuts that light their tall candles in late spring have a small brother that grows as a shrub and is an attractive surprise in large gardens. This is *Aesculus parviflora*, which displays its big, slender white candles in July and August. It grows to about 12ft or more, spreading widely into a thicket of slender stems from basal suckers. The typical palmate leaves colour well in the fall. z4.

The hybrid *A. × mutabilis* is a large plant that may become of tree size, bearing red and yellow flowers in May and June. Its variety 'Induta' is usually pink and yellow.

ALOYSIA. See Lippia

AMELANCHIER

Service berry

The amelanchiers, nearly all of which originated in North America, are deciduous shrubs of some value for enduring sub-zero temperatures and very wet soils. In spring they are crowded fleetingly with small starry blossoms, after which have no great ornamental value. Their small fruits are black or nearly so. In several species a woolly down clothes the young leaves and flowers and, in acid soils, autumnal tints suffuse the leaves.

Amelanchiers may be shrubs of moderate growth or become trees, as in the scented species *laevis* and the hybrid *grandiflora*. There is a fearful imbroglio about names, some having been called *Mespilus* (the medlar), *Pyrus* (the pear) or *Crataegus* (the hawthorn) and the vernacular name "Snowy Mespilus" has often been employed for any of them.

Particular confusion surrounds the identity of **A. canadensis**. Here we follow Bean, but it has also been called *Mespilus canadensis* and other names. It is an erect, stalwart shrub, prospering even in swampy soils and spreading by sucers to form a thicket. The fruits are edible. Rehder, the distinguished American botanist, applied the name *canadensis* to what should now, under modern rules, be called *arborea*. z4.

The only amelanchier from Europe, **A. ovalis**, of 15ft, is no doubt the original "Snowy Mespilus" (and is so identified by Bean), having been named *Mespilus amelanchier* by Linnaeus, who adapted the vernacular Italian amelancier to identify the species. It grows normally to 15ft with an erect carriage. The fruits are first red, then black. z4. Other amelanchiers are of little ornamental value.

X AMELASORBUS

Nature created this hybrid between an amelanchier and a mountain ash. Some leaves resemble those of one parent, some of the other. The white flowers are like those of the amelanchier, but are borne in loose clusters, as in the other parent and turn into dark red fruits. Growing about 8ft high, it is named *X Amelasorbus jackii*. z5.

AMORPHA

Small to medium-sized, deciduous, very hardy shrubs with pinnate, acacia-like leaves and imperfect pea-flowers, followed by typical pea-pods. Most are of limited garden value, many of them die back during the winter, like herbaceous plants, and have to be pruned hard in the spring. Quite the best one is **A. canescens**, the "lead plant", 3 to 4ft, in which the grey, downy leaves provide an attractive setting for the dense spikes, 3 to 6in long, of mauve flowers enlivened by orange anthers for most of the summer. Rated z2 but prospers also in hot, parched conditions, having deep roots.

A. fruticosa, the false indigo, is too big and ungainly. *A. nana* is a pretty little shrub of 2ft, with scented, purple flowers. z2.

ANDROMEDA

The ultra-hardy andromedas only just qualify for inclusion here, being rarely more than a foot or so high, but they are too beautiful to omit in gardens that have a moist, acid, humusy soil. z2.

The usual one is **A. polifolia**, the bog rosemary, a plant with slender stems and narrow, pointed, tough-textured leaves. From the tips of the stems hang clusters of flowers like pink lilies-of-the-valley. There are several variants whose names explain themselves.

A. glaucophylla differs from polifolia mainly in clothing the under-surfaces of its leaves with a white felt. There is a broad-leaved form. A squad of other shrubs previously in-

22.   Andromeda polifolia

cluded in the Andromeda regiment was recently dismissed from its tents by the botanists to form new units, such as the cassiope, leucothoe, pieris, lyonia and others.

ANGELICA TREE. See *Aralia*

ANTHYLLIS

This ancient Greek name represents a small group of quite attractive shrubs with pea-flowers. After the petals fall the calyx persists and becomes inflated, enclosing the seed.

The usual one is **A. hermanniae**, a small deciduous shrub of about 2ft, with zigzag branches and quantities of yellow flowers in clusters at midsummer. As it ages cut back some of the overcrowded branch terminals a few at a time each year. z7.

A. barba-jovis, or Jupiter's beard, is an evergreen best grown on a warm wall, where it will reach 8ft, with silver-tinted, pinnate leaves, very like an old man's beard, and flowers of deep cream in late spring. Acid soil. z9.

ARALIA

Grown mainly for their very handsome leaves, which may be a yard or more long and divided into numerous, pointed leaflets, the aralias are large, rather prickly, deciduous, hardy shrubs, or sometimes small trees, of great ornamental value where there is plenty of room. They stand out with distinction among other plants of contrasting behaviour and, indeed, add a touch of grandeur to the garden. Give them, for preference, a light, well-drained loam, not too rich, in an open position. Stiff clays are unpropitious. They have pithy stems. They spread fairly rapidly by suckers and these you must ruthlessly inhibit, especially on the impressive (and expensive) forms that have variegated leaves. Quantities of small, white flowers are borne in huge panicles in late summer. The

23.   Leaflet of Aralia elata 'Variegata'

central stem of the panicle persists after flowering and should not be mistaken for a disease.

The most popular is **A. elata**, the "Japanese angelica tree", especially those forms of which the leaves are gilt- or silver-edged; these are 'Variegata', with each leaflet margined white, and 'Aureo-variegata', in which the margins start yellow and turn white. The huge leaves are doubly pinnate. Branching freely, the Japanese angelica can become a very large shrub and occasionally tree-like. z3.

A. chinensis, the Chinese angelica, is very similar, but rather smaller, has a less spiny stem, the leaves finely toothed and the panicle of flowers conical. z5. The American *A. spinosa* ("the Devil's walking-stick" or "Hercules' club") is also similar, but viciously spined. z4.

Except for the variegated forms, propagate by allowing a few suckers to develop.

ARCTOSTAPHYLOS

Manzanita, etc.

This rather awkward name for some useful evergreens is derived from the Greek *arctos*, a bear and *staphyle*, a bunch of grapes. They provide us with some of the very best prostrate ground covers, especially the bear-berry (see Chapter 5) and are adorned with pretty pink or white lily-of-the-valley flowers in spring, followed by small, chestnut-red fruits. They are cousins of the rhododendron and need the same acid, peaty soil, but revel in full sun. A characteristic of the taller, shrubby species is that their young shoots and the reverse of their leaves are clothed more or less densely as though with cottonwool. These taller sorts are known familiarly as manzanitas, a name derived from the old Spanish one, though *A. manzanita* itself is very large and not very attractive. They do not like being transplanted after infancy and are not very wind-firm. We note the following, which are all z7 to 8.

Your first choice among the taller species is likely to be **A. stanfordiana**, the Stanford manzanita. Growing maybe to 6ft, the lustrous leaves are accompanied by dense blush-pink trusses of flowers, displayed terminally, followed by chestnut-red berries. Not always an easy plant to establish, needing good drainage and plenty of sun.

A. canescens, the hoary manzanita, is a good shrub conspicuously clothed with white down. Very hardy and successful in Britain. About 6ft.

A. patula, the green-leaf manzanita, a wide-spreading shrub which is happy in Scotland, has a fine down on its twigs, but green leaves, almost round. Flowers white, fruits chocolate. About 5ft.

A. tomentosa, the shaggy-bark manzanita, grows irregularly to about 4½ft, with shaggy bark, grey leaves, white flowers, chestnut berries.

ARONIA
Chokeberry

Aronias are deciduous shrubs that throw up many shoots at or below ground level ("stools") which can be used to replace old,

Aronia melanocarpa, the black chokeberry, its fruits almost hidden

worn-out branches and which give the gardener a good supply of new shoots to replace old ones when necessary. They are hardy ornamental, arching shrubs, contrasting well with those of stiff behaviour. Their white flowers and their fruits are similar to those of the mountain ash. Not for chalky soil.

A. arbutifolia, the red chokeberry, may be as tall as 10ft. The leaves are a dull, dark green, with a thick grey felt clothing the reverse, but glow like flames in the fall, and the red fruits outride most of the winter. z5.

A. melanocarpa, the black chokeberry, is a small, flat-topped, free-flowering shrub of 3ft, with black fruits that drop in September. z4.

A. prunifolia, the purple chokeberry, has lustrous fruits of that colour and is taller than its brothers.

ARTEMISIA

The herbaceous artemisias (from one of which comes the absinthe that has lured many a dissolute old Frenchman to an early grave) are not our concern, but those species that become shrubs are very important indeed in any garden composition for their lacy, silver or dove-grey leaves and for their aromatic breath. The most desirable is *A. arborescens*, but it needs a warm corner in southerly zones. Like most silvers and greys, artemisias are quite happy in a limy soil and are perhaps at their best in a starved, stony one. The flowers have little merit.

You must prune artemisias very hard indeed in the spring if you do not want them to look like crumpled wedding dresses. Propagate from summer cuttings in shade but not in "close" conditions.

A. abrotanum, the southernwood or lad's-love, is a charming old cottager, often seen in Britain at the garden gate, where you brush it as you go in or out, savouring the amorous breath of its dove-grey, openwork leaves. Remove the proletarian little flowers and cut back quite hard in the spring just as a new growth begins. z6.

A. arborescens is a fine shrub billowing

with silver, filigree leaves. It grows to 4ft or to 6ft if on a wall, where it looks particularly well. You must over-winter cuttings under glass. z8.

A. tridentata is the "sage brush" that covers vast expanses in the warmer, alkaline parts of North America in a grey monotone. Cultivated in the garden, it makes a good shrub of 8ft, emitting a stimulating odour from its grey, curiously toothed leaves. z5.

ARUNDINARIA. See under Bamboos

ATRIPLEX

Another genus with grey or silvery foliage, usually associated with the seaside, for they resist salt ocean gales with equanimity, so providing a valuable screen, and they flourish inland also in any dry, sandy soil. Of limited ornamental value, the flowers worthless.

The best is **A. halimus**, the tree purslane, a stiff-branching, semi-evergreen shrub of 6ft and of a silvery-grey appearance, the leaves dusted as though with talc. On reaching maturity the stems open out in loose sprays; cut them back when new growth starts in spring. z7–8.

A. canescens is a sprawling shrub, but quite pleasing in its almost white dress, the sexes separate. z5. *A. portulacoides*, the sea purslane, is a purely utilitarian, straggling shrub for the seashore. z7–8.

AUCUBA

Aucuba japonica is popularly but erroneously called a "laurel", a name that rightly belongs to the bay (*Laurus nobilis*). The vast plantings of it in large or suburban estates in the last century, when it was found to flourish in deep shade, made it something of a joke when the rhododendrons came in triumphantly to replace it. It was a long time before men realized that aucubas were unisexual, the females (which

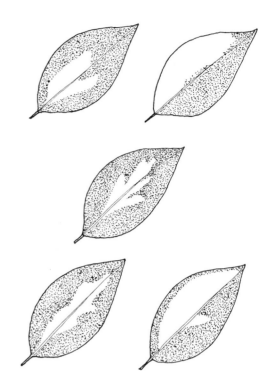

24. Amusing variations in the green-and-gold leaves of Aucuba japonica 'Picturata'

were the first to be introduced) needing the companionship of a male to produce bold red berries. However, in its best varieties the aucuba is a splendid and resilient plant and makes a superlative broad hedge if carefully trimmed with secateurs. Its great merit is that it surpasses all other evergreen shrubs in flourishing in the deep shade beneath large trees, where even grass will not grow, and competing successfully with their roots. z7.

There are quantities of named varieties and some confusion of names. The narrow-leaved forms, such as 'Salicifolia' and 'Longifolia' (both females) have a lighter carriage than the broad leaves. A few have gold markings but the one that arrests our attention is 'Picturata', which displays long, pointed leaves, crazily inlaid with streaks and patches of gold. 'Crassifolia' (male as a rule) is of moderate size and *borealis* is a very hardy dwarf.

AZALEA. See under Rhododendron

AZARA

Very tall, rather tender evergreens from South America embellished with small, yellow, fuzzy flowers that consist of tight bunches of stamens without petals, often scented. If you distrust the climate, grow them on a warm wall, like a ceanothus.

A. integrifolia, the most popular, has oval leaves and flowers abundantly from January till March if the climate allows; the cultivar 'Variegata' has leaves edged pink, turning white. z8 in Britain, z9 in America.

A. lanceolata. The most elegant but the most tender. Very big. Slender leaves. Flowers displayed in little clusters, often double-ranked, all along the stems. April. z10.

A. microphylla. The hardiest, 15ft or more. Small leaves. Scented flowers in February if the season is mild. Accustomed to dry conditions. Again there is a variegated form. Best in some shade and a moist soil. z8.

A. petiolaris. Distinguished by holly-like leaves. Very attractive. Canary flowers in mid-spring.

Azara lanceolata

BACCHARIS

Utilitarian shrub for coastal and other wind-swept places, but must have sun. *B. halimifolia*, the "tree groundsel", deciduous, single-sexed, with white, silky, thistle-like fruits among grey foliage, reaches 12ft. z4. *B. patagonica* is evergreen, smaller and of stiffer habit. z7.

BAMBOOS

Here, for the gardener's convenience, we group the several genera of bamboos together. They are by no means everyman's choice and to some of us are too reminiscent of the jungle, within which, as the tall canes rustle in the wind, you scent a tiger or a snake lying in wait for you. But, of course, we deal here with those accustomed to gentler climes, such as are often delicately painted by Japanese artists. They certainly have their ornamental uses, especially as screens, and some have their own stylish qualities. When rimed by frost they assume a fairy-like raiment. They need, however, to be skilfully sited and look best in the vicinity of water, provided that (with some exceptions) the soil is not sodden, though they do like a moist one, where many of them spread rapidly by suckers. Shelter them from rude, shattering winds. A light woodland pleases them. We omit the swamp-dwellers.

Except in the chusqueas, bamboos have hollow stems, which are wrapped round with a papery sheath when young and sometimes when adult also. They are, of course, simply overgrown grasses, are generally evergreen, and are classified as z6, but fare much better in warmer climes. They have no objection to lime, even chalk. Their flowers resemble those of grasses, but their floral instinct is unpre-

25.   Arundinaria variegata

dictable. Some never flower at all and most of those that do die afterwards. Much botanical argument confounds their identities.

Plant in May during a rainy spell. Propagate by division, but their matted roots make this a tough job. The young shoots (some edible) are called culms.

Arundinaria. Derived from the Latin *arundo*, a cane. The most widely grown of the bamboos. They extend themselves by underground creeping root-stocks, creating dense thickets and throwing out long, arching plumose masses of foliage and needing a lot of room. The following are the first pick. We particularly like the last two, especially for small gardens.

A. anceps. Erect stems of glossy purplish-green of 10ft or more, with arching tips. 'Pitt White' is taller still. Handsome but very invasive.

A. fastuosa. A hefty 20ft or more. Stems dark green.

A. japonica. Hardy and adaptable, the most widely used in Britain. Olive-green canes normally about 12ft high, bending at their summit with an abundance of glossy, dark green leaves.

A. murielae. One of the most handsome. About 10ft tall, often leafless the first year, then bursting out into a thicket of great plumose sprays of apple-green from yellow stems.

A. nitida. Rather like *murielae* in habit, but with empurpled stems, borne down by copious foliage. Not always fully evergreen.

A. variegata (formerly *fortunei*). A good choice for small gardens. Not more than $3\frac{1}{2}$ft high, with zigzag stems bearing dark green leaves, diversified with cream stripes which later turn pale green.

A. viridistriata. Purple-tinted canes up to 5ft, the dark green leaves boldly striped with rich yellow. Highly ornamental anywhere.

Chusquea. This genus, from South America and Mexico, differs from the arundinarias in being more freely branched and in having solid canes instead of hollow ones. The usual one is *C. culeou*, with olive-green stems anything up to 20ft high, densely branched all the way, with small, slender leaves.

Phyllostachys. A genus distinguished by its zigzag stems, flattened on each side alternately. Less invasive than most other bamboos, but often of giant stature.

The species *bambusoides* is a handsome fellow of 15ft and has two dashing cultivars in 'Allgold' (or 'Sulphurea') and 'Castillonis', which is flushed gold in both the stem and the leaves.

The most generally favoured species of the phyllostachys, however, is *P. nigra*, the "black bamboo", especially its variety *henonis*. The mature stems are brown (instead of black as in the wild state) and are laden with luxuriant plume-like foliage, making it one of the finest of bamboos, fit for use as a specimen shrub in a lawn. In the rare 'Boryana' the mature stems are yellow mottled with black.

On the east coast of the USA a much

favoured phyllostachys is *P. aurea*, the golden bamboo, which appears to be the hardiest and most reliable. Its handsome golden stems contrast happily with the green foliage, but in that climate you must expect it to reach 20ft if all things are to its liking, though usually less in Britain. More vigorous still, but a trifle less hardy, is *P. aureosulcata*, the yellow-grove bamboo, often used for fishing-rods. Both are hardy in z6, but must be defended against bitter winds.

Sasa. These resemble the arundinarias, forming dense thickets, but are much smaller. *S. tessellata*, of about 5ft, is a bright, shining green, with leaves so large that the shrub is weighed down by their mass. *S. veitchii* is an invasive dwarf, rarely more than a foot high.

Shibataea kumasasa. A dwarf, less than a foot high, with zigzag stems, forming dense, leafy clumps by creeping roots.

BAY. See *Laurus nobilis*

BARBERRY. See *Berberis*

BEARBERRY. See *Arctostaphylos* in this Register and in Chapter 5

BERBERIS
Barberry

When we enter the thorny territory of the barberries we find ourselves confronted with a very large and embarrassing range of choices and, like the bills of fare of the Ritz and Claridge's, we cannot possibly have them all. So we have reduced them to some 31 species and hybrids, plus their varieties, which should satisfy most appetites.

Widely spread across Asia, Europe and America, barberries may be dwarfs or tallboys and evergreen or deciduous. They are more or less thorny, but seldom aggressively so. The wood is yellow. They are double-event shrubs, giving us small, yellow or orange flowers, dangling in clusters or borne singly all along the twigs, in April and May, followed in autumn by small berries, often brilliant, sometimes sombre but flushed with a delicate bloom in the manner of a peach. The leaves of some species are holly-like, in others lance-like and often very small. The visible leaf is of special interest to the botanist, being in fact merely the terminal of a suppressed pinnate leaf. As a rule the leaves spring from the axils of a group of thorns. Any reasonable soil suits them, but a dry one is preferred. Those originating from S. America are not happy in the eastern half of N. America.

Beyond cutting out dead shoots, no pruning need be done, except as we shall show, but they do not fear being cut if necessary. Several, possibly all, make superlative hedges and many extend themselves by underground suckers. The name comes from the Arabic, whence also the Berber tribe and, anglicised, the 'Barbary Coast', once notorious for piracy and slavery.

Unfortunately, many species of barberry act as hosts for the spread of the rust disease in wheat and their culture is forbidden in wheat-growing areas of North America. In the notes that follow, the term "no rust" means that the species is innocent.

A few barberries are dominant in public favour, notably Darwin's and Thunberg's barberries, and the hybrid *stenophylla*, the last two of which have produced named clones of sterling merit; and from the hybrid *carminea*, mated with other species, we now have a gang with piratical names and loaded with treasures of jewelled berries.

B. aggregata. Deciduous, 4ft. Flowers yellow, handsome red berries. Displaced by its fine hybrid offspring, especially carminea and rubrostilla. z5.

B. buxifolia. An old-stager, semi-evergreen, 8ft, erect, the earliest to bloom (March–April). Flowers yellow, solitary. Berries deep purple. Small leathery leaves in axils of stiff, triple spines. The cultivar 'Aureomarginata' has a gilt edge. z6.

B. calliantha, evergreen, is one of the very best of the smaller barberries, characterized by its holly-like leaves, often as large as theirs but

26. Berberis calianthus in flower

27. Berberis darwinii in flower. Fruit cluster shown on right; note pin-like stigma persisting

elongated and waxy-white on the reverse. Flowers deep cream, very large for a barberry, berries blue-black. About 3ft high (5ft at Wisley), spreading widely and becoming a thicket. z7.

B. candidula. A small, slow barberry recognisable by the vivid ice-blue of the reverse of its small, narrow leaves, springing from the axils of three sharp spines. Flowers bright yellow, solitary. Berries oval with purple bloom. Rarely more than 4ft. z5.

B. × carminea. This is a "collective" name for a group of seedlings of mixed parentage, originating at the RHS Garden at Wisley, remarkable less for their spring flowers than for the exuberance of their berried splendours in the autumn, which often bows down the branches from their sheer weight. The best of them are:

'Barbarossa'. Up to 6ft. Brilliant red berries.

'Bountiful'. 3ft, spreading. Coral berries.

'Buccaneer'. Erect. Large, deep red berries, lasting till December.

'Pirate King' about the same height. Berries brilliant orange.

B. × chenaultii. A neat, evergreen shrub of 4ft that closely resembles its fine parent *gagnepainii*, except that its branches bend like a bow. No rust. z5.

B. concinna. A pretty, compact, deciduous, 3ft shrub, marked by the white reverse of its small leaves, guarded by three basal spines. Solitary yellow flower, red berries. Its offspring 'Concal' has lemon flowers. No rust. z6.

B. darwinii. One of the finest of all evergreen shrubs. Discovered by him on his famous voyage in HMS *Beagle* in 1835, Darwin's barberry is a large shrub equipped with miniature, holly-like leaves, an easily distinguishable feature and vividly green. It suckers freely, making a dense and solid thicket. From its twigs hang showers of flowers in drooping racemes, bright orange, followed by plum-coloured, oval berries. Any reasonable soil will support it but it attains its greatest splendour in a rather moist one and a fairly humid atmosphere, where you may expect it to reach perhaps 12ft, but a specimen at Glenskill, in Scotland, grows taller still and spreads to 24ft. No rust. z7.

B. gagnepainii, evergreen, may be 8ft high, with lance-like leaves of leaden green, which may be 4in long, grouped in rather widely spaced clusters, with slender, forward-pointing teeth. Dense, erect and neat in carriage, the branches barbed with triple spines. Bright yellow flowers in thick clusters and blue-black berries. Makes a fine boy-proof hedge. The variety 'Fernspray' is well-named and has light green leaves. z6.

B. gilgiana, the wildfire barberry. A very hardy, deciduous shrub of 6ft, displaying dangling racemes of bright yellow flowers followed by a brilliant show of blood-red berries and vivid autumn colours. No rust. z5.

A good hardy hybrid that is better known in America than east of the Atlantic is **B. × gladwynensis 'William Penn'**. Born in Pennsylvania of julianae × verruculosa, it becomes a close-packed shrub, broader than high, with rich winter colour.

Though not of the highest order, we must mention **B. glaucocarpa**, a rangy, deciduous shrub of up to 12ft and of suckering habit. In Devon and Somerset it is effectively used in hedgerows. Flowers bright yellow, fruits black but thickly coated with a white bloom.

B. hookeri. A dense evergreen of only about 4ft, rather stiff of carriage, with lance-form, leathery, dark green leaves, white below, in tufts. Flowers pale yellow, berries purple-black, persistent. Very long, sharp spines. The variety *viridis* has uniformly bright green leaves. z7.

B. insignis. A handsome, lusty evergreen, remarkable for its very long leaves of dark, glossy green and its dull yellow, spineless stems; 6ft high but much broader. Pale yellow flowers, black berries. z8.

Where a dense, rounded, evergreen barberry is wanted, a good one is found in **B. × interposita**. It is clothed with tiny, holly-like leaves, yellow on the underside, set among spiny, arching stems. 6ft.

B. jamesiana. A handsome, very big, deciduous, many-stemmed barberry, which can be 15ft high and wide. The carriage is erect, the thorns long, the flowers yellow in 3in racemes, the berries hanging thickly in a wonderful glistening translucent bright red like red-currants. z8.

B. julianae. A sturdy, luxuriant evergreen of about 7ft (10ft at the Royal Botanic Gardens, Kew) equipped with large, spiny, holly-like leaves. Yellow flowers in thick clusters, blue-black fruits. No rust. A hedge of closely planted julianae will stop the most determined intruder. z6.

B. linearifolia. An evergreen that averages about 6ft, with an erect, loose and sometimes ungainly habit and slim, leathery, thornless leaves, with recurved edges. The large, abundant flowers are perhaps the most richly coloured of the true species, being apricot outside and a brilliant orange within. Berries are blue-black. No rust. z7.

B. × mentorensis. Very hardy, yet able to

28.   Berberis linearifolia

stand hot, dry places also. Mentor's hybrid grows to 7ft, with yellow flowers and mahogany berries (thunbergii × julianae). No rust. z5.

B. × lologensis. A group name for several hybrids with darwinii and linearifolia as their parents. The foliage tends towards Darwin's barberry and the flowers to the more brilliant hues of linearifolia. Succeeds in chalk. About 5ft. z7.

B. × ottawensis. This is a group name for some very hardy seedlings raised by the Ottawa Experimental Station from *vulgaris* mated with *thunbergii*, two of the very hardiest species. Bean places it under *vulgaris*, Rehder under the other parent, but, especially in the selected form named 'Superba' (raised in Holland), it is far too important to the gardener to hide its light under a botanical bush.

In this form the Ottawa barberry is truly "superb" and one of the finest deciduous shrubs we have. It is clothed with bronze-red leaves, crimson in autumn, an exuberance of golden flowers, followed by brilliant red berries. Expect it to grow to 8ft or more. Sometimes catalogued as *B. thunbergii* 'Atropurpurea Superba'. z5.

B. prattii, deciduous, best seen in its variety *laxipendula*. A beautiful and ornamental shrub, capable of 10ft, with oblong leaves in thick clusters. Its feature is that the small flowers are carried in large trusses (panicles), which are more or less erect. The prodigal egg-shaped

28a. Berberis × rubrostilla in fruit

berries are bright pink, heavily and persistently borne well into winter. z5.

B. × rubrostilla. A beautiful, deciduous hybrid raised by the Royal Horticultural Society at Wisley early this century. The shrub averages about 4ft and its beauty lies in its berries, which are egg-shaped, a shining, translucent coral, dangling from the branches in remarkable profusion. z6.

B. sargentiana. An evergreen of up to 6ft, sharply armed with three-pronged spikes and very long, lance-form leaves. The scented flowers are pale yellow, opening often in March, the fruits black. No rust. z6.

A small barberry that excels in a dry soil and full sun is **B. sieboldii**, which deserves to be better known than it is. Growing perhaps to about 4ft, it is a bushy, deciduous, suckering shrub clothed with prettily tinted leaves that turn a vinous red in autumn. The bunches of pale yellow flowers fructify as gleaming red berries that may last all winter. z5.

B × stenophylla. An evergreen of great splendour, clothed in small, narrow leaves, reaching 10ft and becoming a dense thicket of slender arching stems, spreading by suckers, the whole 10ft wide. The golden flowers are small but produced exuberantly and the berries are "silvered o'er" with a soft bloom. It makes a superlative hedge but needs a lot of room. Cut back the arching stems after flowering (with secateurs if you have the patience) to a point of new growth. No rust. z6.

Stenophylla (which comes from darwinii crossed with the dwarf empetrifolia) has produced some very attractive children. Most of them, such as 'Coccinea' and 'Corallina Compacta' are too small for us, but 'Etna' is a 5ft dome with fiery red buds that open orange. 'Gracilis' with golden flowers and bright green leaves, will grow to 3ft. So will 'Irwinii', formerly classed as a distinct hybrid of its own, but now included under stenophylla; it is a sterling, compact shrub with yellow flowers.

B. temolaica. A deciduous shrub of 8ft, which is unique in the spring picture, when its pale yellow flowers mingle prettily with the ice-blue of the young leaves and arching stems. Later the stems become purple. Fruits red with a silvery bloom.

B. thunbergii. A deciduous and very hardy shrub (z4–5) of great importance to the gardener, for itself and for its progeny. It is an erect, tidy shrub up to 8ft, not too thorny, with small, spatulate leaves that colour brilliantly in autumn. Yellow flowers and then red berries. We shall glance quickly at its more important progeny, which exceed their parent in popular esteem, the green-leaved ones first.

'Erecta' is a dense, upright but broad strain, specially developed in Ohio for hedging. Five feet high and needs no clipping.

At the other end of the scale is the splendid dwarf 'Minor', miniature in all its parts and slowly reaching 3ft, originating at the Arnold Arboretum.

It is, however, in its bronze-leaved offspring that Thunberg's barberry is usually most valued. They include:

The tall 'Atropurpurea', a great favourite in a reddish-purple dress.

A delightful dwarf, almost thornless, known as 'Atropurpurea Nana', or 'Crimson Pygmy' in America, excellent for the "little low hedges", that Francis Bacon was fond of.

The empurpled form of 'Erecta' known as 'Red Pillar'.

Above all, perhaps, two sparkling varieties of rare ornamental value called 'Harlequin' and 'Rose Glow', in which the young leaves are speckled with pink and cream; to encourage

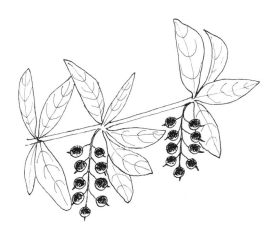

29.   Berberis valdiviana in fruit

30.   Berberis verruculosa, thorns concealed

this pretty young growth, cut back the stems, which are basically bronze, by about one-third every March. The twiggy *maximowiczii* has an even deeper "purple" leaf, but green on the reverse and purple stems, with brilliant autumn colours.

Besides these bronze or "purple" varieties, we have the totally different 'Aurea', with almost golden leaves until late summer, when they become pale green, but still very distinctive.

B. valdiviana. A handsome, sturdy ever-green to 8ft or more, with oval, spineless leaves and profusely decorated with hanging clusters of saffron florets, followed by purple berries. A native of Chile and not in the front line of hardiness.

B. verruculosa. A very useful and attractive evergreen rarely more than 5ft high, with oval, leathery leaves of a dark lustrous green, clus-tered in rosettes along its rough, minutely warty stems, which are its recognition signal. Flowers yellow borne singly or in small clus-ters, fruit blue-black. No rust. z6.

B. vulgaris. The "common" barberry of Britain and Europe, the hardiest of all, is a first-rate shrub, swelling to 10ft high and wide, the stems arching and dripping with clusters of yellow flowers, and laden in autumn with masses of red, oval berries. It is, however, a notorious host for wheat-rust disease. z3. Innumerable varieties or forms have evolved over the centuries, the most attractive being 'Atropurpurea', the purple-leaved barberry One of special interest is the infertile 'Asperma', the berries of which have no seed within, so that the flesh can be used for sweetmeats.

The common barberry has inevitably been mated to others to create hybrids, of which the most outstanding is the magnificent *B.* × *ottawaensis*, above.

B. wilsoniae. A beauty that forms itself into a symmetrical mound only 4ft high but spread-ing rather more broadly. The slender, arching, chestnut-tinted stems carry grey-green leaves and copious straw-coloured flowers, followed by coral berries. A real charmer, but only partially evergreen. z6. The variety *stapfiana* is equally elegant but grows to about 5ft, with elongated fruits; *subcaulialata* is also taller, the leaves larger, the berries globular. z7.

BESCHORNERIA

To the layman's eye the tender *B. yuccoides* does not look very much like a yucca, but is nonetheless an ornamental plant of bizarre beauty. From a basal rosette of sword-like leaves it shoots thick rhubarb stems to an average of 5ft, bending languidly at their tips, from which hang large clusters of bold, red bracts disgorging green, tubular flowers. The rosette dies after flowering but leaves offsets to maintain succession. Give it a hot spot in sandy, stony or chalk soil, preferably on a slope. z9.

BILBERRY. See *Vaccinium myrtillus*

BLACKTHORN. See *Prunus spinosa*

BLADDER NUT. See *Staphylea*

BLADDER SENNA. See *Colutea*

BOX. See *Buxus*

BRIDAL WREATH. See *Spiraea* × *arguta*

BROOMS

Again for the convenience of the gardener rather than the botanist, we group together three genera of similar characters and uses. They are the cytisus, the genista and the spartium. Their butterfly flowers are like those of the pea (consisting of standard, wings and keel as in the sweet-pea), usually yellow and the leaves rather sparse, indicating that they do not need a lot to drink. All are attuned to warm, sunny places, to poor, dry, sandy or stony soils and to long periods without rain; they often do well on clay, however. They like lime if not positively chalky, but can be happy also in a soil that is mildly acid. Most of them flower like mad, but they seldom live very long in a fat soil. Many of the species are unashamedly promiscuous in their relationships, so that there are many of mixed parentage, which we group below under "Popular Hybrids".

Brooms range from prostrate crawlers to large shrubs, almost tree-like, as in the Mount Etna broom. In the garden picture they mingle well with such shrubs as helianthemums, halimiums, lavenders and cistus (all plants for poor soils). Botanists argue continually about their names, but we shall use those commonly accepted. The vernacular one derives from the fact that the twigs of several species, especially *Cytisus scoparius*, make very good implements for sweeping.

The true species come readily from seed. Otherwise, take cuttings with a heel in early August, about 2in long, in very sandy soil in closed conditions; they are ready for potting in spring. After you have planted them out do not attempt to transplant them elsewhere.

Pruning is very important in most cases if you want shapely, well-dressed plants instead of the bare-legged, top-heavy creatures that one so often sees. Not all are treated exactly the same but, in general terms, the important thing is to cut back the stems that bore flowers immediately after they have finished, to prevent the development of seed-pods. We shall note some special cases as we go along. Never cut back into the old, hard wood, but to a point just below the lowest dead flower or thereabouts, except in a sparticum.

Cytisus. These are mostly deciduous brooms and, indeed sometimes have no leaves at all on their green stems. Such leaves as they have are often trifoliate, maybe mingled with very small, single ones. In general terms, leave these unpruned in their first year, then cut back very hard after blossom-fall by two-thirds to where new growth has started. Observing our own rules, we must regretfully pass by the prostrate and very dwarf ones, such as ardoinii and kewensis, usually but not necessarily grown in rock gardens. We are left mainly with the following, the popular hybrids coming at the end.

C. battandieri is totally different from all other brooms and is one of the finest deciduous shrubs you can have where the climate is not too harsh. Sometimes called the pineapple or Moroccan broom, it will grow to 12ft, amply clothed in silky, trifoliate, blue-washed leaves, which are large for a broom, and displaying bold, erect cones made up of tightly packed yellow florets, scented of pineapple. Unlike most brooms, it produces new shoots from its base, so that the only pruning needed is to cut right out the old, decadent ones. This happy faculty gives the pineapple broom a longer life than most others. June. z7.

Also quite distinct and growing fairly tall (to 8ft) is Dallimore's beautiful hybrid broom, *C × dallimorei*. This also has trifoliate leaves, but smaller, and from their nodes come brilliant, pink and crimson flowers of rounded outline, with white keels. Rather rare now. z6.

C. emeriflorus is a delightful Italian, forming a neat, dense hummock of 3ft, with small, silky, trifoliate leaves and yellow flowers in such profusion as to hide the leaves. May. z5.

C. ingramii. A dense shrub of 6ft, with yellow and cream flowers in June. Found in Spain by Captain Collingwood Ingram.

C. multiflorus, the White Spanish Broom, grows splendidly to 10ft, with a dense, brush-like mass of stems, strung with white flowers in May. z6.

C. nigricans. A 4ft shrub distinguished by its long terminal spikes (racemes) strung with small, droopy, yellow flowers displayed throughout July and August. Behead the flowered part of the stems after flowering and prune harder in early spring to new developing shoots. z5.

C. × praecox 'Warminster' is one of the very best, pouring out a 3ft cascade of sulphur flowers in early May, prettily contrasting with evergreen azaleas. Several very good varieties have been raised with this hybrid as one parent, notably 'Allgold' of 5ft, 'Goldspear', of a deeper yellow than its parent, 'Hollandia', in which the mixed colours have an overall effect of rosy-pink, and 'Zealandia', 6ft high and flushed with pink. z7. Prune after flowering.

The pineapple or Moroccan broom Cytisus battandieri

Although *C. purpureus*, the purple broom, grows only about a foot high, we have not the heart to shut it out, for it is spectacular in May and, being well-clad in small, trifoliate leaves, makes a good "ground-cover" or, more artificially, you can get it as a small standard tree, grafted on laburnum stock. Prune after flowering. There are white, pink and violet forms. z5.

C. scoparius, the "common" broom of Britain and Europe, is a glowing shrub of 6ft, erect and green-stemmed, ablaze in May and June with richly golden flowers and seen in great splendour on the hills of northern Scotland. You would place it best in informal, open places, in communities of heathers, on dry banks and anywhere a bit difficult. The most famous of its direct offspring, apart from many hybrids, is 'Andreanus', which has chestnut wings and a yellow keel, a great favourite among gardeners. There are also prostrate and pendulous forms and the pallid compact 'Moonlight', rather rare. All z5. Cut back all the flowered shoots by two-thirds after blossom-fall.

POPULAR HYBRIDS. A whole squadron, or what botanists call a "hybrid swarm", of cytisus, very showy, blooming profusely, usually flowering themselves to death after eight years or so, has been raised by enterprising nurserymen and others. The sap of many parents mingle in their cells, the chief ones being *dallimorei*, *scoparius* and *praecox*. Diverse colours are usually to be found in their standards, wings and keels. To preserve these in decent order you must amputate the flower stems immediately after flowering is over. The following are predominant.

'Burkwoodii'', Cerise, wings crimson, vigorous.

'Cornish Cream'. Shades of pale yellow.

'Donard Seedling'. Pale mauve stamens, wings red.

'Dorothy Walpole'. Cherry and red.

'Firefly'. Yellow and chestnut red.

'Goldfinch'. Yellow and crimson.

'Hookstone'. Distinctive mixture of lilac and orange.

'Johnson's Crimson'. One of the best. All crimson, graceful habit.

'Killiney Red'. Bright, velvety-red dwarf.

'Knaphill Lemon'. All lemon.

'Lady Moore'. Large flowers with standards of cream, flushed rose and wings of flame.

'Lord Lambourne'. Standards cream, wings dark red.

'Minstead'. Ivory with purple wings.

'Mrs Norman Henry'. Like 'Minstead' but darker wings.

Genista. Here again we have some tallboys and some lilliputians. They differ from the cytisus only in botanical detail, but there is often an even more noticeable absence or shortage of leaves, the functions of which are taken over by the green skin of the stems. They are very beautiful shrubs and in general are superior to the cytisus for garden adornment. The flowers of all but one are yellow and are often scented. Several are fiercely armed with thorns. The plant which the Plantagenet kings took for their badge and for their name was *Genista anglica*, the wild, thorny, "petty whin" of England.

The king of them all, but the least hardy, is *G. aetnensis*, the Mount Etna broom, which can become a huge tree-like shrub 20ft high and

even more, rounded in outline and glittering with a great mass of golden, scented sequins in July and early August. It is almost devoid of leaves but throws out long, slender, rush-like stems painted bright green, drooping a little at the tips. Stake it firmly when young and snip back the shoots after flowering for the first year or two to encourage density, after which little pruning is needed. z9.

Growing to about half the size of the Mount Etna broom but likewise laden, in June and July, with showers of gold, also scented, is *G. cinerea*, which, as its name implies, has an ashen complexion from the grey of its tiny leaves to the silky down of its stems. A beautiful shrub. Cut back after flowering in the usual manner to a point where new growth is showing. Some nurseries may send you instead the almost identical *G. tenera*, the flowers of which flutter at the tips of short lateral branchlets. z7.

G. ephedroides is an erect, much branched, green-stemmed shrub of 3ft, virtually leafless, flowering in May and June and fragrant. z8.

G. hispanica, the Spanish broom, is a very thorny creature of about 18in, but gives a brilliant display of massed gold, for a rather short time in May–June. Stems and thorns alike are bright green. You ought, if possible, to plant it in masses in a starved, dry, stony or sandy soil, not rich ones. Give it a light clipping after flowering. As they age, dead patches often occur after a severe winter and replacement is necessary, or you may regenerate them by pegging down living stems hard to the ground. z6.

If the Mount Etna broom is the king of genistas, *G. lydia* is assuredly the queen, the most elegant in form and deportment of them all. Growing to about 2ft high, its slender, lax stems, fairly well-clothed with small leaves, swerve out and down like massed scimitars to form a broad dome, seen at its best when swooping down from a terrace, bank, ledge or mound. The bright yellow flowers come in May–June. z5.

G. monosperma is the only white genista, and delightfully scented too, but not very hardy. Thin, flexible branches make a rather straggly mound of about 4ft, but more in hot regions, and a sandy soil seems essential.

G. pilosa is a low, deciduous broom of about 15in, forming a tangled, twiggy mass with silver-tinted leaves, densely covering the ground or tumbling in the manner of *lydia*. Good in sandy or gravelly soils. May. z5.

G. radiata forms a dense bush of 3ft with evergreen stems and small, trifoliate leaves, the flowers in terminal clusters in June. z6.

When you have an impoverished soil and an almost Arctic climate and you want a shrub that will bloom for months, nothing is better than *G. tinctoria*. This is the old, wild "dyer's greenweed" of England used for centuries for dyeing wool. The dye it provides is, in fact, yellow, but becomes green when mixed with the blue of the woad of the ancient Britons. It flowers from June to September and under cultivation may in warmer zones grow to about 2ft. Many varieties of it have been found, of which the most valuable for the gardener is the double-flowered 'Plena' and the rich 'Royal Gold'. z2.

Besides these chosen genistas, there are several which are fearfully spiny, such as *horrida*, *falcata* and *fasselata*, which we avoid, as we must also the prostrate ones.

Spartium, which derives its name from the ancient Greek one, is our third genus of broom. Almost leafless, but with bright green stems and a little less hardy than most others, it has only one species, *S. junceum*, which shoots up its slender, erect, martial stems to 9ft, covered with relatively large, scented flowers throughout the summer and early autumn. Very good at the seaside and altogether a fine ornamental shrub.

Pruning is a three-year job in order to build a good framework. In the first season get rid of the weaklings and snip off the tips of the main shoots. In the second season, in March–April, amputate last summer's shoots by one-half. Subsequently cut back all new shoots to about two buds annually. A neglected old plant will regenerate if cut right down to the ground. Grown in England for nearly four and a half centuries and naturalised in America. z7.

BRUCKENTHALIA

Although only about 9in high, *B. spiculifolia* is allowed in here because it is an agreeable companion for ericas, which it closely resembles, bearing terminal spikes (racemes) of rose-pink bells throughout the whole of June. The little bells are more open-mouthed than those of heathers. z5.

BUCKEYE. See *Aesculus*

BUCKTHORN. See *Rhamnus*

BUDDLEIA

Celebrated for enticing butterflies and therefore sometimes called "butterfly bushes" by the populace, the buddleias, which were named in honour of the Rev. Adam Buddle, Vicar of Farnbridge, Essex, are rather a mixed bag, some hardy, others tender, some beautiful, others not worth growing, some flowering early in the year, others late, so that pruning is affected. But, with few exceptions, they have three things in common — their leaves are grey or nearly white by reason of the faint down that partly clothes them; their inflorescence is a pyramidal plume (a panicle) of very small, tightly packed florets; and, with one notable exception, their leaves are "opposite". Their flowers are usually scented. They originate from several parts of the world and their ratings vary a trifle. In general, they are among the easiest of the gardener's problems, but do like a rich, loamy soil and a place in the sun. Nearly all are deciduous. We omit the very tender sorts and those of no garden merit.

Pruning is very important and somewhat variable in manner, but the general precepts set out in Chapter 4 apply neatly, namely:

(*a*) on those that flower before July on "old wood" that developed last year, cut away the flowered sections immediately after blossom-fall; the significant species is B. alternifolia.

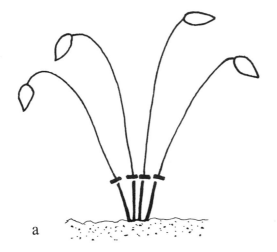

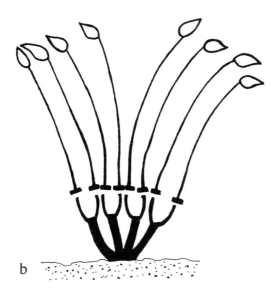

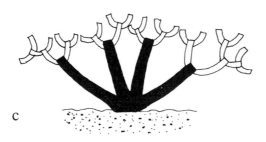

32. Buddleias. Hard pruning of B. davidii and its like. (*a*) first year, amputate by three-quarters; (*b*) second year; (*c*) by the third year you get a knobbly stump like this

(*b*) amputate in March very hard, those that flower later in the year on the "new wood"; typical of their group are the favourite B. davidii, together with the less hardy B. fallowiana and B. crispa.

(*c*) an intermediate group in which the flowers are displayed on short shoots that have developed on growth made in the previous year; here we find the big B. colvilei and the golden balls of B. globosa. We give these no regular pruning but can amputate them severely if necessary.

Most of the true species are easily grown from seed, if you can get it, and others by cuttings in July or August.

The highest in popular favour (but not ours) is undoubtedly Father David's species, **B. davidii**, and its numerous offspring, so we shall get rid of it first. This is the butterfly bush, a tall, upright fellow, with long, tapering greyish leaves, and long, pointed, conical trusses of flowers from July onwards, too often seen as a gaunt creature with unashamedly naked legs. In the first season (having cut right out all weak shoots) amputate the main stems to about 6in off the ground in early spring. Afterwards sever the flowered stems to 2 or 3in of their points of origin on the main stems. In time a dense, woody stump will develop. z5.

In the wild state, the florets of David's buddleia vary from lilac to purple with an orange eye. Several natural varieties have been collected in the wild, to wit:

alba, white

magnifica, the "Ox-eyed butterfly bush", violet-purple, late.

nanhoensis, a lavender dwarf (4 to 5ft) of great beauty.

veitchiana, like *magnifica*, but earlier, deeper colour and a pronounced orange eye.

wilsonii, rosy-lilac in lax panicles.

Besides these, numerous named cultivars have been raised for the delight of the gardener, most of them deriving from the seed collected in China by E. H. Wilson at the start of this century. They include:

'Black Knight', very deep purple.
'Charming', lavender-pink.

Buddleia alternifolia, trained as a tree

'Dubonnet', deep purple in massive panicles.

'Empire Blue', rich violet, orange-eyed.

'Fascinating' (or 'Fascination'), vivid orchid-pink.

'Fortune', long plumes of soft lilac.

'Fromow's Purple', handsome plumes of deep purple.

'Harlequin', leaves strongly variegated cream, flowers red-purple, low growth.

'Ile de France', long, elegant plumes of rich violet.

'Opera', magnificent crimson-purple.

'Royal Red', massive plumes, more purple than red, a great favourite.

Several white clones — 'White Bouquet' (scented and yellow-eyed), 'White Cloud' (pure white) and 'White Profusion' (yellow-eyed). These white sorts are apt to look rather haggard as the blossoms age.

From the most popular buddleia we turn to what is, when well-grown, perhaps the most beautiful. This is the very hardy **B. alternifolia**, in which the leaves sprout alternately on the stems, not opposite. Sometimes called the "fountain buddleia", it does indeed become a fountain of soft lilac-purple. The flowers, instead of being plumes, are composed in small clusters all the way along the elegant, drooping,

willowy wands in May, often smothering the small leaves among which they emerge. In the variety 'Argentea' the leaves adopt a silvery sheen.

Prune the flowered wands back to promising young growth as the blossoms drop, but not too hard in the first year, so that a good framework is established.

When grown as an ordinary shrub, however, *alternifolia* may sometimes adopt an irregular shape. Undoubtedly the way to grow it is as a little standard tree, as in the classic specimen in the RHS garden at Wisley. This is quite easy. I have myself grown it this way from a packet of seed, some of which grew shoulder-high in a single season by keeping them to a single stem, plucking off the side-shoots and retaining only the top tuft. You can do the same thing with a nursery specimen by cutting the plant right back after the first season and subsequently allowing only one stem to develop. z5.

We turn now to a more formal alphabetical sequence;

B. albiflora. Scented, lilac flowers in slender plumes in July and later. Has the same aspect as *davidii* but is inferior to it.

B. colvilei. Very big, handsome and distinctive, the Colvile buddleia is remarkable not only for its great size (up to 20ft) but also for its large individual florets, which are 1in long and bell-shaped and displayed in long, loose, dangling, grape-like clusters in June; they are a beautiful rose-crimson, white in the throat. The green leaves are also very long, maybe 10in, drawn out to a fine, spear-like point and perhaps a trifle coarse. When very young the plant is definitely tender and needs protection, but it soon toughens up enough to withstand zero F. No formal pruning, but remove decadent and weak shoots. z8.

In its form 'Kewensis' the flowers are red.

B. auriculata. An unique and rather tender South African relished for its very sweetly scented panicles of cream florets from September to Christmas — a very rare achievement. The shrub grows to about 9ft in Britain, the lower surface of its leaves thickly covered with a white fur. A severe winter may kill its

31. Buddleia colvilei

B. 'Lochinch'. A charming hybrid originating from Lord Stair's garden in Scotland, the parents being apparently *davidii* and *fallowiana*. Nearer to the latter but much hardier, it wears a soft, grey-green coat, with lavender spikes, erect but drooping at the tips. Prune as in davidii. z6 or 7.

B. salviifolia, the South African sagewood, is only just hardy enough for the north temperate zones. The leaves are sage-like and the very hard wood was used by the Zulus and other aboriginals for assegai shafts. Average 10ft with panicles of soft lilac in July. z9. The other South African is the decidedly tender *B. auriculata*.

branches but its rootstock retains life. Prune in early spring. Easily propagated by summer cuttings. The specific name comes from the ear-shaped appendages (auricles) that clasp the bases of the leaf-stalks. z8 on a warm wall, z9 in the open in Britain, z10 in America.

B. crispa. A beautiful, rounded grey-felted shrub averaging about 10ft, more in width, and providing quantities of small, lilac, scented panicles continuously from June until the frost. Prune as for David's buddleia. z8.

B. fallowiana. Another fine and distinguished but not very hardy buddleia, not often exceeding 6ft, behaving in the same manner as David's, with long panicles of lavender florets, very sweetly scented, among grey-green leaves in July–August. Best against a warm wall. Prune in the same way as in B. davidii. z8.

B. globosa, the Chilean orange-ball tree or "Globe butterfly bush". Unique among all cultivated buddleias in producing bright yellow, scented flowers in June in small, stalked balls grouped together on a 7in plume. Singularly handsome, evergreen in mild places, and its stems covered in a tawny felt, it will reach 15ft. The terminal buds remain leafy all winter. Cut back the flowered sections after blossom-fall. z7. See also the hybrid *weyeriana* below.

Buddleia globosa

B. stenostachys. Notable for its very long, very slender plumes, usually in groups of threes, of lilac, orange-eyed, in late summer. About 9ft. z7.

B. × weyeriana. A hybrid between *davidii* and *globosa*. Of the resulting issue 'Golden Glow' stands out, having orange flowers flushed pink. Very attractive. 'Moonlight' is not so good. z7.

BUPLEURUM

Country folk in England have long known the herbaceous members of this society as "buplevers", but *B. fruticosum* is a lax, more or less evergreen shrub of about 6ft with bunches (umbels) of yellow flowers all summer among blue-green foliage. Not an aristocrat, but valuable for the seashore and other windy places, thriving even on chalk cliffs. When it gets shabby cut it back hard. z7.

BUTCHER'S BROOM. See *Ruscus aculeatus*

33. Bupleurum fruticosum

BUXUS
Box

Beloved of topiarists and other vegetable sculptors, the boxes are evergreen and as tough as you please, often withstanding temperatures far below zero. In their natural forms some become small trees, others low mounds or rounded shrubs, thriving in any reasonable soil, including chalk, and quite happy in shade.

The leaves are usually very small, their growth rather slow, their life long. In England perhaps their most famous and ancient natural plantation is on Box Hill, near Dorking in Surrey, on pure chalk, and commanding a glorious view of many miles. Even in North America, where they were introduced by the early colonists, there are splendid old specimens in Virginia and elsewhere. Some of them have declined sadly due to a nematode infection of the roots, but this is curable chemically.

The wood is hard and bony. The insignificant flowers, devoid of petals, are unisexual but carried on the same plant (monoecious). Cuttings root easily, except in *wallichiana*.

You must plant boxwoods with a good ball of soil. In very cold areas protect them in the first winter. In very hot ones shade them from the sun in the first year and water them well.

When grown naturally no pruning is needed except to keep them in good shape, cutting well back inside the shrub in summer. For hedges and fancy work clip in late July.

At the head of the parade of boxwoods is, of course, *Buxus sempervirens*, the "common" box, which has fathered almost as many offspring as a sultan. We have traced 32 and we list 19 of them, the differences between one and another being often very slight. Generally z5. 'Elegantissima' is perhaps my favourite. Differences in natural habit, as in 'Prostrata' and 'Handsworthensis', must guide your pruning.

'Argentea'. Leaves margined cream. Spreading. Known also incorrectly as 'Argentea Variegata'.

'Aurea Pendula'. Large "weeping" bush with leaves edged and splashed yellow.

'Aurea-variegata'. Leaves striped and

splashed yellow. 10ft.

'Curly Locks'. Branches twist engagingly. Very slow dwarf.

'Elegantissima'. A most attractive little shrub to 6ft, dense, neat, upright, the leaves (some mis-formed) irregularly edged cream. Do not clip it.

'Handsworthensis'. Big, handsome, broad-leaved, of portly figure when mature. Good hedger.

'Latifolia Bullata' (or 'Bullata'). Dense 6ft mound with broad, dark, puckered leaves.

'Latifolia Macrophylla'. Loose, spreading growth to 10ft, with large leaves.

'Latifolia Maculata'. Like 'Bullata' in behaviour, but having smooth leaves splashed yellow.

'Longifolia'. A big fellow (12ft or more) with long, narrow leaves. Very effective when developed on a single "leg", like a tree.

'Myosotifolia'. Dense, compact dwarf with tiny leaves, slow.

'Myrtifolia'. Small, myrtle-like leaves in flattened sprays.

'Newport Blue'. Dense mass of bluish-green, wider than high. Distinctive, but very slow.

'Northern Find'. A Canadian, so extra hardy. z4.

'Pendula'. Graceful shrub of loose and open growth with pendulous branches, ultimately a small tree.

'Prostrata'. Strong 6ft shrub, branches spreading horizontally.

'Rosmarinifolia'. Neat, pretty, dwarf, with narrow leaves.

'Suffruticossa'. This is the famous "box edging", clipped very hard and used for centuries in Europe for defining paths, the margins of flower beds and in old knot gardens. Can be severely disciplined to a mcre 6in but if left to itself will reach 4ft. The leaves are scented.

'Vardar Valley'. Extra hardy, broader than high, growing 2ft by 4ft after many years. z4.

Leaving the common box, we find some other good ones.

B. balearica. A robust, erect Mediterranean, becoming tree-like. Large, matt leaves.

A very old specimen at Kew is 25ft high. z8.

B. harlandii. Rare Chinese dwarf. See *B. microphylla sinica*.

B. microphylla. A dwarf of up to 3ft, with very small, thin leaves. There are several variations, natural or otherwise. Some, such as 'Compacta' and 'Green Pillow', are too small and slow for anything but the rock garden. The natural variety *japonica* is ungainly and *koreana*, though extremely hardy, turns brown in winter in cold places. We are thus left with *sinica*, a good shrub, taller than the parent species, with lustrous leaves, often erroneously labelled *harlandii*. All z5, except *koreana* (z4).

B. wallichiana. A rare but good 6ft shrub, with leaves a good deal larger than those of the common box but not so glossy and the twigs are downy. z8.

CAESALPINIA

These are showy, tropical or sub-tropical, deciduous shrubs that can be grown in z9. They are prettily clothed with fine, feathery, bi-pinnate, acacia-like leaves and gaily ornamented with yellow flowers clustered in long, erect spikes (racemes). The least tender, but formidably armed with fierce, hooked thorns, is *C. japonica*, a plant of about 7ft if grown in the open, twice as high on a wall. The flowers are yellow, striped red, with conspicuous red stamens, in June.

A trifle less hardy, but more benign, is the brilliant *C. gilliesii*, known as "bird of paradise", a real stunner. 25ft on a wall. July–August. z9.

CALICO BUSH. See *Kalmia*

CALCEOLARIA

C. integrifolia is a small, handsome, evergreen, rather tender shrub, usually grown against a wall unless in a warm district. The leaves are sage green and the paunchy, bright yellow flowers thrust out prominently in showy clusters that succeed one another all summer. Happy near the sea. Good value in z9.

CALLICARPA

Though not very effective in the garden picture, some callicarpas are valued for the brilliance of their autumn berries (drupes), which often get prizes at flower shows. They are deciduous, bushy plants, with slender leaves, erect and crowded, throwing freely from the base if cut by frost or by the knife (in spring). Small, tubular flowers, not very significant, assemble if several plants are grown close together in sun. Most are z6. Cultivate as an aronia.

The most favoured is C. bodinieri giraldii, known also more simply as *C. giraldii*, the difference between the species and its variant being trivial. In October, following lilac flowers, its branches become laden with tight bunches of small, jewel-like berries in lavender, amethyst or violet. 6ft.

Other callicarpas that we may note are:

C. dichotoma. 4½ft, pink flowers, mauve berries.

C. japonica. 4½ft, flowers pale pink, berries violet; of its variations, *leucocarpa* has white fruits and *angustata* is taller with longer leaves.

C. americana, the "French mulberry", 5ft, is like japonica, but z7.

C. mollis, 8ft, flowers pale mauve, fruits dull purple. z8.

CALLISTEMON
Bottle-brush

Few shrubs have more appropriate vernacular names than these very distinctive Australians, for their cylindrical floral spikes look just like coloured bottle-brushes, being crowded all along their length with very small, fuzzy florets, in which a thick brush of stamens is thrust out from the tiny petals. Their leaves are very distinctive, being usually very narrow, stiff, spiky and tough. The whole plant, indeed, has a stiff and erect appearance and it is a good example of how a plant has evolved to fit its environment. A peculiarity of their behaviour is that, after the spike has finished flowering, it grows on and extends the stem, leaving behind the old seed capsules, which may hang on for years. They are, of course (like human Australians) inveterate sun-bathers and, except against a warm wall, there is not much point in growing them in any climate colder than Zone 9, except for C. sieberi. They do well in favoured spots in southern England, especially when planted about 3ft (not nearer) from a warm wall, but rarely attain their natural stature. Most do well in dry soils. No pruning.

Callistemon citrinus 'Splendens'

C. citrinus 'Splendens'. Brilliant crimson spikes and lemon-scented leaves (hence "citrinus"). One of the glories of California for landscape planting and can be grown in the open in only the mildest parts of Britain, reaching 6ft (15ft in the wild). Blooms all summer. Known also as *C. lanceolatus*. Closely allied to it are:

C. linearis. Crimson flowers, leaves 5in long but only $\frac{1}{8}$in wide. Decidedly tender.

C. rigidus. 8ft. Flowers dark red, leaves 6in long, stiff and sharply pointed.

C. subulatus, 4ft high, spreading. Crimson flowers, small, sharp leaves, wood mahogany-red. z8 in southern England.

C. salignus. One of the slightly hardier sorts, growing in wet places in its natural home, where it reaches 30ft (9ft in Britain). Flowers and spikes pale pink, leaves willowy, 2–4in long, not spiky. The related species *pallidus* is cream.

C. sieberi, the "alpine bottle-brush", is by all

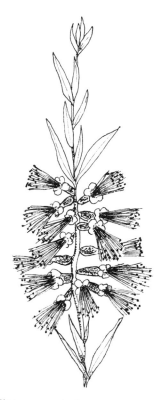

34. Callistemon subulatus

reports the hardiest. Flowers of pale yellow in short spikes, leaves 1in, rigid, awl-like, dense. Can be rated z5.

C. speciosus. A handsome 9ft, with flowers in which the stamens are a brilliant crimson and the anthers golden in dense, 5in spikes above typically stiff, spiky leaves.

CALLUNA. Included under Heathers.

CALYCANTHUS
Allspice

These are deciduous, aromatic shrubs from N. America. Easily grown if the soil is loamy, peaty, moist and in full sun, they make dense bushes throwing new shoots freely from the ground and the lower branches often spreading on the surface to produce good, weed-free ground-cover. The curiously coloured flowers, which are displayed at the tips of lateral twigs, are followed by hard, fig-shaped fruits. Prune, if necessary, in spring.

C. fertilis. A neat, bushy 8ft, with oval leaves of dark, glossy green. Flowers purplish-chocolate. Lacks the characteristic aroma of the allspice. z5.

C. floridus, the Carolina allspice, is a rather straggly shrub of 9ft, with fragrant, chestnut-coloured flowers in early summer. Leaves, wood and roots are camphor-scented. Distinguished from others by the felt on the reverse of the leaf. z4. The closely related species *mohrii* has more rounded leaves. z5.

C. occidentalis, the Californian allspice. Of loose, sprawling habit, but reaches 12ft or more. Flowers tawny-purple, not agreeably scented, but the leaves and wood have a spicy odour. z6.

CAMELLIA

Many people consider the camellia to be the most beautiful of all shrubs, certainly the most beautiful of all evergreens. Its lustrous and luxuriant foliage, densely paraded in holly-green, becomes, in good specimens, scarcely less densely adorned with vivacious flowers of red, pink or white, or parti-coloured, usually enlivened by a central tuft of glittering, golden stamens. The blossoms are displayed over an astonishingly long period; especially some of the williamsii hybrids; indeed, I have one that gleams for five months from mid-December to mid-May every year, amid ice and snow.

Once thought to be the preserve of the rich man and, in the cooler climates, grown only in greenhouses, the "common" camellia (*C. japonica*) now flourishes exuberantly in Zone 8 and very often in colder climes also; a moist maritime or riverine atmosphere is helpful. The snow camellia (*C. japonica rusticana*) is hardier still. Not all are as hardy as these, but it is astonishing how many of the hybrid varieties, raised wholly or in part after the introduction of *Camellia saluenensis* in particular, have proved just as resilient as the japonicas, as seen in the williamsii range and in such splendours as 'Inspiration', 'Leonard Messel' and 'Cornish Snow'. In really genial climes some species will grow up to 40ft high.

Camellias are primarily flowers of the late winter and the spring, their most exuberant period being from early March until mid-May, though some fine species bloom in the autumn. Their rich, varnished foliage, however, is handsome all the year and makes the most impressive of backgrounds to the garden. They luxuriate as wall plants and, for gardeners who have the space and the means, they make sensational hedges of informal bearing. Their ample petticoats, sweeping the ground, serve well to smother weeds. In tubs they are the lords of all flowering shrubs, but need lots of water.

As a result of their newly discovered hardiness, camellias are now being propagated commercially in vast numbers and are to be found in many a small garden. They transplant with equanimity even when quite large (certainly up to 10ft), though they must be cut back fairly sharply, losing a year's flower or most of it.

Camellias expect a rich soil, generously manured. Over and over again one is told by various writers that they must have acid soil, but this advice is much exaggerated. I grow some in a pH of 7. Always, however, assist their establishment with plenty of peat or, better still, ancient leaf-mould. Being nearly always sold in containers of some sort, they can be planted at most times of the year, but the months from September to April are the best, even if they are in flower. Several varieties, particularly 'Donation', will flower when a few inches high.

Consider the siting of camellias with care. They are exposed to damage if, in late winter or early spring, a warm, early morning sun follows suddenly upon a sharp freeze, causing too sudden a thaw, which ruptures the fat buds as they are making ready to open (but without hurting the plant as a whole). Other sudden changes also put the camellia at risk, such as an abrupt change of temperature and, more serious still, a sudden drenching by rain after a prolonged spell of dry weather. These sudden changes may result in the distressing dropping of buds so often observed.

Above all, be absolutely certain that the roots do not become waterlogged. Make quite sure of good drainage. Avoid also the opposite extreme; water them generously when young, although, when they have got their roots well down, they will withstand fairly long dry spells, but not severe drought.

Thus the factors that may cause distress are almost wholly physiological, for the ailments from which camellias may suffer are few. In the southern states of the USA scab is a persistent problem. Occasionally a gall infects the flower, turning the petals into a white, irregular, fleshy mass, and in California and the south-east of the USA a fungus blights the petals with dark brown spots. Remove and burn all affected flowers. Should a yellowing of the leaves occur, due to an excess of lime in the soil, treat the plant with an iron sequestrene preparation. A little light woodland gives them comfort and some protection from extremes, and it is often said that they are safest when facing west or north-west. But the species and the varieties differ somewhat in this respect and plenty of camellias flourish in fully exposed positions, for there the sun ripens the wood and so encourages the formation of buds. Lack of sun discourages the development of flower buds.

Subject to these factors, the actual planting of camellias presents no difficulty. You may plant them 6ft apart, though they are likely to exceed this spacing after some years and 8ft is better. Follow the general precepts of Chapter 4, finishing with a really thick mulch of autumn leaves. Water liberally all the first season, for they transpire copiously. A dressing of sulphate of potash at the rate of one ounce per square yard at the end of August greatly encourages the formation of flower buds.

Camellias rarely need serious pruning, but at need respond well to the gardener's will. Tall, spindly specimens from the nursery will bush out if cut back by several inches. Tie in vertically to a stake the resultant topmost new shoot to create a "leader". Shorten by one-half any shoot that is rivalling the leader and any that may spoil the balance of the plant. Cut fearlessly back by one-third any ancient specimen that has become weak. On very young plants lightly nip back overall the new young growths, to intensify the bushiness of its polished foliage and multiply the flower buds. The time for all this is about April.

Propagation from summer cuttings is usually easy but rather slow, in a compost of peat and sand in equal parts under close conditions. Mist and bottom heat, of course, help and hasten. Use short side-shoots of young wood with a heel or a mere leaf with a basal bud from the stem attached.

Several species of camellia were originally called *Thea*. Hence, of course "tea" (or "tay" by our forefathers), since one of the species has been used for the beverage by the Chinese from time immemorial. See *Camellia sinensis*. The name "Camellia" is after George Kamel, which ought to teach us how it should be pronounced.

A short list to start a collection in temperate climes would include 'Donation', 'Inspiration', 'Brigadoon', 'Adolphe Audusson', 'Apollo', 'Lady Vansittart', 'Leonard Messel', 'Grand Slam', 'Imura', 'Nagasaki' and, in z9, 'Captain Rawes'.

C. 'Barbara Hillier'. A big, distinguished, rare shrub with large single flowers, described as "satiny-pink". Is a clone of the hybrid *heterophylla*.

C. 'Cornish Snow'. A delightful and distinctive hybrid of rather loose and open character, with small, slim leaves and bearing quantities of small, single, white trumpets all along the stems for a very long season. Surprisingly hardy, the parents being *cuspidata* and *saluenensis*. z8. The clone 'Michael' has larger flowers. 'Winton' is blush-pink.

C. cuspidata (formerly *Thea cuspidata*). White cup at ends of tips or in axils. Leaves, coppery when young. Upright twiggy growth of graceful habit, but not quite first-class. 8 to 12ft. z8.

C. 'Inspiration'. One of the most glorious of all the world's shrubs, growing to 10ft or more and massed with large, semi-double flowers of a deep, luminous pink. In spite of its parentage (*reticulata* × *saluenensis*) it is as hardy as the japonicas.

C. japonica. For gardeners this is the dominant species, though now hotly challenged by the williamsii hybrids. All may be confidently reckoned for Zone 8, or Zone 7 in favourable circumstances, certainly against a wall. There are now some thousands of named cultivars but many are too alike to deserve different names. The most important diversity, apart from colour, is in the formation of the flowers, which are classified thus.

Single. Having only one whorl or ring of petals, with the brush of stamens very prominent.

Semi-double. Having two or more whorls of petals, with the stamens bold and prominent.

Double. Numerous petals, but folded back ("imbricated") so as still to show the stamens.

Formal double. Very numerous petals, but with the stamens obscured or absent.

Peony-form. A domed mass of petals or petaloids and occasionally stamens.

Anemone-form. A basal whorl of large, flat petals is overlaid in the centre by a domed and sometimes confused mass of small petals and petaloids, with occasional stamens.

The border-lines between the various forms are not always clear-cut. All are beautiful in their diverse forms, but, to people who prefer form to mass, those that display the glittering stamens have a special appeal. Moreover, the flowers of single and semi-double varieties are more resistant to winter's icy clutches. There are also variations in the deportment of the shrubs; some stand very erect, pyramidal in silhouette; others spread their arms widely and some bend down their branches in a languorous manner, so that they should be planted on a bank or terrace in order for their flowers to be seen (e.g. 'Lady Clare' and 'Drama Girl').

The following list of some 53 is selected after much anguished thought. In most of the white and blush-pink cultivars the petals hang on too long and turn a dusty brown instead of "shattering" and falling cleanly; pick them off early. z7.

'Admiral Nimitz' (or 'Kishu-tsukasa'). Large, formal double of deep rose-pink. Erect and vigorous.

'Adolph Audusson'. A great favourite of long-proven merit. Handsome, blood-red, semi-double flowers in profusion. A top choice.

'Alba Plena'. Formal double white, strong growth.

'Alba Simplex'. Single white. Very good.

'Althaeiflora'. Large, dark red, peony-form, like a double hollyhock.

'Anemoniflora'. Dark crimson, anemone-form. Erect.

'Angela Cocchi'. Bright red flowers of moderate size formed like a rose. Bushy, compact.

'Apollo'. Another red favourite of great merit. Deep rose-red semi-double. Growth open and spreading.

'Apple Blossom' (or 'Joy Sander'). Pretty semi-double, blush-pink, deeper on the rims.

'Are-jishi'. Rose-red peony-flowers, confused centre, open spreading habit, early.

'Berenice Boddy'. Semi-double of clear, soft pink with darker shading. Erect.

'Betty Sheffield Blush'. Charming soft pink double.

'Betty Sheffield Supreme'. Loose, peony-form flowers with white petals, each bordered rose-pink, but somewhat variable; some all white, some all pink.

'Chandleri'. See 'Elegans'.

'C. M. Hovey'. Carmine formal double, of moderate size. Very old and still good.

'C. M. Wilson'. Light pink, anemone-centred, very large growth slow and spreading.

'Contessa Lavinia Maggi'. Crimson and pale pink stripes, double. Popular and easy.

'Debutante'. Light pink, frilly peony-form. Slow to flower.

'Devonia' ('Devoniensis'). Single, white, cupped flowers.

'Donckelarii'. Red, marbled white, variable, semi-double.

'Drama Girl'. Very large, semi-double, salmon-pink. Droops.

'Elegans'. Very large peach-pink, anemone-form. Easy, well proven and popular. Wrongly described by many nurseries as "Chandleri elegans". 'Elegans Splenda', a sport from C. M. Wilson, is a very large, pale pink anemone. 'Elegans Supreme' is light salmon, also very large.

'Fred Sander'. Semi-double crimson, with curled, fringed petals. An old favourite.

'Geisha Girl'. Large semi-double pale pink, speckled rose.

'Gloire de Nantes'. Splendid large rose-pink, with some light speckling. Long-flowering and in high standing. Moderate growth. Very hardy.

'Grand Slam'. Huge, pure red, informal double, with a centre of incurved petaloids, flecked white.

'Guilio Nuccio'. Very large, semi-double coral-pink.

'Imura'. Large, semi-double white of water-lily form.

'James Allen'. Large, fiery red flowers of variable form.

'Jingle Bells'. Charming miniature red anemone.

'Jupiter'. Single scarlet, making a stunning picture with its golden stamens. Old and very good indeed.

'Kelvingtoniana'. Variable semi-double red, with white flecks. Old and well proven.

'Kimberley'. Single cup-shaped carmine flowers, with unusual red stamens.

'Kumasaka'. Large, double, carmine flowers streaked white. Moderate vigour.

'Lady Clare'. Large, semi-double, peach-pink. Most attractive and very popular. Lax, spreading habit, so best placed at the top of a bank or terrace.

'Lady de Saumerez'. Bright red, spotted white, semi-double.

'Lady Vansittart'. Exceptional and beautiful. The semi-double blossoms are formed of pointed petals, forming a neat rosette. The flowers are white, charmingly but unpredictably striped or flecked with pink. Leaf tips twisted.

'Magnoliiflora'. Blush-pink, semi-double veteran.

'Mars'. Rich-red semi-double. Growth open and loose.

'Mathotiana'. Large crimson double. Spreading habit. 'Mathotiana Rosea' is pink. 'Mathotiana Alba' is passing tender.

'Mercury'. Handsome deep soft crimson semi-double. Moderate growth.

'Mrs. D. W. Davis'. Very large semi-double of palest blush-pink. Broad, spreading and pendulous. Needs shelter.

'Nagasaki'. Large semi-double rose-pink, mottled white. Spreading habit.

'Nobilissima'. White peony form. Very early.

'Pink Perfection' ('Frau Minna Seidel'). Shell-pink. Small formal double.

'Preston Rose'. Salmon-pink, peony-form. Vigorous.

'Professor C. S. Sargent'. Large red double. Vigorous and hardy.

'R. L. Wheeler'. Very large and impressive rose-red, variably double. Strong, open, round bush.

'Reg Ragland'. Large, handsome semi-double carmine.

'Rogetsu'. Single white with cream stamens.

rusticana. Small, red flowers on an extra-hardy shrub, known as the "Snow Camellia", from the northern Japanese mountains. Probably z5.

'Tricolor'. White, streaked carmine, semi-double.

'Yours Truly'. Pretty semi-double in pink, margined white. Slender bush, slow to flower.

Here we leave the japonicas and pass to other species and hybrids.

C. 'Leonard Messel'. A hybrid of stunning beauty, having semi-double flowers of a scintillating pink, in which some people detect a faint glint of orange. The surprising parentage is *reticulata* × *williamsii* 'Mary Christian', but it is perfectly hardy in z8 at least.

C. maliflora. Charming shrub of 8ft or so, flowering in mid-winter in mild seasons. Double flowers of soft rose-pink. z9.

C. oleifera. So-called because of the "tea-oil" expressed from its big seeds for commercial use in China. A large, stiff-habited plant that may grow to 25ft, with white flowers all winter. z9.

C. reticulata. Very important indeed to those who garden in Zone 9 at least. A magnificent shrub that can attain 35ft in very favoured places. Distinguishable by its broad, net-veined, dull green leaves and, usually, very large flowers with velvety sepals.

What is known as the "wild form" is specially treasured by connoisseurs. There are single and double forms, both of rich rose-pink, the former being the hardier. From these several clones have developed and we pick the following, all of which will bring you great joy if you have the right climate, flowering in late winter and early spring.

'Buddha'. Rose-pink, semi-double. A pearl.

'Captain Rawes'. King of them all. Huge, deep carmine blossoms of 6in diameter. Brought to England in 1820 by Captain Rawes, a merchant seaman of the old East India Company.

'Crimson Robe'. Nearly red, semi-double.

'Mary Williams'. Single, rose-red. Splendid.

'Noble Pearl'. Very large, semi-double, orient-red.

'Purple Gown'. Wine-red, striped white.

'Robert Fortune' ('Pagoda'). Deep crimson, double. Very fine.

'Shot Silk'. Brilliant pink, semi-double.

'Trewithen Pink'. Deep rose, semi-double.

C. rosiflora. A species unknown in the wild. Close to *maliflora*, but flowers single and leaves thicker.

C. saluenensis. A shrub of luxuriant leafage, reaching maybe 15ft, enamelled with single, blush-pink flowers in profusion in early spring. Once called *Thea speciosa*. z8–9.

C. 'Salutation'. A sparkling hybrid of 10ft or more with semi-double, silvery-pink flowers in winter and early spring and matt green leaves. Offspring of *reticulata × saluenensis*, raised by the late Colonel Stephenson Clarke at Borde Hill, Sussex. z8–9.

C. sasanqua. A big shrub of loose habit and small leaves that, in a suitable climate, enlivens the autumn and winter with scented flowers, which, in cultivation, range from white to red, mostly single. Of delicate beauty, it is said to be the favourite camellia in Japan. There is a famous plantation of them at the Villa Taranto on Lake Maggiore, Italy, established by the late Captain MacEachearn. They need plenty of sun. z7–8. Some 70 varieties have been established, including the following:

'Blanchette'. Single white, tinted pink.

'Briar Rose'. Aptly named. Single, soft, clean pink.

'Crimson King'. Bright red, single.

'Hiryu'. Deep crimson, double.

'Hugh Evans'. Large, single, crimson.

'Mine-no-yuki'. Very large double white.

'Momozono-nishiki'. Curled petals of pale rose, semi-double.

'Narumi-gata'. Perhaps the best of all. Large cream-coloured margined pink, single. October-November.

'Sparkling Burgundy'. Large, double rose-red.

'Tricolor'. White striped pink.

'Usubeni'. Soft pink, marbled white, semi-double.

'Versicolor'. A blend of white, pink and lavender. Single.

C. sinensis, the tea plant. Originally *Thea sinensis* and later *Camellia thea*. When grown in gardens it is usually a plant with small, white, nodding flowers.

C. taliensis (*Thea taliensis*). White, globular flowers and laurel-like leaves. 12ft or more. Not garden-worthy. z9.

C. tsaii. Up to 15ft high, with quantities of small white flowers on lax branches. Not garden-worthy. z9–10.

Lastly we come to a marvellous hybrid which is one of the great successes of modern times. It has enormously broadened the field of camellias available to the average gardener and is being avidly pursued still by the hybridists in all the English-speaking world. This is **C. × williamsii**, bred independently from *japonica* and *saluenensis* by two exceptionally gifted English gardeners in the late Colonel Stephenson Clarke in Sussex and the late J. C. Williams in Cornwall. Their immediate results were quite different. The former gave us the superb semi-double 'Donation' and the latter (earlier in time) gave us the elegant single 'J. C. Williams', 'St Ewe' and others. They have turned out to be probably the hardiest of all garden camellias, quite safe in z7, standing up fearlessly, in some examples at least, to bitter winds in full exposure and sumptuously dressed with flowers for months on end as the fat buds succeed one another. Many of them flower when very young and very early in the year.

The widest acclaim has been given to 'Donation', now propagated in very large numbers and selling on sight in nurseries and garden centres if in bloom. It flowers when a few inches high in the most bewitching tone of soft pink from February till May. It bears a strong facial resemblance to its young sister 'Brigadoon' and to those other beautiful hybrids of different parentage, 'Inspiration' and 'Leonard Messel'. The single varieties open like trumpets or funnels as a rule. Hybridists everywhere have been busily producing other williamsii varieties, using different varieties of japonica. Some closely resemble one another and we have room to list only a few others of the elect.

'Anticipation'. Large, crimson peony-form.

'Bow Bells'. Warm pink, semi-double. Early and long-flowering.

'Brigadoon'. A superlative, semi-double

pink, closely resembling 'Donation' and in some opinions of better floral quality. Very hardy.

'Charles Colbert'. Beautiful semi-double of creamy pink. Slender growth.

'Charles Michael'. Apple-blossom pink, semi-double.

'Debbie'. Fat, peony-flowered in bright rose-pink from New Zealand. Its japonica parent was 'Debutante'. Very early.

'E. G. Waterhouse'. Big, formal double in bright pink from Australia. Slim, erect habit, good for small gardens.

'Elegant Beauty'. Similar in form, colour and habit to the arching japonica 'Lady Clare'.

'Elsie Jury'. Huge, anemone-form flowers of clean pink.

'George Blandford'. Bright crimson, peony-flowered.

'J. C. Williams'. Enchanting single pink, with flared petals, the flowers poured out in rich abandon over a long period. Differing from it in only minor detail, mainly in slightly varying colour tints, are 'Mary Christian', 'St Ewe', 'Mary Larcomb', 'Rosemary Williams' and 'Elizabeth Rothschild', all charming and long-flowering. The blooms of 'St Ewe' are rather like bells.

'November Pink' blooming remarkably from November till May in mild spells.

Other very good well-established williamsiis are 'Bartley Pink' (cherry, single), 'Caerhays' (lilac-rose, pendulous), 'First Flush' (semi-double, pink, early), 'Francis Hanger' (single white), and 'Jermyns' (peach-pink). An attractive curiosity is the deep rose single, 'C. F. Coates', which has fishtail leaves.

CANTUA

Even Bean from his Olympian height apostrophizes *Cantua buxifolia* as a "gorgeous shrub", but it is decidedly tender. In April and May it bursts out from coiled, bright red buds into pendulous clusters of trumpets, 3in long, in a brilliant colour arrangement of many shades of red, with rose predominating.

Averaging about 8ft high, according to conditions, the cantua has deeply lobed leaves, 2in long, in dull green on its lower parts, but on the flowering stems they are very small and box-like. It flowers in Cornwall and seems to like a breath of sea air. z9–10.

Other cantuas are too tender for us.

CARAGANA
Pea-tree

These are extra hardy, deciduous shrubs, usually rather thorny or bristly, with small, feathery (pinnate) leaves and pea-flowers which are nearly always yellow, followed by typical pea-pods. Though not aristocrats, they are useful for windbreaks in the most exposed, even sub-arctic places in all types of soil that are not very damp, their native origins being in dry, cold places, such as Siberia. Certain of them look decidedly decorative when formed into small trees. Most grow easily from seed.

The most favoured of the pea-trees are two varieties of **C. arborescens**, which itself is an erect 18ft shrub. These chosen varieties are 'Lorbergii', with leaves so wispy that they should be measured in millimetres, and the weeping 'Pendula'. For garden purposes you should form them into little trees, the former by running up a single stem, as suggested for *Buddleia alternifolia*, and the latter by grafting high on an arborescens stem. May. z2.

Possibly the prettiest of the caraganas, however (if you can get it), is **C. aurantiaca**, quite a graceful 4ft shrub, becoming pendulous, and richly endowed with orange pea-flowers in May–June. z5.

Also quite attractive, and thornless to boot, is **C. frutex**, a 10ft shrub with bright yellow flowers in May. z2.

C. microphylla is a graceful shrub with tiny leaves on long and slender branches, 10ft high by 12ft broad. z3.

Beware of *jubata*, *brevispina* and *gerardiana*, all viciously thorned.

CARMICHAELIA

Another pea-flowered plant, but from New Zealand and so not very hardy. Many are almost leafless, with flattened stems, and so make no great impact on the garden, but the flowers are profuse and delightfully scented. Give them all the sun possible; none can be trusted below z8. *C. australis*, which can be 12ft high, has small, pale purple flowers in spikes (racemes). *C. petriei* can be anything up to 6ft, with violet flowers.

Other carmichaelias are either too tender or too dwarf for us.

CARPENTERIA

Carpenteria california is one of the most delightful of evergreen shrubs and reasonably hardy. A close relative of the philadelphus, it adorns June and July with terminal clusters of large, scented flowers of pure white, embellished with a scintillating brush of golden anthers. It flowers best in a rather starved and stony soil and wants all the sun it can get. On a warm wall it has been known to reach 18ft, but in the open is usually anything from 6ft to 12ft, according to its environment.

For the finest forms of carpenteria, with big blossoms of good substance and overlapping petals, you must go only to first-class nurseries, who grow them from cuttings. Plants grown from seed are very variable in quality and may produce poor flowers. No systematic pruning, but cut right down to the ground any old stems that become exhausted; new shoots will soon replace them. z8.

CARYOPTERIS

These are delightful small shrubs that flower in various shades of blue among aromatic, deciduous foliage that is often dove-grey. Women seem particularly fond of them and

they are right to be so, for leaf and blossom are nicely complementary. They are happiest in full sun, are relatively drought-hardy, loathing wet feet, and are good plants for chalk. They mingle well with herbaceous plants after a year to establish themselves. You must prune them fearlessly down to within an inch of the woody base at ground level in early spring (Fig. 11). Easily propagated by half-ripe cuttings. Certainly top of the league table are the named varieties of the hybrid **C. × clandonensis**, one of the most popular new shrubs of recent years, raised by the late Arthur Simmonds, former secretary of the Royal Horticultural Society. The inflorescence is a bunch of tiny flowers with a brush of stamens thrust well out, giving a powder-puff effect. The hybrid is a variable one from which the following clones have been fixed.

'Arthur Simmonds'. Lovely, bright blue flowers, with a silvery down on the reverse of the leaf.

'Ferndown'. Flowers of a slightly deeper blue, leaves green.

'Heavenly Blue'. A distinguished American version, of very much deeper blue and more compact habit.

'Kew Blue'. Also of darker hue.

One of the parents of the Clandon hybrid was *C. incana*, itself a pretty, violet-flowered, grey-felted shrub, growing to 6ft if allowed. The form *candicans* has white flowers. Pruning need not be so hard. z7.

The other parent of the Clandon caryopteris is *C. mongolica*, a difficult, 4ft shrub, needing a "continental" climate of very cold winters and very hot summers. z2.

C. glutinosa is a 4ft shrub with leaves that are dark green, fleshy and polished on the surface, but mealy-white beneath. z7.

CASSIA

Handsome, warm weather plants with pinnate leaves. From one of its tropical species the "senna pods" of druggists are obtained. The

99

one that concerns us is *C. corymbosa*, or "flowering senna", a small shrub, wearing clusters of rich yellow flowers from axillary twigs in late summer. z8 if on a wall. In spring prune the flowered shoots nearly back to the parent stem.

CASSINIA

Somewhat heather-like, evergreen shrubs, densely clothed with very small leaves and demanding full sun. They have an untidy habit and you must cut them back hard to a foot from the ground in spring. The small, white flowers are of little account. The best of them is the New Zealand *C. fulvida*, growing 6ft high if allowed, whose garden value is mainly in the yellow glint of the young twigs and under-leaves. Sometimes misleadingly called the "golden heather".

Other cassinias are pretty much the same, but *leptophylla* has a whitish cast and *retorta* is good for growing on sand dunes. All z8.

CEANOTHUS
Californian lilac, etc

Here we have to review a whole regiment, but not many of them are anything like as tough as we should like them to be. Few will stand a campaign in a zone colder than 8 and even there they usually have to be coddled against a wall, where they excel. California is their native parade ground, especially around Santa Barbara. Upon a background of small, dense leaves they burst into a haze of little tuffets, ranging from almost violet to pale wood-smoke blue, which, in due season, almost smothers the shrub as with a cloak. A few are pink or white, not so pleasing. They range also from prostrate crawlers to big, commanding shrubs. A great many hybrids have been raised and, whatever the purist may say, many of them are more ornamental than the species.

It is an absolute command that you plant ceanothus in spring, not autumn. Give them a place in the sun with good, sharp drainage in either acid or limy soil, but not chalk. They are best pleased with a rather poor, stony or sandy soil, not a fat loam. They love the sea air and are considerably drought-resistant, disliking wet feet. In rich, moist soils they grow very fast indeed and are apt to give up the ghost after some years.

Some ceanothus flower in spring, others in late summer or the fall. In general terms, those that flower early are evergreen and of varying degrees of hardiness, those that do so later are deciduous and more hardy and usually easy enough to grow in the open. Each accordingly needs its own manner of pruning. On the deciduous sorts, prune lightly the first year so that a good framework is established about 2ft high; afterwards cut hard back to a bud about 3in from last year's growth. Never cut into the old wood itself.

On evergreen sorts in the open, prune the flowered shoots lightly after the blossoms have withered. We would treat similarly those in

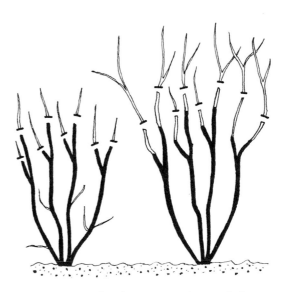

35.   Pruning a deciduous ceanothus. *Left*, first year, tips shortened, whiskers removed. *Right*, second year, main framework established. Extensions proceed next year and are cut back harder. Some gardeners prune much harder from the start

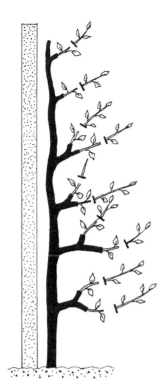

36. Pruning a wall-trained evergreen ceanothus; seen frontally, it is a fan

which the cunning hybridist has married the two groups as in 'Burkwoodii' and 'A. T. Johnson'. Against a wall, however, a little more care is needed for the evergreens, for, if planted in the usual way and left alone, they will flop outwards morosely, so you must plant them hard up against the wall and fan out selected main branches, tying them to wires or canes, as you would a fan-trained cherry or peach. Cut back all breastwood to a few inches of the main framework, unless usable for tying in as part of it. After blossom-fall trim the flowered shoots back fairly hard, but never cut into the old wood. At all times keep the plant tight back against the wall. Afterwards cut the laterals tolerably hard, but never into the old wood. Thin out the sheaf of new young stems that shoot up from the base. Typical examples are *dentatus*, *thyrsiflorus* and *rigidus*.

If any specimen seems to have been killed by frost, chop it down to the ground and it will probably regenerate. They are very resilient shrubs, but will not stand being transplanted. Ceanothus grow easily from seed, but named varieties must, of course, be propagated by cuttings, using young shoots in close conditions in a propagating case. We must reduce our battalion to the following small platoon, ignoring the creepy-crawlers. Count all z8 unless noted otherwise.

C. americanus (New Jersey Tea). Deciduous, 3ft. Dull white flowers at midsummer. Of no merit except for its extra-hardiness.

Ceanothus americanus

Ceanothus arboreus

z4. Much the same sort of flowers are seen in *C. ovatus* (also z4) and *C. velutinus* (z6).

C. arboreus. Evergreen, spring-flowering, towering to 25ft. 'Trewithen Blue' and 'Treasure Island' are fine selections.

'A. T. Johnson'. Evergreen. Rich blue flowers in both spring and autumn. On a wall prune in April.

'Autumnal Blue'. Pale blue, late-flowering evergreen. One of the best and hardiest in Britain.

'Burkwoodii'. Fine, leafy, brightly evergreen hybrid to 6ft, uniting the early and late species. Rich, blue flowers from July to October. On a wall prune in April.

C. burtonensis. A wild hybrid from California doing well at Wisley. Akin to *impressus*, but leaves glossy.

'Cascade'. Beautiful hybrid, evergreen, early. The powder-blue clusters, copiously borne on long stalks on arching sprays, justify its name. On a wall can reach 20ft.

C. cyaneus. A big evergreen with flowers of intense blue on long stalks. From it has come notable clones in 'La Primavera', 'Sierra Blue', and 'Mountain Haze'.

'Delight'. Perhaps my own favourite hybrid and one of the hardiest. Evergreen, with rich blue flowers in spring. The parentage is *papillosus* × *rigidus*. 'Dignity' is akin, often flowering again in the fall.

C. × delilianus. Notable for being the parent of the beautiful deciduous late-flowering French hybrids. Most reach about 8ft, but remember to cut hard back. The best are:

'Gloire de Plantières'. Deep blue dwarf.

'Gloire de Versailles'. Powder-blue, the general favourite.

'Henri Desfosse'. Similar but deeper blue.

'Topaz'. Rich indigo, very handsome.

'Léon Simon'. Light blue.

'Marie Simon'. Rose-pink.

In side-stepping the influence of the hybrid

Ceanothus 'Delight'

pallidus in the pink varieties, we follow Bean.

C. dentatus. One of the few "straight" species that succeed in the garden. It makes an 8ft, rounded evergreen shrub in the open, with bright blue flowers among very small leaves in May.

C. impressus. A small species in high standing. Deep blue flowers from among tiny, crinkly leaves in May. A densely branched shrub 5ft high and wide in the open, 10ft high on a wall.

C. integerrimus, the "deer brush". Very large panicles of pallid blue in June and dull green leaves. Graceful deportment.

'Italian Skies'. A wide-spreading evergreen of brilliant blue.

C. × lobbianus. A natural evergreen hybrid with bright blue flowers, like tiny foxgloves, in May-June. 'Russellianus' is a particularly pretty form of it in powder-blue.

C. rigidus. Evergreen with almost purple florets, copiously borne all along the stems in spring. From the Monterey peninsula, it is the most beautiful and one of the hardier species. In the open is a low, spreading stiff-branched shrub, but on a wall reaches 12ft.

C. thyrsiflorus. One of the hardiest of the garden-worthy evergreen species and parent of several good hybrids. Flowers usually pale blue in great profusion in early summer. A variable plant in the wild state, but very easy from seed and will shoot up to 30ft. In California, because of attacks by scale insects, is tending to be replaced by its variety *griseus*.

A particularly valuable form of the "blue-blossom", as it is sometimes ambiguously called, is its form *repens*, which is usually described as "prostrate", but which, seen in the big rock-garden at Wisley, becomes a low, elegant, broadly spread, tightly packed dome, 3ft high or more. Perhaps the hardiest of all ceanothus.

C. × veitchianus. Evergreen, 10ft or more in late spring, with dense tufts of rich, deep blue. Of uncertain parentage and often misnamed. A fine wall plant.

Ceanothus veitchianus

CEPHALANTHUS
Button Brush

Of use only in swampy places or on a river edge in cold climates, *C. occidentalis* is a 15ft shrub with small, white, globular flowers in July. In spring cut the tips of any flowered shoots that have withered, as far back as new growth. z4.

CERATOSTIGMA

If you like, you can call the most popular of these very pretty little shrubs "Miss Willmott's plumbago", instead of its awful multisyllabic

37.   Ceratostigma willmottianum

botanese, **Ceratostigma willmottianum**. In America it is sometimes "the Willmott blue leadwort". The generic name is simply mongrel Greek for "horned stigma".

The rich, severe old lady who raised this plant from Chinese seed is commemorated in a beautiful 3ft shrub that bears small, blue, plumbago-like or phlox-like flowers in closely packed terminal clusters, opening successively for four months from July onwards. It takes most happily to a dry, rather poor soil, but must have full sun and is not hardy below z8. Let it establish its roots in its first summer, with a light tipping of the stems, and then amputate them almost to the ground every April. Easily raised by late summer cuttings.

Other ceratostigmas there are: *C. minus* is a short version of Miss Willmott's and the rather bristly *C. griffilkii* is decidedly tender. *C. plumbaginoides* is a small herbaceous border plant, and very nice too.

CERCIS

The Chinese red-bud, C. chinensis, is said to be a large tree in the wild, but in cultivation it seldom exceeds about 10ft (20ft in Cornwall). It is a pretty shrub, with clusters of small, pink pea-flowers in May, bold, glossy leaves, broadly heart-shaped, up to 5in long and wide. To flower well it seems to need a continental climate of hot summers. z6. The Chinese red-bud is of course, blood-brother to the better known *C. siliquastrum*, disagreeably known in popular speech as the "Judas tree"; I prefer to call it by the more factually correct name of Judaea tree, as the French do.

CHAENOMELES
Japanese or *Flowering Quince*

Imagine red, pink or white apple blossoms ornamenting brave shrubs of smart deportment parading before the warm weather comes and you have the handsome flowering quinces. They are prime favourites where you cannot grow azaleas, for they tolerate lime and free chalk, though not solid chalk. Our parents and grandparents (or even we ourselves sometimes today) called them "japonicas", irrespective of the truth, but serving to show, by use of such an easy popular name, the esteem in which they were and are regarded by all. They have suffered much at the hands of confused botanists who, even in our lifetime, have repeatedly changed their names. The modern one is a botanical hash-up of two Greek words which imply "split apple". One really ought to pronounce it Ky-no-mee-lees, but few people do, so let us go on calling these ornamental, flowering or Japanese quinces.

The quinces are deciduous, slightly thorny, twiggy and very hardy shrubs of dense, ground-covering foliage, flowering in such profusion as almost to equal that of the azalea, and are rated z4. They produce fruits which are very fragrant but very hard and bitter and which are not ripe until the flesh is yellow.

They make very good jelly and a thin slice gives an aromatic flavour to an apple pie. If you do not want them for such purposes, pluck them off as soon as they form, though they will resist you.

In the open ground the flowering quinces need little pruning, but are improved if you trim back the side-shoots to two or three buds after blossom-fall.

Many of the quinces, especially the speciosa selections and the hybrid superbas, make superlative wall shrubs, but need a little expertise in pruning, treating them as you would spur-forming apples. When planting choose the strongest shoots and tie them in close to the wall, either fan-wise or with a chosen leader and subsidiary stems spaced out either horizontally (espaliered) or angled. Tie in their extension growths and their laterals as they develop. From the very start cut all breastwood and any side shoots not needed as part of the framework. Do this by stopping them at the fifth leaf in summer and the resultant side twigs to two or three in late August. These form the stubby little spurs and produce the flowers and fruits. Expect little flower for the first year or two.

There are three main groups of chaenomeles. Using modern names, these are *C. japonica* (which is not the "japonica" of popular speech), *C. speciosa* (which *was* the old "japonica") and the hybrid between them, *C.* × *superba*, but other hybrids have recently been named. They range from dwarfs to sturdy shrubs of about 6ft in the open. For sheer splendour we favour *japonica* most of all and the similar 'Simonii'.

C. × **californica** is a recently bred strain of hybrids between cathayensis and the hybrid superba, thus bringing three species together. They are erect, spiny shrubs, remarkable for their large flowers, as in the clones 'Cardinal', 'Enchantress' and 'Pink Beauty'. Rarely seen in Britain.

C. cathayensis is a thorny shrub of open habit with sparse, twisted branches, white flowers and huge fruits. A specimen in the RHS garden at Wisley reaches 15ft. z6. *C.* × *clarkiana* is a mixed hybrid strain between this and japonica.

C. japonica. One of the most brilliant of all small shrubs, its colours ranging from deep orange to blood-red, gradually reaching 3ft and spreading widely, and flowering without halt for two months from late March onwards. According to Bean the dwarfer natural variety, long known as *alpina*, no longer exists in cultivation in its true form, so we suggest that you ask the nurseryman for the blood-red form of *C. japonica*.

C. speciosa. These are lordly ones, daring winter's icy rages and, in some varieties, carrying their colours right on till early summer and indeed, occasionally displaying them in autumn. They are very hardy, but like sun and are superb against warm walls. The species, forming a tight mass of interlacing branches may be 10ft high and wide, but the named cultivars grown in gardens are normally much smaller. When we come to these we find some doubt about their affinities, for some might be taken as belonging rather to the hybrid superba, but this matters little to the gardener and the two might easily be lumped together. However, the following seem to belong clearly to the speciosa clan. Nearly all are proven veterans of sterling quality. z4.

'Cardinalis'. Crimson-scarlet, double.

'Falconnet Charlet' ('Rosea Plena'). Salmon, double, 8ft. A favourite in America, where it is sometimes called 'Cameo'.

'Moerloosii' ('Apple Blossom'). Blush-pink, 5ft.

'Nivalis'. Pure white, 4ft.

'Phylis Moore'. Double salmon pink; thinly branched and best on a wall.

'Rubra Grandiflora'. Very large crimson flowers on a low, spreading bush.

'Simonii'. Gorgeous blood-red, semi-double, growing to 2ft by 4ft, with a very long season.

'Umbilicata'. Deep salmon.

C. × **superba**. As we have noted, these are hybrids between japonica and speciosa. Their children are exceedingly handsome, most 4 to 5ft high, occasionally more, but scarcely distinguishable from the speciosas. The red shades predominate. You can use them on walls or in the open. We choose the following:

'Boule de Feu'. Flame, 10ft on a wall.

'Crimson and Gold'. Crimson petals, golden anthers.

'Incendie'. Deep orange-red.

'Knap Hill Scarlet'. Fiery red, 5ft.

'Pink Lady'. Clear rose, spreading habit.

'Rowallane'. Large, vivid red, low and spreading.

C. × vilmoriniana. Both in France and in America marriages between cathayensis and japonica produced sharply barbed children about 8ft high with white or blush flowers. 'Mount Everest' and 'Afterglow' are examples. Rare in Britain.

CHERRY, FLOWERING. See *Prunus*

CHESTNUT, dwarf. See *Aesculus*

CHILEAN FIRE BUSH. See *Embothrium*

CHILIOTRICHUM

Having a distinct resemblance to the rosemary in its leafage, but bearing large daisy-form flowers in summer, *C. diffusum* is a very attractive foliage shrub about 3ft high but spreading widely. The leaves are tiny, beginning grey on account of their down but maturing dark green. The plant known as *rosmarinifolium* is only a variant of *diffusum*, but is even more like a rosemary, except for its big daisies. Allied to the olearias (the "daisy bushes") but much more beautiful. z8–9.

CHIMONANTHUS
Winter-sweet

Only the sweet exhalation of its breath in winter commends this deciduous shrub to the gardener. Otherwise, it is not very ornamental, growing to about 8ft, but more near a warm wall. You have to wait several years for the flowers, which then turn out to be small, nodding, broadly tubular, yellow on the outside, purple within, their development dependent on the weather. The leaves are rough to the touch but a glossy dark green. It is drought-hardy. The scent, when it comes, is delightful and widely pervasive and a twig or two brought into the house puts to shame the concoctions of the perfumer. Long known as *C. fragrans*, it is now *C. praecox*. In most parts of Britain and Northern Europe and corresponding areas of North America (z8) it flowers from December (occasionally November) till March, outlasting the witch hazel, but in colder areas many wait until February. It is too often grown in shade and is far better in full sun.

There are two varieties of the winter-sweet: 'Grandiflorus', with larger flowers but not so sweet, and 'Luteus', all-yellow.

On a wall some pruning is needed before the end of February. Establish a good framework, cut back all outward-pointing shoots and afterwards shorten the stronger twigs. Propagation is by seed or rooted layers; cuttings are very difficult.

CHIONANTHUS
Fringe Tree

The botanist often makes life very difficult for the gardener. Beware of confusing the Chimonanthus ("winter flower") with the Chionanthus ("snow flower"), or fringe-tree. Beware also of its size, for **Chionanthus virginicus** can zoom up to 30ft. A superb creation, it is profusely and lacily mantled in early June with very lax, white, lilac-like panicles beset with bracts and composed of wispy little petals which look as though they had been shredded (hence "fringe"), accompanied by 8in leaves. The flowers come on stems that have grown the previous year. Full sun is best. z4.

The Chinese fringe tree, **C. retusus**, is also a shrub of the first rank, but is usually much smaller though it can occasionally grow just as

Chionanthus virginicus, the American "fringe tree"

big. The leaves and the flower clusters are about half the size of the American and, flowering on stems of the current year's growth, appear in late June and July in erect, loose panicles. z4. Both are deciduous, have fibrous roots and transplant well, but neither is really at its best in the mild British climate.

CHOISYA
Mexican orange blossom

Choisya ternata is a good-looking, dense evergreen with glossy, dark green leaves in triplets and bearing bunches (corymbs) of white, scented, five-petalled flowers in May and occasionally later. Easy, obliging and popular. If damaged by frost or cold wind, it responds readily to the knife; indeed, if the stems are cut back by a frost when the blossoms are spent, it will bloom again. Easy from half-ripe cuttings in any ordinary propagation box. z7.

CHOKEBERRY. See *Aronia*

CHRYSOTHAMNUS
Green-plume rabbitbrush

The American *C. graveolens* is a grey-leaved, aromatic shrub of about 5ft with plumes of yellow flowers, like those of golden-rod. Useful for being extremely hardy and for employment in dry, alkaline soils. z3.

CHUSQUEA. Included in Bamboos.

CISTUS

Ambiguity always arises if you call these very decorative shrubs "rock-roses", or "sun-roses", so let us stick to cistus, which is perfectly easy. They are evergreen shrubs of moderate size, characterised by poppy-like flowers of tissue-paper substance, usually marked with a chocolate, crimson or yellow patch at the base of each petal. The flowers are fleeting, but rapidly succeed one another. The foliage is usually a leaden green, not very effective in the garden picture unless contrasted with such plants as the golden heathers, the bronze barberries and sumachs or suchlike, or among herbaceous plants. Several exude a fragrant, sticky gum (ladanum) used in perfumery and medicine.

Cistus are natives of the Mediterranean lands, where they abound, are drought-hardy, fond of the seaside air and the sun, are happy in lime, including chalk, but will take to other soils also. They will not stand a hard freeze in Britain and must be considered only partially hardy, though Rehder classifies most of them for N. America as z7 (down to 5° F). Sun they must have (with few exceptions) and we think that a lean, dry, stony or sandy soil improves their hardiness. By all accounts the hardiest is laurifolius, followed by the hybrids cyprius and corbariensis, but the most to be admired are purpureus and cyprius.

You must buy cistus in pots and thereafter do not try to transplant them. With few exceptions, all have a short life, but propagation from cuttings in close conditions in late summer is not difficult. No pruning, except to cut back damaged shoots in spring, but do not cut right back into the 'old wood', as new shoots rarely result from there.

C. albidus. A 6ft shrub with lilac-rose flowers, yellow-eyed, flowering most of the summer. Leaves coated with a pearl-grey down. A very good and rather neglected species.

C. × corbariensis. One of the hardiest, but not the most attractive. White, with a yellow eye. June. 2ft.

C. creticus. One of the stickiest of the gum-cistus. Distinctly tender and very variable, the flowers being anything from purple to rose-pink. 3ft.

C. × crispus. Glowing purple-red flowers, May to July. Stems and leaves downy. 2ft. Relatively hardy.

Cistus cyprius

C. cyprius. One of the finest, hardiest and longest lived. Stands about 7ft, with its slender leaves coated with gum. Large, white flowers with red, star-like basal patch, arranged in clusters (ladanifer × laurifolius).

C. × florentinus. White flowers with yellow patches. 3ft.

C. ladanifer (*ladaniferus*) A beautiful but tender gum-cistus, of about 4ft, with large, white flowers, prettily crimped and bearing chocolate patches in June–July.

C. laurifolius, the laurel rock-rose. A reliable but stiff-mannered species of 6ft or more, with erect and open branch system, white flowers, yellow-eyed, from June to August, and glutinous, dark green leaves. Long-lived and generally regarded as the hardiest.

C. × loretii. Large, white flowers with crimson patches. 2ft.

C. × lusitanicus 'Decumbens'. For long one of our favourites and (as Bean well says) "one of the élite of cistuses", this hybrid makes a low, wide-spreading mound 2ft high, with large, white, crimson-eyed flowers, continuously displayed over a long season. Not in the top class for hardiness.

C. monspeliensis, the Montpelier rockrose. Celebrated and much hardier than generally described. A neat, 3ft bush, hairy and gummy, grey-leaved, with white flowers in great profusion.

C. palhinhae. Very handsome, fairly hardy, low-growing and compact shrub of 2ft or less, with very large, pure white flowers in May–June. Grows well under trees in the RHS Garden at Wisley.

C. parviflorus. An attractive shrub of up to 3ft with crisp flowers of clear rose-pink. The floral display is not very long, but the soft foliage is always agreeable. Unharmed at Wisley for twenty years.

Somewhat similar to it is **C. 'Peggy Sannons'**. A charming small shrub of 2ft or more with grey-green leaves and rose-pink flowers.

Cistus purpureus

C. × purpureus. An all-rounder of great ornamental value and the best of all for colour, the flowers being rose-pink with a bold, dark red eye, carried throughout summer. It makes a symmetrical bush 4ft high and wide and will not stand a severe winter. 'Betty Taudevin' is a particularly good form, slighter and hardier and brighter in colour.

C. 'Silver Pink'. Undeservedly the most popular cistus and fairly hardy. A chance hybrid. Clean, soft pink on a grey-leaved shrub of about 2½ft.

CLERODENDRUM

Two species only, entirely different from one another, engage our attention. They are deciduous and useful for coming into flower in August and September, but are not very distinguished when not in bloom. Their leaves, if bruised, stink horribly, especially in the first-named, yet the scent of their flowers is delightful. Both z7.

C. bungei is an 8ft, suckering shrub, developing into a thicket if allowed. It is thickly draped with large, heart-shaped, toothed leaves and decorated in due season with 5in wide orbs composed of fairly tightly clustered, tubular, expanded florets of rosy-red, like red snowballs. In severe winters it may be killed to the ground, but quickly shoots up again. Prune in late winter, lightly in mild climates, severely in cold ones. Propagate from its own suckers and use them as replacement shoots.

C. trichotomum is a large, almost tree-like plant of loose structure and pithy branches, with oval, pointed leaves 6in long, and loose clusters of very small, white, sweetly scented flowers, set off by brilliant red calyces. These calyces persist and the flowers, as they fade, give place to small berries of a brilliant turquoise. Calyx and berry together have a gem-like quality, but later the berry turns black. The dove-grey branches are attractive in winter. If bullied by the hoe the roots produce suckers for propagating.

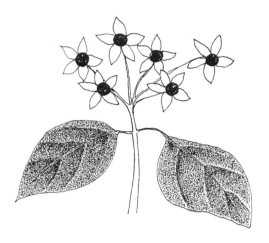

Its tree-like variety *fargesii*, the leaves of which are purple when young, fruits more abundantly but less ornately, the calyx being first green, then pink, and the berry of a paler blue.

CLETHRA

These are aromatic shrubs, often tree-like, pretty hardy, mainly deciduous. You must give them a lime-free soil. The very small florets, which are nearly always white, are clustered densely in racemes or in panicles, with fluffy brushes of little stamens thrust out, and looking like bottle-brushes.

C. acuminata is a large, deciduous shrub of 18ft, with nodding, cylindrical racemes and valued for its smooth, polished bark of cinnamon-brown. July-August. z5.

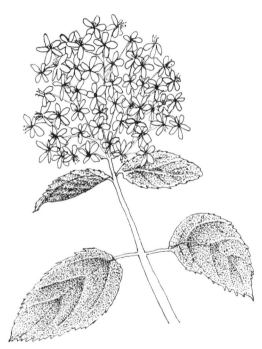

38. Two distinctive clerodendrons. *Above* C. trichotonum fargesii in berry. *Below* C. bungei

Clethra alnifolia, the 'sweet pepper bush'

C. alnifolia, also deciduous, is the sweet pepper-bush or summer-sweet, perhaps the best for the average garden, only 9ft high, with erect, deliciously fragrant bottle-brush spikes in July and slender leaves. Increases by underground stems and becomes a thicket unless thinned. An excellent seaside shrub. Two fine clones of it are 'Paniculata', superior to its wild parent and arranging its flowers in bunches (panicles) rather than spikes, and the pretty, blush-pink 'Rosea'.z3.

Very like the above in most respects is **C. tomentosa**, but the leaves look grey by reason of their woolly coating and the flowers are larger and purer white, coming out a month later. Not, however, quite so bone-hardy.z5.

Akin also, but again less hardy, is the beautiful Chinese **C. fargesii**, which averages about 12ft high and is remarkable for its long spikes, which may measure nearly a foot. z7.

Other clethras are too big for us, but we might admit *C. arborea*, the lily-of-the-valley tree, decidedly tender, of 25ft in Britain and much bigger still in Ireland, clearly enjoying a soft, moist air.

CLEYERA

Evergreen shrubs grown essentially for their foliage, the flowers being inconspicuous. By no means hardy. *C. fortunei* is quite attractive, with dark green, polished, leathery leaves, margined yellow, to 6ft or more. *C. japonica* is twice as big and wholly green.

COLLETIA

Very strange, very spiny, sturdy, boy-proof, but oddly attractive shrubs with scented flowers in late summer and autumn. There are very few leaves and the young branches are really very long spines, and it is on these spines that the small flowers are displayed. These flowers have virtually no petals and it is the calyx that is conspicuous. All about 10ft. z7–8.

C. armata is the usual one, with white tubular flowers scented of hawthorn on grey-green spines. In 'Rosea' the little flowers are pink. *C. infausta* resembles it but lacks the grey down and the rare flowers are dull. *C. cruciata* is grotesquely, but picturesquely, armed and thronged with very small cream flowers at the bases of the spines, without petals.

COLQUHOUNIA

If you are talking to a Scot, you will earn his respect if you pronounce this unfamiliar plant "Cohoonia".

C. coccinea is a tender Asiatic shrub with felted leaves that are olive-green above and grey below, very variable in shape. The scarlet to orange florets are small funnels, tightly clustered together to form a thick, stubby inflorescence rather like a red-hot poker, from August to October. Prune lightly in the first year, then very hard, as in Fig. 11. If damaged by frost, cut hard back. z8 if on a sun-baked wall, otherwise z9.

COLUTEA
Bladder senna

The bladder sennas are rather commonplace shrubs, much seen in old Victorian "shrubberies", but suitable now only when something very easy and hardy has to be used. They have pinnate leaves and small racemes of pea-flowers. Their most distinctive feature (in most examples) is their inflated seed-pods, which children like to pop by squeezing them (quite a sharp report too). Occasionally cut back decadent old wood in February. Too easy from seed. z5.

The usual one is the 12ft *C. arborescens*, with yellow flowers all summer and autumn and 3in pods. Its variety 'Bullata' is dwarf and dense with puckered leaves. The hybrid *media* has bluish-green leaves and copper flowers. *C. istria* is quite a pretty little shrub of 4ft, with very small, delicate leaflets and coppery flowers in late spring.

CORNELIAN CHERRY. See *Cornus mas*

COMPTONIA
Sweet fern

Comptonia peregrina is an extremely hardy, deciduous shrub of 4ft, clothed in downy, frond-like, elegantly chiselled leaves, with the aroma of a bay leaf, but surpassing it in richness, and small catkins, which in the male are brown and glistening, followed in the female by tiny nutlets embedded in fuzzy hairs. It must have an acid peaty soil in sun, is very difficult to transplant and is not suited to a formal setting. z3.

CORNUS
Cornel or *dogwood*

We shall ignore the attempts of certain botanists to monkey about with the names of these well-loved plants and shall stick to the familiar ones. The breed does, however, vary enormously, from the tiny, herbaceous ground-creeping *Cornus canadensis* to magnificent trees 60ft high, as in the superlative *nuttallii* and the wide-flung *controversa*, but we have written fairly fully of these tree-like species in *The Trees Around Us* and shall confine ourselves here to those that are usually counted as shrubs. Even here, however, we find sharp differences between the shrubby types and those that behave like osiers. Inevitably there are some borderline examples, as in *C. florida*, which can reach to 40ft and which sanctifies the memorial planting in Valley Forge, Pennsylvania, but which, sadly, seldom exceeds 12ft in Britain.

The names cornel and dogwood are Old English for a common hedgerow plant native to Britain and Europe and later applied to the "Cornelian Cherry" (*Cornus mas*) brought to England by the Romans.

All are pretty hardy, usually preferring a fertile and reasonably moist soil, but, contrary to general belief, do not all need an acid one and will prosper in lime, some even in chalk. They are lovely in a large landscape or as neighbourhood shrubs.

We come first to those osier-like dogwoods which are distinguished, in a pun that we cannot escape, by their brilliant barks; some have beautiful leaves as well. It is in winter that the majority of them are most fascinating and it is the juvenile stems that give the most brilliant colour. Therefore you must plant them right in the open in a place where you can see them from the house or some other place of vantage. They look marvellous near water or in isolated groups. Because their most vivid display is in their youth, you must, after giving them one year to establish themselves, chop them right down to within 2in of the ground every spring as soon as they show signs of new growth, which is usually late March. However, if you like, you can allow them to develop naturally, when they will become spreading bushes, bearing small, white flowers, followed by small white or pale blue berries.

Propagate by merely cutting down a stem after leaf-fall and sticking it in the ground in a shady spot.

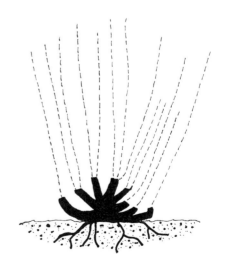

39. A stool of Cornus alba; cut back very hard each spring

First and no doubt best of all is the ultra-hardy Siberian dogwood, **C. alba**, especially its selected forms. The species itself has splendid red legs. If not cut back it becomes a rampant and overpowering thicket, 9ft high. Its selected forms, given below, are shorter, usually 4–5ft. All z2.

'Elegantissima'. Indeed very elegant. Grey-green leaves, margined cream. Bark red. Contrary to what is said above, it thrives in shade.

'Gouchaltii'. Leaves tinted rose-pink and edged yellow.

'Kesselringii'. Stems dark purple-brown, young leaves chestnut.

'Sibirica'. Stems dazzling crimson, leaves copper in the fall. Is celebrated under the popular name of the Westonbirt dogwood, but fallaciously so, those grown at the famous arboretum in Gloucestershire having no separate individuality. Growing to about 4ft, it has a rather weak constitution and needs a rich, moist soil.

'Spaethii'. A beautiful plant, handsomest of variegated cornels, the leaves richly gilded, never scorched by the sun, but the stems not so vivid as in 'Sibirica'. A tough guy, not expecting a rich or moist soil.

'Variegata'. Resembles 'Elegantissima', but more robust and less elegant.

C. amomum, the silky dogwood. Stem a purplish-red, underleaf coated with silken, tawny down. Not as colourful as the Siberians. If allowed to grow on, reaches 9ft, with cream flowers in June and then pale blue berries superior to those of alba. z5.

C. racemosa, the grey dogwood, springing readily from the base. If not chopped down, it reaches to 15ft and is lavishly draped with white flowers after midsummer, and later bears small, white berries on red stalks. z4.

C. stolonifera. Ultra-hardy, extending itself by stolons and creating thickets and giving us an outstanding variety in 'Flaviramea', one of the most handsome dogwoods, with stems of bright yellow that are spirited consorts for the red-legged sorts. Very fine on river banks and in other moist places. z2.

Here we finish with the cornels that can be

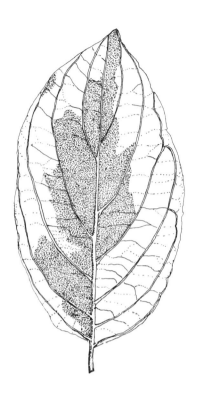

40. Cornus alba 'Spaethii'

treated in the manner of osiers and turn to a handful of others that you do not amputate.

We cannot bring ourselves to omit **C. kousa chinensis**, for, although it can in time become a tree of 25ft or more, it is meantime one of the most beautiful of the smaller, shrub-like dogwoods. In May-June its leaves (which are twisted at their tips) become almost obliterated by a snow-white floral shroud, composed of large, four-limbed bracts underwriting the insignificant true flowers, followed by edible, strawberry-like fruits, produced in a hot, "continental" summer. In China (we are told) it is called the strawberry tree. The shrub is flat-topped, the branches horizontal. Its Japanese version, **C. kousa**, is a duller white. z5.

C. mas, the Cornelian cherry, is also a small tree when full-grown, but may be regarded as a shrub averaging 15ft and nearly as much wide and having a character all its own. "When the hounds of spring are on winter's traces" it bursts into a froth of tiny golden flowers all along its naked branches, followed in due time by fairly large, cherry-like, edible fruits. In the summer it has little attraction except in the cultivars 'Variegata', which is prettily margined white, and 'Aurea Elegantissima', in which yellow and pink tints appear. The Cornelian cherry has been cultivated in England for upwards of 2,000 years. z4.

C. officinalis, the Japanese cornel, is a rather untidy version of the European, but enlivens the autumn and winter by its peeling bark and by its small, cherry-like fruits. z4.

Something quite different from these other dogwoods is an engaging dwarf that sometimes comes in handy for the garden picture. This is **C. hessei**, which keeps down to 18in and is massed with leaves that are almost black. Bluish-pink flowers, dingy berries. z4.

Other shrubby dogwoods are *baileyi* and *rugosa*, neither of great merit.

COROKIA

Decidedly tender New Zealanders which, in the species usually grown, have a very interesting character all their own. In general, they are sparsely evergreen shrubs with small, starry yellow flowers and small red or orange berries. Their name is the Maori one. In doubtful climates they are good wall shrubs.

The most interesting is *C. cotoneaster*, known as the "wire-netting bush", because of its thin, tortuous and entangled twigs, making a dense, interlaced mass of horizontal laterals, with very few and very small leaves. In England it reaches about 8ft. Fruits red, like very small cherries. z8.

C × virgata is a trifle hardier, the twigs not entangled, the leaves spoon-shaped, fruits yellow. Averages about 12ft.

C. buddleioides is a smaller, more tender shrub with willow-like leaves, undercoated with a silvery down, and dark red fruits. z9.

CORONILLA

From both the arrangement of their petals and the resultant botanical name, we could well nickname these attractive plants "crown flowers". Some of them are herbaceous plants, so we have to look at only a handful of shrubs and those not as hardy as we should like. They belong to the pea tribe, and give us bunches of yellow pea-flowers with long, clawed petals, followed by short pea-pods. Their leaves are prettily pinnate with small leaflets. They need a rich soil in sun. Pruning is confined to cutting out any decadent stems or twigs.

The hardiest is the deciduous **C. emerus**, known as the scorpion senna, because its slender pods are jointed like the segments of the tail of a scorpion. It grows about 8ft high, with slender, erect stems, nodding at their tips, flowers throughout the whole of summer and early autumn and is altogether an elegant shrub, with the little trusses of blossom sprouting from the leaf axils. Grown in England for more than 300 years. z6.

Only half its height, but otherwise differing in minor details only is **C. emeroides**. z6.

Not so hardy, but generally more popular in Britain at least, is **C. glauca** a bushy evergreen of 5ft (but twice as much in warm climes) with dainty, sea-green leaves. The flowers are of a richer yellow, are scented by day (but not at night), are more numerous in the clusters and are displayed from April till June. Must be regarded as a wall shrub even in z8. 'Pygmaea' is a charming dwarf of 2ft, often flowering in both spring and autumn.

Very similar to glauca but even a trifle more tender and only half its height is **C. valentina**, a charming shrub, floribundant and graciously scented. Despite its tenderness, is said to have been grown in England for nearly 400 years.

CORYLOPSIS

Close cousin of the witch hazel but less hardy, the corylopsis gives us some big shrubs or small trees of ornamental excellence when, in earliest spring, the bare boughs are hung with pendent tassels, like catkins, of pale primroses, usually sweetly scented. At the base of the tassels are a few bracts. Unhappily the pretty flowers are susceptible to spring frosts, their zone ratings applying rather to the plant than to its flowers. After flowering their value declines to that of a nut-tree, their name, taken from the leaf, meaning "like a hazel". They are suitable, therefore, only in larger places, where their horizontal branches may have freedom to spread out. They need something lively and exhilarating to follow in summer, be it roses, summer heathers (which bear them very good company), hypericums or some spritely herbaceous plants.

A very hardy species is **C. glabrescens**, a big shrub of up to 18ft, but its nodding flower tassels measure only $1\frac{1}{2}$in. z5.

C. griffithii, of about 10ft, is one of the most decorative, the florets, hung in 2in tassels, having purple anthers. z7.

C. pauciflora, known in America as the "buttercup winter hazel", is a very distinctive corylopsis. It has to be grown in woodland, which protects it not only from frost and vicious winds but also from excessive sun, which can shrivel it up. It grows to only about 5ft, twiggy and small-leaved, but spreads widely. It is called "pauciflora" because its pendent spikes carry only a few florets, but they are extra large, bell-shaped, of sparkling quality, borne all along the branches, and scented of cowslips in March-April. z6.

C. platypetala is a big shrub which grows to a good 20ft in southern England and is also one of the best in the USA. Although the flower tassels may be no more than 2in long, they can hold anything up to 20 fragrant florets. z6.

C. sinensis is another fairly big fellow, up to 15ft, flowering in April with a multitude of small, lemon-yellow tassels. z6.

One of the best-known and grown in England for more than 100 years is the interesting **C. spicata**. This is identifiable by the large greeny-yellow bracts at the base of the spikes and the purple anthers that animate the deli-

cately scented flowers, which appear in March unless ravaged by frost. About 6ft high and spreading very widely, the shrub is also recognizable by its crooked branches, silky-haired when young. z8.

About the same size and also equipped with bracts in its flower spikes is **C. veitchiana**. The tassels are nodding rather than directly pendant and enlivened with chestnut anthers protruding from the florets. z6.

In **C. willmottiae** we have a particularly graceful shrub averaging about 9ft with greeny-yellow, scented florets in long tassels, very showy and borne in profusion. The young shoots are chestnut and the leaves red-purple when young. z6-7.

COTINUS

Until recently the Venetian sumach, or smoke-bush, was familiar to most of us as *Rhus cotinus*, then along came some botanist, who pulled it up by its roots, with a few minor satellites, transplanted it in enforced isolation and gave it a menacing new name. This name is **Cotinus coggygria**. You will get your tongue round it fairly easily if you imagine it as two hyphenated words — coggy-gria, with the accent on the y.

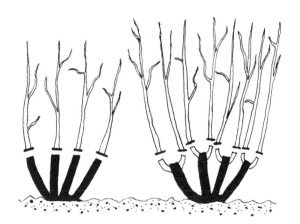

41. Pruning a Venetian Sumach (Cotinus coggygria) for foliage effect. *Left*, first year. *Right*, second year

We have heard it spoken of disrespectfully as the "cock-eyed" sumach. The name is Greek.

However, the Venetian sumach is an unique shrub, remarkably effective in the garden picture in late summer. Reaching an ultimate 15ft in time, broad-shouldered, its sign-manual is the filmy cloud of fine silken threads, loosely but abundantly borne, at first flesh-pink, then smoky-grey, that envelop nearly the whole plant. These filmy threads are in fact elongated stalks of sterile florets. Its best display is given if the soil is not very rich. The leaves colour well in the fall. The yellow wood is used as a dye. The most spectacular foliage displays of those that have coloured leaves result from very hard pruning. In the first spring cut down to about 15in from the ground. In the second spring cut the stem that grew last year to a bud about 2in or so from their points of origin on the original framework. Continue this exercise annually if you wish. z5.

Several exceptionally good forms of the Venetian sumach have been selected, the differences between them being sometimes in the colour of the leaf, sometimes in that of the smoke-puff inflorescences. Take your choice.

'Daydream'. Extra fluffy; hairs dull brown, then pink.

'Flame'. Brilliant orange in autumn.

'Foliis Purpureis'. Leaves tinted purple.

'Notcutt's Variety'. Leaves maroon-purple. Inflorescence purple-pink. Very fine.

'Purpureus' is a green-leaved form ("forma") with an inflorescence like puffs of pink smoke.

'Royal Purple' (or 'Kromhout'). Leaves deeper purple than in Notcutt's. Possibly the finest.

Another smoke-tree, quite different in character, is the huge **C. obovatus** (or *americanus*), which reaches 30ft and is appreciated rather for its autumnal brilliance than for its smoke. z5.

COTONEASTER

Here again we enter a fairly large field, familiar even to non-gardeners, who usually see them as shrubs with small, dark green leaves, clustered in the fall with red berries, quickly gobbled up by birds as winter's breath begins to infiltrate the countryside. The cotoneaster, however, displays itself in diverse shapes and habits, from ground-crawlers to strapping shrubs that may be 20ft or more; it may be evergreen or deciduous and its berries may be yellow or orange instead of red, the yellow berries being the least attractive to birds and so allowed to hang on far into winter. Its species, as grown in gardens, come almost entirely from China or the Himalayan regions and so are mostly of considerable hardiness. The flowers, which appear in May or June, are very small (rarely $\frac{1}{2}$in wide) and are nearly always white, though some are tinted with rose. The name is a mish-mash of dog Latin meaning "something like a quince". It has undergone several changes of sex at botanical hands, having been first masculine then feminine and now masculine again.

Cotoneasters are of the easiest cultivation, content with any soil that is not water-logged. Except when used for hedging, they are much best left unpruned, in order not to upset their natural character, but, should a branch become over-mighty, cut it right out, or very hard back, rather than do any snipping. Propagation is usually very easy from cuttings of half-ripe shoots in July in gentle heat. Seed also is easy from the true species, but not desirable for the finest.

Botanists separate the cotoneaster into two sections, according to whether the petals open our flat, like discs, or are erect. The practical gardener, however, will group them according to their uses, which means whether they are very big, or of moderate size or are dwarfs or are ground-crawlers. We have mentioned the crawlers briefly in Chapter 5 and shall here consider a fairly wide range of others, of which there are more than a hundred in commerce. We consider that the finest of all, provided that there is room for it, is 'Cornubia', but *frigidus*, *lacteus*, 'John Waterer', *salicifolius* and its hybrids are all very fine indeed and *horizontalis*, the fish-bone cotoneaster, is probably the favourite, especially when it has the chance to fan itself out against a wall, though the lesser-known *apiculatus* is better. A little caution is necessary about those that are described as evergreen, because some that are so described may lose their leaves in a very hard winter. We should add, too, that cotoneasters are botanically rather confusing, for their sexual habits are sometimes odd, resulting in what are called "microspecies".

Cotoneasters are one of a group of plants prone to attack by the serious fire-blight disease, which is a killer when allowed to get a hold. It is said to be spread by bees. The first symptom is a blackening of the little flowers, followed by a shrivelling of the leaves and a browning of the stems, as though seared by fire. You must at once cut out the whole branch, or maybe dig up and burn the whole bush. In Britain it is a notifiable disease, being very destructive if it spreads to orchards.

Our descriptions will be confined to only the special characteristics of each species or hybrid, as we have already set out above their general ones.

LARGE AND FAIRLY LARGE

C. bullatus. A 10ft, deciduous shrub of open habit with puckered leaves. Florally of no account but one of the richest of all in its display of red berries. z5.

C. 'Cornubia'. A magnificent hybrid raised by the late Lionel de Rothschild at Exbury, close to the Solent, and one of the finest of all evergreen shrubs. Bears enormous crops of brilliant red fruits that weigh it down by their riches. Appears to be a hybrid between some form of *frigidus* and *salicifolius*, the latter evident in its long, shining, dark green, willow-form leaves. The original plant at Exbury is 25ft high and 20ft broad. z6–7.

C. 'Exburyensis'. Another very fine hybrid from Exbury, more certainly the offspring of *frigidus* and *salicifolius*, but only about half the size and bearing yellow fruits. z6–7.

C. foveolatus. Deciduous, about 10ft. Flowers pink-tinted, fruits red, turning black. Long, glossy leaves that turn scarlet before they fall. z4.

C. franchetii. A picturesque shrub of arching habit, some 9ft, evergreen in mild regions. Leaves soft grey-green, oblong fruits orange, young shoots and underleaves coated with a pale felt. Seen at its finest in the variety *sternianus*, which has rounded berries in great profusion. One of the most ornamental of cotoneasters, often wrongly called *wardii*.

C. frigidus. A noble, deciduous shrub, known best for the handsome offspring that have resulted from its marriages with *salicifolius* and other species. In itself it is one of the most robust of all, normally growing up to 20ft, with blue-green leaves and red berries. In skilled and patient hands it can be trained into tree form, on a single trunk. A specimen at the Westonbirt Arboretum in Gloucestershire towers up to 40ft. There is an improved cultivar in 'Vicarii', a weeping one is 'Pendula' and a yellow-fruited form is *fructu-luteo*. z7. For its more distinguished offspring, see 'Cornubia', 'Exburyensis', 'Rothschildianus', 'St Monica', 'John Waterer' and 'Hybrida Pendula'.

The evergreen **C. glaucophyllus**, known for some reason as the "brighthead" cotoneaster, does not often flower until July and is consequently one of the last to develop its red berries, which may last all winter. At all seasons a handsome and bushy shrub of 10ft. There is a celebrated planting in the Golden Gate Park, San Francisco. The hairy-leaved *vestitus* and the small-leaved *meirophyllus* are varieties of it, but its greatest splendour is the form *serotinus*, which fruits freely and can reach 30ft high. z7.

C. henryanus is a broad, loose-limbed, pendulous shrub of 10ft with long leaves, rather rough to the touch, evergreen in mild areas, and dark red berries. Distinctive and elegant. z7.

C. 'John Waterer' is a splendid hybrid between *henryanus* and *frigidus*, long known simply as *C.* × *watereri*, a name that covers all hybrids of these species. Of stylish and languorous carriage, it grows to 12ft with willow-form leaves and red berries. z7.

C. lacteus. A noble, evergreen globe of 10ft, with rather broad, olive-green leaves, hairy beneath. Late in flower (mid-summer) and in its red fruits. One of the first. z6.

C. lucidus is a sturdy, deciduous, very hairy shrub of 9ft, with pink-tinted flowers, densely cloaked with lustrous leaves and black fruits. A good hedger if not endangered by fire-blight and much used for this purpose in the mid-Western states of the USA. z4.

C. rotundifolius (now **prostratus**) appears in several forms, some of which are almost prostrate, but in the natural variety *lanatus* it builds up into a densely tangled mound of maybe 10ft high, the whip-like branches flicking out in every direction, with large red fruits. Evergreen in mild places. z6. In the cultivar 'Eastleigh' the fruits are blood-red.

C. 'Rothschildianus'. Another sumptuous yellow-berried Exbury hybrid, very like 'Exburyensis', described above, but bigger, its wide-ranged arms weighed down by its heavy burden of fruit. z6–7.

C. salicifolius is one of the dominant cotoneasters, noted for its slim, willow-form leaves, bequeathed to several of its hybrid offspring. Itself, *salicifolius* is a big evergreen shrub of 15ft. Its finest natural form is *floccosus*, a splendid creation, with glossy, leathery, wrinkled leaves on slender branches, drooping slightly at their tips and massed with tiny red fruits. Another natural variety is *rugosus*, with pretty coral berries but with larger leaves and rather coarser general appearance. z6.

We have mentioned the prostrate forms of salicifolius in Chapter 5.

C. simonii. A 10ft semi-evergreen shrub of erect habit, especially favoured for hedging, the red berries conspicuous after leaf-fall. z5.

C. 'St Monica'. Another attractive and distinctive child of frigidus, semi-evergreen, with very long (6in) leaves and hanging clusters of red fruits. Fine autumn tints. Found at the St Monica Home, Bristol. z7.

OF MODERATE GROWTH

C. dielsianus. A decorative 6ft, deciduous shrub of very slender, whippy branches, spreading outwards and downwards, clusters of pink-tinted flowers in June, small leaves that colour well in autumn and bright red berries. z5.

C. distichus. Evergreen in mild climates. A stiffly branched shrub of about 6ft, remarkable for the splendour and abundance of its large, scarlet, flask-shaped fruits, which are usually avoided by birds and hang on well into winter. Its variant *tongolensis* is more picturesque, forming a mound of arching branches.

C. hupehensis, from the Chinese province of Hupeh, has a gracefully arching and widely spreading growth, with an abundance of white flowers in clusters on the upper sides of the stems and showers of bright red fruits. Very handsome.

We include **C. 'Hybridus Pendulus'** here because, although prostrate when grown naturally, it is usually grafted at the top of a 6ft stem, like a standard rose, when it makes the most winsome of small, weeping trees, seen best in a slightly elevated spot, where its long skirts will not trail along the ground.

Cotoneaster 'Hybridus Pendulus' in the main author's garden

C. pannosus is known sometimes as the "silver-leaf cotoneaster" by reason of the white felt on the underleaf and on the young shoots. A very graceful, half-evergreen shrub of some 8ft. z7.

C. racemiflorus is widely distributed from N. Africa to Central Asia, so that its forms vary. The plant usually listed under this name has grey-green leaves and scarlet berries, reaching to 8ft. Its finest and most graceful form, however, is the natural and extremely hardy variety *soongoricus*, which has pink berries and rounded leaves and which thrives even in dry, sandy soils. z3.

Other good varieties are the small-berried *microcarpus*, the very handy *nummularius*, which rarely reaches 5ft, and *veitchii*, in which both flowers and fruit are extra large.

C. splendens, not very well-known, is a handsome, arching, 6ft shrub, with round, grey-green leaves and large, gleaming, orange fruits. The controversial 'Sabrina' arose from it.

In this range we include also **C. zabelii**, because of its great hardiness, its rose-pink flowers and its red pear-shaped berries. About 8ft. z4.

SMALL

These are all normally only about 3ft high, but some spread widely.

Where something really dense is the need, **C. congestus** will meet it very prettily. It makes a compact evergreen dome, with short, stubby branches bearing blue-green leaves, blush-pink flowers and red berries. z6.

C. conspicuus is a very well-known, evergreen dwarf, not flowering until June, followed by red berries, unattractive to birds. It is a variable plant, according to its provenance but, as seen in cultivation, it forms a low, spreading shrub, which may be 4ft high. This is the form that is commonly listed as **C. c. decorus**, but Bean asserts that the varietal epithet is invalid and that those which grow much taller (up to 8ft) or which are nearly prostrate are the ones that should have special epithets. However, if you want to be sure of getting the smaller one, so good for banks and slopes, you had still better specify *decorus*. z6.

C. horizontalis, the herring-bone small cotoneaster or rock-spray, is an old cottage favourite, often seen fanning itself out on walls. Grown naturally, it is a bush with branches spreading quite horizontally, building up to $2\frac{1}{2}$ft. The leaves are reluctant to fall in winter, turning red before doing so. There are several variants, including the very attractive, white-edged 'Variegatus', and some rock-garden miniatures. z4.

Similar in behaviour to horizontalis but in some opinions superior to it is the lesser-known **C. apiculatus**, called in North America the cranberry cotoneaster. Grown naturally, it reaches 6ft and is attired with larger, wavy, minutely pointed (apiculate) leaves and decidedly larger berries, which are scarlet. It is also more cold-hardy than horizontalis and lives where the better-known plant dies. z4.

Last on our list is the wide-spreading **C. microphyllus**, which has very small though lustrous leaves but quite large scarlet berries. Like horizontalis, it will flatten itself decoratively against a wall, but is evergreen and more vigorous. Very good also on sloping banks. The varieties *cochleatus* and *thymifolius* are more prostrate. z5.

CRANBERRY. See *Vaccinium*

CRINODENDRON

Two very choice and distinguished crinodendrons (until recently known as tricuspidarias) are offered to gardeners with mild regions and acid soils. They are evergreen, with slim, tapering and very dark leaves of hard texture, carried on an upright, usually rather slender bush. They most relish a woodsy, peaty or loamy soil, rich in humus, and seem to display their splendours best in a moist atmosphere; very fine specimens are seen, for example, on the west coast of Scotland. They are also at their best in some shade, yet, where their hardiness is in question, they will prosper on a warm wall, though their foliage may be scorched.

Crinodendron hookerianum

The more tender **C. patagua** (or *dependens*) has white flowers, a little smaller than those of the Hooker species and they are a little more open-mouthed — almost bells rather than lanterns. They come at midsummer. Popularly called in America the "lily-of-the-valley tree" — a good example of how misleading such names can be, for there are several other plants with flowers of similar design, notably the sumptuous pierises. z9.

CYRILLA
Leatherwood

An evergreen of distinctive character but uncertain behaviour. Leaves lustrous dark green, flowers in long, slender dangling spikes (racemes) of very small florets in July, issuing from the bases of the shoots that have grown out in the preceding months (the "current year's wood"). In some of its native places (parts of the Americas and the Caribbean) it can reach 25ft, but puts up a poor show in Britain, seldom more than 5ft high. Needs an acid soil. z5.

CYTISUS. Included in Brooms

DABOECIA. Included in Heathers

C. hookerianum is the more arresting and easier of the two. From its dark green recesses clusters of rich crimson-purple flowers, of fleshy texture and almost closed at the mouth, looking like little Chinese lanterns, an inch or more long, hang down from long, drooping stalks. Curiously the stalks and buds develop in autumn but the little lanterns are not lit until May. In America it is liable to be called the "Chinese lantern tree". It is one of those shrubs that, as I have found in my own garden, may appear to be killed by a harsh winter, but remains alive in the roots and regenerates freely if the withered stems are amputated at ground level. Normally its height does not exceed about 10ft, but in very favoured spots it may (we read) soar up to 40ft. z8.

DANAË
Alexandrian laurel

Danaë racemosa is a curious and pleasant little evergreen shrub of only about 3ft, with something of a bamboo about its habits. Its characteristic is that what appear to be leaves on its canes are really flattened stems, slender and finely pointed. Small, "greenery-yallery" flowers of no interest appear in sparse clusters, followed (if the summer has been a hot one) by small red berries, and it then is very good for the flower-vase in winter. Its great merit is that it prospers in deep shade, growing from a spreading rootstock. When the older canes begin to degenerate cut them to the ground. z7.

DAPHNE

The daphnes, who take their name from a legendary nymph of ancient Greece, are creatures of the most refined beauty and the most amorous breath. They are, however, to a large extent unpredictable, maybe sulking in your garden but revelling in your neighbour's. Like gentians and the Madonna lily, they often prefer the cottager's plot to the lord's demesne. We have, therefore, to study with some care their special requirements.

Daphnes are small shrubs, evergreen or deciduous, rarely more than 4ft high. Their tiny flowers, which are tubular until their mouths open to form little trumpets, rather like the floret of a lilac, or, when looked at full in the face, seeming to be four-pointed stars, are crowded in dense little bunches which may form masses at the tips of the branches or may be clustered along the stems. Most are some shade of mauve, pink or white, though a few are yellow. The darlings of the ardent exhibitor are mainly the very dwarf elves that cling precariously to rock surfaces and crevices of steep, stony cliffs, appearing to grow out of the very stone, though their roots, in fact, delve deeply into the soil beneath. Of such are the much-prized *Daphne petraea, cneorum* (the temperamental "garland flower"), *collina, blagayana, arbuscula* and others; likewise that much larger but even more tantalizing beauty, *D. genkwa*, whose place is in limestone rock in hot sun. But, being essentially rock-garden plants, these are outside our brief and we must regretfully pass them by.

Fortunately, there are plenty of other daphnes that are successful as open-garden shrubs, though some are decidedly quirky. A few dwell in light woodland, such as *laureola, pontica, caucasica* and *mezereum*, all of which are easy, though the first two are not choice. Except for these few, all must be in full sun. Gardeners intent on growing daphnes have often been bemused by what Omar Khayyám called "great argument about it and about", some commentators directly contradicting each other, but, where we have been ourselves in doubt, we have followed a splendid little book called simply *Daphne*, by Brickell and Mathew, published by the Alpine Garden Society and available at the RHS Garden at Wisley also. From this it is evident that, with very few exceptions, daphnes are indifferent to the lime content in the soil, prospering in acid as in alkaline soils, and a few, such as *tangutica* and *laureola*, thriving even in chalk.

The most important consideration, however, is that the top layer shall be rich in moisture-holding, humusy soil, but the sub-soil one that gives free and open drainage. These apparently contrary conditions, where they do not exist naturally, can often be contrived by a sloping bed or bank, faced with stone and the soil suitably prepared with plenty of stones, coarse sand or grit. I have myself, however, grown *D. mezereum*, the old mezereon of our forefathers, and the hybrid *burkwoodii* more or less on the flat in stiff clay. Drought is perhaps the worst enemy, but water-logging can also be fatal. Soak the soil-ball thoroughly before planting and maintain the top spit by mulching the plants generously every spring with old leaves, manure or peat. They hate being moved when established; if transplanting is essential take them out with a large ball of soil and saturate the new site.

Do no pruning if it can possibly be avoided. Daphnes shrink from the knife. Should it be essential to remove a diseased or broken stem, treat the cut with a bituminous wound-paint. If a young plant shows a tendency to be lanky, however, you may nip out the extreme tips with finger and thumb.

Propagation is by seed, cuttings, layers or (in experienced hands) grafting.

Seed is by no means always produced by some species in garden conditions. When it is, remove the fleshy coating just before it is apparently ripe, usually late summer, and sow the seed at once. Germination is slow and may not occur until next spring. Seed of the mezereon is often sown when the berries are still green.

Cuttings are faster. As a general rule, take small, young shoots that are firm at the base but soft at the tip in early July. Cuttings with a "heel" apparently root most readily. Use a standard compost of two parts sharp sand and one part peat. Soak thoroughly and house in a close propagating case of some sort.

For gardeners who are anxious to pursue the fairest of the nymphs for the first time, the most wooable are *mezereum*, the hybrid *burkwoodii*, *retusa*, *tangutica*, the hybrid *napolitana* and, where the site is not too chilly, the romantically scented *odora*, especially its variety 'Aureo-marginata', which is a bit more cold-hardy.

The following is a fairly comprehensive list of daphnes that can be grown in the open or in light shade, but for several of them you would have to search with keen diligence. All are deliciously scented, unless noted otherwise.

D. aurantiaca. Evergreen, straggly shrub, to 5ft or more. Slender flowers of bright orange. For warm counties only. April. z8–9.

D. bholua. Semi-evergreen. Can be 10ft high. A fine species that flowers from Christmas to March, but in cooler localities needs a warm south wall. Flowers in small, terminal clusters, variable in colour but usually pale purple-pink, scented of lemons. Leaves acutely pointed. Good in chalk. The clone 'Gurkha', pale mauve and white, is hardier, not quite so vigorous but suckers freely.

D. × burkwoodii. Semi-evergreen, 3ft or more, wide-spreading and dense. Easy and popular. Blush-pink flowers in clusters along the upper parts of the branches in May and June. There are two clones. One is sometimes identified as 'Albert Burkwood' and the other 'Somerset'. The latter is more erect than its brother, reaching maybe 5ft, with larger, blunter leaves, the flowers rather smaller and paler in tone. A French reverse-cross hybrid is known as 'Lavenirii'. Propagate by cuttings in late June. z5.

D. caucasica. Deciduous. Grows fast to 6ft in light shade, with blunt leaves and bunches of glistening white flowers on short laterals in May–June, often repeated in August–September. Berries black, but red in the rare variety *axilliflora*. Seed or heel cuttings in early July. z7.

Differing from *D. caucasica* only in minor details are three other Russians — *altaica*, which suckers freely, and the little-known *sophia* and *taurica*.

D. giraldii. Deciduous. Like a yellow-flowered mezereon, rarely seen but very attractive and not difficult in the right soil. Likes chalk. May–June. To 4ft. Seed. z7.

D. gnidium. Evergreen, grey-leaved, erect deportment to 5ft. Cream flowers in large terminal panicles, borne all the summer. Mix it with other shrubs in sun or light shade. Seed. z8.

D. × houtteana. Semi-evergreen, erect, 4ft, leaves flushed purple. Flowers lilac-purple in spring. Rare and subject to virus. Half-ripe cuttings in July (if plant healthy). z6.

D. × hybrida. Rare but desirable evergreen, having much of the aspect of *D. odora*, growing erectly to 6ft and bearing terminal clusters of purple flowers virtually all the year, but richest in spring and autumn. Half-ripe cuttings in July. z8.

D. jezoensis. A half-size version of *D. mezereum*, but with yellow flowers.

D. laureola. The old "spurge laurel". A very easy evergreen to 4ft. Not showy but useful for a dark corner. Small clusters of yellow-green flowers, not agreeably scented, in February–March. Seed. Good in chalk. The sub-species *philippii* is a dwarf. z7.

D. mezereum. The dearly-loved mezereon of our forefathers. Deciduous, 4ft normally. Flowers soft purple in February–March. A natural woodlander, it prefers a little shade, but does not insist upon it. Thrives in alkaline clay, but highly tolerant of other soils. Berries green, turning red. Propagate by seed when the berries are either green or red, after removal of the fleshy coating.

There are several variants of the mezereon, including the splendid white-flowered, yellow-berried *alba* (especially 'Bowles's Variety'), the rose-pink *rosea*, and *autumnalis* (or *grandiflora*), which flowers in the fall and nearly all winter, flourishing at the head of the Niagara Falls. z4.

D. × napolitana (or *neapolitana*). One of

the best dwarf shrubs for garden use. Evergreen, 2ft, dense and spreading. Rose-purple buds opening pink in terminal clusters in March to May. Thrives anywhere in the prescribed conditions. July cuttings. z8.

D. odora. Perhaps the most bewitchingly scented of all plants. Evergreen, with dark, leathery, polished, pointed leaves 3in long, forming a mound normally 3–4ft high. The flowers, borne in terminal bunches, are purple-red and white and are displayed throughout February and March. Except in the warmer counties, however, it needs some protection, particularly that of a warm south wall, where it may reach 6ft. It fails in chalky soils. To be sure of a bushy plant, pinch out the tips of the shoots when young.

There are many forms of *D. odora*, the best of all (and the hardiest) being the variety 'Aureo-marginata', the leaves of which have a thin gilt stripe along the edges. The flowers are a little paler than the plain *odora* and it is a much better plant all round, needing wall protection only in the colder places. From California comes a fine, white-flowered form, *alba*, but it is less hardy. Other variants are extremely rare. z8.

D. pontica. Easy, evergreen woodlander, succeeding in dense shade if required. To 4ft, spreading widely. Frail, elongated, yellow-green flowers along the stem, usually in pairs. March to May. Berries black. Not choice but useful in heavy soils. Easy from seed as soon as gathered. z6.

D. retusa. An easy and delightful evergreen for anywhere in the garden, given the right soil structure. Shiny, dark green leaves, red-purple flowers, white within, richly scented. Full sun. Occasionally reaches 3ft, forming a dense mound, but of slow growth. Succeeds in chalk. Sow what seeds there are left by the birds in autumn, or take soft cuttings in June or half-ripe ones in July. z7.

D. tangutica. A happy species very like *retusa* and equally good as a garden plant. The carriage is more open and erect, noticeably taller, the growth faster, the leaves pointed and not so glossy. Flower colours vary, but nursery forms are usually red-purple without, paler purple within, and there is a beautiful white form, *alba*. Succeeds in chalk. z7.

DAPHNIPHYLLUM

Robust evergreen shrub with large leaves like those of the rhododendron, but of no floral value. Useful where a dense cover is wanted in partial (not full) shade. Wide-spreading and lime-tolerant. The name is mongrel Greek for "laurel-leaved".

D. humile grows about 7ft high and *D. macropodum* is very much bigger and its little florets are pungently scented. z7.

DECAISNEA

This unusual genus is named after the French botanist Decaisne and the only species normally grown, *D. fargesii*, is for the French missionary Père Farges, who found it. It throws up long, slender but stout stems to about 12ft, very erect and packed closely together, furnished with enormous pinnate leaves that may be a yard long, with 25 leaflets, together with drooping clusters, anything up to 18in long, of small, greenish, bell-formed flowers, followed by long pods coated with a blue bloom. For sun or half-shade. It is deciduous and likes a rich, loamy soil. If late spring frosts damage the young growths, cut the stems back to fresh new growth later in the season. z6.

DENDROMECON

The name means "tree-poppy" and indeed it is a true poppy, producing flowers of bright yellow for a long period on a shrub averaging about 10ft, with slim, pointed, rigid, leathery, willow-form leaves, where the climate is warm enough. In its native home — mainly the California coastal range — it grows in dry, rocky or sandy chaparral, putting down very long, fleshy tap-root, and is very difficult to establish in other conditions. This describes *D. rigida*, the usual one of gardens. *D. harfordii*, the island tree-poppy, differs little from it, and so apparently does its variety *rhamnoides*, except for its paler and less crowded leaves. In doubtful climates grow these against a hot wall, fanning out the stems. Once planted, they refuse to be moved. The only pruning needed is to cut out decadent and spindly stems as new growth starts in spring. z9.

DESFONTAINIA

Where it can be grown *Desfontainia spinosa* is a magnificent but slightly tender evergreen shrub built up of holly-like leaves and glittering all over with small tubular flowers which are a bright crimson, rimmed with a yellow band

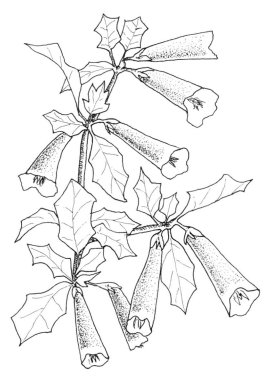

42. Desfontainea spinosa

at the mouth. Its native ground is along the Andes from Colombia down to the Straits of Magellan, so that its reputation for tenderness is founded less on temperature than on the fact that it is accustomed to a moist atmosphere. Its wide distribution causes some variations, but the one generally known under the clonal name 'Harold Comber' comes from Chile under cloudy mountain skies. It grows superbly out in the open on the west coast of Scotland and its islands and in exposed positions in Edinburgh, as well as in Northern Ireland and Cornwall, reaching 10ft high and wide, in its full splendour from July to autumn. In less favourable areas it will be smaller and needs plenty of water plus a thick mulch of autumnal leaves.

DESMODIUM

Rather in the nature of connoisseurs' plants and not at all easy, the desmodiums are members of the pea family, with the flowers and pods typical thereof. The leaves are usually sparsely pinnate or of three leaflets. In nature they are widely distributed in the warmer parts of the world, but those of the gardens are from high altitudes in China. They bloom in late summer. Rehder classes them as z7, but z8 is more realistic. They are semi-herbaceous; cut the old growths down to the ground in spring.

D. spicatum. Laxly branched shrub of about 7ft; rosy-purple bunches, September–October. Flowers well in southern England.

D. tiliifolium. 4ft or more; large bunches of lilac or pink, August–October.

DEUTZIA

Here we return to a race of popular and easy shrubs of modest stature, growable in any decent soil. The name is in honour of Johann van der Deutz, of eighteenth-century Amsterdam, but is commonly pronounced *à l'anglaise*.

Deutzias are deciduous shrubs that fit well

into an herbaceous border, as elsewhere. Most of them flower in June, usually in white or soft colourings. The flowers are cups or bells, often with the tips of their petals turned back to look like stars. They like a little light shade and a fairly moist soil, but are discouraged by a wet, cheerless autumn, which prevents the ripening of new shoots. Some are sensitive to late spring frosts. We think that Rehder's ratings, as given here, are somewhat sanguine.

Pruning is very important indeed. Deutzias grow from "stools", which readily throw up new stems from the base and these flower the next year ("old" wood) on short laterals. In the first year cut right out all trivial, wispy shoots and shorten the main stems a mite. Afterwards cut back the flowered stems after blossom-fall (usually July) to a strong new oncoming growth. (Fig. 10). Decrepit old stems can be cut to the ground.

First choices would include 'Carminea' (a selection from the hybrid *rosea*), *gracilis*, *chunii*, the hybrid *kalmiiflora* and the splendid varieties of *hybrida* raised by the famous French nurseryman Lemoine. The one most commonly grown, because the toughest, is *scabra*, but it lacks refinement.

D. amurensis. A debatable name, but Bean asserts that it belongs properly to a 6ft shrub producing white corymbs from 2–3in wide. Possibly this is the right name for what is often called *D. parviflora*. Not choice. z4.

D. × candelabra is the "candle deutzia" of 6ft. Broad, dense, erect spikes of white, like candles. A handsome hybrid of *gracilis* and *sieboldiana*. z5.

D. chunii. A beautiful shrub, especially welcome for cooling down the hot colours of July with its refreshing white, star-like showers. The shrub has a rather pendulous carriage with drooping, willow-form leaves. The flower buds are lilac and open to form a pointed, white, pyramidal truss, 4in long, in the manner of a lilac, but displayed all along the branches and exposing their yellow anthers. A small shrub with a character all its own, but rather untidy, like an urchin in clean clothes. z6.

Also flowering in July but of a tidier be-

haviour is the uncommon **D. compacta**, which forms a neat, dense bush of 5ft or more, with flowers that are pink in the bud, but open to form tight, white snowballs. Hillier's beautiful variety 'Lavender Time' explains itself. z5.

D. discolor 'Major' is a very showy shrub of 5ft or more with large, many-flowered trusses, faintly tinted pink, on long arching stems. z6.

The flowers of **D. × elegantissima** are fragrant and rose-tinted, but in its form 'Fasciculata' are a deeper pink still and in the lovely 'Rosealind' are positively carmine. The shrubs grow to about 5ft, with an erect deportment and the flower trusses (corymbs) are erect too, z6.

D. gracilis answers to its name, bearing myriads of white flowers in upright racemes on slender stems. Only 3ft high and of close habit.

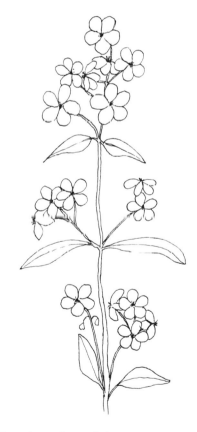

43. Deutzia × elegantissima

Makes a fine informal hedge but should not be sheared. It has a yellow-leaved form in 'Aurea' and a yellow-mottled one in 'Marmorata', z4. Susceptible to both spring frosts and hot American autumns.

D. grandiflora. 6ft. Distinguished by its large flowers, borne in clusters of 2 or 3, and also by its precocious flowering, which may be as early as April, but more often May. z5.

D. × **hillieri**. A fine hybrid of elegant behaviour that grows to 6ft and bears close-set clusters of flowers that are purple in the bud opening to white stars in June–July.

In **D.** × **hybrida** we meet, not an individual, but a group of splendid and colourful hybrids raised by Lemoine, of great delicacy and charm. We need not argue about the parentage. They grow about 6ft or so and you can have any or all of the following first-class clones. z6.

'Contraste'. Large, star-like pink flowers with a dark stripe.

'Joconde'. Purple in bud and outside, opening white.

'Magicien'. Like 'Contraste' but flowers edged white.

'Mont Rose'. Deep fuchsia-pink, with golden anthers.

'Perle Rose'. Quantities of small, soft pink flowers.

D. × **kalmiiflora** is also a Lemoine hybrid, with cup-shaped flowers like those of the Kalmia, deep pink outside, almost white within. A graceful and charming shrub of 5ft. z5.

D. × **lemoinei**. Another "group" with several forms, mostly about 7ft, with white flowers. 'Avalanche' blooms very freely, and 'Boule de Neige' is small and compact with flower clusters like snowballs. Susceptible to spring frost. z4–5.

D. longifolia. 5ft. One of the most stylish Chinese straightforward species, having long, grey-green leaves, felted below and flowers tinted pale purple. 'Veitchii' is a specially good cultivar in deep lilac-pink and *farreri* a white natural variety. z6.

D. × **magnifica**. Erect, branching habit to 6ft, with white double flowers. Several named

clones of good quality. 'Eburnea' has single bell-flowers in loose clusters, 'Longipetala' has long petals, 'Latifolia' has large, wide-mouthed blossoms and 'Erecta' has very large, upright trusses. All single. z5.

D. × **maliflora**. A pretty shrub of about 5ft, with tight clusters of up to 30 flowers, which are frilled at the edges and tinted pink. June.

D. monbeigii. A charming small shrub that does not flower until July, when it becomes weighed down by the abundance of its many-flowered clusters of glistening white stars, each blossom displaying its orange anthers. z7.

D. parviflora. A name we avoid. See *amurensis*.

D. pulchra. Very fine 8ft shrub of great character, but not so hardy as other deutzias. It is adorned with enormous, slender, drooping sprays of flowers like lily-of-the-valley, prettily showing their orange anthers. The dark, leathery leaves may linger until Christmas.

D. purpurascens. A very good, 6ft shrub with white flowers tinted purple and scented, but perhaps more important as one of the parents of fine hybrids, such as *kalmiiflora*, *elegantissima* and *rosea*. z5.

D. × **rosea**. Another Lemoine hybrid group (*gracilis* × *purpurascens*), with several beautiful clones. 'Carminea' is generally the most admired. This is a delightful small shrub of only 3ft, but spreading widely, with petals pale pink within and deeper outside. 'Campanulata' is bigger with large, white bells on purple stalks. 'Eximea' is 6ft, the petals white within and pink outside. z5.

Compared with these and other Lemoine hybrids, the common **D. scabra** is of inferior quality. It grows stiffly erect to 12ft or more and produces large clusters of white bells in June–July. Its brown, peeling bark is quite attractive. Again there are several variants, of which perhaps the most satisfying is 'Plena', for its flowers are double, long-lasting and suffused purple outside. 'Pride of Rochester' resembles it, but its tinting is pink. 'Candidissima', the "snow-flake deutzia", is also double, but pure white in large clusters. z5.

D. schneideriana averages about 7ft, bearing panicles of white flowers like small snow-drops. z6.

D. setchuenensis in its variety *corymbiflora* is another of the "starry" deutzias. There may be 300 tiny stars in the bunches (corymbs), followed by decorative jade-green seed capsules. z6.

Often confused with *scabra*, but half the size, is **D. sieboldiana**. Lax in habit, it produces white flowers with orange stamens and scented of mignonette. z5.

D. vilmoriniae. A fast-moving and more refined version of *scabra*, reaching 10ft, with 6in, grey-green leaves, palely felted beneath, and ice-white flowers in broad corymbs. z6.

DIERVILLA

When a botanical divorce in the diervillas took place some years ago, only the poorest members of the family were allowed to keep the old name. The richest were sent off and called weigelas, but the old name still sticks in some minds today. The diervillas of modern usage have flowers that are two-lipped, yellow and carried on the current year's growth. They are of little interest to gardeners. The best is *D. sessilifolia*, a grey-green shrub of about 4ft (z4) and *rivularis* (z5) is very like it. Prune in early spring to get a mass of summer flowering stems. *D. lonicera* is a tough, scrambling, suckering shrub. z3.

DIPELTA

Cousins of the diervilla and weigela, the dipeltas are large or fairly large, ornamental, deciduous shrubs with long, tapered leaves and flourishing bells or trumpets of soft colours in May–June on stems that have developed in the previous year. Their name is botanist's Greek for "double-shielded", from the fact that the seed capsule (which resembles that of the elm), remains for a long time attached to its floral bract. They like a rather moist, loamy soil and are not scared of lime.

The main branches from the ground are erect, but secondary shoots arch over as the flowers open. From these branches strong growths often develop, but they in turn bend over. The older branches thus are deprived of light and so are liable to die back. Prune out this old wood when it becomes decadent and cut back the more recent ones after blossom-fall, as for deutzias. Propagate by cuttings of half-ripe wood under mist in early July.

Probably the best is **D. floribunda**, which may reach 15ft or more. The flowers are pale pink trumpets, yellow in the throat, developing in profusion from short, lateral twigs in double rows and are scented to boot. Flourishes in chalk. z5.

D. ventricosa, nearly as tall, has broad ("ventricose") bells, deep rose on the outer side of the petal, white within, with an orange throat, produced on twiggy laterals. z6.

D. yunnanensis, 12ft, has slender trumpets of cream, tinted rose, with an orange throat, on long stalks. z7.

DISANTHUS

D. cercidifolius is a deciduous shrub of 10ft, spreading widely and of fleeting splendour in autumn, when its almost round leaves, which resemble those of the Judaea tree (*Cercis*) blaze in a dying glory of crimson and orange. Its small, purple flowers are of no account and smelly. If you yearn for it, you must plant it in acid soil in light woodland, sheltered alike from wind and direct sun. z7.

DOGWOOD. See *Cornus*

DRIMYS

These are large, sometimes enormous, evergreen shrubs, which, when not in flower, look very like rhododendrons, and which are re-

Drimys winteri

markable for their aromatic qualities. They are distinctly tender and their chief liking is for a moist atmosphere.

The most famous is **D. winteri**, known as Winter's bark, which was found on his passage through the hazardous Straits of Magellan by William Winter, one of Drake's captains, in the sixteenth century, who used its highly aromatic bark as an antidote to scurvy for his ship's company and brought it home to England. Formerly it was known by the more apt and euphonious name of *Wintera aromatica*. The rather daisy-like flowers, which may take a few years to appear, are scented too, and are displayed in loose clusters.

Being widely distributed along the southern Andes, Winter's bark appears in a variety of slightly different forms, but the one usually in commerce is quite capable in a soft climate, such as parts of Ireland, of soaring up to 50ft, though in other conditions 25ft may be its maximum. The broad-leaved *latifolia* is a well-

known variety, but far less known is the dwarf *andina*, which does not go more than 5ft. z8 on a big wall, otherwise z9.

D. lanceolata, the mountain pepper from Australasia, differs a good deal from Winter's bark, reaching only 15ft in a broadly columnar shape. The leaves are aromatic and peppery if nibbled, the flowers, some male and some female, white and not very conspicuous, are followed by black berries. z9.

EDGEWORTHIA

E. chrysantha is a tender, thin bush to be attempted only in the milder counties or in a seaside air, which it likes. According to conditions, it grows to an average of 5ft, with rather dull green, pointed leaves, and small, densely packed flowers of rich yellow in a rounded cluster. Its most remarkable feature is that its thin stems are so flexible that they can be tied into knots. Used in Japan for making high-class paper. Hardy on a wall in z8.

ELAEAGNUS
Oleaster

Here we find a small assembly of large or fairly large shrubs, some evergreen, some deciduous, that are of particular value for breaking the force of wind in exposed and coastal regions and often decorative as well. Moreover, they are drought-resistant. The flowers, like tiny fuchsias, are apt to hide themselves secretively, but are often detected by their sweet scent, after which they form small, drupe-like berries.

Oleasters need only a reasonably fertile soil, acid or limy, but dislike chalk; those that have silver-tinted leaves shine best in a sandy one. The botanical name derives in part from the Greek for an olive, hence also oleaster. We must omit *E. angustifolia*, as it becomes a 40ft tree, and confine ourselves to the following.

The most striking and the most often seen are

the yellow variations of the evergreen **E. pungens**, especially the variety 'Maculata'. This is a big, bold thruster of maybe 12ft, whose tough, crinkle-edged leaves are gaily and lavishly splashed with daffodil, leaving the edge green, a most cheering picture in the colourless days of winter. The underside of the leaf is white. It grows almost anywhere, in sun or shade. In 'Dicksonii' the green and gold colourings are reversed. The parent species, *E. pungens* itself, is rather taller and differs only in having an all-green leaf. 'Variegata' has a paler margin. 'Fredericii' is cream-splashed and 'Simonii' has a larger leaf. z7.

No doubt next in popular appraisal is **E. × ebbingei**, a leafy, fast-moving evergreen shrub of 10ft, upright of habit, faintly silvered, very good for screening. Secretive little flowers in autumn, small berries next spring. The name is not a finite one, there being at least two clones of this hybrid group in commerce, one smaller than the other. What is much more definite and striking is its handsome form 'Gilt Edge', in which the leaf is heavily ornamented with gold. z6.

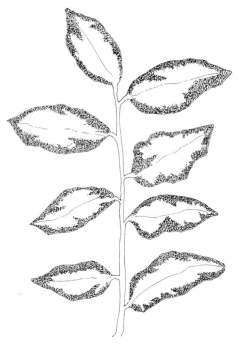

44.   Elaeagnus pungens 'Maculata'

E. commutata, the thornless silver berry, is a remarkable, deciduous, slender, extremely hardy shrub averaging 8ft, being silver-plated in nearly all its parts — leaf, flower and berry, the only other colours being the chestnut of the young shoots and the orange flash on the inside of the flowers, which appear in abundance in May and are sweetly scented. You must site it carefully, not only because of its colour but also because it spreads rapidly by underground suckers. z2.

E. glabra is a big, rambling, thornless, evergreen shrub, 20ft high and more, forming in time a domed or pyramidal mass. Some pruning is needed to keep it in bounds. The underleaf is a shining bronze; white, scented flowers in autumn. z7.

E. macrophylla is a handsome, robust evergreen shrub, averaging 10ft and broader than high, considered by some to be the best of all oleasters, especially in spring, when the broad leaves and the young shoots are richly silvered before turning green, but the silver sheen still remains on the underleaf. The shrub branches thickly right down to the ground, deterring weeds, the upper branches almost horizontal and even pendulous at their tips. Very fragrant flowers in autumn. z7.

E. multiflora is a very hardy but variable creature, semi-evergreen, about 8ft high, with tapered leaves, silvery beneath and scented flowers all along the stems in April–May, resulting in quantities of orange berries like small cherries in July. z4.

E. umbellata is a big, deciduous scrambler, extremely hardy, usually thorny, with light green, tapered leaves, silvery beneath, with visible flowers in May–June, turning to red berries, too much appreciated by the birds. Variable in habit. z3.

ELDER. See *Sambucus*

ELLIOTTIA

E. racemosa is a rare and difficult plant, deciduous, seldom exceeding 10ft, with slim leaves of a dark, leaden green and displaying loose erect spikes (racemes) of small, white flowers at the branch-tips. It needs an acid soil, preferably sandy. Difficult to transplant and seed difficult to come by. z7.

ELSHOLTZIA

E. stauntonii is a rather weedy sub-shrub of 5ft, of value only for its loose clusters of lilac flowers in August–September. It is semi-herbaceous, the stems dying down nearly to the ground in winter. In March cut back what remains of them to the lowest pair of buds. z4.

EMBOTHRIUM

Where they can be grown, the Chilean "fire bush" is one of the great glories of a garden. Multitudes of small scarlet or orange-scarlet, tubular blossoms throng its stems with such intensity and with such dash and spirit that the whole plant looks like a column of fire in May–June. When first seen it brings you to a halt and causes you "to stand and stare". Do not put its life at risk, however, unless you can plant it in a moist, deep, acid soil of not too heavy a texture, not too crowded by other plants. A humid atmosphere is a further encouragement to lengthen and enrich its splendid limbs.

As it has a wide natural distribution in South America, the embothrium varies somewhat in its behaviour and in its colour. There has been a good deal of chatter about its name, but fundamentally it is **Embothrium coccineum**. A variation of it is referred to as *E. c. lanceolatum*. There are botanists who assert that these names are synonymous, but, as generally understood, *coccineum* is orange-scarlet and evergreen and *lanceolatum* full scarlet and not fully evergreen. However that may be, the one to ask for is a dazzler labelled 'Norquinco', from the valley of that name. It is certainly the most vivid of all, but indeed, almost any form

of coccineum will give a thrill to the garden. Recently a seedling named 'Flamenco', deep orange-scarlet, was raised in the celebrated garden at Bodnant, in North Wales, which has just the right moist climate. There is also an excellent form with long leaves, 'Longifolium'. In similar climates in Cornwall and Ireland the embothrium can tower up to 40ft, but most of us would be delighted if it grew no more than half that size, which is more normal. z8–9.

ENKIANTHUS

These are mainly large, or fairly large, deciduous shrubs for an acid, moist, woodsy soil, for sun or light shade. They are curiously branched in whorls, so that they often appear to be in tiers. The leaves also are in whorls. The flowers are small dangling bells or pitchers (like lily-of-the-valley), blooming in May, but their "greatest hour" is the autumn, when the leaves become brightly ensanguined.

The best of them, no doubt, is the rather variable **E. campanulatus** which normally does not exceed 12ft but can be far taller. Bells usually of pale yellow, veined and tipped red. There are several variations, as in the white *albiflorus*, the red *matsudae* and the deeper red *palibinii*. z4.

E. cernuus may be reckoned at perhaps 10ft, with forked branches, white, small bells in hanging spikes, but rich red in the variety *rubens*. z5.

E. chinensis is of about the same size, with hanging clusters of small bells, which are yellow, veined rose. z7–8.

E. deflexus. Much the same character as campanulatus, but can be anything up to 20ft, with larger flowers. The young branches begin bright red. z5.

E. perulatus is a more easily managed shrub of no more than 6ft, with pretty, white, lily-of-the-valley flowers and particularly good autumn colour. z5.

ERICA. Included in Heathers.

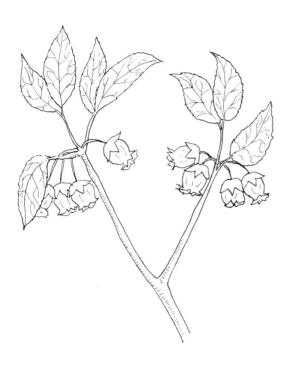

45. Enkianthus campanulatus

Rather more engaging than any of these is the decidedly tender **E. quinqueflora**, a shrub of up to 6ft. Its leathery leaves are chestnut-red before turning green and from among them peep out clusters of five small pink bells borne from pink bracts. Other colours have been reported. z9.

ERICA. Included in Heathers

ERIOBOTRYA
Loquat

One associates the luscious fruits of the loquat with a genial Mediterranean climate, but occasionally they are prooduced in much colder conditions. The plant itself is just hardy enough for sheltered places in Zone 7 and, in the larger gardens, is worth a place regardless of fruits.

In warm zones **E. japonica** forms a tree of up to 25ft; elsewhere it is a tall, strong, rather rangy shrub, with distinct characteristics. The woolly or furry swaddling clothes on several of its parts accounts for its generic name, which is mongrel Greek for "woolly clusters". The young leaves emerge as woolly tufts like rabbits' ears, sandy-coloured, and then gradually become dark green, leathery, ruggedly veined and highly polished, up to 10in long. The small, white hawthorn-scented flowers, borne in winter in closely packed pyramids, peer out of a fuzz of rust-coloured down. The apricot-like fruits (if any) materialise in spring in warm places. There is a variegated form with cream markings on the leaves.

Plant in a deep, well-drained soil in full sun and, in colder climates, on a warm wall.

ESCALLONIA

Somewhat on the tender side, escallonias are handsome, small-leaved, small-flowered evergreens of dense bulk. The leaves are highly polished. The flowers are tubular in appearance (though actually composed of several petals), in red, pink or white. Apart from their individual excellence, they make splendid informal, broad hedges and are particularly at home in a seaside atmosphere. They are drought-resistant and, with few exceptions, are tolerant of lime. Breeders have raised a host of hybrids and these are the favourites of most people. All but a few have curved scimitar stems, becoming in time a congested mass, the tips sometimes touching the ground and taking root there, a tendency to be discouraged. Their favourite soil is a sandy loam, without manure or fertilizer. In suspect climates (anything colder than z8) and in cold heavy clay they must be planted against a protective wall.

When the arching types of escallonias become congested, some surgery is necessary. Do this as the blossoms drop, cutting back to a point just above a promising new shoot. When grown on a wall, occasionally cut outwards-thrusting shoots right out as replacement shoots develop. After a severe winter escallonias have the knack of producing new growth when much of the shrub has been killed, so give them a chance to do so before giving them up as dead. In a genial but wet summer some varieties give a second blooming from short laterals. Prune these lightly after first flowering and hard back after the second. Propagation is easy enough from half-ripe cuttings in a sandy mix in gentle heat in August.

We shall omit all those considered too tender for our purposes.

E. alpina. About 4ft in the open, spreading broadly, but 15ft on an east-facing wall at the RHS Garden, Wisley.

E. bifida. 10ft or more in the open. White flowers in large clusters in September (so prune in spring). Full sun. Not very hardy. z9.

E. × exoniensis. Fast-growing to 20ft or more, with an open habit. Flowers blush-white from June till frosts; prune in spring. The cultivar 'Balfourii' is a beautiful form of pensive carriage.

E. illinita. A big, loose-limbed shrub, hardier than most. Flowers white, leaves malodorous.

E. 'Ingramii'. See under *rubra*.

E. 'Iveyi'. One of the finest, but not the hardiest. Very dark green, highly polished leaves, white flowers in July–August. z9.

E. 'Langleyensis'. 8ft. Splendid, elegant and one of the hardiest. Flowers bright rosy-carmine at midsummer. It is the headspring of a fine array of named clones, of which we note the following, all but two round about 6ft.

'Apple Blossom' (5ft), 'Peach Blossom', 'Donard Rose' and 'Donard White' explain themselves; others are:

'Donard Beauty'. Deep rose-pink, pendulous carriage.

'Donard Gem'. Pale pink, scented.

'Donard Radiance'. Rich pink chalices.

'Donard Seedling'. Pink buds, opening blush. One of the hardiest.

'Donard Star'. Deep rose, spreading petals.

'Edinensis'. From Edinburgh. Very like 'Langleyensis'.

'Gwendolyn Anley'. Splendid. Scarcely 4ft high, but spreading to 10ft. Pink buds opening white. One of the hardiest.

'Pride of Donard'. Red, early.

'Slieve Donard'. Apple-blossom pink, one of the hardiest.

'William Watson'. Deep pink. Dense. Flowers twice. Prune lightly after first flowering, hard back after the second.

E. leucantha. 15ft. White flowers in large clusters.

E. macrantha. See under *rubra*.

E. revoluta. Up to 20ft, covered with a grey down, flowers white. z9.

E. rosea. Averages 6ft. Flowers white, scented, in slender racemes.

E. rubra. 15ft. A valuable but variable species, extending in nature over a long range of the Southern Andes. The forms in cultivation have leaves of variable shape and size and the flowers may be pink or cerise. Parent of some excellent natural or cultivated varieties, including the following.

Macrantha. A natural variety so important as to be often elevated to the status of a separate species. A 9ft shrub of dense and luxuriant leafage. Relatively large leaves, gleaming darkly, flowers rose, in June. A lover of the seaside, tolerant of salt spray and a fine hedger. A handsome wall covering in regions too cold for it to be grown in the open. 'Crimson Spire' is a specially selected form for hedging, growing fast with an erect stance. 'Red Hedger' is nearly as good.

'C. F. Ball'. One of the finest of escallonias, growing to 7ft or more, with large, rich red flowers.

'Ingramii'. Like *macrantha*, but taller, leaves and flowers small. Another favourite for hedging. Of uncertain origin and often listed as a separate species.

'Glasnevin Hybrid'. A Dubliner resembling 'C. F. Ball', but flowers rose, and leaves unpolished.

E. virgata. The only deciduous escallonia of commerce, variable according to its geographical origins. Usually a dense, twiggy shrub of about 7ft, with white flowers in June–July, opening widely, not like other escallonias. Hardiest of all, but should have acid soil. z7.

EUCRYPHIA

The eucryphias are very beautiful plants of the most distinguished presence, but nearly all become trees, even very large trees, of which the most readily wooable and most easily accommodated is the charming hybrid 'Nymansay'. Only one can be deemed a shrub, **E. glutinosa**. Even this becomes a tree in time, but it will be several years before it reaches 20ft, so we can admit it to our pages.

Fortunately for us, glutinosa is perhaps the most enchanting of the species. Like other eucryphias, it has pure white flowers of delicate texture, four-petalled, decorated by a brush of innumerable golden anthers, as you might suppose of a white Rose-of-Sharon. Blossoming in July and August, they grow among pinnate leaves, composed of three or five leaflets of dark, burnished green. The deportment of the tree is erect and graceful. But you must not risk the life of so lovely a creature unless you can plant it in a moist, acid, preferably peaty soil, with its roots in shade. Scorching sun on naked soil may kill it, so some ground-cover plants are needed about its roots, such as prostrate junipers, *Virburnum davidii*, pachysandras or low-spreading heathers. Until these are established and spreading, artificial coverings such as bracken or tree branches will act as nurses, for it is in childhood that glutinosa is most at risk. When well established you need not fear. In mild climates it may be evergreen. z8.

Eucryphia glutinosa

EUONYMUS

This is a versatile genus, providing us with small trees, large shrubs and ground-crawlers, some evergreen, some deciduous. Several make splendid hedges. Their flowers are usually paltry and they are grown mainly for their foliage and, in most instances, for their pretty fruitlets. As in the yew, the seeds are enclosed in a fleshy coating, known as an aril, brightly coloured as a rule, and these are revealed when the capsules split open; the segments of the capsule persist, however, giving the fruit a winged appearance.

The euonymus (a compound word that denotes pregnancy) thrives in almost any soil, in sun or shade, some in deep shade, and is among the best plants for chalk. In parts of the United States it is much preyed upon by scale insects, which can be combated by malathion in June.

There are a lot of euonymus, or spindle trees, but many resemble one another and many are of little garden value; these we shall pass by.

Our chief interests are in the variants of fortunei, japonicus and europaeus.

The very hardy **E. alatus**, deciduous, 8ft, is of interest for the corky ribs or "wings" along its stems. It is quite a good design plant, the branches spreading out far, horizontally in tiers. Vivid autumn colours and mauve fruits. The variety 'Compactus' is excellent and makes a very good hedge; the natural variety *apterus* has wingless branches. z3.

E. americanus, the strawberry-tree or wahoo, 8ft, is upright and straggling, with warty, scarlet fruits. z6.

E. bungeanus, deciduous, grows at high speed to 20ft with a loose habit and is at its best in the variety *semipersistens*, so called because its leaves stay green well into the winter and its yellow-and-pink fruits even longer, but in Britain it may not always fruit well. z4.

E. europaeus. This is the spindle-tree of old, so called because its hard wood was used for the shaping of spindles in the fabrication of cloth. Deciduous but keeping its leaves almost until winter; spreading at the top but almost naked at the base. Can become a tree of 20ft or more. Quite happy in chalk. Pretty and conspicuous fruits. Many variations, of which the most colourful is 'Red Cascade', but it needs a mate for pollination for which the late Rowland Jackman, who introduced it, recommended the big *hamiltonianus*. The brilliant pink 'Aldenhamensis' is also splendid. 'Albus' is white and 'Atropurpureus' has purple leaves. The little-known natural variety *intermedius* is possibly better than any of these, having large leaves and bearing enormous crops of red fruits.

When we reach **E. fortunei radicans** we find something very different from all others. Until recently it was called simply *E. radicans*, but we are now instructed that *radicans* is simply a variety of *fortunei*, not itself of much interest. Radicans behaves peculiarly like an ivy, running along the ground, rooting as it goes, or, if planted close to a wall, climbing it featly. These crawlers seem barren of flower and fruit, but in the form *carrierei* and the natural variety *vegetus* they attain an adult stage, like the "tree ivy", becoming low, fruit-bearing shrubs, the

Euonymus fortunei 'Emerald Gaiety'

former with indifferent, pallid fruits, the latter, orange.

All the radicans are of the easiest culture, flourishing in shade, even in deep shade, as in sun, do not mind how poor the soil and compete well with tree roots. They are as easy as pie to propagate, by plucking off any part and sticking it into sandy soil in shade. The following are at our service, all very decorative.

'Colorata'. Leaves purple in winter, especially in poor soil, spreads widely.

'Emerald Gaiety'. Apple-green, boldly edged white. Bushy and fast of growth. A pretty plant, however grown.

'Emerald 'n' Gold'. Well named and very colourful, the green leaves being splashed with gold. Tawny in winter. Bushy and a good mini-hedger.

'Kewensis'. Small-leaved and dainty, but

will reach 15ft. Good for covering old tree-stumps. 'Longwood' is very similar.

'Silver Queen'. The general favourite. Leaves green and cream.

'Variegatus'. Leaves grey-green, broadly edged white, often tinted pink. Known also as 'Gracilis' and 'Argento-marginatus'.

E. japonicus. Big, bold, evergreen, especially the large-leaved 'Macrophyllus', with smooth, leathery, dark green leaves. Will grow to 15ft and more if allowed. Particularly good at the seaside and frequently grown as a hedge in Britain. Subject to attacks of mildew and by swarms of caterpillars of the lesser ermine moth, for which you need a strong contact poison, such as fenitrothion. Rather sombre as a specimen shrub and, for garden decor, its variegated forms are much to be preferred, apart from their horrible, multi-syllabic names in dog Latin. Watch out for reversion and cut such growths back to their points of origin. z8.

The most favoured of these is 'Ovatus Aureus', which has broad leaves richly margined with gold in the middle; very nice. Others to be recorded are:

'Albomarginatus'. Leaves edged with a white stripe.

'Latifolius Albomarginatus'. Broader leaves and conspicuously broader margin; also known as 'Macrophyllus Albus', etc.

'Microphyllus'. Small leaves, dense, slow, a trifle tender, has also forms edged yellow or white.

E. kiautschovicus (formerly *patens*, known in America as the spreading euonymus). Akin to japonicus, but much hardier, the leaves a lighter green and thinner, with pink fruits. Evergreen in mild climates, it may reach 9ft and is remarkable for thriving in the worst city conditions. Its compact offspring 'Manhattan' is without peer for putting up with all kinds of abuse and neglect. z6.

E. latifolius. A big, handsome, deciduous shrub that can attain 20ft in rich soil, with a loose, spreading top, clothed in large, laurel-like leaves up to 5in long and large fruits of a rich, rosy red on long stalks, but seldom in abundance. Stake it well at first. z5.

E. sanguineus. Another big, deciduous spindle, similar to latifolius, with slightly purple-tinted foliage and large red-and-yellow fruits. z5.

E. yedoensis is the name commonly applied to a fine spindle-tree with several aliases. Its tangled masses of pink fruits are one of the sights of autumn. Bean treats it as a variety of *hamiltonianus* but it (or something very close to it) may appear in catalogues as *E. sieboldianus* or *E. semi-exertous*. z4.

EURYA

E. japonica is a big, stiffly branched, evergreen shrub that can exceed 20ft, though the form grown in Britain, from the more northerly parts of Asia, is much smaller. Flowers of no value, berries black. z7.

EURYOPS

One of the prettiest dwarf shrubs for general use in the garden is **Euryops acraeus**, which originates from high up in the Drakensberg mountains in South Africa. It makes a shapely dome of small, silvery-blue leaves all the year round, from which it puts forth a generous display of canary-coloured daisy-form flowers for a month or more from mid-May. In the gritty soil of its native pasturage it may reach 3ft, but in a fat clay about half that height and often has a life of only about ten years. A splendid and sparkling counterpoint among other shrubs, especially heathers and dwarf conifers. Full sun essential. Very easily propagated from heel cuttings in sandy soil without close conditions. z8, perhaps z7. Formerly mistakenly called *E. evansii*, which is something different.

Other species of euryops are more tender. *E. pectinatus* is ashen-grey with larger, deeply cut leaves, and *E. virgineus* is crowded with tiny, green, cut leaves.

EXOCHORDA
Pearlbush

These are graceful and distinguished deciduous shrubs that put forth clusters of white flowers like large pear blossoms, from the tips of slender stems in May, but for all too short a term. They like the sun if not too intense, deserve a good soil, whether limy or acid and, with one exception, do very well in chalk.

E. giraldii is a big shrub of 15ft, best exemplified in its variety *wilsonii*, which flowers profusely in an erect manner. z5.

E. korolkowii. A robust 12ft or more, the most erect of the exochordas. z5.

E. × macrantha. A 10ft hybrid of great beauty, bearing 4in racemes of relatively large, snow-white flowers. 'The Bride' is a very good form of recent introduction. z5.

E. racemosa is the most sumptuous of all, growing 10ft, spreading widely and throwing out its white trusses (racemes) from short, twiggy laterals from the main branches, thus giving to each branch the appearance of one huge, snow-white bunch of flowers. You must therefore thin it out after flowering, to prevent overcrowding it. It produces suckers, however, and you must get rid of them in winter unless wanted for propagation. Objects to lime. z4.

The rare **serratifolia** has toothed leaves and flowers exuberantly in chalk. z5.

FABIANA

The tender *Fabiana imbricata*, from South America, looks for all the world like a large heather, but is much less hardy. Beginning as a slender upright stripling, it swells to become a rotund shrub 6ft or more high and just as broad. Like those of the calluna or ling, the leaves are very small, closely pressed together and abundant. The flowers are also very small but, instead of being little bells, are tubular, thronging the lateral twigs at high summer. They are white, but in the more desirable form of *violacea* they are mauve in cultivated plants and the shrub is much broader, its flowering twigs growing out at right angles to their parent stems. The useful dwarf variety 'Prostrata' forms a dense, ground-hugging mound, with mauve flowers.

The fabianas are fairly lime-tolerant, but prefer the soil to be light and in plenty of sun. z8–9.

X FATSHEDERA

An entirely pointless mating between a fatsia and a hedera (ivy), both members of the same botanical "tribe". The issue is an evergreen with palmate leaves similar to those of the fatsia but smaller, and a lax, random habit bequeathed by the ivy. Of some use in deep shade and as a pot plant in shade. The name is × *F. lizei* ("fat-headed Lizzy"). z7.

FATSIA

F. japonica is a bold, sometimes over-bold, shrub known for its dark green, smooth, very large (up to 15in wide), leaves, cut into seven to nine deep segments (palmate) in the same manner as those of the horse-chestnut, but pointed, like fat fingers. For flowers it brandishes loose clusters of ivory knobkerries in October, which, if plucked off as soon as they appear, will increase the size of the leaf. Can grow 15ft high, spreading widely, standing a good deal of shade, and prospers in poor soil. Often grown in tubs and within the house. The name comes from an incorrect transliteration of the Japanese Fatsi. The white-splashed 'Variegata' looks diseased. z7.

FEIJOA

F. sellowiana is a big, handsome, tender evergreen, bearing edible fruits in a hot climate. It has decorative, grey-green foliage and an ivory felt on its young shoots. The flowers, borne in July, are remarkable for the large brush of crimson stamens that sprout from the pink petals, making a brave display. An easy plant in sun in any reasonable soil where the climate allows. The plum-shaped fruits are rich and aromatic, but you may need two or more plants of different seedlings, as they tend to be self-sterile. z9.

FENDLERA

F. rupicola wrightii is decidedly a shrub to be grown in such places as the sunburnt mountain slopes of its native New Mexico and Texas. It is then a lively 6ft, deciduous shrub with rose-tinted, four-petalled flowers in May–June. Rarely successful in Britain. z6.

FORSYTHIA

Little need for explanation here. Even non-gardeners are familiar with the golden bells that often ring in the spring before even the daffodil dares, but not all of us are aware of their diversity and how to prune them. They are deciduous, flowering in March–April, and have no soil partialities whatever, but the better you treat them the more they will reward you. They take their name from William Forsyth, who was Superintendent of the Royal Gardens in Kensington in the eighteenth century. In general they are spreading, arching shrubs, for which you must allow plenty of room, unless you want to make a hedge of them, a purpose that they serve fairly well. The most popular is the hybrid *intermedia*, of which there are several clones, but *suspensa* and *ovata* and one or two others deserve our attention. All but *ovata* are z5.

Propagation is extremely easy from cuttings of half-ripe shoots and indeed, 'Spectabilis' and others will root from ripe wood cuttings a foot long in sandy soil stuck in the open ground in late autumn.

Pruning is also straightforward. After blossom-fall sever the flowered shoots to a point where a promising new growth is emerging. Subsequently cut right out all old, degenerate stems once the plant is established. In ancient, neglected specimens cut the whole thing down to 6in from the ground, expecting no flowers next season.

The hybrid **F. 'Arnold Dwarf'** is florally of no consequence, but very useful for covering the ground, especially rough banks, having dense, interlocking branches. It may grow 4ft high in time, with prostrate or arching branches that spread widely and take root as they do so. Any erect shoots can be cut back.

F. giraldiana. Not florally the richest of forsythias, but of tall, graceful habit and often flowering before March.

F. × intermedia. This is everyman's choice, a hybrid between *suspensa* and *viridissima*, mostly 8ft high, the stem erect at first, then bending over at the top. The choicest clones are:

'Densiflora'. Pale yellow flowers in profusion on a plant that is fairly erect.

'Lynwood', an Irish child (sport) of 'Spectabilis', of slightly more erect habit, doubtfully superior to its parent, but perhaps more generous of flowers. 'Spectabilis' is easily the best known and all that we need say is that there is nothing better.

'Spring Glory'. Sulphur flowers in profusion on light brown wood. Valuable for smaller places, rarely exceeding 6ft.

'Vitellina'. Erect growth. Flowers mostly clustered at the base of last year's growth.

F. ovata. Only about 4ft, flowering in early March in mild areas, but of limited floral value. The recent 'Tetragold' (another product of the chemist) is even earlier and smaller and more richly coloured. z4. This species and its derivatives are the only really reliable forsythias in the colder regions of America.

F. suspensa sieboldii, should indeed be "suspended" for, like the winter jasmine, its lax and slender branches never look so well as when cascading down a tall wall or tumbling down a bank, where it will root as it spreads. It is too often grown against a house, where it can grow to 20ft and become an untidy mass unless given constant attention, for it has no climbing mechanism. Another early bird, it begins to flower before March is over and is quite happy in a northerly exposure.

Other varieties or forms of *F. suspensa* are not so lax, as in the very vigorous and arching (but not pendulous) *fortunei* or in the handsome *atrocaulis*, which is decorated with lemon bells on stems of dark purple, and of which 'Nymans' is a particularly beautiful form, erect of carriage and ornamented with soft yellow, nodding flowers on bronze stems later than most other forsythias.

The latest of all to flower is **F. viridissima**, so called because the stems retain their juvenile green for two years or more. Tops 8ft, leaves 6in long, flowers primrose. 'Bronxenis' is a dense, compact dwarf of only 2ft, difficult to establish, but then a prolific bloomer. The variety *koreana* has small leaves and brighter flowers.

Other forsythias, to be mentioned briefly, are 'Beatrix Farrand', a gaunt and ungracious plant, and the tall and lanky *F. europaea*.

FOTHERGILLA

Lime-hating shrubs named after Dr John Fothergill, who made a special collection of American plants in the eighteenth century at Stratford-le-Bow, in Essex. Fothergillas produce white, scented, fluffy-looking bottle-brushes consisting of mere tufts of stamens without petals, on leafless stems in May, are rather dull during the summer and put up their finest show in autumn, when, in a sunny position and sandy soil, their leaves become inflamed with passionate colours before falling. For autumn colour, they are of the first order, but are rather slow of growth. *F. gardenii* is 3ft, *major* (or *major monticola*) is 6ft or more. All z5.

FREMONTODENDRON
Fremontia

Fortunate General Frémont to be so splendidly immortalised! The fremontias, or fremontodendrons as they should now legally be labelled, are tender but big, magnificent shrubs embellished with yellow or orange flowers over a long season. Their adornment consists of five-lobed calyces, within which are five stud-like stamens, radiating on short arms, quite conspicuous. In the most favoured climates they are usually evergreen. Apart from minor species or sub-species, there are only two for us to consider, together with their superb offspring. The sort of home they like is full sun in a light, rather poor but well-drained soil and they are surprisingly successful in chalk. Once planted, do not attempt to move them. No pruning needed.

F. californicum has been known to grow to 30ft but is usually far less. Large, golden flowers glitter on short side-spurs among the leaves, which are dark, dull green on the obverse but clothed with a pale brown felt on the reverse. Seldom lives more than twenty-five years. May to July. z8 on a warm wall, otherwise z9.

F. mexicanum is rather more tender, rarely at ease in Britain. The leaves are similar to those

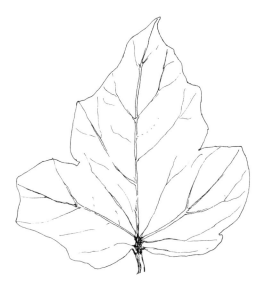

46.   The leaf of a little Fremontodendron californicum

138

of the Californian, but have five or seven vague lobes. The orange flowers, often tinted with red, are on the main branchlets, the sepals of the calyx narrower, and the flowering season extends right into September. z10.

As we have said, the child of these two, **F. 'California Glory'**, surpasses its parents in splendour. Its canary flowers are very large, very abundant and displayed over a long season. Its birthplace was in Orange County, California. It is nearer to *californicum* than to *mexicum*, which shows only in minor detail. z8 on a warm wall, otherwise z9.

Minor species of the fremontodendron include *F. napense*, with small leaves and yellow flowers, and *F. decumbens*, a wide-spreading shrub, 4ft high, with orange flowers.

FUCHSIA

We think it improbable that Dr Leonard Fuchs, the sixteenth-century German, would ever have seen a fuchsia, and it is even more certain that he would have been astonished at the uses to which his name has been put today. We shall not attempt to review the vast field of modern hybrids, which, except in semi-tropical places, have to be treated as so many bedding-out plants.

In general terms fuchsias will succeed in any reasonably good soil and in shade as well as in sun. They are thus very useful plants for any situation that is not sodden nor subject to drought. They bloom continuously from June until Jack Frost nips them and steals their brightly coloured earrings. To foster their chances of survival, be particular to plant the crown about 2in below soil level, especially the hybrids. Their special character is that they display two apparently separate features: the calyx, extended from a long tube, splits into four sepals, usually of a bright colour and curling back. Below the sepals hangs a corolla, which you may liken to a skirt, composed of four petals (but more in the double or semi-double hybrids), usually of a colour in strong

contrast to the sepals, and from this skirt dangles a cluster of thread-like stamens, escorting the demure pistil.

Propagation is extremely easy from cuttings of either softwood or even ripe wood, without any heat. For the amateur the simplest method is to take softwood cuttings of heels or un-flowered tips in August in any sort of close (humid) conditions and, when rooted, to pot them up for the winter in a frost-proof greenhouse or frame before planting out about 1st June.

Pruning of those sorts that will stand the winter outdoors is also very simple — cut them right down to the ground in April, after which new shoots will grow from the crown. In the very warmest regions, however, you may leave the main branches to build up year by year, but cutting back the laterals to their lowest buds.

SPECIES AND THEIR KIN
By far the hardiest is the Magellan fuchsia, **F. magellanica**, of which there are several first-class derivatives and of the identities of which there has been much botanical chit-chat. Its native haunts stretch over a considerable slice of southern South America, thus causing varia-

47.   Fuchsia magellanica

tions, but in general it may be described as a shrub of 8ft, wearing earrings that have a red calyx and a violet corolla, favouring moist, even swampy soils. The gardener, however, is more interested in its smaller, very ornamental derivatives, which are doubtfully rated z6 and comprise the following natural "varieties" (omitting those of only botanical interest).

alba. See *molinae*.

gracilis. The most important of the natural varieties (often quoted as a separate species), which has given two beautiful cultivars and which originated as sports. Both are grown primarily for their beautiful foliage, though they do have ample drop earrings of scarlet sepals which almost hide the small purple petals. These two are known respectively as 'Variegata' and 'Versicolor' (or 'Tricolor'), names which have inevitably led some people astray. 'Variegata', the shorter of the two, has olive leaves with a cream edging, with an overall effect at a distance of pallid gold. In 'Versicolor' the leaves have a light patina of pewter, distinctly tinted rose when young, and irregularly margined cream, the general effect at a distance being of palest pink, but changing with the seasons; in mild climates it will grow perhaps 5ft high and wide from scratch in a single summer.

molinae. A natural albino, not very floribundant.

'Riccartonii'. See under Hardy Hybrids.

Apart from this Magellan fuchsia and its off-shoots, few species are of importance except to the botanist and the hybridist. We may, however, note the following for special interest.

F. procumbens. As you may expect, this is a prostrate creeper with slender stems. The flowers are interesting, being erect, devoid of petals, but pushing out a brush of blue stamens direct from the yellow, recurving sepals. z8–9.

F. thymifolia. (of Bean) is a bit of a headache. It is a rare and tender species with very small leaves, the subject of much botanical debate. From it have come some offspring more attractive than itself, the features common to all being that they are small or dwarf shrubs with very small leaves, and are not proof against frost. The following are its chief progeny.

F. × bacillaris, (*thymifolia × microphylla*). A beautiful dwarf with crimson sepals and coral petals. Also known sometimes as *F. cinnabarina*. For practical purposes we may regard 'Cottinghamii' as a slightly larger version of it.

'Reflexa'. A pretty dwarf with cerise flowers that darken with age. Often wrongly labelled "F. parviflora" or sometimes as a species of its own.

THE HARDIER HYBRIDS

The following are usually found to be hardy in z8, but remember to plant them about 2in deep (about 1st June) and to take cuttings against a hard winter. They are best in a rich, deep soil, with plenty of rain or watering. All succeed in chalk.

Dominating them all in hardiness and size, but with a special character, is 'Riccartonii', believed to have originated in a garden at Riccarton, in Scotland, about 1830, and sometimes listed as a species on its own. It is a big shrub, having flowers with the scarlet sepals and violet corolla typical of fuchsias. It makes a superb hedge in suitable climates, especially near the sea, as seen by anyone who visits Cornwall and other parts of the west coast of Britain. When so used, prune hard back to a formal outline when new growth is about to begin in spring.

Other generally reliable hybrids are as under. We give the colour of the opened-out calyx (sepals) first and that of the petals (corolla) second.

'Alice Hoffman'. Dwarfish. Small flowers, scarlet and white.

'Army Nurse'. Carmine and pale violet. Profuse. Vigorous and upright.

'Caledonia'. Salmon and mauve.

'Chillerton Beauty'. One of the most reliable of all. Rose and violet. 4ft.

'Corallina'. Firmly established veteran, very robust, sometimes becoming a climber. Arching carriage. Scarlet and red-purple. Purple-tinted leaves folded upwards athwart the midrib. Sometimes called 'Exoniensis'.

'Drame'. Scarlet and purple, among pale green leaves.

'Howlett's Hardy'. Scarlet and violet. 2½ft.

'Lena'. Lax, dangling growth. Great favourite for hanging baskets. Blush-white and rose-purple, double.

'Madame Cornelissen'. One of the hardiest and best. Scarlet and white. Elegant, pointed leaves. 3ft.

'Margaret'. Robust and spectacular, 4ft. Rose and pale violet, semi-double.

'Mrs Popple'. An established favourite. Scarlet and violet, ageing to crimson-purple. Leaves tinted purple, 4ft.

'Mrs W. P. Wood'. Flesh-pink and white. Erect.

'Phyllis'. Rose and deeper rose, semi-double. Very vigorous. An old favourite.

'Pixie'. Light red and lavender. Upright and bushy. 'White Pixie' is red and white. Both 3ft.

Three nice dwarfs may also come in handy, though best grown on raised ground. The best is 'Tom Thumb', 15in, light red and mauve. Sometimes sold under the same name, but lower and of much more spreading habit is 'Pumila', crimson and violet. Of more erect carriage is 'W. P. Wood', deep scarlet and red-purple.

If you live in a warm zone, you should certainly consider the brilliant varieties or hybrids of *F. triphylla*. These do not conform to the conventional notion of fuchsia but conspicuously flourish fanfares of very slim trumpets, often drooping, of vivid reds or orange, 2½in long, with no obvious sepals, at the tips of red-veined foliage. Good in z8 but will not over-winter. Very easy from cuttings in a slightly warmed greenhouse. Good examples are 'Mary', 'Thalia', which has dark, bronzy-green leaves, and 'Gartenmeister Bonstedt'.

FURZE. See *Ulex*

GARRYA

Large or medium-size fast-growing, evergreen, dioecious shrubs, bearing male catkins

48. Garrya elliptica

on one plant and female on another. At their best they are good shrubs but, unless in sheltered places, can become distinctly "tatty" under the assaults of rude winds. They resist transplanting. They are named after a one-time secretary of the Hudson's Bay Company.

Dominant over them all is **G. elliptica**, a shrub with prettily waved, elliptic leaves, which averages about 9ft, but, in favoured places, such as the west coast of Britain, can reach 16ft. Grown essentially for its engaging clusters of dangling, grey-green, silky, male catkins, which may be anything up to 10in long and which sway about prettily in the cold winds of mid-winter, until your wife sneaks out and gathers them for a flower arrangement. The catkins of the female plants are much inferior but, if fertilized, produce quite nice little maroon fruits in June. You will get the best results on a dry, stony, sunny bank; it needs little meat or drink. So grown, and protected from cold winds it is reliable in z8. The variety 'James Roof' gives male catkins that can stretch to 14in.

Other garryas are of little garden value. The hardiest is G. *wrightii*, of 6ft, with sage green and acutely pointed leaves and small catkins in summer; doubtfully rated as z6. The hybrid G. × *thuretii* is a mass of long, glossy leaves and small catkins. G. *fremontii* is a rather tender 6ft, with male catkins of up to 6in and females half that size.

X GAULNETTYA

These are evergreen hybrids between a gaultheria and a pernettya, and, we consider, inferior to both. They have dark green, thick, leathery leaves. Some occur in nature but the best-known, occurring in the RHS Garden at Wisley, is 'Wisley Pearl', a neat but suckering shrub of 3ft, bearing clusters of numerous, small, white flowers in May–June, followed by maroon berries, with swollen, fleshy calyces at their bases.

Less well-known, but brighter in its fruits is 'Ruby'. Both may be found listed under × G. *wisleyensis*.

GAULTHERIA

The evergreen, leathery-leaved gaultherias have in nature an enormously wide distribution over four continents, those from New Zealand being the least hardy. They range in size from 3in to 20ft. All have clusters of very small, rather fleeting white flowers like lilies-of-the-valley, often tinted pink, followed by pea-sized berries of various colours. Many extend themselves by underground shoots, a quality which suits some situations but not others. In cultivation their prime need is a moist, acid soil. We must ignore the rock-garden sorts.

To the majority of gardeners the most familiar gaultherias are the ground-carpeters, extending themselves by underground shoots,

two of which we have mentioned briefly in Chapter 5. To these (*miqueliana* and the easier *procumbens*) we may add G. *adenothrix* which makes a rather deeper rug of one foot (z5) and G. *trichophylla*, distinguished by pink flowers and blue berries (z7–8). A little taller than these ground-crawlers is the little G. *cuneata*, a very pretty shrublet of compact growth, reaching to 18in when mature. (z5–6).

Above these we meet a whole range of gaultherias that average about 3ft, most of them pretty like one another as far as garden use is concerned. From these we select a few with qualities of their own.

G. antipoda. Probably the hardiest of the New Zealanders. Very variable, the berries red or white. Usually an erect shrub of about 3ft, but sometimes prostrate.

G. hookeri (or **veitchiana**). An attractive Chinese shrub, marked by its bristly branchlets and bristle-tipped, hard-textured, lustrous, net-veined leaves and ornamented by indigo-blue berries. Spreads by underground stems and can occasionally reach 6ft. z7.

G. shallon, the salal or shallon (a Redskin name) is a remarkable species, found wild all the way along the Pacific coast of North America from the snows of Alaska right down to the genial warmth of Southern California, varying in its behaviour. In full sun and a poor soil it is a thick, low mat, but in a moist woodland it grows to 6ft. In either situation it can be a menace unless your object is to provide a dense, leathery-leaved thicket, for it spreads by underground stems. Its little, blush-white flowers are gathered in a raceme in early June and its hairy, purple fruits are pleasantly flavoured. The cut branches are important florist's "greens" in the USA. z6.

G. tetramera, from China, 2ft or a bit more. Fruits varying from a brilliant violet to China-blue. There are nice examples at Major de Rothschild's garden at Exbury. z8.

Above these in height are some of lesser general interest, such as the 8ft *codonantha*, the tender New Zealander *oppositifolia*, of similar height, and others which often need sheltered positions.

GAYLUSSACIA

Huckleberry

Though they are mostly dwarfs and not of great garden merit, we must allow the huckleberries to creep into our pages, if only in remembrance of young Finn. The botanical name commemorates a French chemist named Gay-Lussac.

The huckleberries are very hardy and have a close relationship with the vacciniums, and, like them, need an acid soil. They have flowers like those of the lily-of-the-valley, followed by berry-like fruits, which are often edible, but they seldom fruit well in Britain. The deciduous specimens often display glowing colours.

Perhaps of most interest is the box huckleberry, **G. brachycera**, a dainty, mat-forming evergreen, averaging 1ft, with glossy, leathery leaves. The little bells are white, sometimes striped or tipped pink, appearing in May and June, followed by blue, edible berries, but the species is self-sterile and two clones are needed for good fruiting. z5.

G. baccata, the black huckleberry, deciduous, averages 2ft, bears dull red flowers in

49.   Gaylussacia brachycero, the box-huckleberry

May and black, shining, edible berries. The best for eating. z2.

G. dumosa, deciduous, grows 2ft or more, spreading by stolons. Pure white flowers in June, tasteless black berries, shining green leaves. Good seaside shrub. z3.

G. frondosa, the handsome, 5ft, deciduous dangleberry, flowers in long, loose racemes of purple-green in June–July, followed by blue, palatable berries, dangling on long stalks. z4.

G. ursina, the bear huckleberry, deciduous, grows to about 4ft, with off-white bells in loose racemes and black berries. z5.

Some vacciniums are also called huckleberries.

GENISTA. Included in Brooms

GORSE. See *Ulex*

GREVILLEA

As Australians, grevilleas expect you to give them a really warm home and an acid soil. Their leaves are often mere needles, but so thickly borne as to give the branch the semblance of a brush. The small flowers are calyx-tubes, without separate petals, and from these very long styles are thrust out. All must be regarded as no hardier than z9. The most amiable in the northern hemisphere is **G. sulphurea**, a 5ft shrub densely clothed with needle-like leaves, and slim, yellow flowers sprouting among them, so that at a little distance and at flowering time in May the shrub looks as though it had golden foliage.

G. acanthifolia, of 5ft, has deeply cut, stiff, prickly leaves instead of needles, and dull pink flowers, with many silky hairs on the stalks.

G. rosmarinifolia is taller and more graceful of bearing, having slim leaves like those of the rosemary, with silvery hairs beneath, and flowers of deep rose with red styles.

G. alpina is a long-flowering dwarf of less than 2ft, with flowers of yellow and dull red.

GRISELINIA

Griselinia littoralis is a rather tender evergreen New Zealander, but a splendid shrub for the seaside, where, with its dense apple-green leaves, it makes one of the most impressive and robust of hedges, impervious to salt winds. Grown alone, it is a round bush about 10ft high, but in a mild climate it can become a tree. Does not mind lime, even chalk. It breaks freely and strongly from the base. Flowers of no account, males on one plant, females on another. Trim in early summer. 'Dixon's Cream' and 'Variegata' are selected forms of lively appearance. z8–9. *G. lucida* has larger leaves and is more tender.

GUELDER ROSE. See *Viburnum opulus*

HAKEA

What we have said about the grevillea applies with perhaps even more force to its fellow-Australian, the hakea. From this very large genus few will put up with our climates, and many stand arid, almost desert conditions; some are rampant weeds. Those that do take to us look uncommonly like conifers, especially *H. lissosperma*, which is probably the hardiest and a branch of which, with its long, needle-like leaves, looks just like a pine, or perhaps a fox's "brush". With us it grows possibly to 10ft with white flowers of little account.

Plants listed as *H. sericea* and *H. microcarpa* differ only in minor detail, but the latter is usually the smaller. The handsomest, the red-flowered *H. laurina*, known to Australians as the sea-urchin or pin-cushion hakea, is often seen on Mediterranean coasts.

X HALIMIOCISTUS

Progeny of an halimium mated to a cistus, these are dwarf, spreading, evergreen shrubs, with small, saucer-shaped flowers, useful for odd jobs, in sun and a dry soil. Generally a bit hardier than their parents but less handsome. They do not respond well to pruning. The best, but unfortunately the least hardy, at some risk in anything colder than z9, is the grey-leaved *wintonensis*, raised in Hillier's nursery at Winchester. This may grow 2ft high, with white saucers that have maroon and yellow zones at the bases of the petals.

The others all have small, white flowers, which usually close in the afternoon. All probably z7.

H. × *ingwersenii*, 15in. May-July.

H. × *revolii*. To 2ft, with a yellow patch at the bases of the petals. June-July.

H. × *sahucii*. 15in. The best known and hardiest. Very good in dry soils. June.

HALIMIUM

Very attractive, small, evergreen shrubs, most of which build up into low domes of small leaves becomingly muted with grey and sprinkled all over in early summer with small saucers that are usually golden. Being Mediterraneans, they expect all the sun you can give them, and make their best floral display in rather dry, sandy soil. In a fat loam they put on a lot of leafage and become even more tender than they naturally are. They enjoy chalk. The flowers have five petals of a rather soft texture. The most brilliant, if you can grow it, is *atriplicifolia*, but the most popular are the easier *lasianthum* and *ocymoides*. None responds well to pruning.

H. alyssoides is a grey-leaved mound 2ft high and 4ft broad, with bright yellow flowers in clusters (corymbs), of variable hardiness according to its provenance.

H. atriplicifolium. A beautiful 5ft mound of silvered leaves with bright yellow flowers that sometimes have a brown dot at the base of each petal in June. Also, too tender for most of us; probably z10.

H. halimifolium. Rather like the preceding, but grey rather than silver, and just as tender. There are some botanical sub-species.

H. lasianthum makes a beautiful grey-leaved dome, 2ft or more high and spreading widely, thronged with a succession of relatively large (1½in) golden flowers with a chocolate spot at the base of each petal, beginning to bloom in May. It has an unspotted form called 'Concolor'. z8.

H. ocymoides is of about the same size, but more erect and compact, sparkling with golden, black-spotted saucers above pewter-coloured leaves. May-June. z7.

H. umbellatum. An 18in dwarf, with slim, dark green leaves rather like those of the rosemary, and clusters of white saucers in June.

HALIMODENDRON
Salt tree

H. halodendron is the frightening name for a remarkable deciduous shrub of 6ft that originates from the salt-laden soils of Siberia and thereabouts. It is as hard as nails and produces purple, scented pea-flowers in June–July among silvery, pinnate leaves on thorny branches. Its best uses are as a seashore shrub, where it defies salt-laden gales, or in excessively limy soils elsewhere, but it is quite elegant, especially if grafted on a 5ft stem of caragana or laburnum. z2.

HAMAMELIS
Witch hazel

Loveliest of all winter-flowering shrubs, the witch hazel has a piquant and captivating charm. From about Christmas to February (but later in the colder American zones) it bears on its straight, naked stems quantities of ingenious, twisted ribbons of spun gold, copper or colourful alloys, making merry bushes that should be the haunts of elves. They make stunning pictures when partnered by the little *Iris histrioides* 'Major' or the mauve *Rhododendron mucrona-*

Hamamelis mollis, the witch hazel

latum or by the winter heathers. You must give them an acid and fairly rich soil, however, and plenty of sun for preference and ample space for their spreading arms. In popular esteem, nothing excels the Chinese species, *H. mollis*. The popular name derives from the Old English *wice*, meaning flexible, as also in witch elm. The botanical name is an ancient Greek one for some sort of fruit.

H. × intermedia. This hybrid results from matings between *mollis* and *japonica* and can mean many things. It is in the nature of a group name, being a pie in which cooks from many nations have had a hand and which has given us the following plums. z4.

'Arnold Promise'. A rather late variety raised at the Arnold Arboretum, Massachusetts, bearing a profusion of sulphur flowers in early spring. The leaves colour richly in the fall. Very vigorous.

'Diane'. Flowers red, rich autumn foliage.

'Hiltingbury'. Pallid copper; leaves colour well.

'Jelena' (also 'Copper Beauty' or 'Orange

Beauty'). Vies with 'Arnold Promise' as the very best of the hybrids. Ribbon-flowers of rich coppery-orange. Very vigorous.

'Feuerzauber' ('Fire Charm'). Coppery-red, fragrant.

'Moonlight'. Pale yellow; rich, sweet scent.

'Ruby Glow' ('Adonis'). Very like 'Fire Charm' and often confused with it in the trade.

H. japonica, the Japanese witch hazel. This is distinguished by having more or less oval leaves, with a wavy margin, and by the plant being sparsely branched and tree-like, especially in the form *arborea*. The ribbon-flowers have little scent. The following varieties or cultivars are of some interest. z5.

flavopurpurascens. Flowers suffused dull red.

'Sulphurea'. Petals pale yellow.

'Zuccariniana'. Pale lemon, seldom flowering before March.

H. mollis. The Chinese witch hazel, still the star of the company. The twisted ribbon-petals are sweetly scented and true, rich gold, sparkling with gaiety in the depth of winter, and a fit model from which a jeweller might contrive a brooch. The leaves, borne on zigzag branches, are broad, resembling those of the hazel, but have no autumnal splendour. In time and in the best conditions the shrub can soar to a spectacular 25ft. z5.

Of its few variations, the pale sulphur 'Pallida', raised by the Royal Horticultural Society, has won considerable acclaim. This invites comparison with the aforesaid hybrid 'Moonlight', but 'Pallida' is considered to be of greater distinction. 'Goldcrest', on the other hand, is a particularly rich gold, suffused with crimson at the base, and is late-flowering.

H. vernalis is valuable for small gardens, as it does not exceed 10ft, but it suckers. In some of its native haunts in North America it grows in very wet ground, but is quite happy in other conditions. The scent of the flowers is pungent rather than sweet. Their colours vary, sometimes having a red flush, as in 'Red Imp'. In 'Sandra', raised by Hilliers at Winchester, the young leaves are flushed with purple and in autumn they blaze with orange and red. z4.

H. virginiana surprises us by flowering in the autumn, often beginning in September, when the golden ribbons are to a large extent hidden until the broad, hazel-like leaves, themselves yellow, fall. A big, broad-spreading shrub that may reach 15ft, good in half-shade. Faint scent. The pharmacist's "witch hazel" is made from the bark and leaves of this species. Often used as an understock for the more decorative Oriental species and then a great nuisance from suckers. z4.

Related to the above but a little less hardy is the big American **H. macrophylla**, which flowers in December and January. The leaves turn bright yellow and drop before the flowers open. Bone-hardy in Britain, a big specimen at Wisley being more than 20 years old. z6.

HAWTHORN. See *Crataegus*

HEATHERS

For the convenience of the gardener and the landscape designer we assemble here all the three genera commonly called heaths and heathers, for they have an intimate resemblance to one another, both in appearance and in usage. They are:

Calluna, or ling

Daboecia

Erica, of which there are several species and hybrids.

Although we set out to exclude dwarf plants in the main, the heathers force themselves upon our thinking. Most of them are very easy to grow, need little attention when established, are in massive flower for exceptionally long seasons and have foliage that is kind and soothing to the eye all the year round. In a great many the foliage is golden, lemon, orange, coppery or dove-grey, often so brightly coloured as to challenge the flowers of many another breed of plants. In size they range from tiny things a few inches high to the "tree heaths" that have been known to reach 20ft. The colours of their flowers also have a wide range, lacking only in true blue. Yellow is seen only in some South Africans, but, with two exceptions, we have to pass by the Cape heaths as being too tender for our pages.

In designing a plantation of heathers, bear in mind the precept of "mass" that we have enunciated earlier. Heathers lend themselves particularly well to this maxim, both in small places and in large panoramas. If you have space for only three plants of 'King George' put them all together. No dotting about. In the middle-size scene think in terms of dozens, all one kind planted together; in large scenes, think in terms of twenty-fives or hundreds. Unless the planting be very small, diversify the heights, breaking up expanses of dwarf sorts with taller ones, such as the ericas *mediterranea* and the tall, slim *terminalis*. Such diversification is of particular importance where the site is flat. If you have any choice of terrain, seize upon any that is broken or mounded. Rocky sites are a particular delight.

It has to be admitted, however, that, on a large scale, a garden that is all heathers can be rather boring to the spectator, but you must be a little careful of what other plants you associate them with. We shall not lay down any laws on this subject, but remark that the dwarf conifers make exceptionally good consorts, and among them we choose the following in particular, briefly described in the appropriate section.

Juniperus communis 'Hibernica', the slim Irish juniper.

Chamaecyparis obtusa 'Nana Aurea'.

C. pisifera 'Plumosa Aurea Compacta'.

C. p. 'Boulevard'.

C. p. 'Filifera Aurea', the gold wire bush.

Thuja occidentalis 'Rheingold'.

Juniperus × media 'Blaauw'.

Taxus baccata 'Fastigiata' the Irish yew or its golden form and the very slow, small 'Standishii'.

Other very good friends are the dwarfer rhododendrons (especially the evergreen azaleas) the berried pernettyas, the small bruckenthalia, itself very like a heather, the rotund fabiana, also heather-like, the dwarf *Hypericum olympicum*, which will give you yellow flowers, the dwarf hybrid brooms *beanii* and *kewensis*, also yellow, flowering in May when few

heathers are out, but needing some elbow-room. Where you think that a sharp, contrapuntal note is needed you will find it in the brilliantly silvered euryops, which is fairly hardy. In acid, peaty, moist soils there are the choice cassiope and phyllodoce (too small for our pages). In the larger scene nothing is more companionable and natural than silver birches and the Scotch pine.

Until the heathers have grown out well and begun to meet each other (three years in most instances) you can fill in with all sorts of small things, among which we find the lithospermums 'Heavenly Blue', the prostrate veronicas and the dwarfer hebes (especially 'Bowles's Hybrid') very useful if the climate is not too harsh.

Culturally, there are a few points to note. First and above all, that the majority of heathers are lime-haters, with the marked exception of the winter-flowering *Erica carnea* and a few others that we shall note. In certain cases it may also be important to note whether the soil is sandy or if clay and whether it is moisture-holding. Second, that full sun is desirable and is essential all day for those with coloured foliage, though the aforesaid carnea will stand quite a lot of shade.

Soil preparation is fairly easy. Given good drainage, only the top spit needs attention, though we prefer ourselves to double-dig. Use no animal manure unless the soil is devastatingly poverty-stricken, but, unless it is naturally so, work in quantities of ancient, decayed leaf-soil if you can get it, alternatively peat. In heavy soil add ample sand, especially for *Erica cinerea*, but try to get lime-free sand, which is not easy everywhere and of which you should get a sample tested for pH before ordering. Limy sand is all right for the ericas *carnea*, *mediterranea*, *umbellata*, the hybrid *darleyensis*, the tall *terminalis* and perhaps *vagans*. Mix all these well with the natural soil, not in layers or patches. The only other thing to add to the soil, and to replenish occasionally, is an artificial fertilizer especially concocted for "woody subjects". In Britain there is a very good (though expensive) one called Enmag, obtained from agents of Scottish Agricultural Industries, Edinburgh.

When the time comes to plant, remember to tease out the roots a bit if container-grown and pot-bound, work some peat into the hole and water well before firming. Finish off with a blanket of leaf-soil or peat. The carneas and some others you can plant quite deeply if you wish, for the low-lying branches will take root and spread out well, enabling you to economise and to provide new plants from the rooted layers. Subsequently you must keep the empty spaces well weeded until the plants all meet in a mass, after which you are unlikely to be bothered with weeds, except perhaps from tree seedlings, for the seeds of oak, ash, chestnut and others are heavy enough to fall through the heather foliage. In autumn you must rake off all the fallen leaves of nearby trees, a tedious operation for which the best, but least pleasant tools are your fingers; alternatively a rubber rake. For this reason choose, if you can, a position reasonably well away from large trees.

Pruning is a matter of some debate. Some people assert that no pruning is needed. Others say prune all in April. Our own opinion is that, unless the expanse is too large, all heathers should be trimmed back to a point immediately below the lowest floret, or thereabouts. Do this trimming as soon as the blossoms have faded, just like most other flowering plants, except perhaps in vagans, the seed-heads of which are attractive all winter. In this way you have trim, bushy plants, continuously producing young wood, and you save the plant's energy from the effort of ripening its seed. Pruning is quickly and easily done by electric hand-shears, but we think that in the formative first year, pruning with secateurs is worth the effort. If the plants are actually in seed at the time you buy them, as they often are, prune them in hand before planting.

Everyone interested in heathers will find benefit from the very friendly Heather Society, whose headquarters are in Britain.

Propagation of nearly all heathers is quite easy and quick if you have the equipment for bottom heat and mist. Otherwise it is still reasonably easy, but much slower, in any kind of propagation box or pot in a warm place in shade. For preference, use unflowered heel cuttings less than 2in long, inserted fairly deeply in a compost of equal parts of peat and sharp sand (lime-free for the lime-haters). Quite tiny shoots will do. There is no need, as in other cuttings, to strip off the bottom leaves, but nip off the soft tip. This you do any time from early June till September. The so-called "silver" varieties are difficult.

The enemies of heathers are few, unless you live in rabbit or deer country. Aphis, if it appears, can easily be eliminated by a systemic insecticide. The deadliest enemy is the soil-borne fungus Phytophthora cinnamomi, which attacks a great many plants but is particularly deadly to heathers if it occurs. There is not yet any positive cure for it, but we have found formaldehyde quite effective, if used as prescribed. A concoction named Mancozeb, intended primarily for the potato blight disease, is also helpful and can be used among growing plants, but may need application two or three times a year. But the first thing is to pull up all plants that are obviously dead or dying and to avoid planting heathers again in the same spot.

Honey fungus is also liable to occur in old woodland soils and callunas may be invaded by Marismus androsaceus, which shows itself as thin white strands, later turning black; burn the whole plant.

CALLUNA VULGARIS

The lings have very dense, branched foliage, the tiny leaves being opposite, blunt-pointed, rather flat and closely packed, not like the tiny pins of ericas. The ornamental part of the flower is its calyx, although the corolla is also decorative. The main flowering season is throughout August and September, but a few are earlier, a few later. The flower spikes are slim racemes, sometimes remarkably long and excellent for cutting. They do very well in rather poor soil mixed with peat or old leaf-soil. There is only this one botanical species, but there are hundreds of varieties, of which we have room to pick only the following handful of well-proven, firm favourites. Several good ones are not in general commerce. z4.

'Alba Plena'. White, double, long spikes. 1½ft.

'Alportii'. Bright crimson, 2ft.

'Barnett Anley'. Soft purple, 1½ft.

'Beoley Gold'. Pale gold foliage, flowers white. Very fine, stunning in winter.

'Californian Midge'. Purple, 9in, tight and compact.

'County Wicklow'. Soft pink, double, 9in. Great favourite.

'C. W. Nix'. Crimson, tall and graceful. 2ft.

'Dainty Bess'. Lilac-pink. 4in. Foliage grey.

'Darkness'. Dusky crimson, compact, 10in.

'Elsie Purnell'. Silvery-pink, double, in long spikes, September-October. Fine for cutting. Similar in kind and of only slightly different tones of pink are 'Peter Sparkes', and 'H. E. Beale', All double, about 2ft and very fine.

'Flore Pleno'. Lilac, double. Old but as good as any. 1½ft.

'Golden Feather'. Outstanding for foliage, feathery gold in summer, bronze in winter, few flowers, 1½ft.

'Gold Haze'. Slightly deeper-tinted foliage than 'Beoley Gold', 2ft.

'J. H. Hamilton'. Pure soft pink, double. Beautifully moulded habit. 9in.

'John F. Letts'. Beautiful old-gold foliage, cyclamen-pink flowers lying flat. Dense, cushioned and neatly moulded. 1ft.

'Joy Vanstone'. Foliage golden in summer, bronze in winter. Pale mauve flowers. Erect habit. 1½ft.

'Mrs Ronald Gray'. Red-purple, prostrate.

'Radnor'. Fresh, clean pink, double. 1ft.

'Robert Chapman'. Golden foliage in summer, turning to copper. 1½ft.

'Rosalind'. Mallow-purple. Pale, yellow-green foliage, 1½ft.

'Serlei'. Long sprays of white on feather-like foliage. 2ft. September-October. 'Serlei Aurea' has golden foliage.

'Silver Queen'. Dove-grey foliage with pale mauve flowers. 1½ft. Generally considered the best of the so-called "silver" varieties, but 'Anthony Davis' is as good and reaches 2ft.

'Sir John Charrington'. Like 'Robert Chapman' but flowers crimson.

'Sister Anne'. Grey foliage, flowers lilac, 9in.

'Sunset'. A remarkable variety, the leaves gilded in spring, deepening to copper, then brilliant crimson in mid-winter.

'Tib'. Rosy-crimson, double, early, 1½ft.

DABOECIA

A small group commemorating St Dabeoc, which Linnaeus misspelt. The leaves are decidedly broader than those of other heathers and are silvered on the reverse. The flowers are relatively large, egg-shaped and dangle loosely from slim, spire-like stems, well above the foliage, each flower dropping its petals as it matures, in sharp contrast to other heathers, whose withered flowers persist with their seed vessels. The daboecias have perhaps the longest flowering season of all, but the blossoms are not densely crowded.

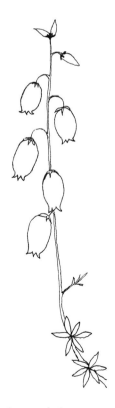

50. Daboecia cantabrica

The usual and best one is **D. cantabrica**, known as St Dabeoc's heath, the Connemara or Irish heath, but native to parts of continental Europe as well. Nearly all can reach 2ft, flowering without cessation from June to November. The noticeably broad but finely pointed leaves are clustered together like irregular six-pointed stars. z5–6.

'Alba' (or *alba*). One of the most beautiful of all dwarf, white shrubs. 'Alba Globosa' has larger globular flowers.

'Atropurpurea'. Rich purple. A splendid plant.

'Bicolor'. A pretty oddity, having some white flowers, some purple, some bi-coloured.

'Cinderella'. White, faintly flushed pink.

'Donard Pink'. Pale pink.

'Polifolia'. Soft purple, variable.

'Globosa Pink'. Pale purple, florets globular.

'Porter's Variety'. Dark crimson, tubular, small leaves, slightly tender and thirsty. 9in.

'Praegerae'. Beautiful, rich pink of the first order, but a trifle tender. Likes a moist atmosphere. $1\frac{1}{2}$ft.

D. azorica. From the Azores. A low-growing, rather tender plant with deep red, egg-shaped flowers, the leaves rolled back marginally and thus appearing to be very slim and narrow.

Daboecia × scotica. Hybrids between the two above species, with the hardiness and continuity of bloom of the Irishman but the shorter stature of the Azorean and sticky stems. A new race officially "published" in 1978, resulting from the success of the deep purple 'William Buchanan'. Others are 'Bearsden', purple-pink, 'Silverwell', white, and 'Cora', pale pink, a poor thing, and 'Jack Drake', not a success with me. All about 1ft.

ERICA

A breed widely dispersed in Europe and a little beyond, with many manifestations and some exceptionally good hybrids. The tiny, spiky leaves, only a fraction of an inch long, are like Lilliputian pins, almost hair-like, thronging the stems densely in fashions varying from one species to another. With two exceptions, we exclude the tender South Africans.

Erica arborea. The largest of the tree heathers, normally of 10–12ft in cultivation, but has been known to reach 20ft. From its roots are "briar" (French *bruyère*) pipes made. It grows very fast and terminates in spires showered with white, sweetly scented, globular flowers in spring. The tiny, densely packed leaves grow in whorls or tiers of threes. One sees it usually as a dark background for other plants. The brittle stems may break under heavy snow. A Mediterranean creature, it is just hardy enough for z8, but the natural variety *alpina*, growing wild in high mountains in Spain, is far hardier, smaller, the foliage bright, fresh green, the stem erect and slender and a better plant all round, except that the flowers which bloom later are of a duller colour. z6.

Erica australis. A tree heath of up to 6ft and of sprawling behaviour. Tiny leaves in whorls of four, flowers in clusters at the tips of the shoots. The most colourful specimen is 'Riverslea', rosy-purple, but 'Mr Robert' is a very fine, upright white.

Erica canaliculata. A big South African, delightfully dressed in pale lilac in our winter, but only in Zones 9 and 10.

Erica carnea. This is the celebrated and much loved winter heather. We decline to accept the diktat of the botanist who wants us all to call it *E. herbacea*; so does nearly everyone else. The carneas are lowly, spreading shrubs, mostly 6 to 9in high, making a dense mat once they have joined one another and creating the liveliest of pictures throughout winter. Many flower for a full three months, though for a much shorter duration in the colder zones of North America. They thrive in a limy soil as in an acid one. Plant deeply, at least a foot apart. From a whole battery we parade the following front-liners. z5.

'Anne Sparkes'. Orange-and-lemon foliage and carmine flowers, sparsely borne. 6 in. February–March.

'Aurea'. Foliage golden in winter, lime-green in summer. Flowers deep pink.

'December Red'. In most regions is really a "January Pink". Flowers till March, 9in.

white, 1½ft; 'Globosa', pale pink, 1½ft; and 'David McClintock', pink-and-white bi-colour, 1½ft. Possibly more distinguished than any of these, but more tender, is the sturdy, well-formed 'Maweana', with larger, purple-pink flowers.

Erica cinerea. Here we have a whole battalion on parade. This is the "bell heather", many of the varieties of which bloom in profusion from June till October, their flowers tightly massed in stiff spikes above the pin-size leaves and sometimes mingling with them. They prefer a rather sandy soil, so, if your soil is heavy, work in plenty of lime-free sand if you can get it. They enjoy a warm, dry home, yet

51. Erica carnea

'Foxhollow'. A superlative, spreading plant of bright gold foliage all summer and pale olive-green in winter. Flowers pale pink.

'King George'. Best of all for vigour, hardiness and length of flowering. Deep pink. Plant at 15in.

'Myretoun Ruby'. Stunning, deep red, the most brilliant of all the carneas.

'Pink Spangles'. Rosy-pink. Vigorous.

'Queen Mary'. Lilac-pink. Begins in December.

'Springwood Pink'. A sheet of soft, pure, lively pink. Very vigorous. Plant at 15in.

'Springwood White'. Lovely sister of the above, enormously popular.

'Vivellii'. Fine old blood-red. Leaves dark.

Erica ciliaris. The Dorset heath is a straggling, almost prostrate plant, but the flower stems spring erect. They are brittle plants, easily damaged, and are a little on the tender side. The leaves come in whorls of threes and the little flowers are daintily hung in similar groups above the erect spikes from July till November. Trim after flowering or in early spring to correct straggling. z7.

The best-known variety is 'Mrs C. H. Gill', a gay cherry-red of 1ft. Other good ones are: 'Corfe Castle', rich pink, 1ft; 'Stoborough',

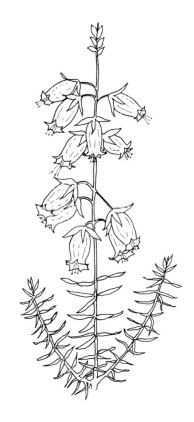

52. Erica ciliaris

53. Erica cinerea

are certainly not tender. The colour of the foliage can be important; generally the darker the flower the darker the leaf. Deploy them in wide expanses if you can, a foot apart in most cases. The following team should satisfy anyone. Assume their heights to be about 7 to 9in unless noted otherwise. z5.

'Alba Minor'. Dwarf white, 6in, neat and trim.

'Atrorubens'. Near to ruby, 6in, June–July.

'Atrosanguinea', Smith's variety. Deep carmine.

'C. D. Eason'. Bright red. Very good indeed.

'Cindy'. Very fine purple.

'Contrast'. Very deep purple; bronzed leaves.

'Eden Valley'. Lilac and white, a good carpeter.

'Foxhollow Mahogany'. Bright maroon, very reliable.

'Golden Drop'. Dense mat of orange leaves in summer, coppery-red in winter.

'Knaphill Pink'. Deep pink, July–August, olive foliage. 1ft.

'Lavender Lady'. A pretty complement to the pinks and reds.

'Pentreath'. Rich red-purple. A stunner and our own first choice.

'Pink Ice'. Deep, keen pink.

'P. S. Patrick'. Purple, good old stager, 1ft.

'Purple Beauty'. Deep, rich purple, 1ft.

'Pygmaea'. Spritely dwarf pink, 6in.

'Rosabelle'. Salmon; leaves dark; 6in. July–August.

'Rozanne Waterer'. Deep maroon-purple, 6in.

'Stephen Davis'. Brilliant scarlet, July–August.

'Vivienne Patricia'. Soft purple, 1ft, never stops.

E. × darleyensis. This hybrid between *carnea* and *mediterranea* is marvellous value and, if we were allowed only one breed, this would be our choice for winter. One may describe it as an enlarged carnea, making 2ft-high domes and maybe more in width. Most bloom from December till April. They are extremely hardy and prosper in the poorest soils and in limy ones. Plant 18in or more apart and prune lightly. The following are the prize-winners.

'Arthur Johnson'. Long spikes of rose; apple-green foliage.

'Darley Dale'. The original. Pale purple. Flourishes in the meanest soil.

'Furzey'. Rose-pink, 1½ft.

'George Rendall'. Deep rose, 1ft, first-class.

'Ghost Hills'. Rose.

'Jack H. Brummage'. Remarkable for its golden foliage, brightest in winter.

'Silberschmelze'. Magnificent white.

E. erigena. See *mediterranea*.

E. lusitanica. Tree heath from Spain and Portugal which is accustomed to poor, thin soils and which, when established, will stand a lot of drought. It can grow 10ft high with plumes of profuse white flowers in both autumn and spring, in some places continuously. Compared with *arborea*, has paler foliage, softer to the touch, and is more plume-like. Rather tender for an erica. Often sold to the credulous by florists as the "lucky white heather". The recent variety 'George Hunt' has gilded leaves. z8.

E. mackaiana. Small shrublets of not much more than 6in that look very like the cross-leaved heath, flowering from July to September. Their natural homes are in damp places. Probably the best-known is the pure white 'Dr Ronald Gray', but the pink 'Plena', being double, is more rewarding.

E. mediterranea. We conserve the good old name and are not lured by the botanist's command to change it to *erigena*. It has also been called *hibernica*, though more widespread in south-west Europe than in Ireland. They are the most becoming of the smaller tree-heathers, growing normally in a neat, conical attitude, seldom more than 4ft high and are just the thing for diversifying a flat expanse of the shorter heathers. They have a wide tolerance of soil conditions, are quite happy in lime and most of them are in flower from early March till late May. A warm fragrance accompanies them and when not in flower they take the part of dwarf conifers. Heavy snow may sometimes break them. There are not very many versions, the following being of the front rank. z7.

'Brightness'. Warm purple-pink. Very neat habit, 3ft.

'Irish Salmon'. Salmon buds, opening clear pink, often before Christmas. A beauty. Plants sold under this name are often 'Irish Dusk', possibly a slightly better plant. $2\frac{1}{2}$ft.

'Superba'. Very fine rose-pink. About 5ft.

'W. T. Rackliff'. Fine white, tight and compact.

E. multiflora. Distinguishable from the Cornish heaths by only minor botanical details and not so hardy. Flowers pale rose, but variable. z7.

E. pageana. A bright yellow South African, flowering in our hemisphere in late winter and early spring to about 4ft. z9–10.

E. × praegeri. Hybrids between *mackaiana* and *tetralix*, tending towards the latter, with very dense foliage. Of Irish origin, flowering all summer in tones of pink. The original (we believe) is 'Connemara', 6in, bright pink, but variable. 'Irish Lemon', soft pink, 9in, is so

called because the tips of the young shoots are of that colour before turning bright green. Of like behaviour is 'Irish Orange'.

E. scoparia. The besom heath. A gypsy among heathers, suitable for only the wilder places. Of random growth, it can reach 10ft, with cheap green flowers. There is a rare dwarf form and we may see some new introductions. z7.

E. terminalis (or *stricta*). A very elegant, slim tree heath, reaching 6ft, with fresh, apple-green foliage and flowers of a clear rose on stiff stems from June till autumn. Perfectly happy in lime. Makes a beautiful hedge of slender carriage. The recently introduced cultivar 'Thelma Woolner' is not quite so tall, with flowers of a deeper hue. z7.

E. tetralix. The cross-leaved heath. Extremely hardy and a very distinctive little shrub, the leaves being arranged in fours to form a cross and grey-hued and the flowers borne aloft in little groups dangling from the tips of the shoots all summer long. They are densely bushy, rarely a foot high, the colours of

54. Erica tetralix, the cross-leaved heath

the flowers usually muted. In their native haunts in Britain they inhabit moist soils but do well in average gardens. z3. Those of the front rank are:

'Alba Mollis'. White. Silvery foliage, 15in.

'Con Underwood'. Crimson. Well-proven favourite, 9in.

'Hookstone Pink'. Muted pink. Strong plants of 1ft.

'Melbury White'. Large white bells, beautifully silvered leaves.

'Pink Star'. The florets look upwards, not dangling.

E. umbellata. Another Iberian, rather tender, but fit for z9. Of rather loose habit, it grows to some 2ft, with grey-green leaves and globular flowers, usually of bright rose, in May and June, when few other heathers are open. For full sun in a dry, preferably stony soil. Fully lime-tolerant.

E. vagans. The Cornish heath, resplendent from early August till October. Not a "tree heath" but in isolation can easily grow 3ft high and 4ft or more wide, dense and compact. The little leaves are in close tiers, slightly bent, and the flowers are in long, plump, cylindrical spikes (racemes), blooming from the bottom upwards. After flowering the russet seed pods are still attractive and may be left on, if you like, until March. The Cornish heath is quite happy in a clay soil and will stand a mild flavour of lime. z5. The front row of this beautiful chorus is made up of the following.

'Birch Glow'. Vivid rose; foliage bright green, $1\frac{1}{2}$ft.

'Diana Hornibrook'. Deep pink, early. 1ft.

'Lyonesse'. Very fine white with brown anthers, $1\frac{1}{2}$ft.

'Mrs D. F. Maxwell'. Deep, warm pink; the *crème de la crème*, 2ft.

'St Keverne'. Like the above, but a shade paler.

'Valerie Proudley'. A quite exceptional little plant of beautiful pale gold all the year round if in full sun. Wins all hearts. Grows slowly to 1ft by 1ft, with small spikes of white flowers. Plant 9in apart.

E. × veitchii. A tree heath, a cross between *arborea* and *lusitanica*. Not of the front rank in a well-ordered garden unless it be the clone 'Exeter', which will reach 6ft, spreading widely, with great plumes of scented ivory-white above fine, soft foliage. z8–9.

E. × watsonii. A natural mating of the Dorset and the cross-leaved heaths. Among its few variations, nothing comes near to 'Dawn', which bears flowers of soft rose, like those of the cross-leaved, at the tips of its dense, widespreading, 1ft-high shoots, for six months.

E. × williamsii. The parents are considered to be the Cornish and the cross-leaved heaths. They are small plants which, like the latter parent, flower the whole summer through. The tips of the foliage start pale yellow and deepen by stages to dark green. 'Gwavas' is pale pink and 'P. D. Williams' is rose, with bronze leaves in winter.

HEBE

Hebe was herself a goddess, but she was also a handmaid to the senior gods, whose goblets she was required to keep filled with nectar. She seems to have been a bit of a tippler herself, for the plants that she has godmothered are a pretty mixed-up lot. Their morals in their antipodean settlements are decidedly promiscuous and even the botanists of New Zealand, where most of them dwell, are puzzled about their lineages. Moreover, in their own pastures they live a soft life and not many of them make good emigrants. Formerly they were numbered among the veronicas and our fathers (and we ourselves) called them "shrubby veronicas", but they were rightly divorced and the name "veronica" is now reserved for the herbaceous species. All hebes are evergreen. Another group called Parahebes are small dwellers of the rock garden, with flowers like speedwell, and outside our scope.

Many hebes have rather fleshy or leathery leaves, some are cord-like, others slim and soft. They may be anything from one-eighth to 6in long and their colours range through various

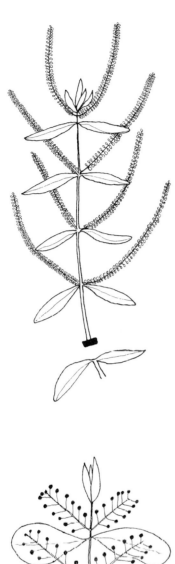

tints of green, grey and bronze. Many make excellent foliage shrubs, spreading widely and deterring weeds. The individual flowers are very small, but usually assembled in packed racemes or spikes.

Hebes are not particular about soil, but are very fond of a seaside air and very often a species or hybrid which is not hardy inland will be happy near the coast and resist the assaults of sea spray. In the USA nearly all thrive on the west coast, but not on the east. They are surface-rooting plants and the only tool you may use near them is a hoe, lightly handled. Fortunately, continuity of supply is easy in most instances, for summer cuttings strike readily and can be potted-up to over-winter in any frost-free glasshouse.

Pruning can be important. Fortunately, hebes make fresh growth freely from the base when cut back, either by frost or by the knife. The tender *H. speciosa* and its offspring may well lose their limbs from freezing but (like other plants that we have mentioned) be alive at their hearts. Leave such plants alone until late spring, by which time new shoots may emerge from the base or part-way up the old stems; if from the old stems, choose a strong-looking new shoot and cut back to there.

Many hebes produce vast quantities of seed, the ripening of which may seriously undermine the vigour of the plant. So behead the flowered spikes, or whole assemblage of spikes in some cases, as soon as the blossom is spent.

In popular eyes the most handsome hebes are the hybrids, but nearly all of these are decidedly tender, and we shall group them separately. According to our brief we must bypass the tinies, often used in rock gardens. Unless noted otherwise, the species (unlike the garden hybrids) all bear white flowers in June–July.

H. albicans. A debatable species in the wild, varying greatly, but we know it as a dense, grey-tinted dome, of perhaps 2ft, but spreading widely. z7–8.

H. amplexicaulis. Distinguished by its close-set, overlapping, stem-clasping, heart-shaped, stalkless leaves. Up to 3ft. z7.

H. 'Andersonii'. See Garden Hybrids.

55.   Pruning hebes. (*Above*) a garden hybrid or species of similar habit; behead the whole inflorescence. *Below*, Hebe × franciscana

H. anomala. A fine foliage shrub densely clad in bright green leaves with a glint of gold. About 4ft. Flowers sometimes pink. z7.

H. armstrongii. See *H. ochracea*.

H. brachysiphon. Perhaps the hardiest of the hebes, growing 6ft high with leaves of matt green. A good hedger. See also *traversii*. z7. Prune hard in late spring if it becomes untidy.

H. buxifolia. A neat, erect shrub, becoming globular, with dark green, burnished leaves, averaging 4ft. z7.

H. canterburiensis. Dark green, polished leaves, spreading, dainty shrub, nearly 3ft high.

H. cupressoides. A curiosity among hebes, looking remarkably like a dwarf cypress, with tiny, scale-like, closely pressed leaves on slender, forked branches, possibly 6ft high. Small, pale blue flowers. z8.

H. dieffenbachii. A tender, 5ft, sprawling shrub with thick, lance-like, sea-green leaves. Flowers lilac or purple. Prune hard if ungainly. z9.

H. elliptica. The genuine article is rare and is normally a shrub a few feet high, but it can reach to 20ft. See next entry.

This brings us directly to one of the most popular of hebes, **H. × franciscana**. It is liable to be sold as *elliptica*, but is a hybrid between that and *speciosa*. It is a "group" rather than a fixed clone. Especially favoured are its forms 'Blue Gem', which speaks for itself, and 'Variegata' which has a broad band of cream around the leaf, both becoming 4ft mounds. Very good indeed near the sea. z8, but can succumb in severe winters.

H. glaucophylla. One of the "mixed-up lot". As we know it, it is a 4ft mass of very small, sharply pointed leaves. Also known as *darwiniana*, which may be something a little different. There is a neat and very pretty variegated form.

H. hectoris. One of the "whipcord" hebes, the stiff branches covered with closely pressed, scale-like leaflets. Shy-flowering. Can be 2ft high, usually less. z7.

The most beautiful of all hebes is undoubtedly **H. hulkeana**, a choice and superlative plant by any standards except that of hardiness.

The key to its heart is to give it a dry, stony, starved, sharply-drained home. It is a loose, straggling shrub, 4ft high and more, with lustrous green leaves and huge, sumptuous, branching panicles, composed of tiny florets of an enchanting tint between lilac and lavender, throughout May and June. Plant it in poor, rubbly soil, at the foot of a hot wall if you are in any doubt, perhaps with a few loose, informal ties, and amputate each panicle complete, as soon as flowering is over. Perpetuate it by summer cuttings. z8.

Closely related to hulkeana are two stockier plants, *H. fairfieldii*, of similar colouring, about 2ft, and *H. lavaudiana*, mauve, shorter still and seeming to need a richer soil.

H. × kirkii. A tall shrub with pointed leaves and branches chestnut when young and very long racemes of white flowers. z8.

H. leiophylla. Of dubious identity, but, as we know it, this is a tender 4ft shrub with narrow pointed leaves and its long racemes of white or pale lavender flowers. z9.

H. × lewisii. A tall, erect shrub of 5ft with pale blue flowers among pale green leaves.

H. matthewsii. Neat, handsome, 4ft. Leathery, oval leaves, flowers sometimes flushed purple. z8.

H. ochracea is the popular, neat, whipcord-khaki-coloured hebe often sold under the name "H. armstrongii". An excellent foliage shrub in the garden picture, its spreading branches of unique colour contrasting well with other shrubs, especially heathers, but not branching close enough to the ground to discourage weeds. The real *armstrongii* is something different, with green leaves. z8.

H. odora closely resembles buxifolia, but is scented of jasmine and is a bit hardier. z6–7.

H. parviflora. A thoroughly mixed-up lot, and tender to boot. The one in commerce is usually an erect, open, slender shrub of $4\frac{1}{2}$ft, with very slim, pointed, spear-like leaves and chocolate branches, flowering from July till November in mild districts. This is the variety *angustifolia*. Another variety, *arborea*, grows 6ft high or more in mild districts, but 25ft in its native land. z9.

H. pinguifolia 'Pagei'. Although a small thing, we must include this because of its general garden use and its popularity. Page's hebe has very attractive, tiny, pearl-grey, waxy leaves, spreading widely. In time and the right conditions it can become a dome 2ft or more high, but the mistake commonly made is to plant it in a rich, fat loam, where it becomes woody and straggly. z7.

Another justly popular hebe, though sparse in flower, goes under the dubious garden name of *sub-alpina*, but is in fact **H. rakaiensis**. It builds up into a lovely, apple-green dome, 2ft high but 4 to 5ft wide; a very refreshing shrub which smothers weed seeds. z8.

H. recurva. The plant in circulation under this name makes a tender, 3ft, spreading shrub, slender and open in character, with very slim leaves and rich in flower. In the best nurseries the stock is from a clone called 'Aoira'. z9.

Rather more hardy, particularly at the seaside, is **H. salicifolia**, with long, very slim, willow-like leaves of bright green, and reaching 12ft or more, festooned with an abundance of long clusters of flowers, which are sometimes tinted with pale lilac. 'Spender's Seedling' is smaller and scented. z8.

H. speciosa is a small, tender shrub with leathery leaves and purple-red flowers, important as being one of the chief parents of the colourful garden hybrids.

H. sub-alpina. See *H. rakaiensis*.

H. traversii. Very like *brachysiphon*, but the true traversii is more closely related to *sub-alpina*. Hardy and popular. z7.

H. venustula. Also closely related to *brachysiphon*, but smaller and equipped with dense, brightly shining leaves. z7.

H. vernicosa. Like *canterburiensis*, but more generously flowered. z7.

GARDEN HYBRIDS

These are of mixed parentage, usually giving us brightly coloured flowers in long or fairly long, tapering and pointed racemes, which we shall call spikes, because they look so. The most vivid carry the sap of *speciosa*, often with leathery and colourful foliage also, but are the most tender and we should hesitate to plant them in any climate colder than z9, unless it were by the seaside or in some sheltered spot.

'Alicia Amherst'. A *speciosa* hybrid. Violet in crowded spikes. Leaves dark and leathery. Also known as 'Royal Purple' and 'Veitchii'.

'Amy'. Deep purple. Leaves also empurpled. An erect shrub up to 4ft, named after Lady Ardilaun.

'Andersonii' (*salicifolia* × *speciosa*). Lavender. 4ft. Leaves of soft leathery texture. Eclipsed by its beautiful sport 'Variegata' which wears leaves broadly edged with cream, and there is also a golden-edged variety. Tender.

'Autumn Glory'. Purple-blue in short, plump spikes; leaves red-edged. Stems bronze, $2\frac{1}{2}$ft. One of the hardiest, July–autumn.

'Balfouriana'. Pale purple with erect, purple-tinted stems, 18in.

'Bowles's Hybrid'. Charming low shrub of 2ft, with multiple spikes of lavender; leaves soft, light green.

'Carl Teschner'. A carpeter, 9in by 4ft. Small violet spikes. Very popular, but the name is suspect. Is identical with what is called *youngii* in New Zealand.

'Carnea'. Beautiful pale pink with narrow leaves. May–September. 3ft. The cream edge to its form 'Variegata' gives it added beauty.

'Ettrick Shepherd'. Magenta turning quickly to white. $3\frac{1}{2}$ft.

'Gauntlettii'. Long, rose-pink spikes, long leaves on a splendid shrub of $4\frac{1}{2}$ft; of *speciosa* type. 'Red Ruth' is similar.

'Gloriosa'. A *speciosa* hybrid with long spikes of bright pink.

'Great Orme'. Like 'Carnea' but a deeper pink.

'Highdownensis'. Long, deep blue spikes, narrow leaves. Long season, 6ft.

'Hielan Lassie'. A *speciosa* hybrid. Violet, July onwards, neat habit.

'La Séduisante'. Crimson-purple, leaves also flushed purple. July onwards. *Speciosa* hybrid. Beautiful but tender.

'Lindsayi'. Good all-rounder. Flowers pale pink on short, dense spikes, spoon-like leaves, chestnut stems, 3ft. One of the hardiest.

'Margery Fish'. Violet and white, repeating in autumn. Leaves bronze in winter. Virtually identical with 'Primley Gem'. Relatively hardy, a nice shrub. 2½ft.

'Marjorie'. Pale violet and white version of 'Andersonii', 3ft, wide-spreading.

'Midsummer Beauty'. A great favourite, also from 'Andersonii'. Long spikes of pale violet throughout summer, with soft, pale green leaves. 5ft by 8ft.

'Miss E. Fittall'. Very like 'Midsummer Beauty', but mauve. From this comes the "Wand Group", tall shrubs in pink, lilac or violet.

'Mrs Winder'. Bright mauve-blue. Leaves bronze-purple and chestnut stems. A pretty and popular shrub of dense, soft growth. 4ft.

'Simon Delaux'. Rich purple-red in long spikes. Leaves edged purple. Very colourful small shrub, but with the tenderness of *speciosa*.

'Tricolor'. Long, red-purple spikes of *speciosa*. Pretty leaves of sea-green, flushed purple when young, edged cream. Tender.

'Waikiki'. Like 'Mrs Winder', but spreading widely.

HELIANTHEMUM
Sun-rose or *Rock-rose*

The invented English names for these popular dwarf evergreens are highly ambiguous, for they are applied to other plants also, notably the cistus; but, since *helios* is Greek for the sun, there should be little doubt.

We would consider these lowly shrublets as outside our brief if it were not for the fact that their hybrids are one of the gardener's most useful handmaids, ready to do all sorts of jobs in odd places, of easy culture and pretty hardy. In North America they are really happy only west of the Rockies. We must turn our backs on the tiny, rock-garden species, so that we are left with little more than the popular hybrids.

Helianthemums are essentially sun-lovers,

accustomed to lime, giving their best floral performance in a lean, stony soil, quite happy, indeed, in a gravel path. Except for the few doubles, they have five simple petals, each flower lasting no more than a day, but following one another successively from the curling cymes at the tip of each branchlet, beginning in late May. It is a positive command that you cut the stems back hard after each cyme has exhausted its treasury; otherwise you will get a mat of bare, woody stems in the middle. Their useful life is sometimes rather short, but propagation is very easy from late-summer cuttings.

One species to be noticed is **H. apenninum**, which grows to 18in, is dusted nearly all over with a white powder and crowned with pure white moon-flowers, but silvery-rose in the variety *roseum*. z6.

H. nummularium is the most important species, being the dominant parent of a large family of garden hybrids. It forms a low hummock about 10in high, spreading to nearly 3ft, with the lowest branches prostrate and bearing yellow flowers. We can overlook a clutch of sub-species, but its variety 'Amy Baring' is a little charmer of a rich orange. z3.

The said garden hybrids are very numerous, in reds, pinks, yellows and white, and we can give only a brief list of those that have some significance. The name itself often tells you its colour. Several are named after Scottish mountains (as in 'Ben Nevis'), all reliable. Those with double or semi-double flowers are good value, giving a long season of bloom. z6.

'Alice Howarth'. Mulberry purple, semi-double.

'Cerise Queen'. Double.

'Henfield Brilliant'. Brick-red; grey foliage.

'Jubilee'. Primrose, double. Extra good.

'Mrs C. W. Earle'. Scarlet, double.

'The Bride'. White with yellow centre. Foliage grey.

'Tigrinum Plenum'. Tawny orange, double.

'Watergate Rose'. Dark red, orange centre; foliage grey.

'Wisley Primrose'. Robust plant that may be 18in high and 2ft wide, with grey leaves. 'Wisley Pink' has similar foliage but is sparser and less flowerful.

HELICHRYSUM

A mixed genus that includes some shrubs, herbaceous perennials and annuals, and daisy-form flowers, many of them cut and dried as "everlasting" or "immortelles". They must have all the sun possible and prosper in poor stony soil.

Strictly speaking, the only one eligible for our ranks is **H. splendidum**, a brilliantly silvered shrub of 3ft by 6ft. The clusters of small, yellow daisies are worthless. Prune hard in April and trim lightly to shape in July. Should over-winter in z9.

We must, however, take the opportunity of mentioning the prostrate, wandering *H. petiolatum*, because of its decorative value in the garden scene. Its small leaves look just as though they were cut out of white lamb's-wool, but the faintly yellow-tinted 'Sulphureum' is perhaps even better. Excellent in tubs as in the open ground. Easily perpetuated by cuttings of small side-shoots taken with a heel in late summer in a sandy mix in a shady place, without top-cover but kept moist, over-wintered in pots and planted out about 1st June. So treated, will succeed in z8. Cuttings of *splendidum* can be treated in the same way.

People who live in sun-drenched climates can enjoy several other dwarf helichrysums garbed in silver or pearl-grey, such as the handsome *italicum*, the curious *scutellifolium*, with stems like stag's antlers, the sage-green *serotinum*, smelling of curry and *stoechas*, known for its flowers as "Goldilocks".

HESPERALOE. See *Yucca parviflora*

HETEROMELES
Christmasberry or *Tollon*

H. arbutifolia is an evergreen shrub of dense and compact growth, with leathery, glossy leaves 4in long, growing perhaps 10ft high, with flat clusters of small, white flowers in June–July, followed by bright red berries in autumn and winter. Nice for Christmas decorations. May also be labelled as a photinia. z9.

HIBISCUS

Blood-relation of the mallow and the hollyhock, as may often be recognised in the single-flowered specimens with their projected stamens, the hibiscus has some stalwart flowering shrubs of the first order, an adornment to any garden, tolerant of most soils, good in towns and needing the minimum of attention. They make splendid hedges. They must, however, have all the sun possible and good drainage. The only pruning necessary is to cut out decadent or overcrowded stems.

The most glamorous is the summer-flowering **H. rosa-sinensis**, which so often adorns the hair of dusky maidens. It can grow very large indeed – up to 25ft in the right sort of climate, which means the Mediterranean, Florida and similar regions, as well as its native Orient. The flowers are huge, often expanding to 6in wide, with their stamens carried on very long, projecting columns, and they come in named varieties of many colours, some single, others double. We particularly like 'Californian Gold', which is rich yellow, with a red shading in the centre. z9, but rarely prospers in Britain.

Much hardier, though also from China, is **H. sinosyriacus**, a fine introduction by Hilliers of Winchester. Of similar general character to the "Syrian" hibiscus (our next entry), it has rather larger flowers, sage-green leaves, reaches 10ft or more and is valuable for flowering from September until frost clamps down. Three clones have been established, all having a red or pink flash in the centre; these are 'Autumn Surprise', white, 'Lilac Queen', pale lilac; and 'Ruby Glow'. For warm spots in z8.

Far hardier than either of these and much

159

more widely grown is **H. syriacus**, which originates in fact from the Far East, not Syria. Here we have a robust shrub of rotund outline, generally reaching 10ft, with small variable leaves, some lobed, others not, and bold, wide-open flowers distinctly like hollyhocks, mainly in September. Though able to withstand a hard freeze, it will not flower well unless in full sun and is often a slow starter in the first year. There are single- and double-flowered varieties, but the doubles (besides lacking the charm of simplicity) need hot weather to open properly. The Syrian hibiscus flowers on the current year's growth and, if you are so minded, you can get extra-large blooms by cutting back the old stems very hard in early spring, leaving only three or four new buds on the shoot, as they do at Versailles, but this spoils the character of the plant.

Rehder's hardiness rating is z5, but in such a climate the shrub really needs wall protection, and we think that a good flowering in the open needs z7–8. Of the numerous varieties available, the following are the cream.

'Admiral Dewey'. Double white.

'Ardens'. Rosy-purple, double, very flowerful.

'Blue Bird'. Finest of all, a glorious bloom.

'Comte de Hainault'. Lively double flowers of marbled pink and white.

'Diana'. Very large, very beautiful white.

'Duc de Brabant'. Deep crimson, very double.

'Hamabo'. Blush-pink, crimson eye.

'Lady Stanley'. Palest blush, crimson eye, semi-double, erect habit.

'Red Heart'. White with crimson eye.

'Woodbridge'. Large, rose-pink with crimson eye.

HIPPOPHAË

Sea buckthorn

Slender, willow-like silvery or sage-green leaves and orange berries are the marks of these very large, thorny, very hardy shrubs, which

56. Hippophaë rhamnoides, the sea-buckthorn, in fruit

are of most use as bulwarks against harsh winds, especially sea ones. You may sometimes see them on the seashore half-buried by blown sand, yet unhurt. They are drought-hardy also. They are deciduous and the flowers inconspicuous, but their splendour is in the small, orange berries (too bitter even for birds) which thickly encrust the stems of the females. For male and female flowers are on separate bushes, which are distinguishable only by trial and error, but the nurseryman should know. One male will serve five females, the pollen windborne. The species nearly always used is the silvery-leaved **H. rhamnoides**, which is capable of towering up to 20ft, yet you can also chop it to the ground if necessary. It throws up suckers, creating a thicket if allowed, but good basal shoots can be used as replacements of old ones. z3.

160

H. salicifolia is a much rarer, much bigger tree-like plant, with sage-green leaves, pendulous branches and deeply furrowed bark.

Hippophaë is the ancient Greek name for a spiny plant.

HOHERIA

Beautiful little trees and large shrubs from New Zealand, massed with white flowers in summer, their name being derived from a Maori one. The two that are shrubs can themselves become almost tree-like in favoured places. They are both very much alike and deciduous, with an upright bearing, branching from ground level. Full sun. z7.

H. lyallii can be 20ft high. Its slender branches become weighed down by quantities of pensive, white, saucer-flowers, almost translucent, with purple anthers, dangling prettily in July from among grey-coated leaves that are like an elongated heart with a roughly wavy edge.

H. glabrata differs from Lyall's species only in its leaf, which is smooth rather than downy-grey, its tip stretched out to a very fine point, its edges toothed. It blooms a few weeks earlier.

HOLLY. See *Ilex*

HOLODISCUS
Ocean Spray

Huge, drooping, feathery plumes of massed creamy-white flowers, reminiscent of a spiraea, adorn **H. discolor** in July. Deciduous and grey-leaved, the shrub grows 12ft or more high, but the arching stems spread wider still. The flowering occurs on shoots springing from the previous year's growth. Prune back after blossom-fall as for deutzias (Fig. 10). z5.

H. dumosus is denser and more twiggy in behaviour, bearing its plumes erect. It can be pruned in the same way to get a good floral display.

HONEYSUCKLE. See *Lonicera*

HUCKLEBERRY. See *Gaylussacia*

HYDRANGEA

Hydrangeas have a very important purpose in the garden scheme, for they flower mainly in July and August, when there is no great abundance of other flowering shrubs. In their various forms they suit both formal and informal settings and consort particularly happily with the golden hypericums, the more informal roses and with clematis behind them.

For the gardener's purpose hydrangeas can be assembled in four groups:

The climbers (*H. petiolaris, anomala* and *integerrima*), which do not concern us here, although the first-named can, in fact, be grown as large, free-standing shrubs
the plume-helmeted (*paniculata* and *quercifolia*)
the mop-heads
the lacecaps

All the last three are first-class garden shrubs, colouring our picture with large bouquets of red, pink, blue or white from July to September and ranging in hardiness from Zones 4 to 7, though many need a bit of coddling in their first winter.

The dominant species in most gardens is *H. macrophylla*, which embraces nearly all the mop-heads (known somewhat confusingly also as the 'hortensia" section) as well as several splendid lacecaps. The hortensias, which most command popular esteem and which often adorn mayoral functions and hotel lounges, arrange themselves in large orbs of tightly packed florets that are almost entirely sterile, being calyces composed of sepals without any true petals.

The lacecaps embrace nearly all other species of hydrangea, as well as one important section of the macrophyllas. In them the inflorescence, or flower-truss, is flat or slightly domed and is composed of two quite different sorts of floret.

In the centre of the truss is a crowded disc of very small, fertile flowers, usually of some shade of blue or pink, each miniature blossom opening to thrust out a tiny brush of stamens, and surrounding them is a ring of large, sterile blossoms, which may be white or brightly coloured. These, often called ray-florets, occasionally intrude into the inner sanctum of the fertile discs.

Hydrangeas range in height from 6in to 12ft, occasionally more. In general they like most of all a rather moist situation. Some are wood-landers in origin and most others are first-class seaside shrubs, enjoying the humid atmosphere. The mop-headed hortensias flourish almost anywhere, subject to climate, but the lacecaps look most at home in the dappled shade of thin woodland. Their susceptibilities to this or that situation differ a trifle, but all are likely to be distressed in frost-pockets and hill bottoms exposed to biting winds, which may ruin flower buds without killing the whole plant.

A factor of particular importance to the gardener is the degree of lime in the soil, for the blue shades that most people so much admire will appear only in acid soils, though they can be induced in mildly alkaline ones by repeated dressings of aluminium sulphate. Not all will so react and, indeed, their tints are to a large extent unpredictable. No white hydrangea can be induced to change its complexion (though some do blush!). In limy soils the reds, pinks and white of the hortensias can be gorgeous.

Give all hydrangeas (with a few exceptions) a good soil enriched with organic matter before planting and, every autumn, give them a thick mulch of leaves, underlaid with a good sprink-ling of nitrogenous fertilizer. If the soil is so strongly alkaline that the leaves turn yellow, give them a foliar feed of iron chelate or a dressing of iron sulphate at $\frac{1}{4}$oz per gallon of water per square yard, though Mr Haworth-Booth considers magnesium sulphate better. Iron is a plant food and has nothing to do with blue-ing, for which you need aluminium sulphate.

Except as we shall see, hydrangeas need little pruning. In general terms we have only to cut

right out whole stems that have lost their virility. Spring is the time.

Propagation by summer cuttings is in most cases extremely easy, either from small side-shoots with heels or from soft tips. Many hydrangeas also layer themselves very conveniently.

In the lists that follow all are lacecap types, except where described otherwise. There is an awful mix-up about names, but we follow in the footsteps of Bean, whose editors have studied the earlier researches of Mr Michael Haworth-Booth and Miss Elizabeth McClintock.

H. acuminata. See under *H. serrata* 'Bluebird'.

H. arborescens. Of loose growth, with cream flowers. Rarely of decorative value, except in the 3ft white variety 'Grandiflora', originating from Ohio, which has the mop-head form of the hortensias, but lacks their strength of stem to hold the truss erect and becomes what Dr Donald Wyman calls "a rolling mass of white". Its American nickname is "hills of snow". Its sub-species *radiata*, is distinguished by the snow-white felt on the underface of the leaf. The new clone 'Annabelle' has larger snowballs and is dwarfer and more compact. z4.

H. aspera. A very lusty and rather hairy, but variable shrub that has large, velvety leaves and may be 12ft high and wide. In the big, lacy flower truss the ray florets are white or are some shade of pink that becomes purple in acid soils. The asperas thrive surprisingly in chalk and, unlike their brethren, can put up with a reason-ably dry soil. In cold climates cosset them for the first two years. z8.

There is a maddening disagreement about names but, as now defined, the best form of the asperas is that which is usually labelled *H. villosa*, a splendid creature that can be blue even in a mildly limy soil. Another is usually listed as *H. strigosa*, which may not flower until October, is a slow starter and not quite as hardy as we should like.

H. heteromalla. Another species with a long list of aliasas, due to its diverse geographi-

Hydrangea macrophylla 'Lilacina'

cal origins. Some can grow 20ft high or even more. The flowers are white throughout. 'Bretschneideri', hitherto listed as a separate species, is a sturdy 9-footer, distinguished by the peeling of its second-year bark. 'Snowcap' is a fine selection by Hilliers, unusually hardy to sun, wind and drought, with flower-trusses like large, china-white plates.

H. involucrata. A pretty dwarf, exceeding 18in only in the mildest counties. Leaf-like bracts enclose the truss of flowers and persist after they open. The inner, fertile florets are lilac or rose and the outer ray florets cream, but in the variety unfortunately called 'Hortensis' the latter are tinted with rose if grown in sun and much more doubled. The whole plant may be killed to the ground in winter but new stems shoot up. z7.

H. longipes. All-white, about 7ft, of lax habit and hairy leaves, identifiable by its very long leaf-stalks and its very large ray-florets. A sub-species, *robusta*, is of debatable provenance.

H. macrophylla. This, the dominant species, is one which is buzzing with arguments of botanists, but we shall stick to simplicity. As we have seen, it is divided (by Michael Haworth-Booth) into two sections, to wit, the plate-like lacecaps, which are thought to be the original wild type, and the mop-headed hortensias, a term derived from the early French name for hydrangea, which was *Hortensia opuloides*, believed to have been in honour of a lady named Hortense. Other changes of name that took place need not bother us.

The flat or slightly domed "cymose corymbs" of the lacecaps are generally most at home in an informal setting and are charming in the company of a few small trees, if their shade is not too dense.

The "globose corymbs" of the hortensias,

opulent and extrovert, are very well suited to a formal setting, though there is no need at all to regiment them so, and indeed, they mingle very well with other shrubs. Both classes are supremely good within a mile or two of the sea.

Pruning. Behead the lacecaps after flowering to prevent weakening the plant by formation of seed, but retain the withered heads of the hortensias until April, however "untidy" they look, as a small protection against frost. On both sorts act as follows in spring before growth from the buds has advanced: cut right to the ground all feeble shoots; cut to the ground, or to a point low down where a good bud is developing, all antique and degenerate stems; shorten remaining stems to a strong bud, say 8in or so from the tip. This process gives sumptuous blooms, but you can still have a good show of smaller blooms if you omit the shortening.

In the two lists that follow (which we are obliged to abbreviate) expressions such as "pink/blue" mean that the sterile florets are pink in limy soils and the blue in acid ones. In heterogenous soils you may get a mixture of colours. The little disc florets are usually some sort of blue in any soil.

See also *H. serrata*.

THE LACECAPS

'Blue Wave'. The most celebrated of the lacecaps, 6ft high and broader still, rarely flowering before August. Light pink/blue needing aluminium to be a really good blue. Plant in light shade.

'Lanarth White'. A superb shrub of only 2ft, flowering profusely. The pure white ray-florets encircle a bevy of tiny blue beauties. Happy in full sun and satisfied with rather poor soil.

'Lilacina'. A delightful hydrangea, not more than 5ft high but somewhat broader. The flower truss is smaller than in 'Blue Wave', but of superior colours, the ray florets prettily serrated and of bright pink or blue, the disc florets sparkling with a mass of tiny stamens of brilliant amethyst in all soils.

'Mariesii'. Rounded trusses, half-way to a mop-head. The pink ray-florets, mingling with

the central disc, become blue in very acid soils only. May reach 6ft.

'Veitchii'. Very hardy and very lime-tolerant, but of rather lax carriage and desirous of light shade. Ray florets white. 5ft.

'White Wave'. Large, beautifully formed, pearly-white ray florets surround a pallid pink/blue disc. Very happy in full sun and altogether splendid, 5–6ft.

Avoid 'Tricolor' and 'Quadricolor', which have variegated leaves but are poor things outdoors.

THE HORTENSIAS

Hundreds of these mop-heads have been reared in France and Germany, specially intended for pot work in conservatories and salons. Fortunately a good many have proved hardy enough to plant outdoors, though this hardiness is variable. They make first-class tub plants, in which, if you hunger for the blue tints, you can get them by choosing the right varieties and filling the tub with acid soil or treating it with aluminium sulphate. But you must keep them well watered, for no shrub is quicker to wilt.

The hortensias are also splendid foundation plants for house walls, the ideal aspect for most of them being north-west. Due south may be too dry and hot, unless there is a moist atmosphere from the sea, lake or river. Due east may be too cold for some, according to where you live. North may be good for the shade-lovers, but not in North America.

The following is a selected list of the best all-rounders outdoors. z6 in general.

'Altona'. Pink/blue. Big trusses on strong stems, 3–4ft. One of the finest but not the hardiest. Splendid on a westerly wall.

'Amethyst'. Pink/purple. Double ray-florets, prettily frilled. Very long-flowering, $2\frac{1}{2}$ft.

'Ami Pasquier'. Deep red/vivid purple. A firm favourite, $2\frac{1}{2}$ft.

'Domotoi'. Pink/lilac. Frilled florets, sometimes double. Rather loose habit and often reluctant to blue. 2ft.

'Europa'. Like 'Altona' but with looser deportment.

'Frillibet'. Pale pink/azure. Pretty, frilled flowers. 2½ft.

'Générale Vicomtesse de Vibraye', usually shortened to "Vibraye". Hardy, freely flowering and highly popular. Pink in limy soils, but blues with eagerness in acid ones. Rather lax. 5ft.

'Goliath'. Pink/mauve. Small trusses on 4ft stems. Exceptionally good near the sea.

'Hamburg'. Rose/purple. Strong growth. Some shade preferred.

'Harry's Red'. Good red for limy soils.

'Heinrich Seidel'. Deep cherry-red, for a shady place.

'Holstein'. Pink/azure. Large, frilled florets. Rather lax.

'Kluis Superb'. Deep pink/dark blue. Semi-shade. 3ft.

'Mme. E. Mouillière'. Magnificent white to 6ft. Very long-flowering. West or north wall.

'Maréchal Foch'. Rose/deep gentian blue. Early and very free. 3ft.

'Miss Belgium'. Rose, for lime soils. 2½ft.

'Parsifal'. Crimson/deep blue, variable. 3ft.

Hydrangea paniculata

'Pia'. Pink. Only 6in.

'Sir Joseph Banks'. The original hortensia introduced into England in the eighteenth century. Huge cream trusses. Not a choice garden shrub, but useful for its tough resistance to the rudest sea winds. 'Seafoam' is a lacecap sport from it, suggesting a reversion to the original wild form.

'Violetta'. Vivid red/violet. 3ft.

'Westfalen'. Richest colouring of all — vivid crimson/violet. Abundant shapely trusses. 2½ft.

In the ruggedly hardy **H. paniculata** we turn to something totally different in character from the lacecaps and the mop-heads. Instead of these types of inflorescence, it throws out fat, conical plumes of innumerable small flowers in the manner of a panicle, as in the lilac. It is a tall, rangy shrub, the massed ivory florets of which wane from white to fawn-pink. It is tolerant of all kinds of soil, including chalk, and thrives in sun or half-shade. In the wild it can reach tree size. It flowers in late summer from new shoots that start their growth in spring, a fact that controls their pruning. Follow the normal practice for late performers. In the first spring, having got rid of feeble shoots, snip back the top 2in of the main ones. In the second spring cut back the new shoots by two-thirds. In subsequent years cut the new growths hard back to two buds at their bases. Occasionally amputate to the ground any old, exhausted stems.

Propagate from small side-shoots with a heel. We have several forms to consider. z4.

'Floribunda' A handsome shrub with erect plumes of mixed male and female florets, July–September. 9ft if unpruned.

'Grandiflora'. This is the huge variety known in America as "Hydrangea Pee-Gee". It throws out spectacular plumes that can be 18in long, and if you want that sort of thing you amputate the flowered stems to a pair of new buds near the point from which they originated last year and reduce the number of stems as the plant ages. So treated, the heavy trusses may droop down dismally into the mud when rain falls, and as a garden plant it is better to prune it as ordained above. Plant it behind something of more graceful foliage.

The late-flowering Hydrangea paniculata 'Tardiva'

'Praecox' is a fast mover of up to 8ft, starting to flower early, with a mass of frilly fertile florets. A fine garden plant, but unsightly in autumn.

'Tardiva' is the opposite of 'Praecox', delaying its flower until September, but just as pretty.

H. quercifolia. The oak-leaved hydrangea has scalloped leaves like those of the red oak (*Quercus rubra*), colouring ruddily in the fall. Flower trusses like those of the panicled hydrangea but more stumpy. A lover of shade in rich soil and shelter from coldest winds. $3\frac{1}{2}$ft. The new American 'Snow Queen' has extra-large trusses with quantities of lively sterile florets. z6.

H. sargentiana. A fuzz of hairs and little bristles gives a mossy look to this much abused hydrangea. Considered a "woodlander", it is too often crowded in among trees. Give it a fairly open position, with oblique shade at midday, in a rich soil and it will develop into a splendid shrub of 10ft, bearing very large lacecaps composed of white sterile florets surrounding a blue disc. Vulnerable to frost when very young, and always to strong winds, which may tear its huge velvety leaves. It throws up suckers, which may be a nuisance but provide an easy means of propagation. z8.

H. serrata. More confusion here, for this species is very close to macrophylla. It may be described as an uplands version of the maritime macrophylla. It is therefore a little hardier, but usually smaller and admirable for small gardens. All but one of those in cultivation are lacecaps. Prune the same way as the macrophyllas.

'Bluebird', often called *acuminata*. One of the most beautiful of hydrangeas, pale pink or pale blue. Drought resistant. Perhaps 5ft.

'Diadem'. Clear pink or blue, flowering June. In the open the leaves become purple. $2\frac{1}{2}$ft.

'Grayswood'. Ray florets white at first, turning pink and finally crimson when in sun. 5ft. A pure white exists.

'Preziosa'. This is a small mop-head, at first pink, deepening to crimson. Not always easy. Keep it away from the macrophyllas, which make it look a weakling. $3\frac{1}{2}$ft.

'Rosalba'. Ray florets at first white, becoming crimson. Never blues in any soil. $3\frac{1}{2}$ft.

In addition to these garden cultivars, we should note the natural variety *thunbergii*, which is a dainty little shrub of about $2\frac{1}{2}$ft, with almost black stems and pink or blue lacecaps in July-August.

H. villosa. See *H. aspera*.

HYMENANTHERA

Curiously, these antipodean shrubs are related to the violet. The orotund name means simply that the anthers are joined by a membrane (*hymen*). They are darkly evergreen or half-evergreen according to the climate, the rigid stems densely crowded with small leaves. The flowers are trivial but are followed by heavy crops of white berries. Full sun, no pruning. z8–9, except the last.

H. crassifolia is a very ornamental shrub of 5ft, splaying outwards to twice that size, congested with smooth, leathery leaves. *H. angustifolia*, on the other hand, is an erect shrub of about the same height with very small, spiky leaves and a purple marbling on the berries (though the flowers are often unisexual). *H. dentata* is very similar. *H. obovata* can reach 10ft or more but is z9.

HYPERICUM

Golden bowls, filled with posies of stamens of like colour, surrounding a fat, globular pistil, are the hall-marks of the hypericum, one of the easiest shrubs at the gardener's command. We may find it prostrate at our feet or reaching to the crown of our heads, but in these pages we must step over the prostrate and the very lowly, such as reptans, olympicum and buckleyi, which are charming creatures of the rock garden, as well as the herbaceous sorts. What is left is a squadron that is always dressed in a uniform of some shade of yellow and, to the average gardener seeking a shrub of average height, there is little point in looking further than the hybrid 'Hidcote', unless one lives in a climate where 'Rowallane' or *leschenaultii* will be comfortable. Only the collector is nowadays likely to hunger for such species as forrestii, hookeranum, wilsonii or the true patulum; the weedy androsaemum, proliferating by seed, should certainly be avoided. However, apart from colour variations, there are diversities in size, habit and general behaviour that warrant the use of other species, and if you can, you must certainly have the pretty little 'Tricolor' of Moser's hybrid.

Hypericums thrive in any reasonable soils, including dry, sandy ones, though the American ones seem to shrink from chalk. One of their great virtues is that most of them are entirely happy in shade, even deep shade. The foliage is commonplace but abundant and is usually evergreen in mild places, after turning a rusty pink in autumn.

Propagation is very easy from small side-shoots taken with a heel in summer in a normal propagating box or pot, with or without heat. Some pruning ought to be done to the larger sorts and a useful rule for them is to chop off about one-third of the growth early every spring with the shears and to cut out entirely any elderly and exhausted stems.

We limit our list to those species and varieties that have some special characteristics.

H. acmosepalum. A pretty, arching shrub, 4ft high but wider, with slim, close-set leaves and golden, slightly drooping flowers. Sometimes incorrectly labelled *H. patulum* var. *henryi*. z6.

That label is, however, a valid synonym for what is now **H. beanii**, a plant of very similar behaviour and best demonstrated in its cultivar 'Gold Cup', which has lance-like leaves and long flower buds, in which, when they expand, the blooms are pale yellow on the margin. z6.

A rare but attractive species is **H. bellum**, a 2ft shrub with cup-flowers, broad leaves, chestnut branchlets and bronze berries.

H. calycinum, although scarcely 1ft high, must come into our list because of its general usefulness and popularity, to which its several vernacular names testify — St John's-wort, Aaron's beard and rose-of-Sharon (in Britain). Whether in bright sun or in deep shade, it is a galloping ground-cover. The expanded petals resemble five-pointed, broad-rayed stars, not bowls. Keep it away from anything precious. Clip it hard with the garden shears to within 2in of the ground every March. z6.

H. densiflorum. True to its name, this American is smothered in blossoms, which, though very small, are arranged in clusters ("cymose panicles"). The leaves are of fine texture. 4ft or more. z5.

H. elatum. See *H.* × *inodorum*.

H. frondosum. A deciduous American of distinctive character, often looking rather like a miniature tree of 4ft when mature, as the lower branches fall off. The leaves have a blue rinse

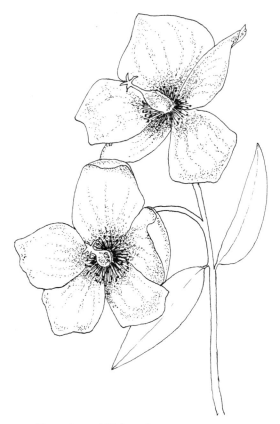

57.   Hypericum 'Hidcote'

Hypericum 'Hidcote'

and the flowers are tinted orange, with a thick brush of stamens. It flowers in clusters and bears berries in great profusion. In nature chooses rocky ground. z5.

H. 'Hidcote'. This famous hypericum is a hybrid of uncertain origin (formerly classed as a variety of *H. patulum*), which takes its name from the Warwickshire home (not far from Stratford-upon-Avon) of Major Lawrence Johnson, the American whom we have noted and there made an original garden of outstanding beauty. 'Hidcote' is a stalwart shrub that will easily reach 6ft high and wide in mild climates if allowed, bearing large, debonair, golden saucers, sometimes 3in wide, from early July till October. It prospers not only in full sun but also in full shade even right up to the boles of trees. Prune it hard, cutting it back thigh-high when it gets big. If you have only one or two plants and are finicky, you will prune to a pair of buds. In severe climates where it may not exceed 3ft, it may be killed to the ground, but will sprout again. z6–7.

H. × inodorum (formerly *elatum*) is worth growing only in its cultivar 'Elstead'. Its flowers are very small but its bright red, ovoid berries mature rapidly, so that both flowers and berries appear at the same time. z7.

H. kalmianum is of interest for its hardiness, growing wild in the cliffs of rivers north of Niagara. Named after the Swedish naturalist Kalm, who found it in 1710. 3ft. July. z4.

H. kouytchense. A 3ft shrub, with large, elegant flowers of pale gold with an audacious brush of stamens, reflexed petals, from early July to October, followed by bright red fruits of curious design. z7.

Of the true species **H. leschenaultii** is surely the finest in flower but the least hardy, coming from Java and thereabouts. The shrub can grow anything up to 8ft high in a rather lackadaisical manner, bearing very large flowers of rich gold. z10.

H. × moseranum. A good little shrub, flowering from July to October with broad, overlapping petals, but outclassed by its beautiful child 'Tricolor', in which the leaves are a blend of olive-green, cream and rose, to which it adds its little gold cups. One of the prettiest of all small shrubs, growing about 15in if pruned back half-way at the end of March. If the top growth is killed by a hard winter cut it to the ground, and fresh shoots will spring up. z8.

H. prolificum. A healthy and vigorous American of dense and rounded form, averaging 4ft, with dark green, shining leaves and quantities of small flowers in July and August, followed by a large crop of berries. z4.

H. 'Rowallane'. A great splendour. Just a little finer than 'Hidcote', but not so hardy. It originated in Northern Ireland and produces big, richly golden bowls, 3in wide, beautifully moulded and can reach 6ft if allowed, but prune as for 'Hidcote'. The parentage is *H. hookeranum* 'Rogersii' × *leschenaultii*. If cut down by frost, it regenerates from the base. z8–9, but Dr Wyman gives z6 for America, which we find surprising.

HYSSOPUS
Hyssop

The medicinal herb of antiquity is *H. officinalis*. Its sub-species *aristatus* is a pretty little shrub from which many gardens would benefit. Growing to perhaps 18in, it is a half-evergreen shrub with green leaves and spikes of tightly packed blue flowers from early July to September. Very good as an under-planting for other shrubs, especially roses, in a warm, light soil. Prune hard in April. Easily propagated from late summer cuttings. z7–8.

ILEX
Holly

Prickly leaves and bright red berries form the popular image of the holly, but there are plenty that have no berries, several that have yellow or black berries and a few are even deciduous. To the undiscerning eye those that have very small leaves do not look at all like hollies. The many variations are due to the fact that in their native state they are to be found in almost all parts of the world except Australasia. They are adaptable to most soils, but prefer a moist, loamy one, and the Americans must not have a limy one. They prosper in the shade of trees as in full sun, they defy the pollution of cities and they face the salt-laden gales of the sea with composure. They make superb hedges. With these manifold virtues one may excuse them for their unimpressive floral display, which consists of a mere fuzz of cream.

The really important thing to bear in mind is that nearly all hollies are dioecious, bearing male flowers on one plant and female on another. Contrary to ancient superstition, the holly has no occult powers of divining the weather to come, so that, if you see a holly bearing berries, the explanation is the prosaic one that it is a female that has been pollinated by a male within reasonable distance. There are, however, rare instances in which a lone female will bear fruit that has no seed in it, but such parthenocarpic fruits do not persist.

Pruning. Except in a wild or woodland situation, hollies need at least some shortening to keep them shapely. Do this with secateurs ("garden shears" in America) in July or earlier. Do hedges early in August, when you may use hedging shears if the job is a big one. When hard cutting-back of old shrubs is necessary, do so in April, cutting back to the bone if you like, but spread the job over two or three years, cutting the sides back first. Plant in September or late April, using preferably container-grown plants with a good ball of soil. Hollies transplant with reluctance after juvenility.

Most hollies seed themselves freely, germinating slowly, but named cultivars must be raised from summer cuttings under mist or autumn cuttings in a cold frame.

Goodness knows how many species, varieties and forms there are in this vast field, but we list below the shrubby sorts that have some special character. Sticking to our brief, we leave out those likely to grow more than about 20ft, which unfortunately excludes some of the splendid Highclere hybrids, a few aquifoliums and such hefty species as *cassine, decidua* (the

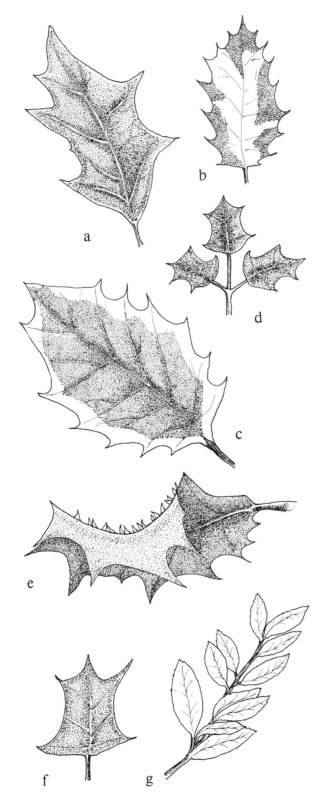

58. Holly leaves, (a) Ilex aquifolium sp.; (b) I. a 'Myrtifolium Aureomaculatum'; (c) I. a. 'Argento-marginatum'; (d) I. pernyi; (e) I. a. 'Ferox'; (f) I. cornuta; (g) I. crenata 'Golden Gem'

possum berry), *pedunculata*, the handsome, small-leaved *pernyi*, *opaca* (50ft), *rotundifolia* (70ft) and several more. Likewise the prostrate species *rugosa*, *montana* and *intricata*, which are of little garden value. The berries (drupes) of all are red unless we say otherwise.

H. × altaclarensis, the Highclere holly. The botanical name is a Latinization of the English garden where the original hybrid occurred (believed to be *aquifolium × perado*). Since then about 20 named cultivars of the first order have appeared, the majority signalised by their great vigour, their pyramidal outline and their large leaves, often almost free of thorns. Good in towns and near the sea. Excluding those that become large trees, such as 'Hendersonii', 'Wilsonii' and 'Hodginsii' (50ft), we are left with the following. z7.

'Camelliifolia'. Female. Very large, dark, glossy, almost thornless leaves, up to 5in long, with dark red berries. Of pyramidal, rather loose and open construction.

'Golden King'. Female, despite its name. One of the great favourites. Leaves brightly margined gold, with few spines.

'Lawsoniana'. Female. Almost spineless leaves splashed with gold in the centre. Watch for reversion to the dark green of 'Hendersonii', of which it is a sport, and cut them out at the point of origin.

'Mundyi'. Male. Very vigorous. Very large, spiny leaves.

'Silver Sentinel'. Female. Sparsely thorned, leaves with cream margin. Handsome and vigorous.

'W. J. Bean'. Female. Dense and neat. Small, very spiny leaves. Bright red berries.

I. aquifolium, the "common" or "English" holly of the British Isles. Its name implies that its leaves are like the claws of an eagle, so you know what to expect. 'Ferox', the hedgehog holly, is indeed ferocious and 'Fisheri' nearly as fierce, but there are a great many with beautifully variegated leaves, as well as many fine, straightforward greens. The leaves of all are handsome, usually undulating between the spines and highly polished. Some become tree-like, even up to 80ft, and in these, curiously, the leaves often lose their spines at the top. Because of its custom of clothing itself densely down to the ground it makes one of the best of all shelters and is a superb hedger. There are some 50 or so cultivars in commerce, which cannot possibly all be included and the names of which are often bewildering, especially when pompously latinized. What a pity it was when bogus Latin names displaced such charming ones as the Painted-Lady Holly, Fine Phyllis Holly and so on in the nineteenth century. We use the spelling of Bean.

Watch those sorts that are colour-splashed in the middle of the leaf and cut out the whole twig if it reverts to green; those with a coloured edge are usually well fixed. z6.

'Amber'. Berries burnt-orange.

'Angustifolia'. Leaves lance-shaped, thorns weak. Pyramidal.

'Argenteo Marginata', the "broad-leaved silver holly". Leaves edged white. A choice and popular variety that may grow to 20ft. Usually female, but there are some males.

'Argenteo Pendula', Perry's Weeping Holly. Similar to the above, but of "weeping" habit, imitating a mushroom. Female.

'Aureo Marginata Ovata'. Leaves almost round, spiny, edged pale yellow. Male.

'Aureo Pendula'. Gilt-edged weeper. Female.

'Bacciflava'. Handsome yellow berries.

'Donningtonensis'. An elegant shrub with purple stems and lance-shaped leaves. Male.

'Elegantissima'. Milky margins, faint marking, spiny. Male.

'Flavescens', the "Moonlight Holly". Leaves lightly suffused canary, old leaves turning dull gold. Female.

'Golden Queen'. Very striking. Broad yellow margin, the most popular of its kind. Compare with 'Golden King' and 'Silver Queen'. Male.

'Grandis'. A very handsome holly with black twigs, green leaves tinted grey and a broad cream margin. Male.

'Handsworth New Silver'. Purple stems, long leaves mottled grey and margined cream. Very elegant. Female.

'J. C. Van Thol'. Of the very first order. Large, almost spineless leaves. Self-fertile, with bright red berries, richly produced. Often listed under altaclarensis. 'Golden Van Thol' is a gilt-edged sport from it.

'Madame Briot'. Also of the very first order. Purple twigs, long, slender leaves, mottled and margined gold, strongly armed. Female. To 12ft.

'Ovata'. Thick, leathery, oval leaves, purple stems, neat habit. Male. 'Ovata Aurea' is prettily edged yellow.

'Pyramidalis'. The name explains its posture. Broadens with age. Some leaves very spiny, others faintly, of mid-green. Handsome female, fruiting freely. 'Pyramidalis Fructuluteo' has yellow berries.

'Scotica'. Quite thornless. It has gold-rimmed and gold-centred forms.

'Silver Queen'. Cream-edged. Male, a classic consort for 'Golden King'.

'Watererana'. Almost thornless, gilt-edged. Starts as a broad bush then becomes conical. Male.

I. ciliospinosa. A trim, slender and erect holly, averaging 15ft, with small, oval, leathery leaves and red, egg-shaped berries. z5.

I. cornuta. A neat, compact 9ft of rounded outline. Leaves rectangular and needle-pointed, of varying sizes, the terminal spine downward curved, except in the excellent variety 'Burfordii' which has only the terminal spine. In 'D'Or' and 'Jungle Gardens' the berries are yellow. In 'Shangri-La' the berries hang on for six months. 'Rotunda', though sterile, is a very fine dwarf, making a dense mound of glossy, bright green. z7.

A few hybrids have been produced in the USA. A mating with *I. pernyi* gave the dense small-leaved 'John H. Morris' and the loose-limbed 'Lydia Morris'. A cross with *I. aquifolium* produced 'Nellie Stevens'.

I. crenata. Only its black berries detract from the value of this shapely holly, in which the very small, sparingly spiked leaves are closely crowded on rigid stems. The male flowers are in clusters, the female solitary. Capable, we are told, of reaching 20ft, but seldom met at more than 9ft. Stands clipping very well and forms a dense low hedge, very firm and hard. z6. Outclassed by its beautiful offspring 'Golden Gem', a small shrub in which the little leaves are all-gold if in full sun. Other garden varieties, omitting the very dwarf ones, are:

'Convexa'. Broader than high, the leaves convex above.

'Green Island'. Low, spreading very widely and loosely.

'Helleri'. A splendid dwarf, low and spreading, but slow.

'Hetzii'. A broad, rounded shrub with convex leaves, better than 'Convexa'.

'Kingsville'. Like 'Green Island' but larger each way.

'Stokes'. Low, dense, mounded.

The natural variety *latifolia* is a vigorous, upright shrub that may reach 20ft, with large leaves. Var. *longifolia* has slim leaves.

I. glabra, the rugged inkberry. Black berries on willowy stems of 9ft. Leaves spineless. Among the hardiest of all broadleaf evergreens. For wet soils. 'Compacta' is a dwarf, female clone from Princeton Nurseries. z3.

I. × messerveae. A group of extremely hardy hybrids, forming round, 8ft shrubs composed of small, glossy leaves. 'Blue Prince' is male and 'Blue Princess' female. The parents are *aquifolium* and the tough *rugosa* from the Kurile Isles. z3–4.

I. serrata. Deciduous. Leaves finely toothed, downy beneath. Berries hang on long after leaffall. To 15ft. z5.

I. verticillata, the winterberry. Deciduous and generally a more ornamental plant than the preceding, branching at ground level with rather fine, stiff growth and the berries hanging on in the same way. 9ft. z3. In *chrysocarpa* the fruits are yellow. In *fastigiata* the carriage is upright. In *tenuifolia* the leaves are thin and the

garden cultivar 'Nana' is a pretty female dwarf of 3ft, with large berries.

The hybrid 'Sparkleberry' is a female of the marriage between verticillata and serrata. It is a semi-dwarf and remarkable for the sheer brilliance of its red berries.

I. vomitoria (the yaupon) is so called because the American Indians used an infusion of its leaves as a vomit. It may reach 20ft, is neat in habit and bears its berries densely the year after flowering. z7. The dwarf 'Nana', though infertile, is an excellent low evergreen for hot, dry climates.

ILLICIUM

Illicium floridanum, the Florida anise, is an evergreen, aromatic shrub of about 8ft, displaying in May and June red-purple flowers contrived in a manner to remind us of the star magnolia (*Magnolia stellata*), consisting of many, very narrow, ribbon-like, sharply reflexed petals, from which is thrust out a small

Illicium anisatum

cluster of carpels, not conical as in the magnolia, but squat and raggedly star-like. The aroma is in the leaves, which are pointed ovals, leathery, 4–6in long. For acid soil in partial shade. Cut out any old, weak shoots. Propagate by layers. z8.

The Asiatic *I. anisatum*, with yellow and green flowers, and *I. henryi*, pink, become small trees.

INDIGOFERA
Indigo

The dyer's indigo of old repute is *I. tinctoria* and in popular speech other indigoferas tend also to be called indigos, the botanical name meaning simply "indigo-bearing". They are very decorative shrubs with fine, pinnate or feather-like leaves and pea-flowers in summer. Give them full sun in a rather light soil, acid or alkaline. Except in the mildest counties, top growth is liable to be killed in winter, but new growth shoots from the base in spring. So prune back hard almost to the ground in early spring, as for hardy fuchsias and perovskia (Fig. 11).

Propagate from cuttings of half-ripe shoots in a close frame with some heat and do not plant out before late spring. The most popular was long known as *I. gerardiana* but in orthodox terms is *I. heterantha*.

Known as the pink indigo, **I. amblyantha** is a 6ft shrub with tiny, rose-pink flowers held erect in compact spikes (racemes) from the leaf-axils in a continuous succession from June to October. z5.

I. decora (or incarnata) is a pretty dwarf, averaging 18in, with copious foliage and quantities of bi-colour flowers in white and pink in July and August on shoots that have grown during the current year, so that no harm is done if last year's top-growth is killed in winter. The all-white variety *alba* is of special charm. z5.

I. heterantha (or **gerardiana**), the sovereign choice, though not very hardy, is a splendid ornamental shrub with luxuriant foli-age, the leaflets in the pinnate leaves small. Normally, it grows to about 4ft in the open, much more against a wall, with racemes of rosy-purple flowers from midsummer till late September. It may not break into leaf until June. A cruel winter may cut it to the ground, but it resurrects eagerly. z7.

Hardier than any of these is Kirilow's indigo, **I. kirilowii**, a 3ft shrub with rose pea-flowers on erect, 5in spikes. Spreads by underground stems and throws up suckers. Leaves bristle-tipped. z4.

Largest of the cultivated indigos is **I. pendula**, which will grow to 9ft, with rosy-purple flowers on slender, dangling racemes which may be as much as 18in long. The leaves likewise are long, with sometimes 27 leaflets. The plant behaves the same way as *decora*, so the same conditions apply. z8.

Some ambiguity surrounds the indigo listed as **I. potaninii**, for it may be confused with amblyantha. Whatever the truth, it is an indifferent garden plant, with insignificant racemes of pallid pink florets. The leaflets are much larger than those of heterantha. z5.

The pink **I. pseudo-tinctoria**, a 4ft shrub rare in cultivation. z5.

ITEA

These are impressive shrubs of varying performance with prickly leaves, for moist soils. Oddly, the name is Greek for a willow. No doubt the handsomest is **I. ilicifolia**, which is an elegant, evergreen and rather lax shrub, averaging 10ft, with spiny, holly-like leaves, dripping with cascades of large, dangling, catkin-like streamers of minute, sweetly scented green-and-white florets in August. On a warm wall in z8 it may grow very big, and once the framework has been established, you must cut out the older and weaker branches. In the open z9 is safer. Propagate by cuttings of half-ripe shoots. **I. yunnanensis** is very similar, with larger leaves, white flowers, and rather more tender.

I. virginica is quite different, far hardier, deciduous and a very desirable small bush that seldom exceeds 3ft. The white, scented florets, which flourish in June–July, are gathered in stiff, slender, erect spikes, and the leaves, which turn red in autumn, are not prickly. The erect shoots branch freely in their second year, and you should cut right out sufficient of the older ones in spring to encourage the young. It needs an acid, damp soil. z5.

KALMIA

Close cousins of the rhododendron, the kalmias grow wild in vast quantities in North America. In Europe they yield place to the rhodo, but are much admired when seen, their coloured cups an adornment to any garden, their hardiness beyond question, and they are sun-lovers rather than shade-lovers, but do need a moist, acid soil and ample mulching. They are named after the Swedish naturalist Kalm. The leaves are poisonous to cattle and sheep, as in many rhododendrons.

What we have said applies particularly to the big **K. latifolia**, which is popularly known in America as the mountain laurel or calico bush and which can there be almost tree-like. When not in flower it looks just like a rhodo, but in June, when most of the rhodos are over, it throws out big bouquets of small, cup-shaped flowers, usually pink, very distinct and charming. In its native America the mountain laurel can tower up to 30ft, but in Britain seldom exceeds 10ft, a fact which Bean suggests may be due to inferior seed from America or to the fact that kalmias like the "Continental" type of climate not experienced in Britain.

There are a few forms, of which the red 'Clementine Churchill', raised at Sheffield Park, in England, is perhaps the finest. Of others, *rubra* is a deep pink, 'Fuscata' has a broad purple band, and *myrtifolia* is a very pretty dwarf averaging 3ft. In America Richard Jaynes has raised a number of charming hybrids. z4.

All other cultivated kalmias are small. The most attractive is the ultra-hardy **K. angustifolia**, known as the sheep laurel or lamb-kill because it is poisonous. This varies in height but averages 2ft, with small clusters of rosy-red flowers. For very moist, acid soil, where it spreads by suckers. The form *rubra* is a deep red form, *candida* is white and *ovata* has broad leaves. z2.

Closely related to the sheep laurel and perhaps only a variety of it is **K. carolina**, distinguished by having flowers of clear pink and leaves coated in a velvety down. z5.

K. polifolia. A dwarf averaging 18in with clustered flowers of a beautiful, pale rose-purple in April. Hard as nails, growing wild in Labrador and Alaska. z2.

Avoid the worthless *K. cuneata*.

KERRIA

Kerria japonica is a very hardy, kindergarten shrub that almost anyone can grow. Very jolly in April with its buttercup flowers on slim, erect stems up to 6ft high, accompanied by saw-edged leaves. Most favoured in its double, long-flowering form 'Pleniflora'. There are also forms with vari-coloured leaves, that named 'Picta' having an attractive tracery of branches.

The kerria flowers on stems thrown up from the ground level in the previous year and spreads by suckers. Therefore, when the blossoms fade, cut down their stems to ground level or to a point where a strong young shoot is emerging. z4.

The name commemorates William Kerr, once a gardener at the Royal Botanic Gardens, Kew, and afterwards Superintendent of the Ceylon gardens.

KOLKWITZIA

Named in honour of the German professor Kolkwitz, but corrupted by some gardeners in America into the fancy name of "beauty bush", **K. amabilis** is one of the prettiest and easiest of deciduous shrubs for everyman's garden, if he has room for it. It grows up to 10ft high, but wider still, with long, graceful, scimitar, twiggy branches and is thronged in May and June with quantities of small bell-flowers of soft pink tints, arrayed in small clusters on short, lateral twigs. Owing to the variability of seed, one had better order one or other of the named clones, such as 'Pink Cloud' or 'Rosea'. Plant it in full sun in any reasonable soil, including chalk, for which it is one of the very best plants.

Pruning means no more than the normal rule for early-flowering deciduous shrubs, cutting back the flowered shoots of each stem after blossom-fall (Fig. 10) and amputating exhausted stems to the ground or to a good new growth. Propagation is by cuttings of half-ripened shoots in gentle bottom heat. z4.

LAURUS
Bay or *Laurel*

The tree laurel or bay, employed by the Romans to adorn the brows of heroes or, when berried, for poets (as in poet laureate and the French baccalauréat) and by the modern cook to give pungency to a casserole, is *Laurus nobilis.*

59. Pruning Kerria japonica. After blossom-fall prune to ground level or to promising new buds low down. The two outside shoots in the sketch are new growths, to be retained

The "laurel" of common speech is something else, either the aucuba or the "Portuguese laurel", which is a prunus.

If allowed, the bay will grow 40ft or higher, but it is one of the easiest shrubs to restrain according to one's needs, for it suffers the knife with equanimity, as you may see in the trim little specimens in tubs outside the doors of restaurants. But you must trim it patiently in May with secateurs, please, not hedging shears. Within the axils of its dark green, aromatic leaves, the bay breaks into clusters of small, yellow flowers in April and black berries follow on a female tree if pollinated by a male. Try a pair at your front door or a slightly larger pair as sentinels at the entrance to your drive.

If cut by a particularly hard frost or seared by ocean winds, the bay sprouts again readily when pruned back, even to the ground. z7.

Laurus azorica is even larger still and, as you would suppose, much more tender, but 50ft specimens are to be seen in the south of England. z9.

LAURUSTINUS. See *Viburnum tinus*

LAVANDULA
Lavender

It might well surprise you, Reader, to learn that this apparently simple friend of old days, grown in the gardens of Europe for many centuries, is, to the botanist, a very complicated creature, of which there has been a great deal of name-swapping and discarding. But we shall strive to be simple and are helped to be so by the botanical conclusion that most of the lavenders that we grow in gardens are hybrids. We are left with very few species and are expected to forget such old names as *vera, officinalis* and *spica*, though they are still used by some good nurseries.

Lavenders have all kinds of virtues in addition to their aroma. They will grow in almost any soil that is not water-logged, flowering best in a poor, stony one, are pretty drought-hardy and are first-class seaside plants. Their grey-tinted foliage is soothing to the eye and they make splendid dwarf hedges.

To prevent them from becoming straggly, however, you must prune them regularly. When the blossom has fallen, cut back the spike and, next spring, trim over the shrub fairly sharply with shears. Propagation from cuttings in late summer is extremely easy, even in the open ground if in sandy soil in shade.

The general terms, the **Garden Forms** of lavender are hybrids between two species. One is now called *L. angustifolia*, a variable species formerly *spica* or *officinalis*, also known as the "true" or "common" or "old English" lavender, though grown more widely in France for extracting oil of lavender. The other parent is the spike lavender *L. latifolia*, likewise formerly known as *spica*; this has leaves a shade broader than the other, has a more slender spike, flowers three weeks later and adds a spice of camphor to its breath.

Unless one is a specialist, there is no point in growing either of these when their hybrids are to our hand. Those that begin to flower in June are the most strongly influenced by the true lavender, especially 'Hidcote', which is probably not a hybrid at all. For the average gardener and for general purposes, one need look no further than 'Hidcote'. All may still be listed in catalogues under *spica*. z5.

'Alba'. Nearly white. July. 2ft.

'Folgate'. Purple. July. 12in.

'Grappenhall'. Pale purple. Late July. 3ft.

'Hidcote'. Rich purple. Long, stems, spikes dense, leaves silver-touched. Exceptionally good. Introduced by Lawrence Johnson (see reference in Chapter 2). June. 15in. 'Nana Atropurpurea' is similar but paler. 'Hidcote Pink' is a wan pink.

'Hidcote Giant'. Resembles 'Grappenhall'. Sumptuous aroma.

'Loddon Pink'. Pale pink. July. 18in.

'Munstead'. Blue-purple. Late June. 18in.

'Twickel Purple'. Bold, open, the stems spread out. 2ft.

We turn now to the species, all of which are much less hardy and need a fairly hot sun.

L. dentata. Leaves green with a toothed edge, the pale flowers embraced by conspicuous bracts. Scent faint. For dry, rocky places. July. 2½ft. z9.

L. lanata. Woolly leaves. Flowers violet. Richly scented. 2ft. z9.

L. pedunculata. A handsome, grey-leaved lavender, with a short spike, of which the most conspicuous features are the violet bracts, which nearly conceal the purple corolla and which also crown the flower spike. For dry, chalky soils. 2½ft. z9.

L. stoechas, the robust, pine-scented French lavender, resembles *pedunculata*, being covered with a fine, grey down, and carrying a short, stumpy flower spike in which the purple bracts dominate the deeper purple, closely set florets and in which a tuft of leaf-like bracts surmounts the blossoms, in the manner of a pineapple. Grows in chalk and blossoms in April on its home ground, early summer elsewhere. 3ft. z9.

DISCARDED SPECIES

L. spica is an ambiguous name (*nomen ambiguum*) formerly used for both the true and the spike lavender. *L. vera* was often called the "Dutch" lavender, but is a superfluous name for inferior forms of *angustfolia*.

LAVATERA
Mallow

Simple, open-faced flowers in pink or purple among lobed leaves on plants of moderate size and fast growth with an astonishingly long season of bloom sums up these very useful but not very hardy shrubs, named after the Swiss brothers Lavater. Most of them are creatures of coastal regions, and enjoy the sea air, provided it is not icy, and are efficient guards of other plants against salt spray. The flowering stems shoot from at or near ground level in spring, so that the old ones ought to be cut back at that season nearly to the ground, as for hardy fuchsias and Russian sage. (Fig. 11). Their life is often short, but they are easily perpetuated by summer cuttings, potted up and over-wintered under glass. We have no concern here with the pretty herbaceous and annual species.

The one usually grown is **L. olbia**, a 7ft shrub with red-purple flowers from midsummer till November. It goes very well among herbaceous border plants. The form 'Rosea' is the best for colour. z8–9.

L. arborea, the tree mallow, assumes the likeness of a small tree of about 7ft. Grows wild along the western and southern coasts of Britain and the Atlantic seaboard of Europe. Flowers purple, in great abundance. There is an attractive form with vari-coloured leaves. z9.

L. assurgentiflora. The name means that the cerise flowers curve upwards. Native of the Santa Barbara and Santa Catalina islands. Used as a barrier against salty winds. Blooms all the year round, averaging 6ft.

L. maritima. Evergreen, averaging 4ft. Pale pink with crimson patch. May till November. Palmate, grey-hued leaves.

A compact form of Ledum groenlandicum, the 'Labrador tea', used as a cut flower

LEDUM

Except for the last named, these are small, tough, aromatic, sub-arctic, white-flowered evergreens of use in very cold, damp, lime-free places where nothing else will prosper. In mild conditions they are good companions for other shrubs that also need peaty, damp conditions. They produce new growth during and just after flowering. Behead the flower trusses carefully at blossom-fall.

The most favoured species is **L. groenlandicum**, the "Labrador tea", a pretty, 3ft, erect shrub, with rounded clusters of small white flowers carried at the tips of the stems in the manner of many daphnes from April till June. The fragrance is in the leaf. Its dwarf form 'Compactum' is a neat 18in. z2.

Similar but inferior, and having smaller leaves, is **L. palustre**, a marsh dweller, sometimes called the "wild rosemary". Young shoots furred as with rust. There are several geographical variants. z2.

L. glandulosum is florally much the same, but can reach 6ft and is much less hardy. There are better plants for its zone, which is 6.

LEIOPHYLLUM
Sand myrtle

L. buxifolium, akin to the ledums, is a small, very pretty evergreen shrub of up to 2ft for well-drained acid soil only. The leaves are small, rounded, glossy, dark green. The little flowers, blooming in May–June, are rose-pink in the bud, opening white, animated by the chestnut anthers of their numerous stamens, and clustered in small trusses in such profusion as almost to obscure the leaves. There are a few geographical variants, including a prostrate one forming close-packed pincushions. Behead the flower truss after blossoms fall. When the shrub gets old and shabby cut it back hard. z6.

LEPTODERMIS

Deciduous shrub of moderate size with tubular or funnelled flowers, some in lilac-form trusses in late summer, for all soils.

L. kumaonensis. 5–6ft, dark green, downy leaves, 2in long, a grey, peeling bark and clusters of small, slim trumpets, jasmine-like, white ageing to purple. July to October. For full sun in a sheltered place. z8–9.

L. oblonga. 3–4ft. Clusters of very small, violet tubes from July to September. z5–6.

L. pilosa. Averages 8ft. Flowers scented of daphne, lavender in colour, shaped like the florets of a lilac and collected in panicles also like a lilac. July till frost. z7.

L. purdomii. To 5ft. Long, wiry slender shoots, bending under the weight of their pink, lilac-form panicles in August and September. z7.

LEPTOSPERMUM

Delightful in their floral simplicity, but decidedly tender, some of the leptospermums of Australasia are charming shrubs for warm, maritime climates or warm walls in cooler ones, doing pretty well on the west or south coasts of Britain, in California and in similar places. The little flowers, seldom more than half an inch wide, cling closely to their stems and have five rounded petals, opening flat, within which is a tuft of stamens. The leaves are very slim and pointed, sometimes almost hair-like. The soil must be acid or neutral. Except for the varieties of the last named, which are decidedly the most popular, all have white flowers. Lots more botanical debate here about names.

L. flavescens. A rare species in northern latitudes, reaching 15ft in z9.

L. humifusum (or **rupestre**) begins as a ground-hugger, but can in time build up into a dense, 3ft mound with tiny, packed leaves.

L. lanigerum (or **pubescens**) is a variable and debatable species with hairy leaves, having at least two different forms, one of which is known horticulturally as *L. cunninghamii*; this starts to flower in late July, two weeks later than what is considered to be the type. z8.

L. liversidgei, the lemon-scented tea-tree, is a 10ft shrub of slender, stooping deportment, with small flowers in June and leaves scented of lemon if the climate is warm. z8–9.

L. rodwayanum. A tender, 10ft, grey-leaved shrub of arguable identity. Sometimes called *grandiflorum*, which Bean says is a variety of *flavescens*.

We are on surer ground when we come to **L. scoparium**, the manuka or tea-tree, from the fragrant leaves of which, it is said, Captain Cook's sailors made an infusion. It is a rangy, straggly 20ft shrub, with needle-like leaves, but what most gardeners are interested in are its numerous varieties and cultivars, which oddly seem to be a trifle more hardy than their parents and easily perpetuated by cuttings. Two natural varieties, with flowers and leaves slightly larger than usual, are *eximium* and the pink-tinted *incanum*. z8–9.

Of the cultivated forms, the usual favourite is 'Red Damask', a most attractive shrub that can reach 6ft, with doubled, red flowers in profusion. 'Ruby Glow', of the same Californian raising, is almost as good. Others of high quality are:

'Album Flore-pleno'. White double, erect.

'Boscawenii'. White with rose centre.

'Chapmanii'. Rose. Leaves tinted bronze. Hardier than most.

'Leonard Wilson'. White, double.

'Nichollsii'. Crimson. Of high class.

'Roseum'. Large pink, centre crimson.

'Nanum, pink, and 'Nicholsii Nanum' are cheerful dwarfs.

LESPEDEZA

Bush clover

Small pea-flowers, trifoliate leaves on semi-woody plants, of easy cultivation in any reasonable soil. They die down every winter but throw up a crowd of shoots in spring, flowering

60. Leptospermum scoparium

in late summer. Cut away the old, dead stems in spring.

L. bicolor. Rosy-purple racemes, 9ft. In warm places dies back only half-way. z4.

L. cyrtobotrya. Purple racemes, 3ft upwards. z5.

L. juncea. White umbels tinted blue, 3ft. September.

L. thunbergii. Elegant and luxuriant, averaging 6ft, arching and sweeping to 10ft in width, its slender stems bowed down by their mass of rose-purple panicles in September. z6. *L. japonica* is a white version; October.

LEUCOTHOË

Small, choice, usually evergreen shrubs for moist, peaty, acid soils and a moist atmosphere in part-shade. They have dark green, glossy, leathery leaves and from their branches dangle little clusters of the most charming, white, tiny doll's bells or cups, like those of the lily-of-the-valley. Not a beginner's plant unless he has the ideal conditions.

We think that the most beautiful leucothoë is **L. davisiae** (commemorating a Miss Davis), for it is a neat, sturdy little shrub of up to 3ft, holding its clustered, erect racemes well above the foliage in June. z5.

It is under challenge, however, from the new American clone 'Scarletta', in which the leaves turn crimson in the autumn, remain so all winter, turn green again in spring, when a new crop of crimson leaves appears. $2\frac{1}{2}$ft.

L. fontanesiana (better known as **catesbaei**) is quite different, having a drooping posture with very long (6in) leaves drawn out to a fine point, which partially obscure the little bunches of flowers, unless propped up in some seemly way. It spreads by underground stems. Cut out the old ones occasionally. It grows anything from 3ft to 6ft, flowering in May–June. There are forms with variegated leaves — 'Rainbow' and 'Trivar' — and a dwarf. z4.

L. axillaris. Resembles the above but is less hardy, more dwarf and compact. The leaves are more blunted. z6.

L. keiskei. 3ft. Zigzag branches, slender, graceful habit, flowers larger than most but not abundant. z5.

L. populifolia. Elegant foliage plant, sparsely flowered, hollow-stemmed. 4ft or more. z6–7.

L. racemosa. Erect shrub, 6–10ft. Abundant flowers tinted pink in May–June, satisfied with fairly dry soil and naturally a woodlander. z5.

LEYCESTERIA

Nicknamed "Elisha's tears" by old-time gardeners in England and commemorating William Leycester, who was Chief Justice of

Bengal in the days of British rule and a keen horticulturist, *L. formosa* is a Victorian shrub of no great distinction but often of practical use and of fast growth. From its green, hollow, leafy stems, hang down, in the manner of catkins, curious streamers composed of leafy, wine-tinted bracts, from which peep out very small, stalkless pale mauve flowers from July to September, when they fructify as tiny, rose-purple gooseberries. Much used in Britain as cover for pheasants, who like the berries. The stems break out freely from the base and reach their full 5–6ft in one season. Cut out all the old, flowered stems almost to the ground in spring. Easily propagated from its abundant seed. z7–8.

L. crocothyros is quite different and a much more tender creature, having arching, terminal spikes, 6in long, of small trumpets in rich yellow, without the bracts, and slenderly pointed leaves. z9–10.

LIGUSTRUM
Privet

If, Reader, your acquaintance with privets is limited to hedges of *Ligustrum vulgare* or *L. ovalifolium*, you must read on a little for there are some 10 hardy species of privet, though we shall name only a handful. The factor common to all is that their flowers are white or off-white, not of the choicest perfume, followed by black or blue-black berries if unpruned. Most are deciduous. All fulfil themselves as freestanding shrubs rather than as hedges and as such we describe them. They will grow under almost any conditions.

L. delavayanum. 6ft. Evergreen, of good texture, flat-topped and so good for hedging. (Others should be rounded or ridged). z7.

L. × bolium. Vigorous hybrid from *ovalifolium × obtusifolium*, reaching 12ft. Valuable for its hardiness, and for hedging. z4.

L. japonicum. Very distinctive. Large, deep green, glossy, camellia-like leaves. Flowers in large, pyramidal, lilac-form trusses. Averages 10ft. 'Lustreleaf' is a selected form,

'Macrophyllum' has broad leaves. Ignore 'Rotundifolium'. z7.

L. lucidum. Often confused with the above, because it also has large, dark green leaves, but is far more powerful. Seen at its best as a free-growing specimen, when it will develop into a very fine tree of up to 50ft, covered in August and September with big, erect panicles of white. A splendid street tree when grown on a single trunk. Good variegated forms are the yellow-edged 'Excelsum Superbum' and 'Tricolor', pink edges turning white. z7.

L. obtusifolium. A very ornamental, deciduous shrub, exceptionally hardy, of graceful deportment and luxuriant foliage. Of special interest in its variety *regelianum*, the Regel privet, which throws out its branches horizontally up to a height of about 4½ft and is exceptionally tolerant of the polluted air and poor soil of inner cities. z3, but much better in warmer climes. Named after a Russian called Regel.

L. ovalifolium. Known in America for some reason as the "California privet", but is, in fact, Japanese, and is grown for thousands of suburban miles in Britain and western Europe as a hedge. Part-evergreen, according to the climate. Better than the "common privet", though itself common enough. 'The "golden privet" is 'Aureum'. Watch for reversion. z5.

L. sinense. Notable for its foaming masses of flowers in July. Part-evergreen, 12ft. Used also for hedges and favoured as such in hot cities. 'Multiflorum' is even more flowerful. Var. stautonii is smaller. z7.

L. × vicaryi. The great merit of this hybrid privet is that it retains its bright golden leaves all the season. It is one of the few golden shrubs to do so in a hot, continental climate. Very fine hedger. Occurred in the garden of the late Hon. Vicary Gibbs at Aldenham. Believed to be *ovalifolium* 'Aureum' × *vulgare*. 12ft. z5.

LILAC. See *Syringa*

LINDERA

Big, aromatic shrubs for acid soils. Some become tree-like and are too big for us, especially as male and female flowers occur on separate plants. Black or coloured berries on females if fertilized. Good foliage shrubs, especially in the fall, otherwise undistinguished. In China some species are used for making joss sticks. Ensure a good initial framework, as in Fig. 8.

The most accommodating is the **L. benzoin**, the "spice bush", averaging 12ft, rounded in outline. Clusters of greeny-yellow flowers in April. Berries red, juicy, $\frac{1}{2}$in long. Leaves very pungent if crushed, deciduous. z4.

Also of manageable size and more attractive, though it may reach 25ft, is **L. praecox**. Flowers again greeny-yellow. Leaves oval, deciduous. Berries chestnut. z6.

LIPPIA CITRIODORA
Lemon-scented verbena

With respect, we do not here follow Bean for the name of this old favourite. We are told that it should now be *Aloysia triphylla*, but we prefer the old, more euphonious and more expressive one, which is still actively in use by the best people. It has, indeed, had several other aliases imposed upon it.

Of all the plants whose leaves one loves to pluck for their sweet odours, none is more ambrosial than the lemon verbena. It subtly combines the aromas of both the verbena and the lemon, breathing, as it might have seemed to Keats, of the warm South and sunburnt mirth.

Unfortunately for other counties, it is the warm South that it prefers, but it will be content enough in z8 if it can bask in "sunburnt mirth" on a hot wall, but z9–10 is much safer. It has, however, a strong will to survive and, in Britain, when cut back by a severe winter often regenerates from the base. One thinks of it in old southern cottage gardens, snugly ensconced

in an outdoor inglenook and breathing sweetly as it strokes the passer-by.

The lemon-scented verbena is deciduous and not often seen more than 12ft high. In August it bears slender panicles of small, tubular, pale purple flowers, which will win no prizes.

LONICERA
Honeysuckle

The climbing honeysuckles, or woodbines of Shakespeare, are not our concern. Of the bushy ones there are cohorts, but many are so like one another, or have so little merit for garden and landscape purposes, that there is no point in calling the whole roll, so we detail only those of special character or merit. In Britain many of them are not happy, and, indeed, are not widely appreciated, because we have so many more alluring shrubs on display in the honeysuckle season, which is short and usually in May. But in very cold regions, even sub-arctic ones, they earn our regard.

The flowers of the shrubby honeysuckles are tubular with prominent lips or are bells. After them come small, fleshy berries of one colour or another, quickly gobbled up by birds. In small gardens they may be awkward customers, many of them flinging their arms very wide and being of limited ornamental value when not in flower. A few are evergreen or partially so, according to the climate. The botanical name comes from the old-time German naturalist Lonizer.

Give the shrubs a good loamy soil; fairly moist. They grow well in some shade but are happier in sun. They throw up shoots freely from the base, so that the only pruning you need do is as for deutzias (Fig. 43) and to cut exhausted shoots hard down to a promising new growth. Propagate the deciduous sorts by simply sticking a twig in the open ground after leaf-fall or in early spring, the evergreens by ordinary cuttings in August, or the true species by seed.

The general favourite is the sweet, winter-flowering *fragrantissima*, but *tatarica* is a better all-rounder. Others in high standing are *maackii*, *korolkowii* and *morrowii*. Take May as the flowering time for all, the berries red and the foliage deciduous, unless we note otherwise.

L. × amoena 'Arnoldiana'. 9ft. Flowers blush. A graceful plant with delicate leaves. A clone listed as 'Rosea' by Hilliers of Winchester may be the same thing. Both are *tatarica × korolkowii*. z5.

L. × bella. An erect 6ft, fast-growing. Flowers blush fading yellow. Several clones, such as 'Candida', white, and 'Rosea', deep pink. A hybrid from *morrowii × tatarica*. z4.

L. chaetocarpa. A neat, erect 6ft. Flowers yellow, like winter jasmine, in June. Leaves oval, bristly. z5.

L. chrysantha. Erect, ornamental, extra hardy, 10ft. Twin, pale yellow flowers. Berries coral. In *regeliana* the flowers are a deeper colour. Other variants differ in leaf. z3.

L. deflexicalyx. 9ft, gracefully spreading, flowers yellow, well and profusely displayed on upper side of feathery branches in June. Berries orange. z5.

L. fragrantissima. This is the popular sweet-scented honeysuckle of winter, flowering continuously but not profusely from December to March (much later in USA). The cream-white flowers come on twigs from stems grown in the previous season, 7ft high, with stiff, leathery leaves, half-evergreen, good in cities. Not a choice plant at other seasons, so drape it with one of the shorter clematis, such as *C. × durandii*. z5.

L. korolkowii, the blue-leaf honeysuckle. One of the best, 10ft high, with blue-tinted leaves, but widely spread. Flowers rose, two-lipped, in June, not always produced in abundance. Berries orange. z5.

L. maackii podocarpa. Exceptionally hardy, of great vigour, reaching 15ft and spreading widely, with large, dark green leaves. Fragrant white flowers, yellowing, and brilliant red berries in profusion. z2.

L. morrowii. A dense mound, 6ft high and twice as wide. Flowers cream. Excellent for mass planting along highways and on banks.

Berries yellow on the variety *Xanthocarpa*. z4.

L. nitida. This is the familiar Chinese honeysuckle with very small, dense, dark, evergreen leaves, much used and abused for hedging. Grown in isolation, it becomes a shrub of about 10ft, with scented, cream flowers and purple berries. There are several varieties and a confusion of names. For an open-ground plant take 'Fertilis', distributed by Hilliers, or the gleaming 'Baggesen's Gold'. For a hedge, either 'Fertilis' or plain 'Yunnan'. Avoid 'Ernest Wilson', the common "nitida" of the nursery trade. Tailor trimly, clip frequently and feed generously. Can be cut to the ground if shabby. Very easy from cuttings. z7.

L. × purpusii. Sweetly scented flowers in February. 10ft high but broader, resembling its parent *fragrantissima*. z5.

L. quinquelocularis, the mistletoe honeysuckle, 12ft. Of interest for its white, translucent berries, the seed visible within. Flowers cream. z5.

L. standishii. Another valued for its scent all winter, but florally inferior to *fragrantissima*. 8ft. Bristly-edged leaves. z5. Evergreen in warmer zones.

L. tatarica. Perhaps the best of all, extremely hardy, very drought-resistant. Flowers blush, not fragrant. Named clones excel the parent. Fine displays are made by the red 'Zabelii', 'Arnold Red' and the Canadian 'Hack's Red'. In 'Lutea' the berries are yellow and 'Morden Orange', also from Canada, speaks for itself. 'Virginalis' has the largest flowers, in rose-pink. z3.

L. thibetica. Begins low and spreading, developing as a dense, twiggy and rounded mass, 5ft high but 10ft wide. Good on a slope. Flowers lilac in colour and in scent. A good choice. z4.

LOQUAT. See *Eriobotrya*

LOROPETALUM

L. chinense may be described as a white-flowered witch hazel, but with oval, pointed, evergreen leaves, 2in or less in length, somewhat tender. Not often more than about 6ft high, with its lateral twigs crooked, it blooms profusely in March and prefers an acid or neutral soil. z8–9.

LUPINUS
Lupin

The "tree" lupins, which have the same sort of pea-flowers as their herbaceous brethren, are very pretty, long-flowering and of luxuriant growth, well suited to small gardens and of the easiest culture. The compound leaves are composed of several finger-like leaflets ("digitate"). They like the sea and their native home is in the wind-swept sands of California.

The usual one is the evergreen **L. arboreus**, of 6 to 8ft, which grows very fast and flowers madly from late May to August, if in full sun. The flowers are nearly always yellow and faintly scented, carried in erect spikes averaging 8in tall. Such is its exuberance of flower and seed that it exhausts its life in four to five years, unless you prune away its vast quantities of seed-pods and if the soil is not too rich. Easily perpetuated by heel cuttings in summer in mild heat or by its own seed in sandy soil. 'Golden Spire' is deep gold and 'Snow Queen' white. Other colours are also to be had. Plant in spring, using small specimens. z7–8.

L. chamissonis is a 3ft dwarf with silvery leaves engagingly ornamented with flowers of lavender and blue. All possible sun. z9.

LYCIUM
Box-thorn

Lax, rambling, usually spiny shrubs of value for clothing banks, especially sandy ones, and enlivening waste ground. The name is from the Greek *Lykion*, a thorny shrub.

The Chinese box-thorn, **L. barbarum**, has become naturalized in many parts of the world

Loropetalum chinense

and so is very variable. In Britain it sprouts in seaside cliffs and in cottage walls. Small, purple funnels, May to July, then a splendid display of brilliant scarlet berries. It abounds with aliases, of which *chinense* and *halimifolium* are the best known, but Kew herbarium shows that all are forms of the variable *barbarum*. z4.

Several other box-thorns are fearful entanglements of identities, as well as of growth, but **L. pallidum** is distinctive and quite decorative, having slim trumpets of green flushed with purple, dangling from spreading, spiny and often tortuous branches. Berries sparse. z5–6.

From South America comes **L. chilense**, a 5ft tangle with small mauve and yellow flowers and small red fruits.

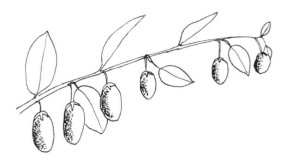

61.   The red berries of the Chinese box-thorn,
Lycium barbarum

LYONIA

Closely related to the pieris, and endowed with
the same pendulous clusters of ivory, lily-of-
the-valley flowers, but not quite up to the
standard of that sumptuous genus. Plant in a
woodsy or peaty, rather damp soil. Leaves oval,
dark green, glossy and mostly deciduous.
Flowers borne on last season's stems, often at
their tips. Named after the eighteenth-century
explorer John Lyon, who discovered it in the
Eastern USA.

The best, we think, is *L. mariana*, the stagger-
bush, of 6ft, the flowers profuse, continuous
from May to early July and sometimes blushing. Succeeds in acid, boggy ground. z5.

The least attractive, but extremely hardy, is
L. ligustrina, flowering June and July. z3. In
between come the evergreen, rather lax *L.
lucida*, flowering in late spring, z7, and the big,
tree-like, half-evergreen *L. ovalifolia*, also of
late spring and of which there are two dwarf
forms. z7–8.

MAGNOLIA

We have investigated the magnificent tree
forms of the magnolias in *The Trees Around Us*,
so here we have a much reduced plantation to
explore. The shrub forms, which are all deciduous, have not the same nobility, but they
can have an exhilarating influence in any scene,
large or small. They do not demand so much
faith in the future as the tree forms, which may
not flower for many years. Their name comes
from the seventeenth-century Frenchman
Pierre Magnol.

What one would naturally call the petal of
the magnolia is technically a tepal (an anagram
of petal), implying much the same thing as a
perianth, the petals and sepals being similar in
shape and size, though not fused together.
Within the waxen heart of these tepals is a
dense, hair-like circlet of stamens of brilliant
colours and thrust up through this mass is a
short pillar crowded with the carpels of the
female pistil, which gradually becomes
elongated.

A good start means everything. Some species
expect an acid soil, others are quite suited to
lime. Except in the warmer areas, choose a place
sheltered from whatever wind prevails, to save
their large and handsome leaves from being
"ribboned and rolled and torn" by rude winds.
The blossoms of those that flower early are
susceptible to damage by frost, so avoid frost-
pockets. The roots of all are fleshy and sensitive,
so that they must be planted when very young.
Spring is the best time, as the roots start into
activity. Prepare a hole of ample proportions –
at least 4ft wide and 8in deep. Enrich it with
organic matter and lace the top spit well with
peat or old, well-rotted leaf-soil to ease the way
for the roots. Handle the young plants with
care, for the stems as well as the roots are brittle,
and do not plant too deep. When returning the
soil firm it with care, but do *not* harshly stamp it
in with the heel, as so often wrongly advised.
Water copiously (itself a good way of firming).
Thereafter never harry the soil with a hoe, fork
or spade and allow no other plant to encroach
on its immediate root areas, except maybe for
the scattering of a few seeds of annuals. Mulch
heavily each autumn, with a fair sprinkling
underneath of a nitrogenous fertilizer or a
"complete" one free of lime.

Magnolias fork naturally from ground level,
thus often becoming very broad. If they encroach on to a path, prune the outermost
branches low down. They respond well to

pruning and regenerate readily if damaged wood has to be cut. Do the pruning at the end of July or early August, and protect cuts ½in or more with a dressing made for that purpose; the heartwood is soft.

Magnolias sometimes set seed in vast quantities, thereby seriously undermining their vitality. Tedious though it is, we ought therefore, within reason and within reach, to pick off the flowers as they wither.

The smallest magnolia is the popular star magnolia, **M. stellata**. The scented flower is made up of a quantity (up to eighteen) of very narrow, ribbon-like tepals, which unfold rather raggedly before reflexing. It flowers unfailingly and profusely in March and April on naked stems, beginning when about 10in high. Frost may kill the early blossom, but a second crop then usually breaks out. The deep pink from 'Rubra' is charming. 'Rosea' begins pink and turns to white. 'Waterlily' is pink in the bud, opening white, with longer and more numerous tepals. The new 'Centennial', from the Arnold Arboretum, is pure white, large and doubled. The star magnolia forms a widespread dome, its lower branches hugging the ground, not often more than 10ft high but capable of much more. Tolerates a little lime. z5. Some good authorities consider that stellata is not a true species but a dwarf form of the big M. kobus.

Another small magnolia, of totally different habit, being much less expansive than other species, is the lily magnolia, **M. liliiflora**, seen at its most handsome in the cultivar 'Nigra'. This is of the tulip-form species, the tepals being deep purple on the outside, white when open, often starting in late April and going on till June and even later. It seldom grows more than 9ft high and needs an acid soil. 'Gracilis' is a slender and erect form. z6.

Hybrids. An interesting new race of hybrids between *liliiflora* and *stellata* has recently been raised by the U.S. National Arboretum, Washington, and is in commerce. The best of these clones is the luxuriantly coloured 'Susan', a fairly large shrub of erect growth. The large tepals are deep red-purple on the outer surface

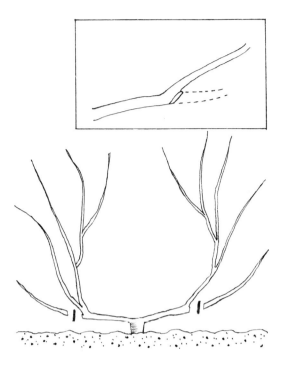

62. Pruning a ground-forking magnolia (or other shrub of similar behaviour) that is growing too wide. *Inset*: the actual cut

and the inner is white, stained a paler red-purple, in late April. Almost as good, according to report, is 'Betty', also flowering in late April, the outer surface of the tepal grey-purple at the base shading to red-purple at its tip, the inner surface white. In Britain 'Ricki' has also been good, having white tepals, flushed purple on the exterior. Other clones, both cup-shaped, are 'Jane', red-purple outside, white within, and 'Pinkie' of paler tone. All need a moderately acid soil and may be classed as z6.

The most generally popular of all the slightly larger magnolias is **M. × soulangiana** (*denudata* × *liliiflora*). In the best conditions this can become a 25ft tree, but for many years it will be no more than a broad shrub and a spectacular one too, flowering when quite young. Its opulent, erect, tulip-form flowers begin to open on naked branches in late April, making a superb shrub for town or country, tolerant of a mild element of lime and easy to cultivate.

There is a whole trugful of clones, of which

the favourite is 'Lennei', which has tepals of a rich rose-purple on the outside and white within. It flowers in May and occasionally later also. Other of the first order (all white within) are:

'Alexandrina'. White, flushed purple, but variable.

'Brozzonii'. Very large white.

'Picture'. Very long, red-purple tepals; will rival 'Lennei'.

'Rustica Rubra'. Rich, rosy-red.

'Speciosa'. White, tinted purple. Very free.

'Verbanica'. Rose-pink, late, usually escaping frost damage.

We turn now to three magnolias which, like the Soulange hybrid, can in time exceed 20ft but which are florally of quite a different character, being devised in the form of saucers or shallow bowls and which nod graciously at you as you approach, exhibiting brilliant profusions of carpels, so that, to get a good view of them, you should, if possible, plant them on slightly elevated ground.

The most beautiful, and one which, indeed, often does not become more than a large shrub, is **M. wilsonii**, named after the famous plant explorer who found it and so many other oriental treasures. The lovely, white bowls, encrusted within by a circle of brilliant crimson stamens, dangling on long stalks, are sweetly scented and open with the young, elliptical leaves in May. It can grow 8ft in six years from seed and comes into flower quite young. The elegant flowers are seen in their full beauty if you discourage the plant from its shrubby character by gradually suppressing all but the main stem until it is six feet tall, when a tree-like attitude develops.z5–6.

Not quite so demure but just as beautiful is **M. sinensis**, but it does spread excessively widely, though not more than 20ft high. The flowers, large, fragrant, white, purple-centred, come out seven or eight years from seeding. Thrives in limy soils, including chalk. z7.

Probably a hybrid between the two above species is **M. × highdownensis**, remarkable for thriving in chalk and having originated in the famous chalk garden "Highdown" of the

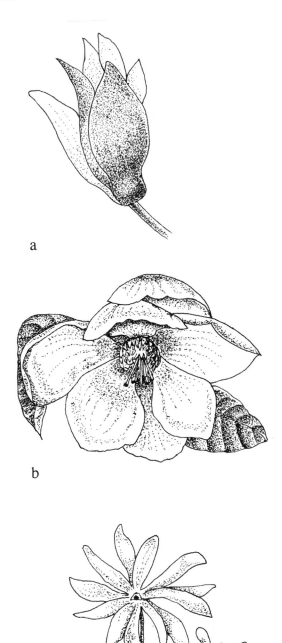

a

b

c

63.   (*a*) Magnolia liliflora nigra; (*b*) Magnolia wilsonii; (*c*) Magnolia stellata

late Sir Frederick Stern in Sussex. The leaves are like those of wilsonii and the flowers like sinensis.

Another bowl-shaped magnolia is **M. sieboldii**, a large, wide-spreading shrub. The flowers, though displayed on long stalks, have not the same modest bearing, but look boldly straight at you. They are scented and the tepals are concave and, in the best form, enclose a tonsure of rose-crimson stamens. They blossom intermittently for two months from early June and fructify as brilliant red seeds. z6.

Very like sieboldii but not of the same quality, is **M. × watsonii**, recognisable by its short, stout flower stalks, the rose tint of its tepals, its powerfully aromatic breath and its stiff carriage. It blooms freely in June and July. z5–6.

On the borderline between a tree and a shrub is **M. virginiana**, the "sweet bay". In Britain and the southerly parts of the USA it is tree-like and evergreen; in sterner climates a deciduous shrub. The rather small, waxy flowers form bowls, richly scented, from June to September. The leaves, blue-washed underneath, are aromatic and last well into winter. z5.

We take this opportunity of briefly mentioning a remarkable new hybrid with yellow, tulip-form flowers raised by the Brooklyn Botanical Gardens. This is **M. 'Elizabeth'**, begotten by heptapeta out of acuminata, flowering in April and May with 9in leaves. After 22 years the plant, trimly pyramidical, is about 19ft high at the time of writing, so will probably in time become quite a large tree. z5–6.

X MAHOBERBERIS

We enter this race of hybrids between a mahonia and a berberis only as a matter of record. It is inferior to both of its parents. The best is × M. aquisargentii, an erect evergreen, 6ft high, we have seen it hitherto, curious rather than beautiful, with spiny, bronze-tinted leaves of diverse shapes and flowers of soft yellow, followed by

black berries. Another, known shortly as miethkeana, raised in Tacoma, Washington, is similar.

MAHONIA

Prickly, evergreen leaves and very small yellow flowers in bunches or sprays, nearly all borne in winter or early spring, are the marks of these very useful and often very handsome shrubs. They adapt themselves to any reasonable soil, including chalk, and are among the best shrubs for planting in quite deep shade of deciduous trees, except for some species from the southern regions of North America. They range from ground-huggers (which are not our business) to big, bold specimens with enormous, pinnate leaves as prickly as holly, notably the expensive clones of M. × media, which dominate the modern scene, though there are plenty of others for both decorative and useful purposes, particularly, we suggest, M. undulata. Some are rather tender. Mahonias submit willingly to pruning, even hard pruning, and if one of the bigger sorts throws out an obstructive limb, its yellow wood can be amputated at ground level or at a growth point near it. They take their name from the eighteenth-century American Bernard M'Mahon. All leaves pinnate, all inflorescences composed of tiny yellow cups.

The biggest is the tender **M. acanthifolia**, which can exceed 20ft, with leaves 2ft or more long and often comprised of 27 leaflets. The spectacular flower sprays may also be 2ft long, starting erect, then swooping downwards and finally tilting up at the tips, in autumn.

M. aquifolium, the "Oregon holly-grape", is an everyman's shrub, particularly valuable for growing in quite heavy shade under trees. Normally about 3ft high, but sometimes taller, it flowers from February to May and spreads by suckers, making a good ground-cover thicket and tolerant of the most unpromising conditions. Blue-black berries, like small grapes, follow the flowers. Of its various selections, 'Atropurpurea' has red-purple leaves in autumn, 'Compacta' and the Mayhan strain are dwarfs. z5.

M. bealei is a stout shrub of 6ft or more, with stiff stems and big, lustrous leaves, which may be 18in long and composed of 19 spiny leaflets, each about 2in long. The floral performance is a bold, brush-like cluster of long, erect, slightly spreading spikes at the tips of the stems, sweetly scented and produced in mid-winter. z6.

Nowadays Beale's mahonia (named for Mr T. C. Beale, in whose Shanghai garden it was brought on last century) is considered by many to be less ornamental than **M. japonica**. To the gardener the only difference between the two is that japonica is a little less hardy and that, instead of erect bunches, it displays itself in long, lax, drooping sprays, richly scented. Both are fine shrubs and will flourish under quite heavy tree-shade, like aquifolium, but are more luxuriant in sun. Prune after blossom-fall if they become overpowering. z7–8.

M. fremontii. A handsome shrub from Texas and thereabouts with blue-green leaves. The leaflets are stalkless, except for the terminal one. Pale yellow flowers in spikes, 2 to 3in long. Very variable in height, averaging 7ft. Full sun in this case. z6.

M. haematocarpa, of about 9ft, strongly resembles Fremont's mahonia, but is "special" for its juicy, blood-red berries, from which jam is made. Full sun. z7–8.

M. 'Heterophylla'. Very like aquifolium, but with curiously twisted leaflets. Many aliases.

Of greater floral splendour than any of these, but tender, is **M. lomariifolia**, which stands 10ft or more high. Of the same general character as Beale's mahonia, it throws up a cluster of very bold, erect, cylindrical, truncheon-like spikes. There may be twenty such spikes in a cluster, each one up to 8in long. The leaves may be 2ft long, with 18½ leaflets, stalkless and spiny. A very handsome fellow. z8–9.

M. × media is the name now given to a clutch of superlative hybrids begotten by japonica out of lomariifolia in England, including second generation seedlings. The best-known is 'Charity', the original plant of which now stands 15ft high in the Savill Garden, Windsor Great Park, blossoming in succession all winter, with quantities of spreading flower spikes in lemon-yellow a foot or more long. 'Charity' has produced some notable offspring of its own, including the bright yellow 'Hope' and the soft-tinted 'Faith'. Both very fine, with more to follow.

In our opinion, however, these Windsor mahonias (which originated, in fact, in Northern Ireland) are excelled by 'Lionel Fortescue', raised by the skilled gardener of that name in Devonshire. Not yet easy to come by, this throws out gorgeous, golden sheaves of branching spikes, 16in long. 'Buckland' is another splendid clone by the same raiser. The erect 'Winter Sun' raised in Northern Ireland, is also of high order. z8–9.

M. nevinii. 7–8ft. Small, slim leaves only 2½in long with five leaflets, tinted pink when young. Flowers in loose clusters. Egg-shaped, blue-black berries. From California.

M. trifoliata glauca. Unique in having almost white, spear-like leaflets, only three to the leaf. Flowers in bunches (corymbs), fruits black with blue bloom. Stiff growth to about 7ft. From Texas mainly.

M. undulata. An excellent, decorative mahonia for all sorts of uses, not as well known as it deserves to be. One could describe it, in appearance, as resembling aquifolium, but slim, 6ft tall, with flowers of rich, deep yellow in abundance in spring and glossy, wavy-edged leaves. Rarely suckers. z7–8.

We by-pass those mahonias that are of dubious identity and uncertain behaviour, such as *pinnata* and *schiedeana*.

MAPLE. See *Acer*

MELIOSMA

The name is mongrel Greek for "honey-scented", though not all are. The meliosmas, which derive mainly from China and are often quite big trees, are characterized by large, pyramidal plumes, in the semblance of an astilbe or some spiraeas, crowded with quantities of small, white or off-white florets. Their leaves have diverse forms and they are not very hardy. We shall consider only the shrub forms, all deciduous, all scented and all simple-leaved with bristly edges. All z8.

The most accommodating is **M. pendens**, a graceful 16ft, bearing dangling plumes at the tips of the branches in July.

M. cuneifolia. To 20ft. Leaves 6in long. Flowers in July. A good choice.

M. parviflora (not *parvifolia*) is a little taller, with small leaves, flowering sparsely in August.

M. myriantha. Up to 20ft, with minute, very fragrant, creamy flowers in 6in trusses in July.

MENZIESIA

Some lovely little aristocrats mingle with rather plain commoners in this mixed breed, which takes its name from the surgeon-botanist, Archibald Menzies, who discovered so many American and other plants when serving in the British naval survey expedition led by Captain Vancouver in the 1790s.

Menziesias call for a moist, acid, peaty or loamy soil, not in heavy shade, and, like many other plants accustomed to such conditions, produce dainty little bell-flowers resembling lily-of-the-valley. They are deciduous.

The choicest species, however, are not the Americans — *M. ferruginea* (which was the one found by Menzies), *pentandra, pilosa* and *glabella* — but the Japanese, so we are left with only a handful, all probably z6.

The usual one is **M. ciliicalyx**, especially its variety *purpurea*, a charming little shrub of about 2½ft, with small leaves grouped at the ends of the twigs and small, nodding pale purple bells in May.

Unfortunately there is also a species called **M. purpurea**, which causes much confusion. This can be a much bigger and even finer shrub, in which the hanging bells are bright red rather than purple, the brightest coloured of all the menziesias, flowering in May and June, yet

plants sold under this name are more often *M. ciliicalyx purpurea*.

Also very like ciliicalyx is *M. multiflora*, in which the flowers vary from white to pale purple.

MESPILUS. See *Amelanchier*

MEZEREON. See *Daphne mezereum*

MICHELIA

Large, rather tender, evergreens, some tree-like, resembling magnolias, but bearing their flowers in the axils of the leaves not at the tips of the stems. Named after the Italian botanist Micheli. For acid soils.

We have to note only **M. figo** (*fuscata*), a shrub that averages 15ft. The young leaves are coated as with rust, becoming dark, glossy green. Flowers green-white, flushed purple, of no great beauty but of the richest fruity scent, sparsely but continuously borne all summer. Rated z7–8 by Dr Wyman in America (where it is called the "banana-bush") but in our experience is more like z9.

MIMULUS

The popular annuals and perennials of the "monkey flowers" have a few shrubby brethren for warm places. M. aurantiacus is an evergreen of 4ft or more, with narrow, shining, dark green leaves and trumpets of bright yellow or orange, 1in long, opening successively all summer. *M. puniceus* differs only in having red flowers. z9.

MYRICA
Gale or *Bayberry*

Known especially for the spicy aroma exuded by their leaves rather than for their beauty of flowers, these are very tough shrubs best thought of as plants for the open and informal scene rather than the conventional one. They are hung with uni-sexual catkins but sometimes male and female catkins grow on the same plants. A few, such as the waxy-fruited *M. californica* and *cerifera*, soar up to trees of 30ft and more, and so are not our business. Their culture is easy.

M. gale is the deliciously aromatic sweet-gale or bog-myrtle of Britain and Europe. Of arctic hardiness, it is a small bog plant, spreading by suckers, with warm, golden-brown catkins in spring, males and females on separate plants. Cut tall and straggly branches right down to the ground. Z1.

M. pensylvanica, the bayberry, almost as hardy, is a half-evergreen shrub of 9ft from Newfoundland, eastern Canada and southwards, with matt-green but richly aromatic leaves and bearing white or grey waxen berries, from which candles are made. It thrives in a poor, sandy acid soil and beside the sea. Males and females on separate plants. Z2.

MYRICARIA

M. germanica is a useful plant for river banks and other places of light soil liable to occasional inundation. Very small, pink florets are carried in loose, 6in spikes at the tips of erect wands beset with tiny, blue-green leaves, having the semblance of plumes throughout summer. Tolerates lime, but prefers acidity. It flowers on the current year's growth and becomes ungainly if not very hard pruned in early spring. Z5. *M. dahurica* differs only slightly.

MYRTUS
Myrtle

To Goethe the myrtle belonged to the lands "Where the wind ever soft from the blue heaven blows". To Byron (as one might expect) it spoke of passion and for English brides a sprig of the common myrtle traditionally added a spice to her bouquet. Yet myrtles other than the "common" or European species luxuriate in the south-west corner of England and in Ireland, where the winds are by no means "ever soft"; one prostrate species (*M. nummularia*) endures the icy blasts of the Falkland Islands. We think that, when considering the hardiness of myrtles, a moist atmosphere has to be taken into account, for certainly they like the sea air.

Apart from the European species, myrtles originate mainly from Chile and New Zealand. When the conditions are right they are of easy culture, some becoming quite large. Any well-drained soil, including chalk, will suit them and they will endure considerable drought. They are evergreen, the leaves usually very small, dense and breathing a sweet incense, thus making one of the best of hedges in warm climates. The flowers consist of a fuzzy throng of stamens, often tipped with yellow anthers, such petals as there are being always white, except in one instance. Small, juicy berries follow, often edible.

If planted in the open myrtles must be given a place in full sun. In doubtful climates they will stand a good chance against a warm wall, planted 18in away from it. As a rule they break freely from ground level, and if apparently killed by frost will break afresh from the base, when you must cut the old stems right back. Otherwise no pruning unless a branch becomes obstructive, then cut back well inside the shrub, to conceal the wound, in spring.

By far the most widely grown and the most hardy is **M. communis**, the myrtle of the ancients, to whom it was an emblem of the Goddess of Love. Normally it grows to about 10ft, frothing with blossom in July and August, with 2in leaves, fragrant in both flower and leaf, and inky berries in the fall. You will remember that Milton went out to "shatter your leaves before the mellowing year", and we still today shatter them in the hand to savour their aroma.

There are several variants, of which the most attractive is a clone of the natural variety

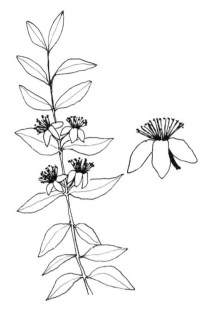

64. Myrtus communis

Myrtus communis, the common myrtle

tarentina called 'Jenny Reitenbach'. This is a charming, wind-hardy, dwarfish, compact shrub with a fine pattern of small leaves and white berries. In 'Flore Pleno' the flowers are double and in 'Variegata' the leaves are edged cream.

Splendid as a wall plant, the common myrtle can, as seen in Devonshire, shoot up to the very eaves of a small house, if clipped every spring and perhaps later also. Cuttings root quite easily in gentle heat. z8–9.

Other myrtles, discovered only after European man had begun to explore or to colonize, are less hardy and should be classified for z9–10. The leaves of all are very small. Consider *ugni*, which is distinctive.

M. bullata. To 15ft. Leaves puckered ("bullate") and chestnut-tinted. Black, egg-shaped berries.

M. chequen. Relatively hardy, densely clothed in very small leaves. Blooms late summer. Berries black. A big shrub.

M. lechlerana. A hefty, wind-hardy shrub clothed to the ground. Young leaves golden-brown, then green. Blooms May. Berries red, turning black, edible. In the famous National Trust garden at Nymans, in Sussex, it grows 25ft, and at Trewithen, in Cornwall, is a stunning hedge of the same height. z9.

M. luma (or *apiculata*) is the "tree myrtle" of superlative beauty, with a gleaming cinnamon bark, peeling to reveal its pale new skin, over which hangs a snow-like canopy of multitudinous little flowers. As it ages "the trunk has a sinuous grace and power rivalled only by the Madrona, the Californian *Arbutus*" (Arnold-Forster, *op. cit.*). In such climates as those of Cornwall and Ireland it reaches nearly 30ft, seeding freely and "going native". The purple berries are sweet and edible. z9.

M. obcordata. A graceful shrub of 15ft, neat and twiggy, but sparing of flowers. Berries dark red or violet.

M. ugni, the "Chilean guava". A shrub of 6ft or so, slow, erect and stiff in growth, with pale pink, bell-like flowers, followed by aromatic berries of a mahogany colour and a wild-strawberry flavour. Wind-hardy. z9.

Nandina domestica

NANDINA

Nandina domestica, the "sacred bamboo" of China, looks like a bamboo hung with red or purple berries in autumn and winter. It is not in fact a bamboo. The long, erect stems, up to 8ft tall, carry multiple-pinnate leaves, the leaflets loosely dispersed, slim, fine-pointed, lance-like, darkly evergreen, tinted red in spring and a deeper hue in autumn. At the tips of the stems are plumes of small white florets in July, before fructifying.

The nandina must have a fairly moist soil of good quality in sun, protected from cold winds. A rough winter may knock it about, in which event cut damaged shoots right to the ground in spring; for it does not branch and new stems will come from the base.

There is a white-fruited clone and an attractive dwarf, 'Nana Purpurea', which has purple-tinted leaves all the year. The name is an adaptation of the Japanese Nanden. Propagation by any method is slow and uncertain. z7–8.

NEILLIA

Long, slim, elegant sprays of small, tubular flowers emerge from bright green, heavily veined leaves with toothed edges on spreading, slightly zigzag branches. Deciduous and of easy culture in all but very dry soils. Named for the Scottish naturalist Patrick Neill.

Pruning. New stems shoot freely from the base; so, when the plant begins to age, cut worn-out stems right down to the ground and less mature ones part-way.

The best-known is **N. thibetica** (or **longi-racemosa**, now declared by Authority to be synonymous), a pretty shrub of 6ft or so. The slender flower sprays are up to 6in long, massed with small, rose-pink tubes in May and June. The leaf is like a slender heart, drawn out to a fine point, heavily veined, the edges slightly toothed. z6.

N. sinensis is a trifle shorter, of equally graceful habit, but the nodding flower sprays, white or blush-pink, which appear in August and September, are only 2½in long. The leaves are finely toothed. z5.

N. thyrsiflora, of 3ft, is of neat and rounded form, with deeply incised leaves and rather insignificant spikes of white flowers in August–September. z7.

NEMOPANTHUS

N. mucronatus, the "mountain holly" of very cold regions of North America, is a deciduous shrub, averaging 6ft, with leaves like those of an almost spineless holly. Insignificant flowers in May June, followed by gay red berries after a hot summer. Fails in Britain except in the colder parts of Scotland. z3.

NEVIUSIA
Snow wreath

N. alabamensis is a deciduous shrub, averaging 5ft but wider, with erect stems, spreading branches and oblong, finely toothed leaves up to 3in long. The white flowers are a froth of feathery stamens, without petals, in May. Sometimes blooms lavishly, at other times sparingly. The shrub has a stool-like growth, spreading outwards as new canes arise. Cut back all decadent stems to ground level or to promising new growths low down after blossom-fall. Discovered by the Rev. R. D. Nevius. Flowers poorly in Britain. z5.

NOTHOPANAX. Now included in *Pseudopanax*

OLEARIA
Daisy bush

The daisy bushes are Australasians with very little resistance to cold weather and many of them have little or no ornamental value. They become smothered in due season with small daisy-form flowers, usually with a yellow central disc and white (or off-white) ray-florets and are sometimes pleasantly scented. The leaves of nearly all are coated underneath with a white, ashen or fawn felting. Some species form quite sizeable trees. They are among the best of all maritime plants, resisting sea salt and violent gales and being by all accounts hardier at the seaside than inland. This, indeed, is their best use, for they fit well into a wild and windy scene in the milder counties and look out of place in a formal picture. Rock and sand become them well and they make good "nurse" shrubs for the protection of more sensitive creatures.

You must, however, give them all the sun possible and plant them where their feet will not get very wet for long. They are excellent in chalk. One has to say, however, that when the daisies wither and give place to the dirty-grey or buff of their fluffy seeds the shrub can look very shabby. So you must crop them with the shears before that happens.

Olearias respond very willingly to more severe pruning also, so that old, worn-out shrubs can be cut back very hard in spring and so that damage from frost can be made good, if any growth develops low down. Propagation of the hardier sorts is fairly easy from half-ripe cuttings even without heat.

There is enormous variety among olearias but the most widely grown, because the most hardy, is **O. × haastii**, normally an 8ft shrub with leaves dark green and leathery on the obverse, white-felted on the reverse. It becomes smothered with its daisies in July and August, scented of hawthorn, but otherwise it is a dowdy, commonplace creature and should make way for hydrangeas, hypericums, etc. Parentage: *avicenniifolia* × *moschata*. Resistant to city fumes as to salt. z7–8.

Other daisy bushes are but precarious in our regions, yet succeed where there is some shelter, and many have flourished in Commander Dorrien-Smith's garden where the Scilly Isles ride the Atlantic and in similar places. The following have usually been found satisfactory in milder parts of z8, especially near the sea, but z9 is better. We omit those of little ornamental value.

O. avicenniifolia. Possibly 20ft. Leaves grey-green. Large, erect, rounded flower clusters, which soon lose colour. One of the hardiest. Said to be inferior to *O. albida*, but, according to Bean, the true albida is very rare.

O. ilicifolia. 10ft, spreading. Hard, leathery leaves, the edges wavy and sharply toothed (i.e. like holly, *Ilex*). Musk-scented flowers in June. z8–9.

O. × mollis, offspring of the above mated with *O. lacunosa*, 4–5ft high, of rounded outline, is a fine foliage shrub, with an overall aspect of silvery-grey. Leaves only slightly spined, densely coated on the reverse with white wool, and all young parts silvered. The clone 'Zennorensis', of 6ft, is better still, the spiny leaves olive on the obverse. z9.

O. macrodonta. 10ft or more. We think this the most handsome. Sage-green, holly-like leaves up to 5in long. Scented flowers in loose orbs in June. Crop it well as the flowers wither, or it will get leggy. 'Minor' is dwarf in all its parts, rarely flowering, 'Major' is the opposite (22ft high at Rowallane in N. Ireland). z8–9.

O. nummulariifolia. Almost as hardy as haastii, possibly 10ft. Very small, thick, leathery leaves, set very closely together on stiff branches. Off-white flowers in July scented of heliotrope. z8–9.

O. phlogopappa (or **gunniana**) is an aromatic May-flowering shrub of 9ft or more, which has given way to its progeny, next described. The strain known as Splendens has flowers of various colours, like Michaelmas daisies, but they are tender.

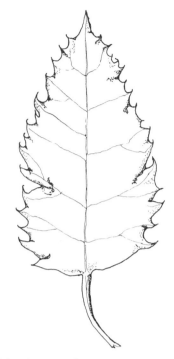

65.   Olearia macrodonta

Olearia macrodonta

O. × scilloniensis. This grey-green, fast-growing hybrid from the Scilly Isles has attracted much attention recently. It is a solid, rounded bush, 6ft high so far and is so smothered with the purest white daisies in May that the leaves, though 4in long, are obscured. You must decapitate the dead flowers. Parentage: *lirata × phlogopappa*. z8–9.

O. semi-dentata. One of the most popular and most beautiful in flower, growing fast to 9ft, but decidedly tender. Very large, pendent flowers with violet disc-florets in June, surrounded by pale purple ray-florets and accompanied by thick, tough, grey-green leaves, with its young shoots a brilliant white. Safest in a rather poor, sandy or stony soil. z9.

Some other olearias are either too tender for us or not sufficiently ornamental. Thus *arborescens* is a good nurse-tree of 12ft, with loose, drooping plumes of off-white; *colensoi* is a good, very big foliage plant; *traversii*, reaching 25ft, makes a good weather screen, growing in pure sand; and the yellow-hued *solandri* is also useful in sand.

OLEASTER. See *Elaeagnus angustifolia*

ONONIS

Pretty, deciduous, dwarf shrubs, mainly for the rock garden but useful and decorative elsewhere also. Other members of the genus are herbaceous plants and include wayside wildings in Europe. The shrubby ones have long-blooming pea-flowers, trifoliate leaves and crooked branches and do well in any reasonable, well-drained soil, including chalk, but want full sun. Cultivated for centuries in England. If the seed pods are excessively produced, as they often are, give the shrub a light clipping after blossom-fall.

O. aragonensis. Up to 2ft. Erect spikes of yellow pea-flowers over a long season, starting May. Propagate by half-ripe cuttings or by seed. z7–8.

O. fruticosa. More often grown, a little

bigger and of spreading habit. Flowers rose-purple from June to August. Trifoliate, stalkless leaves closely hug the crooked branches. Increase by seed. z6.

O. rotundifolia. Bright rose-pink flowers all summer, leaves round on zigzag branches. Pretty but not long-lived. It is semi-herbaceous, so cut the old stems to the ground in winter. Increase by seed. z5.

OPLOPANAX
Devil's club

O. horridus must be included merely as a matter of record. It is viciously thorny, even along the veins of the leaves, which are bright green and shaped like a maple's. Loose, elongated sprays of greenish-white flowers in August followed by conspicuous red berries. z5.

There are japanese (*japonica*) and Korean (*elatus*) species which differ a little.

ORIXA

O. japonica is a graceful, densely foliaged, deciduous shrub to 8ft, throwing out horizontal branches which hang down at their tips and touch the soil, where they take root, like blackberries. Thus a dense, outward-spreading mass is formed, but it can, of course, be checked, or the rooted tips used as a means of propagation. The slender leaves are a lustrous, bright green and aromatic. Essentially a foliage plant. The flowers are insignificant and unisexual, males and females on separate plants. Small brown fruits on the female if pollinated. In 'Variegata' the leaves have cream margins. z5.

OSMANTHUS

Among the finest of our garden shrubs, darkly evergreen, of shapely form, of sturdy bearing, rich in its bounty of small, white, jasmine-like flowers, resembling little silver trumpets, that embalm the air with the sweetest of scents. Some have holly-like leaves. A few are unisexual. Small oval berries, usually dark blue, follow the flowers. They grow well in any good garden soil, acid or alkaline, including chalk. Growth, however, is rather slow. The name is Latinized Greek for fragrant flower (*Osme* and *anthos*). Refuse any plants that have been grafted on privet. Plant in spring rather than in autumn.

Most osmanthus flower in spring on growths made in the previous season. Should any pruning happen to be necessary for such species, it has to be done immediately after blossom-fall; but in early spring for the few that flower late. They regenerate freely from the older wood. Unless noted otherwise, all in this list have white, scented flowers in April.

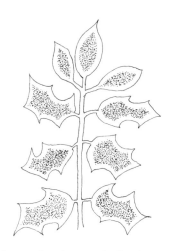

66. Osmanthus heterophyllus 'Variegatus'

Osmanthus delavayi

Osmanthus × burkwoodii

We think that the most handsome osman-thus, though not the hardiest, is **O. delavayi**. We may normally expect it to grow about 8ft in time, but in warm climes it can be a great deal more. Except in severe conditions, it is drought-hardy. The spreading stems are attired in small, dark, oval, glossy leaves and the elegant little trumpets cluster both at the tips of the stems and in the leaf axils. z7–8. In doubtful places you can grow it on a wall, training out the main branches fanwise.

O. × burkwoodii was until recently label-led × *Osmarea burkwoodii*, being a hybrid between *delavayi* and what used to be called *Phillyrea decora*. We can forget all that and say simply that it is a fine evergreen, not quite up to the standing of Delavay's species to the dis-cerning eye, but similar to it and a good deal hardier. z6.

O. decorus. Averaging 8ft but spreading more widely with stiff branches.

O. × fortunei. Spiny, holly-like leaves and amorously scented flowers in autumn on a hardy, neatly rounded shrub, which is 6ft in z7, but much bigger in warmer, moister counties. Parentage: *heterophylla × fragrans*.

O. fragrans. Tiny flowers of bewitching scent on a large, very tender shrub. The "frag-rant olive" is one of the glories of coastal gardens in the south-east of the USA. z9–10.

O. heterophyllus (until recently **ilici-folius**). A very popular and hardy shrub of strange behaviour, with shining, prickly, holly-like leaves until maturity is reached, when the top-most leaves lose their prickles and become "entire", thus justifying the epithet "heterophyllus".

The "recognition signal" is that the leaves are opposite, whereas those of the holly are alter-nate. In favoured climates the "holly os-manthus" can reach 18ft, but elsewhere about 10ft. The tiny flowers wait until the end of summer before casting their sweetness on the air. Blue oblong berries may follow. It makes a fine hedge. z6. There are many variants, of which perhaps the best is 'Variegatus', which has a shining white edge, like a silver holly. Others are:

67.   Osmanthus × burkwoodii

'Aureus' (or 'Aureomarginatus'). Gilt-edged leaves.

'Gulftide'. Leaves small, twisted, dark, dense, very thorny; a very good cultivar.

'Latifolius Variegatus'. Leaves broad and white-edged.

'Myrtifolius', the "myrtle-leaved" osman-thus, propagated from the topmost, spineless leaves and looking rather like a myrtle.

'Purpureus'. Young leaves black-purple, extra hardy.

'Rotundifolius'. Dwarf, very slow, leaves wavy-edged, spineless and very dark.

O. serrulatus. Averages 8ft. Slender, dark, leathery leaves, very prickly. Berries blue-black. z7.

O. suavis. Up to 12ft, more in mild climates, very like delvayi. z8–9.

O. yunnanensis. A 30ft tree with cream flowers.

OSMAREA. See *Osmanthus × burkwoodi* above

OSMARONIA
Oso berry

More mixed-up Greek about sweet savours! *O. cerasiformis*, from California, is quite a nice plant with a character of its own. It shoots up tall, erect stems to 8ft or maybe 16ft, clothed with lively, bright green, deciduous leaves from which dangle clusters of spikes made up of very simple, five-petalled, white flowers like those of a bramble, but which fructify in the form of small purple plums. Both flower and fruit are strongly scented of almonds, but the fruit is very bitter and (to us) suggests prussic acid. As a rule, male and female flowers are borne separately, the males finer than the females.

The oso berry, with its stiff, erect stems, is useful as a variation of form in the larger scene, flowering in March, and makes a good screen. It spreads avidly by suckers, forming a thicket in any soil that is not very alkaline. Propagate by seed or by suckers. z6.

OSTEOMELES

One might interpret this name as "bony apple". Those that we cultivate, coming from hot, dry parts of China, are not very hardy, but are picturesque in their finely pinnate foliage, in which the leaflets are stalkless. Both the white flowers, opening in June in terminal clusters, and the berries resemble those of the hawthorn, except that the berries ripen to deep purple. Both z8.

The grey-green **O. schweriniae**, of which the small-leaved variety *microphylla* is the prettiest, grows to about 7ft with us. Where the climate is doubtful, it is a delightful wall plant, the long flexible branches conforming well to being fanned out tight to the wall. When it matures cut out some of the old branches to encourage the new.

O. subrotunda is a dwarf, compressed, slow-growing version of it with fern-like leaves, covered with silky hairs.

OSTRYOPSIS

Related to the big ostryas, or hop-hornbeams, *Ostryopsis davidiana* looks rather like a hazel,

with broad leaves and male and female catkins. Deciduous, it suckers and grows to about 10ft. Of little ornamental value. z5.

OZOTHAMNUS

Greek *ozo*, scented, and *thamnos*, shrub. Hailing mainly from Tasmania, these are half-hardy, rather hairy creatures, mostly sheathed in tiny leaves, so crowded as to resemble the brush of an animal's tail, and crowned with massed clusters of small, daisy-form flowers. Formerly they were labelled helichrysums. Their floral peculiarity is that what appear to be the rayflorets of a real daisy are, in fact, bracts closely hugging the central disc like a collar. Several of them have been listed for z8, but, as we have seen them, are liable there to get straggly and unkempt and need determined pruning. z9 in a hot, rather dry spot is better, except as noted below.

Ozothamnus rosmarinifolius

The most wooable and most to be desired is the surprising **O. ledifolius**, known as the kerosene or paraffin shrub, because it exhales a gas that is not only aromatic but also inflammable. This gas is given off by a yellow substance that oozes from the underside of the tiny, leathery, re-curved leaves and from the stems. Yellow is seen also in the bracts, so that the whole shrub, which grows to about 3ft, has a dusky yellow flush. Dense bouquets crown each stem. Usually safe in a sheltered place in z8.

Very like the kerosene shrub in these strange characteristics is **O. ericifolius** (perhaps not a valid name), but this has an erect, close carriage of 9ft or more and the leaves are sticky.

O. rosmarinifolius speaks for itself in its name. Here, however, we have a plant that in its natural haunts lives in wet, peaty soils. Said to grow to 10ft but, as we know it in conditions of z8–9, is apt to straggle widely. The rosemary-like leaves form dense plumes and the bracts form a collar of chestnut-red as the massed bunches of flowers begin to open in late June.

Ozothamnus thyrsoides

O. secundiflorus is a hairy shrub of about 6ft, with woolly branches and sweetly scented, outward-facing flowers.

O. selago holds its minute leaves close-pressed to the stems, as in a cypress, but the young branches are slender and lax. Very variable in height to 15ft.

O. thyrsoideus, one of the plants known as "snow in summer", is a beautiful shrub where conditions suit it, growing to about 8ft, with a cluster of daisies at the tip of each shoot, enveloping the whole shrub as with snow from June to August. It gives us some of the best "everlasting" flowers if the flowered stems are hung upside down for several weeks, after which, in a waterless vase, they will last for several years.

We keep quiet about what is sometimes called *O. purpurascens*.

PAEONIA
Peony

The blushful peonies of the herbaceous border have a few fine, upstanding brothers with wooden arms to qualify them to be classified as shrubs. These are distinguished from the herbaceous sorts by the name of tree peony, but in popular speech that term usually means the gorgeous *Paeonia suffruticosa* or moutan and its derivatives. None of them, however, is really a "tree"; they are shrubs and not very big ones.

In general terms peonies are happy in any reasonably good soil, acid or limy, including chalk, and they are of easy culture, except as we shall observe from the moutan. Normally no pruning has to be done. They are deciduous, with elegantly cut leaves, particularly handsome in delavayi and lutea, and their splendid flowers are animated with innumerable stamens. Their flowering is rather short, but the foliage remains decorative and they can be followed up prettily by lavender, fuchsia, summer ericas, golden callunas or anything small from the treasury of herbaceous plants.

In **P. delavayi** we have a 5ft shrub of great

beauty in all its parts but inclined to sucker. The elegant, doubly-pinnate leaves are a foot or more long and persist on the plant all winter after they have withered. The big, cup-like flowers, which open in June, may be up to 4in wide at the mouth and are the richest of reds, enamelled with a throng of golden anthers but, being somewhat pendulous, are partially hidden by the foliage when the plant is young. The large fruits, surrounded by the persistent coloured sepals, are also decorative. Give it a rich soil.

P. × lemoinei (*lutea* × *suffruticosa*). Enormous flowers in differing shades of yellow in May or June on bushes up to 6ft high. Cultivars with gorgeous colour combinations have been raised in France by Louis Henry and by the famous nursery of Lemoine and in the USA by Professor A. P. Saunders. They include:

'Alice Harding'. Lemon-yellow, fully double.

'Argosy'. Huge primrose, splashed carmine.

'Chromatella'. Pure sulphur.

'La Lorraine'. Double yellow.

'L'Espérance'. Huge, pale yellow, semi-double, splashed crimson.

'Mme Louis Henry'. Big double, deep cream, suffused red.

'Souvenir de Maxime Cornu'. Yellow flushed deep orange. Richly scented but so heavy in petals that it droops.

In some lists these are shown under P. suffruticosa.

P. lutea. A variable dwarf, sub-shrub of which by far the best exemplar is *ludlowii*, a natural variety often catalogued as a separate species. This outgrows the dwarf and reaches 7ft, bearing very large, single, golden bowls in June on a sturdy, symmetrical shrub clad with handsome leaves. Give this a rather poor, dry soil.

P. lutea × delavayi was a rather obvious marriage to make, but only a few children of note have resulted. These include 'Anne Rosse', which has big, lemon flowers streaked red, raised by the late Earl of Rosse.

P. potaninii. A suckering shrub of only 2ft.

68. Ornamental (pedate) leaves of shrub peonies. *Above*, Paeonia lutea ludlowii. *Centre*, P. delavayi. *Below*, P. suffruticosa

The foliage is handsome, but the flowers are only small imitations of those of delavayi.

And so we come to the most glorious or (as some might think) the most flamboyant, but certainly the one with the most panache. This is

P. suffruticosa, the historic moutan, bred for more than a thousand years by the Chinese and then taken over and refined by the Japanese. Moutan is the Chinese name for it. Splendid indeed it is but it has its fallibilities, too.

In winter the moutan is a cluster of stiff, gaunt and naked rods, but in spring it puts on a dress of doubly pinnate leaves and in May and June (after a few years) there appear a few magnificent and audacious flowers of rather short-lived splendour that may measure anything from 6in to more than a foot from rim to rim, but not many of them. At the base of each petal there is often a splash of some bold, contrasting colour, with a circle of countless stamens crowned with golden anthers. The flowers may be single, double or semi-double and are occasionally scented, not always pleasantly. It may take some years before the plant reaches 4ft, but in time it will grow a few more feet and aged specimens may have a considerable girth. Few plants are more desirable, but few are so unsuitable to the impatient gardener or the one with a shallow purse.

This said, one is happy to add that, in the right conditions, the moutan is not a difficult, wayward or temperamental shrub. The late Sir Frederick Stern, for example, in his famous chalk garden in the Sussex downs, received a small plant from Canada which flowered after two years and twenty years later was 8ft high and 12ft wide. Similar successes are reported elsewhere.

Oddly, the moutan is grafted by nurserymen on to the rootstock of an herbaceous peony. Plant it in October in a rich, deeply dug loam, preferably a limy one, with the crown a good 4in or more below ground level, so that the scion can form its own roots independently of its herbaceous foster-mother. It is a gross feeder, but never give it any animal manure, unless very ancient. Mulch heavily with a quilt of leaves in autumn, underlaid with a fertilizer strong in phosphates and potash.

The moutan is a perfectly hardy plant where conditions are not extreme and it needs no coddling, no "warm and sheltered position", but in climates such as those of Britain it may be excited into premature activity in a mild winter and, if night frosts follow in spring, both its buds and its young foliage may be shattered. So give it a place where the sun will not reach it until about noon. This means oblique shade, not anything like wall protection, for the plant should be in an open, well-aired spot, where there is less danger from the grey-mould disease (*Botrytis paeoniae*). If this attacks, cut back to clean wood and spray twice with a copper fungicide.

The moutan can readily be transplanted, especially after the scion has formed its own roots after two or three years, when the old herbaceous roots can be cut away, but the stems must be cut back to about a foot or so. It can then also be increased by division of the roots, with two or more buds or eyes per division. Propagation by seed is also not difficult, but the plants are slow to mature. The progeny, though unpredictable, are lovely.

In addition to the old, established cultivars, American nurserymen are now busy raising quantities of new ones crossed with other species (see also under Lemoine's hybrids above). We suggest the following "starters" as fairly readily available.

'Bijou de Chusan'. Famous old double white.

'Black Pirate'. Deep maroon-crimson. Often listed under lutea × delavayi, but we are advised otherwise.

'Elizabeth' (or 'Reine Elizabeth'). Double pink.

'Jeanne d'Arc'. Double pink.

'Hana-kisoi'. Red, large.

'Hinode-sekai'. Brilliant rosy-red, double.

'Jitsu-getsu-nishiki'. Red-purple.

'Gessikai'. Huge double white, crinkled petals.

'Godaishu'. White, yellow centre, semi-double.

'Higurashi'. Vivid crimson, semi-double.

'Saku-rajishi'. Lustrous pink, petals fringed.
'Shunkollon'. Rosy-violet, semi-double.
'Tama-fuyi'. Blush-pink, semi-double.
'Yachiyo-tsubaki'. Vivid, two-tone pink, petals ruffled.

PALIURUS

P. spina-christi is one of the plants imagined to have provided Christ's crown of thorns. Not unworthy of cultivation, it is a big, deciduous, wide-spreading shrub, possibly 18ft high, with flexible, fiercely armed stems, often flopping to the ground, small, oval leaves and thronged in July and August with quantities of small, yellow-green flowers, followed by curious fruits of the same colour, imitating a pastor's hat with low crown and wide brim. z7.

PENSTEMON

The popular bedding plants have some good woody relations, not very hardy, prostrate or nearly so, best fitted for the warm rock garden in a light, well-drained soil. But the evergreen *P. cordifolius* is a pretty shrub that will grow to about 5ft on a warm wall in mild districts, where it will produce large, pyramidal clusters of scarlet, tubular flowers with pouting lips from midsummer to autumn. Its habit, however, is loose and floppy, so it must be tied back. Prune moderately hard in April.

PERNETTYA

Pernettyas are of very high standing among evergreen, berry-bearing shrubs. Indeed, their berries, in a wide range of colours, are perhaps the most beautiful of all and, when seen in a vase by a non-gardener, look for all the world as though made of the finest porcelain. They are under threat of a take-over bid by the gaul-

therias, who are their relatives, which would be a pity, for, to the gardener, they are quite different.

Most pernettyas are ground-crawlers, so that, in effect, we are left with **P. mucronata**, a dense, dark green, small-leaved, glossy, slightly prickly shrub. The prickliness is in the tips of the stiff leaves, which measure only three-eighths of an inch. In the spring the shrub bursts out into a fuzzy mass of cream florets, which, if pollinated, fructify as gem-like berries, white, pink, red or mauve. The flowers however, are nearly all unisexual, so that although there is a hermaphrodite clone, the most handsome display occurs only when a known make is planted among about half a dozen females. The gleaming berries, borne in clusters, last nearly the whole winter and are splendid ornaments in the house. Though they originate from Chile and southwards towards Cape Horn, we owe their sparkling diversity to a Northern Ireland nurseryman named Davis just a hundred years ago.

Pernettyas must have an acid and fairly moist soil, preferably peaty or leafy, in a mild but cool climate which, in the USA, restricts them to west coasts. Though often recommended for shade, they fruit much better in sun and keep to

69.   The porcelain berries of Pernettya mucronata

a compact shape, seldom more than waist-high. The following are some good named varieties, the colours being those of the berries. z6–7.

'Atrococcinea'. Large, deep ruby.

'Bell's Seedling'. Dark red hermaphrodite.

'Cherry Ripe'. As named.

Davis' Hybrids. Good choice for those who want a mixture of unspecified colours.

'Lilacina'. Rosy-lilac.

'Pink Pearl'. Paler than the above.

'Rosea'. Deep, rose-pink.

'Sea Shell'. Charming soft pink.

'White Pearl'. Gleaming white, a gem.

The natural variety *rupicola* is a wilding of loose build and berries of various colours. *P. angustifolia*, though said to have been used by Davis, is of uncertain status. Pernettyas are named after the eighteenth-century Frenchman Pernetty.

PEROVSKIA
Russian Sage

Not quite sure whether to be a shrub or an herbaceous plant, and despite its heavy-weight name, **P. atriplicifolia** is a delightful plant of airy and delicate grace, which sends up very slim, erect, pointed wands sheathed in silvery-grey, with grey-green, trimly cut leaves and terminating in slender panicles of lavender florets, agape like those of a sage (to which family the plant belongs) to a height of 3ft. It is seen at its best in the aptly named 'Blue Spire', in which the leaves are deeply chiselled and the floral panicles larger. You can plant it in any good garden soil, including chalk, but give it as warm a spot as you can. It flowers in August and September. On no account put it near plants of a strong colour. It keeps good company with lavenders, artemisia, campions and such-like, fits very nicely into an herbaceous border and looks aristocratic on its own on top of a bank. z6.

P. abrotanoides has lavender flowers and branching stems, only lightly powdered, is slightly hairy and needs more heat. A hybrid between the two species has been raised by Hilliers. z7.

As sub-shrubs, perovskias are not wholly woody in their stems, which may partially die back in winter. Amputate them to the ground in March (Fig. 11). Their name commemorates the nineteenth-century Russian Perovski.

PETTERIA

A fine, shapely shrub that we should like to see more often, *P. ramentacea* is remarkable for looking like a shrubby laburnum, with the same trifoliate leaves, but with flower trusses standing erect instead of drooping. It is deciduous, growing to 7ft and flowering abundantly in May and June. The spikes (racemes) are 2–3 inches high and are scented. Known as the Dalmatian laburnum, it is named after the nineteenth-century botanist, Petter.

Propagate from its seeds, which (like those of the laburnum) are poisonous. z6.

PHILADELPHUS
Mock-orange

The uninstructed multitude (and some people who should know better) still persist in calling these beautiful white-flowered shrubs by the invalid name "syringa". The reason is an historical one. Before the systematic classification of plants by Linnaeus in the mid-eighteenth century this name was oddly applied indiscriminately to the philadelphus, the lilac and even some jasmines. Linnaeus, putting the seal of his approval on the judgement of the earlier botanist Bauhin, established the name "philadelphus", leaving "syringa" to apply only to the lilac. Philadelphus is a conjunction of the Greek *phyllos* and *delphos*, meaning brotherly love, and is said to be the name that the Greeks used in honour of an Egyptian king. If there is any justification whatever for a nickname, then "mock orange" is the most appropriate.

The philadelphus occur naturally in many parts of the northern hemisphere. The main flowering season is June–July, though a few open in May and some wait till late summer, so that the bee has created many hybrids in the wild and man has made his very significant additions, resulting in some confusion of identities. All have white or off-white flowers, but some have a small patch of a contrasting colour at the bases of the petals. By no means all have a fragrant breath. Otherwise, they vary a good deal in size and habit. Their failing as garden plants is that each species or variety is on-stage for only two weeks and for the rest of the year is of little interest, being sometimes gaunt and half-naked, and, though a few do clothe themselves to the ground, notably *P. inodorus* and its five varieties, their foliage is commonplace. This failing can be overcome by giving them the society of other shrubs and they are particularly effective among herbaceous plants, or with shrub roses and the small blue Hyssopus aristatus. However, all philadelphus are easy to grow in any reasonable soil and begin to flower when quite young, but are all the better for generous feeding. Because of their willingness to inter-marry, they are not easy shrubs to classify.

The great name in the mock-oranges is that of the inspired French nurseryman Lemoine, who, as in several other genera, produced what one might call a whole *corps de ballet* of sparkling hybrid ice-maidens. Other distinguished hybrids have been created in Britain and, more recently, in the USA. In approaching this problem of classification we shall, in general, follow the example of Bean. We suggest that, for general purposes the outstanding ones are 'Virginal', 'Belle Etoile', 'Beauclerc' and the charming 'Sybille'; do not overlook the pretty dwarfs *microphyllus* and 'Manteau d'Hermine'.

Pruning can be very important. The philadelphus is typical of those shrubs that flower early on growths put out in the previous year. Therefore, immediately after blossom-fall, we cut back the flowered shoot to a point where a promising new one is developing. Occasionally amputate down to the ground or near it, any old, worn stems. Bear in mind, however, the natural habit of the species or variety. The philadelphus throws new stems freely from the base, forming a "stool". This habit is encouraged by planting a trifle deeply.

Propagate either from young cuttings under mist in summer or by hard-wood cuttings in the autumn in sandy, shaded soil in the open.

THE SPECIES AND THEIR SIBLINGS

P. argyrocalyx. A charming New Mexican of 6ft, of graceful bearing with flowers of a fruity fragrance, clasped by silky calyces and having overall a silvery patina from the white hairs on the reverse of the leaf. z5.

P. brachybotrys. Cream flowers on a rounded, dense plant. 8ft. z5.

P. californicus. Small flowers crowded in showy panicles, a distinctive feature. 9ft. Little scent. z6.

P. coronarius. The original European "mock-orange" of ancient usage. A 10ft shrub with flowers of very rich, pervasive, almost cloying scent, "troubling and molesting the head" if brought indoors, as was said by the classic English herbalist John Gerard, of Shakespeare's day. The flowers are not quite pure white and open in early June. Good in dry spots. Prune it conscientiously to save it from getting too lanky. z4. In the USA the true *corronarius* is rare in the trade and has been supplanted by more showy but quite scentless species.

Valuable in small gardens (as in others) are a few variants of *coronarius*, not exceeding 3–4ft. 'Aureus' starts with brightly gilded leaves, which gradually turn pale green, with insignificant flowers, good as a foliage shrub in cool climates. 'Variegatus' has leaves boldly edged cream, attractive all summer. 'Deutziiflorus' has double flowers.

P. coulteri. See under P. mexicanus.

P. × cymosus is a term used by Rehder for a group of variable hybrids equipped with "cymose racemes". See under Garden Hybrids.

P. delavayi. Large, richly scented saucers arranged in racemes on a thrustful shrub that may reach 15ft. It flowers early and fleetingly in full sun and is best in partial shade. There are several forms, the best one, having rich purple calyces and large, heart-shaped leaves, being often called 'Nymans' Variety', from the famous Sussex garden of that name, or *calvescens*. Prune hard. z6.

P. 'Falconeri'. Distinguished by its narrow, twisted petals. Little scent. 12ft. z4.

Useful for flowering in late July is **P. incanus**, an 8ft shrub of erect deportment with blossoms scented of hawthorns and carried in racemes. Leaves hairy. z6.

Another late starter, but a little earlier than incanus and of more spreading character, is **P. insignis**, an attractive 10ft shrub with faintly scented cups clustered numerously with pronounced orange stamens in panicles and accompanied by glossy leaves. z5.

As its name implies, **P. inodorus** of 8ft, is scentless but, as a garden shrub, makes up for this fault by its dark glossy leaves, by clothing itself with them right down to the ground and by the striking form of its flowers, which have large, pointed petals overlapping in such a way as to make them look square. Its natural variety *carolinus* is of the finest quality, but better known, and often counted as a separate species, is the large-flowered *grandiflorus*. Another natural variety, of distinctive habit, is *laxus*, which bows gracefully down to the ground from a height of 6ft. Reckon all as z5.

P. × lemoinei. See under Garden Hybrids.

P. lewisii is a variable shrub, but the form in commerce is usually a lusty 12ft, gracefully pendulous, with flowers in racemes, unscented, except in the variety *gordonianus* (sometimes counted as a separate species). z4.

One of the earliest mock-oranges to blossom is the Chinese **P. magdalenae**, a dense, free-flowering shrub of prime quality distinguished by its grey-green, hairy leaves, rough to the touch. White racemes in late May. Some noses detect a sweet scent. z6.

For warm climates **P. mexicanus** is a handsome and distinctive philadelphus, with cream-tinted flowers, richly scented of roses, usually displayed singly, and with slightly hairy leaves on a 6ft shrub. It is particularly attractive in the cultivar from Ireland unfortunately called by the traditional name "rose syringa", in which the bases of the petals are pale purple. It has also been erroneously called "P. coulteri". Just hardy enough for sheltered nooks in parts of Britain, but cannot be rated hardier than z9.

P. microphyllus is a charming little shrub of not more than 4ft, densely arrayed in flowers very sweetly scented of pineapples, complemented by small, neat foliage. In winter it becomes a mass of chestnut twigs. Slow. z5.

The huge, "hairy mock-orange", **P. pubescens**, can grow 20ft high and even more in width. Its flower-stalks, calyces and the reverse of its leaves are coated with a soft down. The large, faintly scented flowers, in clusters of seven or eight, are liable to be partly hidden by the foliage. z4.

Its offspring, *P. × nivalis*, differs only in minor details, but there is a double-flowered form.

P. intectus differs from pubescens only in being free of down. z5.

P. purpurascens. A graceful shrub related to delavayi, but only half its size, with the same attractive purple-tinted calyx, but the flowers and leaves are smaller. z5.

P. satsumi (or *satsumanus*). Though this Japanese mock-orange is variable, its overall character is one of slender and erect carriage, both in the stems, which may reach 8ft, and in the inflorescence which forms a many-flowered raceme. z6.

P. schrenkii. The first of the mock-oranges to bloom, often starting in late May. Very sweetly scented flowers on a shrub that resembles coronarius, reaching perhaps 12ft, the blossoms borne in racemes. z5.

P. sericanthus. Horticulturally resembles magdalenae, but flowers in late June, with less hairy leaves. z5.

P. 'Splendens' is a handsome, natural hybrid, growing 8ft high, but with wide-flung branches bowing to the ground, forming a mound, and richly robed in mid-June with single, unscented blossoms enlivened by gilded stamens. z5.

P. tomentosus. Resembles coronarius, but

the leaves wear a soft grey down beneath. z5.

P. × virginalis. A group name covering many fine hybrids. See Garden Hybrids.

P. zeyheri. 8ft, spreading. Of no floral value. z4.

THE GARDEN HYBRIDS

As we have noted, most of the popular mock-orange hybrids were created by that great floral marriage-maker Victor Lemoine. He began by mating the European *coronarius* with the small American *microphyllus*. From these he obtained 'Lemoinei' and others classified by Rehder as *P. × lemoinei*, marked by small leaves, rather small flowers distilling a celestial fragrance and smooth-edged leaves. Other crossings soon followed and many were classified by Rehder in such names as *P. × virginalis*, *P. × cymosus*, *P. × polyanthus*. Inevitably the sap of *mexicanus* was also introduced, resulting in handsome flowers with purple patches at the base of each petal, but best regarded as no hardier than z7. Otherwise, all the following are safe in z5 and two of them in z3.

'Albâtre'. Scented, double, early July. 5ft.

'Argentine'. Scented, very double, 4ft.

'Atlas'. Slight scent, single, cup-shaped, 5ft.

'Avalanche'. Richly scented, single, low, arching, and resembling a 5ft mound of snow. A fine creation.

'Beauclerc'. (Pronounce it Bo-clear). One of the finest, raised in England by the late Hon. Lewis Palmer. Large, fragrant flowers with a small, pale pink flush in the centre, cup-shaped before opening fully and enamelled with conspicuous golden anthers. 6ft. Parents: 'Sybille' and 'Burfordensis'.

'Belle Etoile'. In the front rank. Lovely blossoms with pink eye, delightfully scented, in thick clusters, produced in profusion. The young stems are mahogany, peeling off in the next year. 6ft.

'Bicolor'. A dwarf, bearing single, cup-shaped, scented cream flowers with a purple patch in the centre.

'Boule d'Argent'. Slightly scented, semi-double, in thick clusters. 5ft, bushy.

'Bouquet Blanc'. Is perhaps synonymous

Philadelphus 'Beauclerc'

Philadelphus 'Beauclerc' in full splendour

206

with 'Albâtre'.

'Burfordensis'. Vigorous, upstanding English variety of high quality. Big, single, abundant, scentless flowers, with a bold brush of yellow anthers. 10ft.

'Burkwoodii'. Clusters of scented flowers, pale purple at the throat. Petals too narrow. 7ft.

'Cole's Glorious'. Large, single, lovely scent. 6ft. American.

'Conquête'. Very fragrant, single or semi-double flowers (having petaloid stamens) in small clusters on slender, arching stems. 3–4ft. Is the type plant of Rehder's "Cymosus" group.

'Coupe d'Argent'. An elegant, erect 4ft, with flowers resembling those of 'Beauclerc', but borne sparingly.

'Dame Blanche'. Double flowers in dense clusters, faint scent.

'Enchantment'. Small double flowers in crowded spikes, profusely borne on arching branches. 7ft.

'Erectus'. Creamy-white, richly scented, single in threes or fives. Erect, slender, close-packed stems. Very good where space is limited. A good hedger. 5ft.

'Etoile Rose'. A pretty dwarf, with small, scented, single flowers tinted rose at the base.

'Favourite'. Very large, single, cup-shaped, with a cluster of yellow stamens. 6ft.

'Frosty Morn'. An exceptionally hardy American, double and scented. 4ft. z3.

'Girandolle'. Double, milk-white in crowded clusters. 5ft.

'Glacier'. Scented, fully double, in clusters. 4ft.

'Innocence'. Single, very fragrant flowers exuberantly borne. Leaves mottled cream.

'Lemoinei'. Rather small, pure white, richly scented flowers in clusters at the ends of short, lateral twigs. Rounded shrub of 6ft.

'Manteau d'Hermine'. A charming and popular dwarf, smothered with small, creamy-white, scented blossoms. 2½ft.

'Minnesota Snowflake'. Scented, fully double, in many-flowered racemes. Extremely hardy, of rounded shape and clothed to the ground. 8ft. z3.

Philadelphus 'Belle Etoile'

The double-flowered Philadelphus 'Enchantment'

'Monster'. Very vigorous, coarse shrub that has reached 25ft in England. Large, single flowers and very large (6in) leaves.

'Mont Blanc'. Single. A shapely dome of 4ft. Very hardy.

'Norma'. One of the finest single-flowered varieties, with scented, bowl-shaped flowers on slender, swaying stems. 5ft.

'Patricia'. A Canadian, raised by F. L. Skinner. Flowers single, scented, in fives or sevens. Tough, dark green leaves.

'Purpureo-Maculatus'. A dwarf of 2–3ft, with fragrant, solitary flowers, rose-tinted at the base.

'Rosace'. Scented, semi-double flowers in arching sprays. 4ft.

'Silver Showers'. Single, solitary, scented, cup-shaped flowers on a round bush. $3\frac{1}{2}$ft. German.

'Sybille'. One of the most beautiful and accommodating of all mock-oranges. Large,

Philadelphus 'Virginal'

scented, saucer-shaped, usually solitary flowers, with fringed petals, dyed rose-purple at their bases. The shrub is full of grace and opulent in flower. 4ft by 6ft.

'Velleda'. A beautiful little philadelphus that should be better known than it is. Large, saucer-shaped flowers, scented of roses, usually solitary. About 4ft.

'Virginal'. One of the best-known of all mock-oranges. Large, cup-shaped, very fragrant, double or semi-double flowers, often appearing in scattered clusters all summer. This is the "type" of the Virginalis group. Its fault is that it is of gaunt and leggy habit, up to 8ft high. Put it at the back of a border to hide its naked legs and prune it hard.

'Voie Lactée'. Large, single, petals becoming slightly reflexed at the edge. $4\frac{1}{2}$ft.

Philadelphus 'Sybille', small but lovely

PHILESIA

Philesia magellanica, the "Magellan box-lily", is a darkly evergreen, suckering shrub of 3ft, developing into a thicket, to be grown only where the conditions are moist, peaty or woodsy and partially shaded. The flowers are half-open trumpets of a rich rosy-crimson, 2in long, in late summer. If planted near a tree or wall, it may behave as a climber, like *Euonymus fortunei*. z8.

PHILLYREA

Large, evergreen shrubs, sometimes small trees, the use of which is primarily to provide that background of "rich, harmonious masses" which William Chambers prescribed for the larger scene, not a small garden. Their flowers, white or tinted green, are of less importance. Prune as you will or clip as a hedge. Easily propagated by cuttings from young shoots in July.

Hitherto the best has been *P. decora*, but this has now been classed as an osmanthus (*O. decorus*). Less hardy, and of close growth to 10ft, is *P. angustifolia*. Leaves narrower, flowers creamy-green in May and June. In its form *rosmarinifolia*, the leaves are only $\frac{1}{8}$in wide and grey-tinted, and the growth so dense that, with age, there is a build-up of dead growths inside. Very good seaside shrubs. z7 8.

P. latifolia is too big for us.

PHLOMIS

Clothed in soft furs and easily recognisable by the whorls or circlets of hooded flowers that ring the stems in loose tiers, the phlomis are useful, small evergreen shrubs for creating that community of difference that helps to prevent monotony in any kind of border. Several phlomis are herbaceous plants and a herbaceous element lingers in the shrubby species also, their

Phlomis fruticosa, the 'Jerusalem sage'. An example of flowers in whorls

tips being soft and liable to shrivel up in winter. However, they make new growth quickly from their old wood, if not too aged, so you cut back any frosted tips in spring and also occasionally cut back a few of the older stems slightly harder. Dry, well-drained soil and a warm patch are their primary needs. They come from the Mediterranean and their name is straight Greek for a woolly plant.

The hardiest is **P. fruticosa**, the Jerusalem sage, which has been grown in England ever since Shakespeare's day. It reaches about $3\frac{1}{2}$ft in a loose, widespread fashion, with sage-like leaves and rings of yellow flowers in June and July. Easily propagated by cuttings of young growth in summer. 'Edward Bowles' is a clone with much larger leaves and paler flowers. z7.

Less hardy but of attractive foliage is **P. chrysophylla**, a $2\frac{1}{2}$ft shrub, with its fur faintly tinted with gold and flowers of bright yellow. It can become weighed down to the ground by its heavy growth. z8 in a warm corner.

In some opinions **P. italica** is the most desirable, but it is decidedly tender. The fur is white and the flowers lilac in terminal spikes. Control it firmly with the secateurs or it will become ragged. *P. purpurea* is much the same but less furry.

PHORMIUM

New Zealand Flax

Strictly speaking, the phormiums are "evergreen herbs" and not shrubs, having no woody parts and their leaf-blades springing from a very tough rhizome, but they are treated as shrubs horticulturally.

Being New Zealanders, they are of limited hardiness in the northern hemisphere, but in most parts of Zone 8 they have an important place in gardening design, as a contrast to other kinds of foliage, especially the bigger of the two species, **P. tenax**, which provides very long, sword-like leaves, standing stiffly erect with uplifted blades. The other species, **P. cookianum** (or *colensoi*) is much smaller with usually laxer leaves. Both are essentially foliage plants, the flowers, which somewhat resemble those of the day-lily and stand high above the leaves, being usually rust-coloured and of no great account.

Apart from their frost-tenderness, they are remarkably tough creatures, standing up fearlessly to salty ocean gales, in which their big leaves clash together like a rattling of sabres, and they are immune to the pollution of cities. They take to any reasonable soil, but are at their best in a wet one. The term "flax" derives from the fact that their leaves, like hemp and sisal, are very fibrous and are used for making ropes and the like. They thrive exceptionally in coastal California.

The forms of both species and their hybrids that have coloured or striped leaves are too numerous to set out here and can be found only in the most up-to-date or specialized catalogues. But we must mention *P. cookianum* 'Tricolor', a delightful garden plant of but 2ft

(not to be confused with the 6ft *P. tenax* 'Tricolor') and the really outstanding hybrid 'Dazzler', blood-red and rose-pink, 18in high. For tall, variegated forms of *tenax*, first choices might be 'Purpureum', 'Veitchii', 'Variegatum' and 'Purple Giant'.

PHOTINIA

This is a mixed breed of trees and shrubs, some evergreen, others deciduous, some highly ornamental, others commonplace. We have to deal only with the shrubby species, of which we may say at the start that 'Red Robin' is the star. All bear clusters of small, white flowers, frothy with numerous stamens, followed by berries like those of the hawthorn.

The needs of the photinias are fairly simple, but the deciduous sorts, which are the hardier, dislike lime and the evergreens will fail in both flowers and fruit unless the climate is warm, but are of special value in chalky soils. All like the sun.

Outstripping them all as garden plants is a group of evergreen hybrids that go under the collective name of **P. × fraseri** (*glabra × serrulata*) which originated by chance in the Fraser Nurseries of Birmingham, Alabama. The original selected clone, introduced in 1955, was called 'Birmingham' and was remarkable for the coppery cockades of its young foliage, as in the more colourful forms of *Pieris formosa*. Others followed, the most brilliant of all being the New Zealand clone 'Red Robin', a superb shrub which, as we know it, is rather low and wide-spreading. Another fine clone, from Australia, is 'Robusta', a lusty shrub and perhaps the hardiest. All make splendid hedges.

A great virtue of these Fraser hybrids is that they will flourish in limy soils, including chalky ones, and are very good substitutes for the pieris, which must have an acid soil. They are also less tender than the said pieris and keep their red cockades much longer. z7.

One of the parents of Fraser's photinia was **P. glabra**, a 10ft evergreen shrub of loose habit, the young leaves of which are tinted bronze before turning a glossy, dark green. The June flowers are scented of hawthorn, with red berries later, but otherwise it is of no distinction. The New Zealand clone 'Rubens' is a brighter red. The other Fraser parent, *P. serrulata*, becomes of tree size, with laurel-like leaves, similarly cockaded.

P. parviflora is a deciduous shrub of 8ft, flowering in May, followed by scarlet berries in October. Of graceful demeanour but not remarkable. z6.

P. villosa, deciduous, 12ft or more, deserves some consideration for its hardiness and specially for its brilliant autumnal colouring, but it is very variable and does not like chalk. Most of those grown seem to be the narrow-leaved natural variety *laevis*. The much more distinctive variety *sinica* is a slender shrub of 20ft or more, of spreading behaviour and carrying its large, orange-scarlet berries in dangling clusters.

Another form of villosa is generally known as *maximowicziana*, a very big shrub with pale green, puckered leaves, turning a rich yellow in the fall, which Mr R. L. Lancaster regards as a separate species under the name *P. koreana*. z4. All the species are easily grown from seed cleared and sown in the fall as soon as ripe.

See also Heteromeles

PHYGELIUS
Cape Figwort or Cape Fuchsia

These South Africans are further examples of "sub-shrubs". In climates colder than their natural ones the top growth, which is soft and pithy, can be killed by frost, but, to some extent, the root system remains inviolate and the plants will send up fresh growth, like herbaceous perennials. Plant in a rather dry, stony soil in full sun. Prune by cutting the old stems right down to an inch or two of the ground in winter.

The only one generally cultivated in the northern hemisphere is **P. capensis**, a pictur-

esque shrub whose floral habit is to throw up small, loose pyramids of elegant little hunting-horns, an inch or more long, dangling from the tips of slightly bent stalks in late summer. They are red with a yellow throat, the variety 'Coccineus' being the most brilliant.

The Cape figwort will reach 6ft in z9 in the open ground. In z8 against a warm wall is said to aspire to 20ft. Propagate by summer cuttings or by its suckers.

P. aequalis is far more rare and a trifle more tender. It is a pretty sub-shrub of 3ft with stiff leaves. The flowers are a yellowish-pink with a bright red margin and are almost straight tubes, not bent like the little horns of its brother.

PHYLLOSTACHYS. See Bamboos

PHYSOCARPUS

Utilitarian deciduous shrubs, usually wide-spreading, bearing small, white flowers in small clusters (corymbs or umbels) in June, followed by inflated fruits, which is exactly what is meant by the Latinized Greek name (*physa*, bladder, *karpos*, fruit). In some species the pods are bright red. In flower they often resemble spiraeas, but the leaves, having three to five lobes, look more like those of a currant. The bark peels off. Hardy and useful for filling in, but not refined. Moist soil and full sun. Prune back the flowered stems as for deutzia, Fig. 10.

P. opulifolius, the 9ft, "nine-bark", so called because its bark is constantly peeling, is phenomenally hardy, enduring z2 in Quebec, Michigan and thereabouts. The flowers have a pink tint. The variety 'Luteus' has leaves that begin yellow, turning green. The dwarf version *novus* is a very useful shrub for the harsh prairie states of North America.
Others to be noted are:

P. amurensis, 7ft. Leaves 3-lobed. z4.

P. bracteatus. 6ft. Leaves 5-lobed. z5.

P. capitatus. Very big, for wild scenes only. z5.

P. intermedius. 4ft. Perhaps a variety of

opulifolius, and more refined. Leaves with shallow lobes, scalloped. z4.

P. malvaceus. 5ft. Leaves lobed and toothed. z5.

P. monogynus. 3ft. A small, pretty shrub from the Rockies, with lobed and toothed leaves. Flowers often pink-tinted. z4.

PIERIS

Where the conditions are right, the pieris are among the greater glories of the garden, challenging the rhododendrons and the camellias, unifying in their various forms the qualities of both strength and elegance. Luxuriantly robed in foliage of different patterns, their skirts sweep the ground when well grown and suppress the germination of weed seeds.

Formerly known as andromedas, they bejewel their robes with the same sort of lily-of-the-valley flowers, which look like sprays of pearls, sometimes in the form of pendent necklaces, sometimes of little fountains, occasionally tinted with rose. Botanically they are racemes or panicles.

Pieris grow rather slowly, prolonging their youth, and must have an acid soil, whether of loam, peat or ancient leaves and some like a little shade. Except in warm counties, all are best seated where they will escape the early morning sun in winter. Their flower buds are formed in late summer and will occasionally open in autumn, but usually wait until spring, so that a harsh winter "when Marion's nose looks red and raw" may rob them of their jewels, without damaging their robes. All are evergreen. Where the soil is not acid and the climate mild, think instead of Fraser's hybrid photinias.

Do not fear to prune pieris, if necessary; spring is the time.

The most opulent of the pieris (using the name now generally accepted) are **P. formosa forrestii** and its selected clones and a hybrid derived from one of them. Due to the importation of seed from different regions of Asia,

70.   Pieris formosa

there has been a good deal of doubt about identities and names, with which we need not involve ourselves. It is enough to say that all become noble, many-stemmed shrubs, normally about 12ft high in time, occasionally much more, their leaves slender, pointed, dark green and firm of texture.

What particularly distinguishes them are the brilliant cockades of their young leaves throughout the whole of spring, which make a regal setting for their floral string of pearls. In the best examples these cockades are almost a true red, always at least a bright chestnut.

Of its few selected clones, all of which occurred in southern England, 'Wakehurst' is the one that has excited the most admiration, but we have to utter the warning that, unfortunately, there are two claimants to this famous name. One is a cultivar of *P. formosa*, and the other (superior to it) came from what was of late separately designated *P. forrestii*. The difference between various specimens of *formosa* and *forrestii* are so indeterminate that *forrestii* is now classed as a natural variety of formosa, so that we now have "*Pieris formosa* var *forrestii* 'Wakehurst'", and this is the one to demand. In this the young shoots unfold a brilliant red, slowly fade to salmon, then to blush before becoming grey in high summer. The large, dangling panicles of flowers are borne profusely in some years, meagrely in others.

Other handsome clones are 'Charles Michael' with bronze cockades and upright panicles, and 'Jermyns', which has distinctive wine-red plumes and the same colour pervades the flower clusters before they open. All z7.

A chance but very happy offspring of the formosa group came into the world in **P. 'Forest Flame'**, a superb pieris, of which one parent was *P. japonica*. The formosa parent, it has been claimed, was 'Wakehurst'.

'Forest Flame' has very much the same character as 'Wakehurst', comes into growth a little earlier, is a little more graceful in its carriage and inherits the hardiness of japonica. Very similar to it but of unspecified parentage is 'Firecrest'. These hybrids are probably z6, definitely hardier than P. formosa.

The only American pieris is perhaps the least ornamental, but much the hardiest and much to be desired in colder regions, as in others. This is **P. floribunda**, a 6ft shrub sometimes called the "mountain andromeda". It bears its flowers in nodding pyramids, 4in high, in April, but in areas that combine summer heat and humidity it is very susceptible to a dangerous stem canker and to root rot. 'Elongata', where the climate allows, is an improved form providing much taller and later pyramids. z4.

These perils do not appear to affect the very interesting new American hybrid **'Brouwer's Beauty'** (floribunda × japonica), which combines the cold-hardiness of floribunda with the much longer, pendant flower clusters and greater tolerance of summer heat displayed by japonica. z4.

Almost as hardy and a great garden favourite is **P. japonica**, which becomes a 10ft shrub clad in slender, lustrous, dark green leaves and prettily decorated with drooping clusters (panicles) of pearl-like flowers all the way from March to May. Several cultivars have been selected or created, of which the loveliest in popular esteem is 'Variegata', one of the most beautiful of all small shrubs (though it reaches 12ft in southern England). The young, slim shoots are a beguiling pink, gradually maturing to a soft green, boldly bordered in cream. Charming at all seasons, but very slow at first. One is often told that it should be grown in diapered shade, which is certainly true in the USA, but we have it in full sun.

Other cultivars of *P. japonica* (all z5 in general) are:

'Bert Chandler' or 'Chandleri'. A beautiful Australian in which the young growths are bright salmon, fading to cream before maturing a normal green. In the USA it is suitable only for the west coast.

'Christmas Cheer'. Flower tips and stalks flushed deep rose, in great abundance in midwinter. Very hardy.

'Compacta'. Leaves small, habit close.

'Crispa'. Leaf-margins wavy.

'Daisen'. Buds deep pink, opening pale pink.

'Dorothy Wycoff'. Buds dark red, opening deep pink. There are a few others on similar themes. 'Purity' and the long 'Whitecups' are what you would expect. 'Pink Bud' is pink at all stages.

P. taiwanensis is a lordly mound of dark green, rarely more than 6ft high, so that it is an ideal pieris for the smaller garden. Its young shoots open a bright bronze in the manner of the formosas. In March and April it becomes richly decorated with large, boldly displayed flower trusses of slim and erect carriage. It is sun-hardy and altogether a very fine shrub indeed. z7.

PIPTANTHUS
Evergreen laburnum

These evergreen or half-evergreen shrubs are curiously neglected in gardens and parks, for

Piptanthus laburnifolius

Other species grown, but not easy to find, all about z8, are:

P. concolor. About 9ft, flowers a little smaller, with a maroon patch on the standard petal. Hardier than the above.

P. forrestii. 6ft or more. Flowers bright yellow. Perhaps hardier than the others.

P. tomentosus. Leaves velvety.

PITTOSPORUM

Every "flower arranger" knows the value of a few twigs of pittosporum in a vase, but to the gardener their uses are only as foliage shrubs or as something sweet to sniff in their due season. Their flowers, though scented, are paltry. So one must decide for oneself whether they deserve a place in one's garden picture, bearing in mind that they are all rather tender, that there are foliage shrubs of greater pictorial value and that some of them become unexpectedly large trees in places particularly to their liking, as splendidly seen in Cornwall and Ireland, and other districts near the sea, the breath of which stimulates them. You must also site them thoughtfully, for they are easily overpowered by shrubs of larger foliage. But where subtlety of colour and delicacy of form are needed, one or other of the pittosporums may be the answer. In doubtful circumstances plant them 2–3ft away from a warm wall, but they will not submit to being tied back. Their name means merely that the seed is coated with a sticky substance (*pitta*, pitch, and *sporus*, seed); such are the heights of imagination to which taxonomists can aspire. Any reasonable soil will do. Prune as you will, either for shaping or to remedy frost damage. Pittosporum regenerate well from the old wood. Propagate by late summer cuttings or by seed.

The most generally accepted, though not the hardiest, are **P. tenuifolium** (the Kohuhu of New Zealand) and its varieties. They have slender, tapering trunks and a pyramidal outline. Their attractions lie in the happy conjunction of their black twigs with their ivory-

they are of easy culture in any soil that is not waterlogged, grow very fast but not too big and are decidedly decorative where the wind is not too vicious.

Imagine a laburnum growing in the form of a bush, with its pea-flower clusters growing erect instead of pendulous and its individual florets much enlarged, and you have the picture of **P. laburnifolius**, which is the one usually grown. It quickly reaches up to 12ft high and wide, with the typical trifoliate leaves of a laburnum. The flower trusses are 3in long and slightly hairy and the individual florets $1\frac{1}{2}$in, in May. The stems are soft and pithy, but in z8 in full sun it is usually safely evergreen in the open. If in doubt, give it a wall, but do not train it thereto. Not long lived, but easily perpetuated from seed, and then brought on in pots, as it disapproves of root disturbance. Cut worn-out stems to the ground in spring.

edged, olive-green leaves and in the honey-sweet scent so unexpectedly exhaled from their maroon flowers in spring. In warm, sheltered places, especially near the sea, they can reach 30ft, but elsewhere, in z8, they rarely exceed 12ft.

Of the several varieties of Kohuhu, the one which commands popular acclaim is the Northern Irish 'Silver Queen', in which the dainty leaves are prettily margined white. 'Warnham Gold' is all-yellow, cheerful in winter. 'Purpureum' is purple-leaved all winter. 'James Stirling' has small, rounded, silver-touched leaves.

Closely associated with the Kohuhu and hitherto classed as one of its varieties is **P. 'Garnettii'**, now considered to be a hybrid. This is a picturesque plant, very like 'Silver Queen', but with a pink, crinkly margin.

We have said that pittosporums have paltry flowers. This is not quite true of **P. tobira**, which is prettily festooned with clusters of small, five-petalled, creamy-white flowers scented of orange-blossoms among its dark green, blunt-tipped ("obovate") leaves from April onwards, but it can grow 20ft high in favoured places as in the Mediterranean lands. The tobira is of rather stiff posture, but well clothed and makes a fine, thick-set hedge. It is drought-hardy, and, unlike tennufolium, seems by all accounts to need a continental climate to ripen its wood, rather than a maritime one. In 'Variegatum' the leaves have cream edges. 'Wheeler's Dwarf' is a good, close-set foreground shrub of a foot or more. z8–9.

Other pittosporums within our discipline are:

P. eugenioides 'Variegatum'. We really ought not to include this, as it is decidedly tender and, in the right circumstances, can reach 30ft or more. But it is one of the most beautiful of variegated plants, with clean-cut margins of white on the 4in, undulate leaves and a heavenly scent from its small, densely packed clusters of tiny, dirty-white flowers. z9–10.

P. patulum is one of the hardiest and the most sweetly scented of all as its sombre little flowers open in May. Of slender growth, it is recognised by its very narrow leaves edged with blunt, shallow teeth. About 10ft, more in warm spots. z8.

P. ralphii is outstanding as a wind-screen, standing extreme exposure in sand near the sea. Its grey-green leaves and silvery shoots are decorative, but it must be planted when very young, before its tap-root becomes twisted.

We include **P. dallii** only because it is one of the hardiest, growing to 12ft in a neatly rounded fashion of stiff growth and leathery, toothed leaves of 4in. Rarely flowers. z8–9.

Other pittosporums are either too tree-like, too tender or of too little interest, often differentiated from one another in minor detail only. But we may note that *buchananii* and *colensoi* are excellent wind-breaks.

PLUMBAGO, shrub species. See *Ceratostigma*

PONCIRUS
Japanese bitter orange

Ferociously armed with dagger-like thorns, often 2in long, *P. trifoliata* is not merely boy-proof but almost commando-proof. It is deciduous, green-stemmed, densely twiggy but often only scantily vested in pinnate leaves, fleetingly ornamental between the thorns in May with large, white, single, sweetly scented flowers, which turn into bitter but pretty oranges that may be of 2in diameter. Despite its fierce weapons, it is a handsome and shapely shrub that may slowly reach 30ft high and wide, though we have seen none much more than 12ft. It throws readily from ground level and makes a formidable hedge if clipped in June. Full sun. Known in my youth as *Aegle sepiaria*. z5–6.

'Citrange' is a name given to a hybrid between the poncirus and a true citrus, raised in both Florida and France. It is less hardy and no more ornamental than the spiny parent.

POTENTILLA
Cinquefoil

A most confusing jungle of names confronts us when we step into this field of easy, popular, extremely hardy shrubs. The cause of the confusion is the enormously wide distribution of the cinquefoils over the greater part of the northern hemisphere, overlapping each other with little more than geographical differences. We walk with Bean in what is the most recently defined path, but Mr Christopher Brickell, the Director of Wisley, is very near the mark when he says that, for gardening purposes, they might very well all be included in the omnibus name *Potentilla fruticosa*.

Most potentillas belong to the herbaceous border, but we are concerned only with the shrubby species. For most gardeners the main interest lies in those selections that we group here as Garden Forms, which are of indeterminate origins but are usually catalogued under *P. fruticosa*. To the botanist the distinctions between one species and another are determined mainly, though not wholly, by the hairiness of the leaves, a factor that interests the gardener only when the effect of the hairiness is to give a silvery patina to the leaf.

Otherwise, all have a strong family resemblance and an almost arctic hardiness (z2). They are as easy as pie to grow, whether in sun or in quite unpromising umbrage. Seldom more than thigh-high, they make dense little thickets and good little hedges. The leaves are nearly always pinnate, having very small leaflets, usually in fives, hence "cinquefoil".

Set among them are small, simple, five-petalled, strawberry-like flowers, but nearly always some shade of yellow, and, with rare exceptions, flowering the whole of summer without intercession but never in absolute profusion. In winter the brown stems look as dead as old bracken. They ignore conventional pruning, and the only way to rejuvenate them is to amputate old stems at ground level. The botanical name, applied rather to the herbaceous species, simply means medicinally potent.

P. arbuscula has a list of aliases that occupies three lines of print. As now understood, it is a plant of about 2ft, of slightly shaggy appearance with (usually) trifoliate leaves and relatively large flowers, borne with most abundance in late summer. The almost identical varieties *albicans* and *bulleyana* have leaves of a silken, silvery coating. See 'Elizabeth' in the list of Garden Forms.

P. davurica grows to about 4ft with shaggy and hairy stems when young and smooth pinnate leaves with five leaflets and (usually) white flowers. Like all these potentillas that botanists have unwisely tried to segregate into separate species, it is confusingly variable, but is seen at its best in its variety **mandshurica**, a very attractive dwarf, with silken leaves, excellent in shade, formerly treated as a separate species. Var. *subalbicans* is much stronger, and var. *veitchii*, very hairy in the leaf, can grow to 5ft.

P. fruticosa is the one that matters most, fathering or mothering many fine offspring. In itself, it is usually a 3ft shrub, with shredded, brown stems, pinnate leaves with five leaflets and flowers of bright yellow, with numerous stamens, native to Britain, parts of N. America and many other countries, growing in all sorts of soils, and so adopting many diverse forms, one of which is unisexual.

P. parvifolia is a dwarf of varying propensities, with small flowers, and small, bright green leaflets in sevens (usually). In the wild the colours of the flowers vary greatly and they may have had an influence in the rearing of the orange-tinted garden hybrids.

P. × sulphurascens. Pale yellow flowers, somewhat bell-shaped. 'Logan' is a good selection of 4ft.

P. salesoviana. Perhaps the most distinct but rarest of all, having blush-pink flowers in June and July on a 3ft shrub. It seems to need a harsh, stony soil.

GARDEN FORMS
These named cinquefoils are either garden-bred or else selections from seed collected in the wild. P. fruticosa is the dominant parent. Unless noted otherwise, all have pinnate leaves

and yellow flowers. We list the group of orange-tinted varieties at the end hereof.

'Beesii'. A pretty shrub of less than 2ft with leaves lightly silvered, and small, bright yellow flowers. Once treated as a separate species.

'Elizabeth'. Generally regarded as the best of all and once taken as synonymous with P. arbuscula. Large flowers of rich, soft yellow, paler on the backs of the petals. Leaves densely hairy beneath. The most remarkable for its continuity of blooming. Makes a very attractive floral hedge. 3ft. Watch for mildew and spray twice with malathion against red spider.

'Friedrichsenii' ('Berlin Beauty'). Pale flowers on too big a shrub.

'Gold Drop' (farreri). Neat and dwarf. Very small leaflets in sevens. Small, cheerful flowers.

'Goldfinger'. Large flowers. Leaves tinted blue, seven leaflets. 4ft.

'Jackman's Variety'. Like the above, but taller and the flowers not quite so large.

'Katherine Dykes'. Small primrose flowers, freely produced. A dense shrub 4ft by 5ft. A good hedger.

'Klondyke'. Like 'Gold Drop' but with larger flowers of bright, deep yellow. Slow but good.

'Lady Daresbury'. Arching branches, forming a dome.

'Longacre'. Low and spreading.

'Moonlight' ('Maanelys'). Soft yellow flowers on grey-green leaves. 4ft by 8ft. Danish.

'Munstead Dwarf'. 18in. Close and dense. Good.

'Mount Everest'. 4ft. White, intermittent.

'Ochroleuca'. 6ft. Cream.

'Parvifolia'. 3ft. Flowers bright yellow. The main display is in early summer.

'Primrose Beauty'. Well-named and one of the best. A picturesque shrub with arching branches, 4ft by 6ft. Silken, grey-green leaves. Flowers cup-shaped at first, opening flat, paling, but with a darker eye.

'Vilmoriniana'. 5ft, stiffly erect, with silken, silvered leaves and cream flowers, borne sparingly over a long period.

'William Purdom'. ('Purdomii'). 4ft by 5ft, erect. Leaves bright green, Abundant canary flowers. A form of P. parvifolia.

Orange-tinted varieties. Several of these have found favour. They differ somewhat in the intensity of their tints, but all are inclined to be unpredictable and pale in hot climates. With the possible exception of 'Red Ace', all are commonly said to colour best in partial shade or cloudy weather, but this has not always been our experience and they are often just yellow in shade. All are about 2ft high. 'Tangerine' is well named. 'Sunset', a sport of it, is more deeply tinted. 'Day Dawn', another sport, is, at its best, prettily flushed with pale apricot. 'Red Ace' has some flowers that are really red in Britain, others of varying hues of orange, a good but variable cinquefoil, not colouring fully in hot weather.

PRINSEPIA

Dense, tangled, thorny, deciduous shrubs, of lax, arching, spreading growth, good for hedging. Simple flowers of five petals. Small, cherry-like, edible fruits. On old branches the bark peels off. Any reasonable soil. Named after James Princeps.

P. sinensis, 7ft, with slim, 2in leaves. Flowers yellow, among the thorns in May. Fruits in August. z4.

P. uniflora. Disorderly growth to 6ft. Leaves dark, polished green. Very small, white flowers liable to damage from late frosts. Fruits, if borne, like Morello cherries. z5.

P. utilis. 9ft high by 12ft wide. Leaves up to 4in long. Flowers cream, scented, in racemes in autumn and, if not hit by frost, the fruits develop next May. z8.

PRIVET. See *Ligustrum*

PROSTANTHERA
Mint bush

These evergreen Australians are decidedly for Keats's "warm south" only, some being of little account, but others as pretty as you please, thronged with small bells, and clothed with small, aromatic leaves. For light, acid or neutral soil, though a mild flavour of lime seems acceptable. Full sun. Not easy to come by. Those mentioned here succeed in such climates as those of Cornwall and Devon, especially if given the comfort of a warm wall, though they must be grown "free", not tied in. They normally break from low down, producing fairly erect, but branching stems, forming a bushy plant. None is hardier than z9.

If necessary to restrain growth, prune after flowering. If damage from frost is feared, wait to see if new growth starts and cut back to there. Propagation is easy from soft summer cuttings in sand and peat.

Perhaps the most desirable of the mint bushes is **P. rotundifolia**, which may grow anything up to 10ft, flowering in imperial splendour of rich purple in April and May from nearly black buds among tiny, rounded leaves of polished green.

Generally considered to be a trifle hardier is **P. cuneata**, a 2ft shrub, with flowers of pale lilac, spotted with purple in May and again later.

P. lasianthos is a very large shrub with panicles of pale lavender, spotted red in the throat.

P. melissiflora parvifolia (*P. sieberi*) is probably as favoured as rotundifolia, but is a big plant of 12ft, of fast growth with very small, papery, dark green leaves and terminal clusters of several lilac bells.

PRUNUS

Flowering Cherry, Almond, Peach, Plum, Apricot

We have described the larger sorts of "the loveliest of trees" in our previous book, so that here we have naturally to exclude the sumptuous Japanese cherries, the exquisite almonds that dare the ice of February, the charming *Prune mume* and the big bird cherries. However, we are left with a pretty enough barrow-load of

shrubby ones, several of which are astonishingly hardy. Several (in addition to the specific orchard varieties) are valued for their fruits and others make fine hedges. All but one or two flower in the spring, those that have doubled blossoms lasting the longest. In general, they prosper in loamy soils, whether acid or alkaline, but we shall note a few that take kindly to sandy or stony ones. The plums, as we judge, seem happiest in lime.

Botanists group the prunus (which is the Latin name for a plum) into a number of subgenera, often sub-divided into "sections". Thus plums and apricots are sub-genus Prunus (with several sections). Almonds and apricots are subgenus Amygdalus; cherries are sub-genus Cerasus; the bird cherries are grouped under Padus and the cherry-laurels under Laurocerasus. There are also some hybrids. These groupings are of some help to the gardener where pruning and use are concerned and they can be of critical concern if the nurseryman grafts an almond, for example, on an incompatible stock. In passing, we may note that the almond itself, formerly familiar as *P. amygdalus*, is now *P. dulcis*.

By and large, with the inevitable exceptions, prunus are best left untouched by the knife, but they vary a great deal in their behaviour, so that we have to consider carefully what to choose and where to plant it, so that natural growth can be developed. Peaches and apricots, however, make a better show if the flowered shoots are cut back to some promising new growth in order to give a good display next spring. Cherries are a special case and it is dangerous to prune them (if at all) much before or after 1st June. We shall note some other exceptions as we go along, but when in doubt follow the golden rule of pruning: don't.

A few enemies have to be watched. Aphis can be kept at bay by a systemic insecticide. The most serious, attacking cherries and almonds in particular, is peach-leaf curl, in which the leaf becomes blistered, twisted and distorted by a fungus. Spray with Bordeaux mixture or some other copper fungicide just as the leaves are about to fall and again just before the new ones emerge. Silver-leaf of cherries, which explains itself, is a notifiable disease in Britain and you must lop off and burn whole branches or possibly burn the whole tree. Occasionally another disease makes the plant burst out into "witches' brooms", consisting of dense bunches of shoots before the leaves open. Remove at once and burn and spray with Bordeaux mixture or an equivalent. Feeding and mulching greatly fortify plants against disease.

Propagation of prunus is not always easy, but most can be done in gentle heat by heel cuttings of young shoots just beginning to get firm. Many a good tree has been raised simply from the nuts, if they are first half-buried on their sides to get well frosted, after which, if protected from mice and squirrels, they will germinate in the spring.

Not all the plants we list below are what a gardener would call "choice", but, in accordance with our brief, we make a fairly comprehensive catalogue to suit many situations and to hint at what to avoid as well as choose. Those that have no value at all are omitted. Assume all to be deciduous except where shown otherwise (the cherry-laurels). The sub-genera are noted in brackets.

P. alleghaniensis, the Alleghany plum or American sloe. Straggling shrub of 15ft. Saw-edged leaves. Clusters of small, blush flowers in April. Small, purple fruits dusted with a blue bloom. (Prunus). z5.

P. arabica is an almond of 5ft, with green, almost leafless stems and small, white flowers, accustomed to arid country.

P. besseyi, the Western or Rocky Mountains cherry, of 5ft, extremely hardy, grown particularly for its small, sweet, purple-black fruits, which are produced in great abundance (though sparingly in Britain). To thrive it needs cold winters and dry summers. Leaves grey-green, slightly toothed. Very small, white flowers in May. (Cerasus). z3.

A very useful hybrid of sub-arctic hardiness came into being when, early in this century, Dr Nils Hansen, of the South Dakota Experimental Station, produced **P. × cistena**, known as the purple-leaved sand-cherry. Its

distinction lies in its leaf, which opens crimson and turns to coppery-red, growing to 7ft high and wide. The small white flowers fructify as purple cherries. Taking kindly to pruning, it makes a colourful hedge. The breeding is *P. pumila* (or perhaps *besseyi*), both of which are "sand cherries", crossed with the purple-leaved *P. cerasifera* 'Pissardii'. It roots well from hardwood cuttings, unusual for a plum. "Cistena" is Red Indian (Sioux tribe) for "baby". z2.

P. concinna. A pretty shrub of only 7ft. White or blush flowers in great profusion on naked stems in March or April. The leaves, when they appear afterwards, are at first purple-tinted and finely toothed and drawn out to a point. (Cerasus). z5.

P. fruticosa, the ground-cherry, becomes a neat, spreading mound not more than 3ft high, composed of slender branches clad with green, shining leaves, small white flowers and tiny red fruits. There is a variegated form. The practice of grafting it on a standard stem destroys its character (Cerasus). z3.

More popular than any of these so far is **P. glandulosa**, the slender, willowy dwarf

Prunus glandulosa 'Sinensis'

flowering almond or Chinese bush-cherry, particularly its double-flowered forms, which are among the most charming of small shrubs. Growing to about 4ft, their branches sparkle all the length of their stems in white ('Alba Plena') or pink ('Sinensis' or 'Rosea Plena') in early May. Give them a warm spot and prune the flowered shoots very hard back, almost to the ground after blossom-fall. (Cerasus). z4–5.

P. ilicifolia, the holly-leaf cherry, is very distinctive, being evergreen and having broad leaves of dark, glossy green, sharply toothed all round the edges. The very small, white flowers are clustered in dangling spikes (racemes) in late spring. Small, purple fruits follow. A Californian of 10ft, it needs to bask in the sun, is slow of growth and accustomed to dry soil. (A cherry laurel). z8–9.

P. incana, the willow-cherry. Loose, open shrub, averaging 6ft, with toothed, tapering leaves, very woolly underneath and very small flowers borne singly in April (Cerasus). z5.

For a dry, sunny place, unlike most prunus, yet happy in a cold climate, the pretty, fast-growing Afghan cherry suits our purpose. This is **P. jacquemontii**, which is a slender, 10ft shrub, with broad, toothed leaves and clusters of small rose flowers in late April, followed by red juicy fruits (Cerasus). z6–7.

A prunus that will be welcomed for its very early flowering, weather permitting, is the very distinctive **P. kansuensis**, which may wreathe its naked branches in white as early as January. It is a tall shrub that may reach 20ft. (Amygdalus).

Of a totally different character from all those reviewed so far is the evergreen cherry-laurel, **P. laurocerasus**, known sometimes in America also as the English laurel, but it is neither a true laurel nor English. In the main, it is primarily a utility shrub, making an exceptionally good shelter-belt up to 18ft. It is often used also as a formal hedge, but clipping with the shears, which cut through the large leaves, causes disfigurement to the discerning eye. On the other hand, as it regenerates freely, it can in certain circumstances be cut back very hard indeed and coppiced. As an isolated specimen it

makes a good, but not choice, tree, with erect spikes of white flowers. The roots are very hungry. z6–7.

Nurseries list quantities of varieties of the cherry-laurel, of which the finest is the large-leaved 'Magnoliifolia', but 'Caucasica' is also very good indeed. 'Otinii' has almost black leaves. The German 'Herbergii' is erect, dense and very hardy, but for sheer hardiness nothing beats 'Shipkaensis'. z5.

The cherry-laurel also has several dwarf forms, very useful for clothing the ground, especially on banks. 'Zabeliana' spreads in horizontal tiers, thickening up to 3ft and spreading 12ft or more, with willow-like leaves. The recent 'Otto Luyken' has made a distinct impact, eventually making a dark green mound nearly 4ft high, the leaves 4in long.

The handsome, evergreen Portuguese laurel (again, not a laurel), **Prunus lusitanica**, is put to much the same uses as the cherry-laurel and is of the same classification, but is, in all, superior to it, making very fine, dark-leaved, informal hedges or screens of 12ft or so and, if not harshly pruned, putting out a profusion of 10in racemes of off-white flowers in late May from the previous summer's growth. In Britain it too often suffers from the fate of familiarity. Among its few cultivars is 'Myrtifolia', with very small leaves. 'Variegata', very attractively bordered white, is less hardy. Like the cherry-laurel, the Portuguese will make quite a big tree if planted in isolation. z7.

One of the very hardiest of the prunus is **P. maritima**, the beach-plum or sand-plum, so called because it is "as happy as a sand-boy" on the seashore (and elsewhere). It grows to about 6ft in compact form, rather broader than high, with toothed leaves and a profusion of white flowers in twos and threes in May. In its best forms the red or purple fruits are juicy and delicious. In 'Flava' they are yellow (Prunus). z3.

P. persica is the peach, in which our concern will be only in those grown for the rich beauty of their flowers rather than for their juicy fruits. They seem to do better in a somewhat lean, stony soil rather than a fat loam and they must have plenty of sun. They are fortunately just caught within our net, rarely reaching 20ft and being of bushy habit. April is their flowering time, those with double or semi-doubled flowers being the most favoured. Beware of peach-leaf curl and (in America) the peach-borer. (Amygdalus). z5.

There are a great many named varieties, of which the sovereign choice is the queenly, double, pink 'Klara Mayer'. Others of great charm, all opulent of their floral treasures, are:

'Aurora'. Rose, semi-double, petals fringed.

'Helen Borchers'. Deep rose, semi-double.

'Iceberg'. Charming white, semi-double.

'Palace Peach'. Deep crimson, double.

'Russell's Red'. Large, semi-double, crimson.

'Windle Weeping'. A sweeping, purple crinoline.

P. pumila, the original (we suppose) "sand-cherry" or dwarf American cherry, is very hardy. Its behaviour is rather uncertain, it being often only 2–3ft high, but sometimes rising to 8ft. The grey-green leaves are almost toothless, colouring well in the fall, and the shrub is crammed with clusters of white blossoms in mid-May, but a good form must be sought for, because sometimes the flowers are but a dirty white. Very small, purple fruits, scarcely edible. The natural variety *susquehanae* keeps to below 3ft; *depressa* is quite prostrate. (Cerasus). z2.

P. spinosa is the sloe or blackthorn, a spiny bush of up to 15ft, not at all choice, but very useful for clothing waste ground and exposed places, where, growing in the meanest soils, it will quickly colonise by suckers. A wilding of Britain and other parts of Europe, it is of some fame for its black, bitter fruits, which make that exhilarating drink, sloe gin. The wood is extremely hard and makes a strong, knobbly walking-stick or, for the wilder Irish, a shillelagh. Normally the small, white flowers appear before the leaves, and there is a doubled variety, but quite the best one to have is 'Purpurea', which has beautiful purple leaves, pale pink flowers and fewer spines than the whites. (Prunus) z4.

P. tangutica. A large, dense, uncommon

beauty of up to 15ft or so. Charming, solitary, rose-pink flowers in March, leaves round-toothed, fruits nearly 1in wide, coated with a peach-like bloom. (Amygdalus). z6.

The dwarf Russian almond, **P. tenella**, is a great favourite of extreme hardiness, yet fond of a warm spot, averaging 4ft. The rose-red flowers appear in rich abundance in twos and threes in April–May among saw-edged leaves, and the fruit is a small almond. It is a very pretty bush, but one of those that should be grown on its own roots, which is easy enough from layers, but is too often grafted by nurserymen on a plum stock. This little almond is very variable in its details, with several varietal or group names, but undoubtedly the finest of all is the brilliant cultivar 'Fire Hill'. The leaves are thick and dark green and look well all summer. If you want a white, there is 'Alba'. No pruning needed. (Amygdalus). z2.

Another of extreme hardiness is the Manchu or downy cherry, **P. tomentosa**. This grows

Prunus triloba

to about 8ft, its branches filmed with a pale down and its toothed, matt leaves densely woolly on the reverse. Unfortunately, the small, pink flowers of April fall all too soon. The red fruits, though small, are delicious in a pie. (Cerasus). z2.

P. triloba is one of the gems of the smaller prunus. The shrub is reported as growing to 15ft and in early April is wreathed with pink, doubled, rosette-like flowers, before the leaves unfurl. Enchanting at that time, it is rather a plain Jane for the rest of the season. The fruits being of no account, prune the flowered wood hard back almost to the ground immediately after blossom-fall to provide next year's display. In cold districts it makes a delightful wall plant. The term "triloba" approximately describes the shape of the leaf.

On no account accept *triloba* if grafted on a plum stock, nor be enticed by the beguiling little half-standard on which it is often grafted, or you will get a forest of suckers, as I know to my cost. Propagate by cuttings of firm wood or by layers. (Amygdalus). z5.

PSEUDOPANAX

We include these tender, evergreen New Zealanders, so strange to northern eyes, as a matter of record. Most make sizeable trees and are remarkable for the changeability of their leaves, altering as they age, especially in *P. crassifolius*, which has four distinct leaf stages. They like the moist air of Ireland. However, *P. davidii*, which comes from China, not New Zealand, and is hardier, can earn a place here. This is a slow-growing shrub, averaging 15ft, with dark, leathery, slender leaves, borne singly in compound form. The flowers are green-yellow, in small pyramids, in July. z8–9.

PSEUDOWINTERA

An uncouth sort of name that shows the plant's comradeship with Winter's-bark (*Drimys win-*

teri). This is one of the most handsome of variegated shrubs, its leathery, elliptic leaves being a blend of purple, pink and silver-gilt, and aromatic to boot. Very small, cup-shaped yellow flowers peer in clusters from the leaf axils. This is **P. colorata**. It grows only head-high, but is regrettably tender. z9.

P. axillaris is very much bigger and plain green.

PSORALEA

Deciduous, tender shrubs of the pea order, with small, typical pea-flowers and pods and compound leaves. For warm places only, but easily maintained by seed or cuttings. The branches are dotted with wart-like glands (Greek *psoraleos*, a wart). Reckon all as z9.

The usual one is the South American *P. glandulosa*, a slender, erect shrub of 8ft, giving us spikes of small white-and-blue flowers in abundance from May to September from among trifoliate leaves. Any reasonable soil.

P. pinnata is a larger plant with beautiful pinnate leaves and blue flowers in June, growing very fast. For sandy-peaty soil. The same soil suits *P. aphylla*, which has varied foliage, single white-and-blue flowers all summer. Both from South Africa.

PTELEA

This rather awkward name is ancient Greek for the elm, the botanists having purloined it to describe a breed of plants which the Greeks knew not but which has a very similar seed. The pteleas are deciduous and rather large for us, particularly the most favoured and hardiest, *P. trifoliata*, the hop-tree or wafer-ash, which becomes a spreading tree of 25ft. Others, however, deserve a place as foliage plants, with trifoliate, aromatic leaves, though their flowers are of small account. Thus *P. baldwinii crenulata*, the western hop-tree from California, reaches

15ft or so with slim, trifoliate leaves, not quite as handsome as its big brother. z7–8. *P. nitens* has glossy, rather broad leaflets like stiff writing paper from yellow-tinted twigs (z5). *P. poly-adenia* has leaves like soft leather, very aromatic. z6–7.

Maybe a better candidate and certainly more distinctive than any of these, however, is *P. lutescens* from the Grand Canyon, which has branchlets of shining silver-grey (pewter col-our). The trifoliate leaves have slim, lance-form leaflets, which are thickly sprinkled with aro-matic oil-glands, clearly visible against the light. A shrub of modest size, 10ft at Kew, probably more elsewhere. z6–7.

PUNICA
Pomegranate

We should be misleading our readers if we were to suggest (as some writers appear to do) that they could get full value from the pomegranate (*P. granatum*) in any but a really warm place.

The plant as a whole seems to be hardy in z7, certainly in z8 (which means most of Britain), but it seldom dares to open its red, crumpled funnels in real abundance where the tempera-ture falls below freezing-point. Nor does it ripen its fabled red-gold fruits below z10, unless toasted on a warm wall. However, it is a very handsome, deciduous-foliage shrub, especially in its brilliant autumn dress, and if cut to the ground by winter's knife, usually regenerates well. Expect it to grow 15ft or more. To the Romans it was the Punic or Carthaginian apple.

PYRACANTHA
Firethorn

These count as some of our finest berrying shrubs. Nearly always evergreen, obedient to man's will in many ways, not excessively thorny, fast-growing, tolerant of all sorts of soils, they are the most easy-going of shrubs and are often the only answer to a difficult problem. Though they may lack the floral glamour of a camellia, a rose or a rhododendron, they can, however, cause you to "stand and stare" when seen robing the walls of a whole house with their dense shroud of white flowers in spring or their coloured berries in autumn and winter. The name comes from the Greek *pyr*, fire, and *acanthos*, thorn.

The firethorns can be grown naturally as open-ground shrubs or constrained to form the densest of hedges or trained on house walls by either espalier or fan methods. In Britain and western Europe they are entirely hardy and evergreen, facing the bitterest of winds with equanimity, and are likewise hardy in most parts of North America from Zone 5 south, but may lose their leaves in cold places. They emulate the ivy as a cloak for a cold, sunless wall and are, of course, more colourful.

The flowers of all species break out from their green background in a white froth of little bunches (corymbs), forming as spurs on stems that grew in the previous summer, and the berries (which are pomes) are nearly always some shade of red or orange, though we shall note some that are yellow.

The pruning of firethorns is a simple matter. When grown as open-ground shrubs, leave them alone generally. As hedges, clip back the sides only after flowering and in August until they reach the height you want, then clip them back fairly hard all over whenever they become shaggy. On house walls or fences the espalier method is best, using wires fixed to the host. Select and tie in the leading and horizontal stems, removing all others and cutting hard back any outward-growing shoots ("breast-wood" or "foreright" shoots). Subsequently, just keep them cut back hard, especially after flowering. You will need a ladder before many years have gone by.

Propagate from summer cuttings in misty conditions.

Pyracanthas are prone in some areas to two serious maladies — the deadly fire-blight (see in Cotoneaster) and the debilitating scab, which is seen as a sooty coating of spores on leaf and fruit, causing the leaves to wither and fall. The usual treatment for scab is to spray with captan three times in March and April and again twice in June. Some American sorts, however, have recently been raised which have so far been resistant to both diseases. Birds can also be a nuisance, gobbling up the red berries, though often ignoring the yellow.

The biggest firethorn is **P. atalantioides**, which will sometimes reach 20ft in the open and is almost thornless. It is one of the finest of all plants for a sunless wall, which it will cover to a considerable height. The leaves, rather large for a firethorn, are broadly oval. It can be built up into a small tree by confining it to a single stem for its first few years, removing the lower shoots a few at a time. The small fruits are very long-lasting. It achieved its fame when grown by the late Hon. Vicary Gibbs, in his garden at Aldenham, in Hertfordshire, and for some time was accordingly called P. gibbsii. z6.

P. angustifolia, the narrow-leaved firethorn, is rather less hardy, but can make a fine 12ft shrub with orange berries, retained all winter. Prone to degenerate into a low, sprawling plant. z7.

P. 'Buttercup' is a hybrid, with rather small berries, but perhaps the brightest of the yellow. Spreading habit.

Perhaps the best-known firethorn, because it has been cultivated for centuries, is **P. coccinea**, known of old in Britain as simply the pyracanth. It is a very fine shrub that can grow to 15ft, but is usually much smaller, unless grown on a wall, for which it is really splendid. Birds gorge themselves on its bright red berries. z6.

Several varieties of the pyracanth have been raised, the most famous of which, surpassing its parent, is the French-raised 'Lalandei'. This is a superlative and popular variety, with broad leaves and extra hardy. z5. Other varieties, all rated z5 and all but one having orange berries, have been raised more recently, nearly all in America, notably:

'Monrovia'. Orange berries. Upright habit. For open-ground planting.

'Loboy' (or 'Lowboy'). Only 2–3ft high, but spreading widely.

'Kasan'. From Russia. Orange. Of moderate size, upright but spreading. The hardiest clone of all in the USA but not a success so far in Britain.

Others are 'Thornless' which explains itself, and 'Wyattii', a useful one for poor soils. In addition, several American varieties or hybrids have been raised of particular value for their resistance to fire-blight and scab. They include:

'Mohave'. A fine hybrid of upright carriage with orange berries in August, unfavoured by birds (*koidzumii* × *coccinea*). z6.

'Rutgers'. Like 'Loboy' but highly resistant to disease.

'Fiery Cascade'. Scarlet berries in August. The hardiest true red and very resistant to disease.

From the old pyracanth and its offspring we turn to the less exciting, but still very good **P. crenato-serrata**. This is a big 15ft shrub, rather like atalantioides, but flowering in June and having a blunter and serrated leaf. 'Knap Hill Lemon' is a good yellow, of strong growth. z7.

Despite its name, **P. crenulata**, the Nepal white-thorn, is something different, which we can consider simply as an orange-berried version of the common pyracanth but much more tender, and a deal more thorny. z8.

P. koidzumii is the least hardy of the firethorns, but a fine, showy 10ft shrub which is a great favourite in the south-eastern United States and, of course, quite hardy in most parts of Britain. As suitable for training on a wall as in the open. Among some excellent selections are 'Victory', which has very dark red berries, the wide-spreading 'San José' and the prostrate 'Santa Cruz'. z8.

Two orange hybrids, both flowering in mid-September and both apparently scab-free, are high-ranking firethorns, but not very well-known. 'Orange Charmer' from Germany, comes from *rogersiana* × *coccinea*. 'Orange Glow', from Holland, makes a very fine specimen shrub, from *crenato-serrata* × *coccinea*. 'Golden Charmer' is a German newcomer, of the same parentage as 'Orange Charmer'.

What sets one firethorn apart from another is often difficult to define, but we have a strong predilection for the Chinese **P. rogersiana**. You can say that it has very small leaves, that it is pyramidal when grown alone and that it is rather prickly. But these points do not alone explain its merits, for it has a distinctive character. The flowers, which do not open until June, are decidedly the most attractive of any, and are borne in profligate abundance. The berries are red, except in the excellent yellow form 'Flava'. It grows very fast to 10ft and makes one of the finest, densest of hedges, but when so grown, needs frequent trimming to keep it in good shape. z7.

P. 'Shawnee'. Another American which has so far resisted fire-blight and scab. A fine, big, spreading shrub with berries of light orange. It is a second generation seedling of the hybrid *crenato-serrata* × *koidzumii*. z7–8.

P. 'Taliensis' is a handsome hybrid with bright yellow fruits, but they fall all too soon.

Another example of how hard it is to explain the difference between one firethorn and another except in minor botanical detail is seen in the English **P.** × **watereri**, a very fine shrub indeed of dense and tight growth. As a hedge, it is curiously springy if leant against, like a mattress. If you have a choice, you cannot go wrong with this one. Parentage unstated. z6–7.

QUICKTHORN is *Crataegus monogyna*

QUINCE, flowering. See *Chaenomeles*

RAPIOLEPIS. See *Rhaphiolepis*

RHAMNUS
Buckthorn

With two exceptions these are ragamuffins of no ornamental quality. Those that will endure an almost arctic climate have some use for gardens in such places. These include *R. alnifolia*, a low, spreading, deciduous, bright green mound, and *R. frangula*, the alder-buckthorn, native of England, from which the best gunpowder is made, and of which a selected form known as 'Columnaris' or 'Tallboy', is used in America for hedging, and esteemed for its glossy dark green foliage. Both z3.

However, there is certainly a decorative quality in the variegated form of the big *R. alaternus* named 'Argenteovariegata', which becomes a cheerful mass of silvered evergreenery, but it is much less hardy (z7–8). Striking foliage is also found in *R. imeretina*, which has leaves that may be more than a foot long, and in *R. fallax*. Both z5. Plenty of better shrubs are at our command, but these buckthorns have some use in derelict sites.

RHAPHIOLEPIS

Often spelt without the first h, the mongrel Greek name meaning "needle-scaled", from the small, sharp growths on the bracts.

Excellent as foundation plants, the rhaphiolepis are pretty, evergreen, well-mannered but rather lazy shrubs, with small, leathery, dark green, usually oval leaves and small, slightly scented, white or pink flowers like very small wild roses gathered together in clusters, followed by small, black berries. They need plenty of sun and a good loam and are favoured garden shrubs in California.

The hardiest is **R. umbellata**, which, in favourable conditions, can reach 10ft, but is usually much less. The young leaves emerge in swaddling clothes of grey felt before turning dark green, very stout and leathery. The flowers are pure white, in stiff trusses in May–June. z7–8.

Less hardy but more beautiful is **R.** × **delacourii**, a French hybrid of shapely and well-bred carriage, 7ft tall, and bearing flowers of a lovely, fresh, rose pink in erect, 4in trusses, usually appearing in spring. 'Coates' Crimson' is a selected clone. Parents: umbellata × indica. z8–9.

R. indica, a graceful shrub with lance-shaped leaves and blush flowers, accentuated by

71. Rhaphiolepis umbellata

bold tufts of pink stamens, is the least hardy. Three favourites in California are the dwarf 'Enchantress' with large, pink flowers, the round-formed 'Fascination', with deep pink flowers, white-eyed, and the spreading 'Snow Dwarf'. z8–9.

RHODODENDRON
(including azaleas)

To attempt a full review of the regiments of the rhododendron (including the azalea squadrons) within our limited arena is out of the question. Their numbers are vast. Many volumes have been written about them, including one by ourselves (*The Rothschild Rhododendrons*). All we can do here is to pass swiftly along their ranks, like an impatient general anxious to get away to his polo and his port. We shall ignore altogether those in tropical uniforms and posted in Java, Borneo and suchlike stations and others that can perform only limited duty, and shall confine ourselves to those fit for general duty in everyday operations.

Thus our notes here will serve as no more than an introduction to what can become a highly technical subject for those people who are dedicated enthusiasts of all the subtle differences that can be discerned, not only within the numerous species, but also in the "series", subspecies, natural varieties, "formas" and almost microscopic diversifications, about which your rhododendron fanatic will argue with the fervour of a hot-gospeller. In short, we shall be simple.

The behaviour of rhododendrons varies considerably. They may be ground-creepers or tree-like or mounded bushes of all sorts of sizes. The leaves may be huge, as in *R. sinogrande* (up to $2\frac{1}{2}$ft long) or minute, as in many dwarfs. In general they are like broad-bladed lances, but they may be round, as in *R. williamsianum*, or anything in between. Many have a felt-like undercoating, called an indumentum, cunningly designed to control the supply of water vapour. Except for the deciduous azaleas, nearly all are evergreen. The flowers, which may be in the shapes of bells, trumpets or occasionally tubes, are clustered together in trusses at the ends of twigs, but unhappily are on parade for a very short time.

Fundamentally, the culture of rhododendrons (among which azaleas are included) is quite easy if the conditions are right; if they are not right it is usually better to forget them. The prime need, except in two unimportant species, is an acid soil or at least a neutral soil of some sort, whether loam, peat or ancient leaf-soil; a pH reading of 7 is about the limit and even that is too high for some of the Asiatic species and hybrids. See further in the section on "Rhododendron Maladies". It is entirely fallacious to assert that rhododendrons fail in clay. What is more dangerous is a soil that is excessively sandy, where the best remedy is to chop up some turves and mix them in 6in or so deep.

The second need is a reasonable supply of water, a commodity which some need more than others. Thirdly, fairly generous feeding; if the soil is not naturally rich give it a good dressing of rotten manure or compost. As always, good drainage is necessary, though there are, indeed, one or two species that prosper in swampy ground, such as *R. hippophaeoides*.

After these needs, common to all rhodos, we come to some special needs. One is shade. Many bask happily in full sun, particularly the azaleas, but others, particularly the choicest, need some protection from it. The shade should not be too heavy, nor is a place immediately beneath a tree a happy one, for the rhodo will be drawn up and become long-legged and there will be root competition. Oblique or dappled shade or filtered sunlight are best for the plant and for the picture.

Another crucial factor is temperature. Though they may come from the Himalayas, they are not always as successful as we should wish in the western world, a frailty that debars many of the most beautiful from the colder zones of North America. In Britain the Royal Horticultural Society and in America the American Rhododendron Society have systems of "ratings" for cold-hardiness. These generally tally well with one another. Britain has for long been far in the lead in the raising of hybrids but it is unfortunate that many of our finest, especially some of the Rothschild introductions, though they have proved hardy enough as plants in the US, do not always flower as they should. In return, as it were, Britain and Europe are now receiving some beautiful American-raised azaleas, notably 'Rosebud', which captures all hearts.

A third factor in the culture of the rhodos is the humidity of the atmosphere. It is probably true to say that all rhodos are happiest where the air is moist and balmy and that the choicest are miserable without it. According to accounts, nowhere in the world are finer rhodos grown than in the west coast of Scotland, in Cornwall, North Wales and parts of Ireland. Here the sea air and the ample rainfall compensate for that enemy of the rhodo — wind. If your allotted portion of the Earth is a dry-air one, keep your rhododendrons out of the worst wind.

Cultivation

These natural elements are to a large extent imposed upon us, but we now go on to matters more under our control. Having first prepared the soil, examine the plant. After making sure that it is otherwise in good shape, look at the root-ball. The fine root-tips must be exposed, in order to make intimate contact with the soil of their future, so tease out any soil that obstructs them. This precaution is especially important for container-grown plants which otherwise are loath to root out into their new location.

Prepare a hole in the ground somewhat wider than the root-ball, but not deeper. Line the hole with peat or ancient leaf-soil about an inch deep, peppered with a fertilizer specially made for acid-loving shrubs and containing magnesium. If the weather be dry, flood the hole and let the water then drain through. Put in your plant so that the root-ball is at about the same level as the soil, not lower; rhodos are shallow-rooting. Water thoroughly all round the perimeter of the plant. After a little while fill in the space all round and firm the soil, rather lightly at first. Never pound it in or the soil texture will be destroyed. Shape the soil so that a little rim or ridge is built round the perimeter to act as a catchment area for rain.

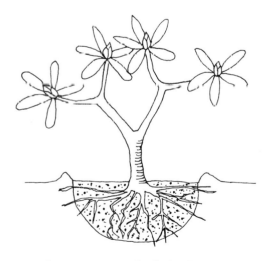

72.   Planting a young rhododendron: note top of soil-ball not sunk below ground level, tips of rootlets exposed to contact new soil and lip of earth to form catchment for water

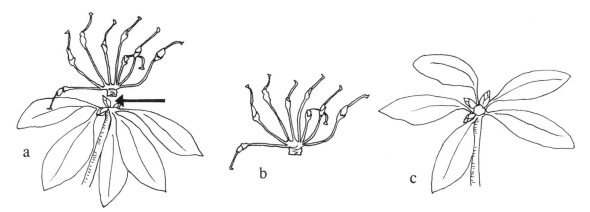

73.   Dead-heading a rhododendron; (*a*) snapping off the truss of seed pods without damaging the immature new buds; (*b*) the seed truss removed; (*c*) emerging new buds

Thereafter you normally have only two main and regular tasks to carry out: see that the plant is kept well watered and dead-head the spent flower trusses. The latter is a very important task especially for young plants and you must do it as soon as you can after the blossoms have fallen. With thumbnail and fingernail hold the truss of seed-pods at its base and snap the whole thing off sideways, taking great care not to damage the embryo growth immediately at the base of the foot-stalk and in the angle of the top leaves. These buds are usually clearly visible, but may be dormant; they are the shoots that will give you next year's flower. Obviously as the large-growing rhodos approach maturity dead-heading becomes impracticable. Only the most spiteful of Greek goddesses, however, would put you to the appalling task of dead-heading the dwarf rhodos and the evergreen azaleas, for they get sheeted with small flowers beyond numbering, so the human being leaves them alone; nor are the seed-trusses of some deciduous azaleas always easy to snap off.

A further small task of cultivation arises if a rhodo fails to flower well, a failing to which some of the deciduous azaleas are prone. They can be encouraged by a dressing of sulphate of potash, applied to the root perimeter at the rate of one ounce per square yard at the end of June.

As in roses, keep a sharp look-out for suckers. In many European nurseries named varieties of rhododendrons are commonly propagated by grafting them on to the "common" stock of *R. ponticum*, although this practice is happily declining. In such plants any shoot coming from below ground level will be a ponticum sucker and must be sliced or ripped off (not cut by secateurs) at the point of origin. Neglect of this precaution explains why so many old plantations have "gone to ponticum", for the mauve wilding is very vigorous and soon overwhelms the named variety. It has a long, pointed leaf, but so have others. Deciduous azaleas are often prone to the same danger. However, the increasing skill of modern propagators in the best nurseries is gradually reducing the problem of grafted plants.

Rhododendrons, with their mass of fibrous roots, are easily moved from one part of the garden to another. Move them in early autumn with a good ball of soil according to their size and be sure to water them copiously. In the harsh, dry winters that prevail in many parts of Northern America, however, spring transplanting is safer.

PRUNING

When it may be necessary, rhododendrons have not the least objection to the pruning knife. The need may occur if a branch is trespassing or has been broken or if the shrub has become gaunt or misshapen. The time to do it is immediately after blossom-fall. For a light trimming, simply cut back to a point just above one of the whorls, or rosettes, of leaves. For harder pruning, feel down the stem for a small swelling, giving promise of a new bud. If there is none, cut back at random, await the emergence of a new shoot and then trim back to this. A few rhodos do not respond to pruning. They include the species *thomsonii* and its hybrids, *lacteum*, *calophytum* and the hardy hybrids 'Alice', 'Bagshot Ruby', 'C. B. Van Nes' and 'Mrs C. B. Van Nes'.

In the eastern USA ageing rhododendrons retain the same vigour as they do in the west coast of the British Isles. Quite often old plants show signs of senile decay, exhibiting progressively shorter annual growth and fewer flower-buds. Such plants if on their own roots (not grafted) can be completely rejuvenated by cutting them down to 6in stubs, just like rejuvenating a superannuated lilac. This drastic treatment is best done in November, so that the cut stubs will dry out and make the first movements towards healing long before the rush of sap in the spring. If the cutting is made later in the winter the plant will often "bleed to death". Properly done, old root-stocks will thrust out a beautiful cluster of new basal shoots and, a couple of years later, produce the full, rounded plants which are the envy of every gardener.

The fabulous, dense greenery of rhododendrons and kalmias which grow wild in the Great Smoky Mountains of North Carolina and Tennessee are plants rejuvenated by nature in this way. They are often hundreds of years old, having been burned off by forest fires on countless occasions. Garden rhododendrons and azaleas re-grown in this manner respond well to applications of a broad-leaf evergreen fertilizer plus a mulch of oak leaves, pine needles or old wood chips.

RHODODENDRON MALADIES
Rhododendrons are preyed upon by few serious enemies. The commonest, not prevalent in all districts, is "bud blast". This is a condition in which the flower buds turn brown and become shrivelled and bristly. This is caused by the gnawings of the maggot of the leaf-hopper, which lays its eggs in the young bud. Pick off and burn the infected buds and spray with a systemic insecticide about 1st July and again a fortnight later.

Discoloration of the leaves indicates some chemical deficiency or excess. Technical advice should be sought, but the condition usually known as "lime-induced chlorosis" is easily recognised, the leaf turning yellow except in the veins, which remain green. It is not true, as often said, that lime is a "poison" to rhododendrons. Put simply, the fact is that their roots, and those of most other related plants, are not equipped, in the presence of lime, to absorb the soluble iron that is necessary for the production of the green chlorophyll of the leaves. Plants showing this form of chlorosis are thus suffering, not from poisoning by lime, but from iron starvation. The usual reason is simply that the soil is too alkaline, but even an acid soil may be deficient in iron. The remedy is to give the plant a dressing of an iron sequestrene.

The rhododendron white fly is a frail pallid creature, the larvae of which suck sap from the under-surface of the leaf, secreting a honeydew which, dropping on the lower leaves, results in a "sooty mould", which impairs the functions of the leaf and saps the plant's vitality, ruining its appearance. A similar white fly sucks away at azaleas. Spray at midsummer with a systemic insecticide.

Several species of weevil prey on rhodendrons, the adults nibbling the leaves and their larvae the roots. They spend the day hidden under débris on the ground and attack at night. Rake up and burn all débris and drench the soil with fenitrothion. In America, where weevils and beetles are more damaging than elsewhere, a poison bait is widely used.

Rhododendron bug is another tiny, frail creature that sucks the "soft under-belly" of the leaf from May onwards. It reveals itself by a speckling of the upper surface and a chocolate spotting below. An allied species is a very serious pest of pieris in American gardens. Spray with an insecticide in mid-May.

Leaf-spot is seen as purple spots turning black. Spray with captan or a copper fungicide.

Petal blight is the name for an ailment in which the flower collapses in a slimy mess. Pick them off and burn them and spray with benomyl. It is especially serious south of Washington, DC, in the USA.

Azalea gall is a fungus that causes fleshy swellings of the leaf, pink or dirty yellow, turning white. Burn the affected leaves and spray with a copper fungicide.

Rust occasionally appears as orange pustules, later brown, on the reverse of the leaf. If widespread, spray with a copper fungicide. The Exbury and Knap Hill azaleas exhibit a wide range of resistance and susceptibility to rust in humid climates, some being immune and some very prone to the fungus.

SELECTIONS

We are now ready for our own hasty review of our regiments of rhododendrons. These comprise the wild or natural species, the Asiatic or woodland hybrids derived from the species, the "hardy hybrids", the deciduous azaleas and the small evergreen azaleas. There are, of course, some borderline rhodos. We are grateful to Mr William Flemer III, of Princeton Nurseries, for his selections of those most suitable to American conditions.

There are roughly two rhododendron belts where the evergreen species and hybrids thrive in America, one on the East Coast from the ocean to the Appalachian chain of mountains and including the mountains themselves from Pennsylvania south to Georgia. Rhodos also thrive in a narrow band along the south shore of Lake Erie and in the small Niagara peninsula of Ontario, Canada's "banana belt". In the lowlands south of Washington, DC, summers are generally far too hot for any but a few tolerant hybrids and species to succeed. The winter weather in the eastern rhodo area is much colder than in most of the British Isles and in consequence only the very hardy "iron-clad"

species and hybrids are reliable.

The West Coast of North America from northern California north to southern British Columbia has a narrow moist rain belt along the coast with a climate like the milder parts of England, though not quite as temperate as the West Coasts of Ireland and Scotland. In this favourable strip most of the choicest English and European hybrids grow vigorously. However, every ten years or so a really bitter freeze does come down from the north, and the Oregon growers at least have modified their production lists in favour of hardier clones, although they are not confined to the "iron-clads" as are the easterners.

In general the American enthusiast is less sophisticated than his English counterpart. The American wants a dense, compact plant with lush foliage, because the plants are in bloom for only a short period and are merely broadleaf evergreens for the rest of the year. He prefers clones with full, round trusses of flowers conspicuously displayed well above the foliage. Many cultivars esteemed in England which have small trusses of drooping flowers, sparse foliage, and an open branching habit with many bare stems are not saleable in the USA.

In both areas, but especially in the East, the soil-borne fungus-like *Phytophthora* are much more serious diseases of rhododendrons than east of the Atlantic. A major reason may be the higher soil temperature of American summers. *R. ponticum* is especially susceptible to this devastating fungus and losses were so serious that rhododendron culture was in real danger of dying out until cutting propagation was mastered during the early years after 1945. Countless experiments, especially using newer and much more concentrated rooting hormones, have resulted in successful own-root propagation of all the most important hybrid clones, and the garden use of this lovely genus is consequently increasing each year.

The species

These vary considerably, not only in flower, but also in size and behaviour. Those that belong to the azalea "series" are in the list of deciduous azaleas. We omit the identifications of other series, as they are of importance only to the specialist. Many of these natural wildings have been valuable as parents of hybrids but are also desirable for their own sakes, none more so than the last in this list. The following is a mere handful from a large barrow-load:

R. arboreum. Of tree size. Red, pink or white. Early.

R. augustinii. Varying from pale lavender to rich violet. To 15ft, April–May. Delightful.

R. campylocarpum. Yellow, compact. April. R. c. elatum is taller.

R. catawbiense. Mauve, pink or white. Very hardy. Many varieties. June. z4.

R. carolinianum. Mauve and other colours. z5.

R. cinnabarinum. Flowers trumpet-shaped, red or orange. The var. *roylei* is outstanding. Needs some shelter. May–June.

R. decorum. White or pink, scented, 15ft. Needs light shade. In USA succeeds on both coasts. z5.

R. discolor. Blush-pink, scented. Tall. June–July. z6.

R. fortunei. Pale pink. Scented. To 30ft in Britain, less in USA. May–June. z6.

R. falconeri. Pale yellow. Leaves 12in long, with rusty coating below. Needs ideal rhododendron conditions. To 30ft. April–May.

R. griersonianum. Bright red, 8ft. Needs sheltered place. June.

R. griffithianum. White, scented. Big shrub for mild places only.

R. keiskei. Pale yellow. z5.

R. lacteum. Pale to deep yellow. For ideal conditions only. 15ft.

R. lutescens. Primrose, of great beauty, young leaves bronze. March.

R. mucronulatum. Rosy-mauve. 6ft. 'Cornell Pink' is pure pink. z4.

R. neriiflorum. Red shade. 8ft. April–May.

R. orbiculare. Rose, in loose trusses. April–May.

R. oreotrephes. Mauve or rose. 15ft. April–May.

R. ponticum. The "common ponticum" of Europe, but excellent for mass planting or as a

Rhododendron 'Lady Chamberlain'

windbreak. Pale mauve, June.

R. pseudochrysanthum. Beautiful pink spotted crimson. To 9ft. April.

R. racemosum. Distinguished by bearing its small, pink flowers all along the branchlets. 'Forrest's Dwarf' is particularly good. Prune away the flowered sections. z5.

R. russatum. Deep purple. 4ft. Splendid.

R. souliei. White to deep rose, of elegance and grace. 10ft.

R. thomsonii. Blood-red. 20ft. April.

R. wardii. Bright yellow. Good forms are scarce and coveted. 10ft. May.

R. williamsianum. Shell-pink. A 6ft dome with small, rounded leaves. April.

R. yakushimanum. Deep pink buds gradually opening white. A great treasure, magnificent in full flower. Young leaves like white rabbit's-ears. Slowly forms a spreading 4ft dome. Full sun or part shade. May–June. Not cheap. The clone 'Koichiro Wada' is considered by some to be perhaps the best.

The heraldic splendour of species with very large leaves such as *sino-grande*, *macabeanum* and *fictolacteum* can be enjoyed only under the ideal conditions of a mild and moist climate.

Woodland Hybrids

These expect to be grown in dappled sunlight, with not too heavy a canopy of trees, but often succeed in the open if the atmosphere is moist and balmy. All quoted are hybrids.

'Albatross'. Huge, luxuriant mound of white in June. 'Exbury Albatross' and 'Townhill Pink' are pink clones.

'Beauty of Littleworth'. Pure white with some red speckling in the throat. Vigorous and spreading. Hardy. May.

'Blue Diamond'. Blue. 6ft, rounded bush in April. For open ground also.

'Curlew'. Yellowish green with green eye. Small compact plant with very large flowers in May.

'Cornish Cross'. Rose-pink to over 20ft. The Exbury form is a deeper colour than others. April–May.

'Crest'. Brilliant gold. Flowers profusely for a prolonged period. One of Rothschild's great achievements and the finest yellow so far. May and well into June. Moderately hardy.

'Elizabeth'. Blood-red. A top-ranking hybrid from Bodnant. Semi-dwarf, compact, profuse flowering, easy to grow. A great favourite. April–May.

'Elizabeth de Rothschild'. Deep cream with chestnut spotting. Large truss on a noble plant which will one day become famous. June.

'Fred Wynniatt'. Maize-yellow. A new hybrid with several named clones. Will become much sought after.

'Jalisco'. Dusky yellow with faint green undertone. This modern Exbury hybrid and its many clones are of the highest order and much coveted. Pretty hardy. June.

'Loderi'. The clones 'King George', 'Venus' and many more are all in shades of white or pink. All exquisite and scented. Probably the

Rhododendron × loderi 'King George'

most successful hybrid ever raised. April to May.

'Lionel's Triumph'. Deep rich cream, flushed pink. Of impressive stature, carrying large trusses with up to eighteen florets. The clone 'Halton' is tinted green in place of pink. April–May.

'May Day'. Scarlet. 5ft with equal spread, flowering into June. Suitable for most gardens as well as the woodland.

'Moonshine'. Yellow. A group of six clones from Wisley, all good. Still difficult to obtain but will become popular. April–May.

'Muy Lindo'. White, pink in the bud. Fragrant. A fine new hybrid. June.

'Naomi'. The Exbury form is biscuit-tinged lilac-pink. Other clones of this well-known cross are in diverse shades of pink. Hardy, probably the best known of the Exburys. Reliable and always flowers profusely in April–May.

'Penjerrick' Pale cream. An old but beautiful hybrid. Bell-like flowers hang in loose trusses and should be viewed from below on the tall trees against a blue sky. Hardy. April–May.

'Queen Elizabeth II'. Greenish-yellow from Windsor. Worthy of its name. April–May.

'Red Admiral'. Bright red. A sight to behold in February–March with the flowers protruding from a snow-covered plant. 25ft high.

'The Dowager'. White flushed pale purple, with red-purple patch. Another good entry from the Loder stable. April.

'The Master'. Creamy-pink, dark throat. Bold and hardy plant from Slocock. April–May.

'The Queen Mother'. Greenish-white. Small-flowered hybrid from Windsor. April–May.

'Vanessa Pastel'. Cream, flushed shell-pink. Medium-sized plant of upright habit. May.

'Yvonne'. Pale pink. Large flat-topped trusses held loosely. There are 4 clones all of equal merit. Real woodlanders. April–May.

Hardy Hybrids, Europe

These we may grow in full sun or light shade. Many are of old raisings:

'America'. Good dark red. Neat deportment. June.

'A. Bedford'. Lavender. Dark eye.

'Betty Wormald'. Red bud opening pink with a speckled eye. June.

'Bow Bells'. Two-tone pink. Elegant, dense foliage. Young leaves in chestnut cockades. 6ft by 8ft. May.

'Britannia'. Crimson. 6ft by 6ft. One of the great favourites. Bred in Germany. May–June.

'Blue Peter'. Light lavender-blue. May.

'Cynthia'. Huge rose-pink. Tall, old favourite. June.

'Chevalier Félix de Sauvage'. Red with dark spots. May–June.

'Doncaster'. Dark red, well-proven. May–June.

'El Alamein'. Deep red with brown patch. Good tight trusses. May.

'Earl of Donoughmore'. Bright red, orange glow. June.

'Fabia'. First-class scarlet, with orange throat, brown speckling. The clone 'Tangerine' has a subtle blending of colours and 'Waterer' is salmon.

'Fastuosum Flora Pleno'. Mauve double flowers. June.

'General Eisenhower'. Carmine, elaborately ruffled. Vigorous. June.

'Janet Blair'. Pastel mauve-pink. Golden-bronze marking. Tall. May–June.

'Kluis Sensation'. Bright vermilion. June.

'Lamplighter'. Salmon-red. Large trusses. June.

'Loder's White'. White, scented. Very free. June.

'Lord Roberts'. Dark crimson. Fine old warrior. June.

'Mrs Betty Robertson'. Pale yellow with pink flush turning to cream. May–June.

'Mrs Furnival'. Pink with crimson patch. Handsome. June.

'Mrs A. T. de la Mare'. White spotted green, slightly scented. Good habit. May.

'Mrs Chas. E. Pearson'. Blush-mauve with brown spots. June.

'Nova Zembla'. Dark red. Upright growth. June.

'Old Port'. Plum-coloured old-timer. June.

'Pink Pearl'. Huge trusses of fresh clear pink. Best of the lot, but rather loose structure. 10ft. June.

'Purple Splendour'. Deep purple with darker patch. Very striking. June.

'Princess Elizabeth'. Crimson. Fine erect plant. June.

'Professor Hugo de Vries'. Resembles 'Pink Pearl' but less open habit. June.

'Souvenir of W. C. Slocock'. Pale yellow. Low and wide. May.

'Susan'. Nearly true blue. Big, handsome shrub.

'Sappho'. White, purple patch. Hardy. May–June.

'Temple Belle'. Pink buds opening paler. Small, round, tightly packed leaves. Modest stature.

'The Hon Jean-Marie de Montague'. Bright scarlet. May–June.

Hardy Hybrids, American West Coast

Several of these appear in the European list. All are hardy to at least 0°F.

'Anah Krushke'. Lavender. Large conical trusses. Compact grower with dark green foliage.

'Anton Van Welle'. Deep pink, very large upright truss. Vigorous and tall.

'Blue Ensign'. Light blue, maroon patch. Like 'Blue Peter', but much denser.

'Beauty of Littleworth'. See European woodland list.

'Cynthia'. See European list.

'Elizabeth Hobbie'. Waxy, scarlet flowers. Compact.

'General Eisenhower'. See European list.

'Full Moon'. Brilliant canary-yellow in a full globular truss. Low and compact.

'Jan Dekens'. Enormous trusses of rich pink, frilled flowers. Rapid, vigorous grower.

'Loderi King George'. See European woodland list.

'Marchioness of Lansdowne'. Pale violet with dark purple patch.

'Mars'. Deep red, full truss. Splendid, compact, low grower.

'Maryke'. Pink with yellow throat. Dense, rounded habit.

'Mrs A. T. de la Mare'. See European list.

'Mrs Furnival'. See European list.

'Odee Wright'. Bright yellow in ruffled trusses. Low, dense habit.

'Pink Pearl'. See European list.

'Purple Splendour'. See European list.

'The Hon. Jean-Marie de Montague'. See European list. The most popular standard red.

'Unique'. Yellow tinted with pink. A charming colour.

'Vulcan'. Bright brick-red flowers in abundance.

American East Coast

Few of these are now grown in Britain, but may be seen in the colder parts of Europe.

'America'. See European list.

'Besse Howells'. Red. Large trusses of ruffled flowers. Low, dense habit.

'Boule de Neige'. White. Low mounded growth.

'Catawbiense Album'. White. Well-furnished bush of medium height.

'Catawbiense Grandiflorum'. Lavender pink. Medium height, dense, very hardy.

'Chionoides'. White, late blooming. Low and dense.

'Dora Amateis'. White. Small but abundant trusses. Low growth.

'English Roseum'. Clear rose-pink. Vigorous and rounded growth.

'Great Lakes'. Pale pink, turning white. Yakushimanum hybrid. Dwarf and dense.

'Lee's Dark Purple'. Rich purple. Excellent dark green foliage.

'Nova Zembla'. See European list.

'P. J. Mezitt'. Rich magenta. Very early. Small foliage turns purplish in winter. Hardiest of all hybrid rhodos. To minus 40°F.

'Parson's Gloriosum'. Lavender-pink with yellow patch. Tall.

'Purpureum Elegans'. Lavender-pink. The most adaptable and easily grown of all the hybrids. In habit and tolerance the standard by which all others must be judged.

'Ramapo'. Blue shaded lavender. Tiny but abundant flowers on a dwarf plant.

'Scintillation'. Strawberry-pink, waxy texture. Showy. Best of the Dexter hybrids.

'Venus'. Early, bright pink with dark centre.

Deciduous Azaleas

These constitute one of the rhododendron "series". There are several species and a host of hybrids. Normally they average about 6ft in height and often spread widely. They have a wonderful range of colours, opening their mouths wide and often displaying a contrasting patch of colour in the throat. The foliage is not dense but, in most examples, glows with "the exquisite chromatics of decay" before it falls. Most of them enjoy full sun.

The ancestry of the hybrids is extremely complicated, but they are horticulturally classed in the following groups (not all easily distinguishable).

The Mollis azaleas, flowering in May before the leaves open, with a strong element of orange in their colour and somewhat inclined to tenderness. Derived mainly from R. japonicum (formerly Azalea mollis).

The Occidentale azaleas, flowering a fortnight later in pastel shades and scented.

The Ghent azaleas (originating from the town of that name), in which the sap of American species is mixed with that of the Pontic Azalea (*R. luteum*). Rather small flowers.

The Rustica Flore Pleno group, believed to be derived from the double forms of the Ghents crossed with the Mollis.

The Knap Hill azaleas, which include the celebrated Exbury azaleas, a race of scintillating brilliance, lively and dancing poise and often scented.

SELECTIONS FOR EUROPE

Unless otherwise noted, these flower in May–June. Those printed in italic type are species.

R. albrechtii. Deep purple-rose with olive-green spots. Unlike most deciduous azaleas, this seems to prefer woodland conditions and a moist humusy soil. The clone 'Michael McLaren' is red-purple. z5.

'Annabella' (Exbury). Gold, flushed orange.

'Adriaan Koster' (Mollis). Deep yellow.

'Basilisk' (Exbury). Deep cream with golden flare, large truss.

'Berryrose' (Exbury). Beautiful rose with yellow patch.

R. calendulaceum. Orange or red. Wild plants may exhibit yellow. From eastern N. America. z5.

'Cécile' (Knaphill). Deep pink buds opening to soft pink with yellow flash.

'Clarice' (Exbury). Pale salmon with orange patch.

'Coccinea Speciosa' (Ghent). Brilliant orange, growing in tiers. April.

'Christopher Wren' (Mollis). Large orange.

'Edwina Mountbatten' (Exbury). Deep yellow. New.

'George Reynolds' (Knaphill). Large, buttery-yellow with greenish throat. A classic.

'Gog' (Knaphill). Orange with yellow flash. Good autumn colour.

'Hotspur Orange' (Exbury). Brilliant orange.

'Homebush' (Ghent). Beautiful double pink.

R. kaempferi. Salmon-red. 'Eastern Fire' is a beautiful clone from Windsor.

'Klondyke' (Exbury). Very fine deep gold. Bronze leaves.

R. luteum (formerly *Azalea pontica*). Bright yellow, richly scented. Trusty old favourite. Good autumn foliage. May.

'Narcissiflora' (Ghent). Pale yellow, double, scented.

R. occidentale. Pale pink with orange patch. Valuable for late flower (June–July).

'Silver Slipper' (Exbury). Beautiful white, flushed pink with orange patch.

'Sun Chariot' (Exbury). Rich yellow with orange eye.

'Strawberry Ice' (Exbury). Two-tone pink with orange flush. One of the most beautiful.

R. schlippenbachii. Very delicate, pale rose. April.

'Sunte Nectarine' (Exbury). Deep orange with yellow flash. New.

R. vaseyi. Rose-pink. April. z4.

FOR NORTH AMERICA

Although all but one of the wild species which entered into the complex parentage of the Knap Hill and Exbury deciduous azaleas came from North America, these hybrids are still "new plants" to most American gardeners, with a great future ahead of them. They thrive in all the cool temperate areas, but languish in the heat of the southern states. However, even in the humid south there are beautiful native deciduous species awaiting the genius of a latter-day Waterer or Rothschild to create a group of hybrids for these conditions.

In the cooler areas, the Knap Hill and Exbury hybrids in general do well, but not all are of equal value as garden plants. The combination of summer heat and humidity causes many cultivars to become badly infested with mildew and with rust fungi on the leaves. This results in disfigured leaves and at worst in defoliation which greatly weakens the plants and shortens their life expectancy. There are over 100 Exbury hybrids alone, in addition to the multitudes more of Knap Hill, Ilam, New Zealand and Windsor hybrids. Obviously it will take decades to assess them all for American conditions. The following list is composed of those which have shown special vigour and freedom from foliar diseases in North America.

'Berryrose'. See European List.

'Exbury Crimson' (Exbury). Crimson, vigorous, upright.

'Gibraltar' (Exbury). Best of all for American conditions. Strong grower, frilled flame-orange flowers.

'Klondyke'. See European List.

'Oxydol' (Exbury). Unfortunate name for a splendid white. Very strong growth.

'Persil' (Knap Hill). Pure white with yellow splash. Splendid deep green. glossy foliage.

'Pink William' (Ilam). Very large silvery-pink with a delicious scent.

'Red Velvet' (Ilam). Deep rich crimson. The deepest red of all. Splendid fall colour.

'Satan' (Knap Hill). Rich red. Completely disease-free foliage.

'Windsor Buttercup' (Windsor). Brilliant, clear canary-yellow. Vigorous grower and heavy bloomer.

Evergreen azaleas

These are mainly low, spreading shrubs, densely clothed with small leaves, though a few grow, in tiers, to 7ft. They are evergreen only in the sense that they grow two sets of leaves — the spring leaves, which fall in the autumn, and the summer leaves, which last through the winter. They flower like mad, often obscuring the leaves. There are three groups:

The so-called "Indian azaleas", deriving mainly from what used to be called Azalea indica (*Rhododendron simsii*) and intended especially for the greenhouse, but a few will grow outdoors in mild climates.

The famous Kurume azaleas from Japan, of obscure parentage, in all sorts of colours, both brilliant and tender. Greeted with rapture when E. H. Wilson brought them to the West, but not all have proved as hardy as he claimed. Of low and spreading habit, with very small leaves, densely packed, which in many instances are completely obscured by the multitudinous flowers.

Modern hybrids. New fields were opened up this century when splendid varieties of diverse habit were bred by the late Lionel de Rothschild in England, by B. Y. Morrison of the U.S. National Arboretum, and J. B. Gable in the USA and the Dutch nurseries of Koster and of Vuyk Van Nes (who gave us the incomparable 'Palestrina'). The Glenn Dales were designed for the warm states, but several prosper in Britain. The Gables, on the contrary, were bred for cold-tolerance and are among the hardiest of all the evergreen azaleas.

For Europe

'Addy Wery' (Kurume). Vermilion with orange glow. April–May.

'Alice' (Malvatica × Kaempferi). Orange. May.

'Blaauw's Pink' (Kurume). Salmon. April–May.

'Betty' (Malvatica × Kaempferi). Salmon with dark eye. April–May.

'Bengal Fire' (Exbury). Vivid orange, late (June–July).

'Eddie' (Exbury). Orange-red. Upright habit. June.

'Hatsu-giri' (Kurume). Dazzling red-purple; the flowers completely hide the densely set foliage.

'Hino-degiri' (Kurume). Like the above but bright red. A great favourite.

'Hino-mayo' (Kurume). Also like 'Hatsu-giri', but a sparkling silvery-pink. A top choice.

'Iro-hayama' (Kurume). White, edged lavender.

'John Cairns' (Malvatica × Kaempferi). Deep orange-red in tiers. Hardy.

'Lorna' (Gable). Double pink. Dense growth.

'Martha Hitchcock' (Glenn Dale). Large white, edged magenta.

R. mucronatum (formerly *ledifolium*). Profuse white, sometimes with a faint mauve flush. Several clones. 'Lilacina' is soft lilac. 'Bulstrode' a faint yellow-green. z5–6.

'Mothers' Day' (Kurume). Splendid, bright red, semi-double, of the highest merit, but single in some forms.

R. obtusum. Bright red, of low growth,

usually preferred in one of its clones. 'Amoenum' is taller and magenta. 'Amoenum Coccineum' is carmine and the best, but liable to revert to magenta. 'Amoenum Splendens', mauve, and 'Macrostemon', orange-pink, are dwarf spreaders. April–May. z6.

'Palestrina' (Vuyk). Superlative white, green-eyed, to 5ft. A prime choice.

'Rosebud'. A real charmer, delightful in its clean, pink dress. Very aptly named. Extremely hardy.

'Vuyk's Rosy Red'. The name describes a very showy, large-flowered, low-growing azalea, of great garden merit. April–May.

'Vuyk's Scarlet'. Like the above except for colour.

FOR NORTH AMERICA

Although the west coasts of the British Isles have a climate which produces rhododendrons which are the despair of American enthusiasts, Americans have their revenge in the field of the evergreen azaleas. Particularly from Washington, DC, south on the east coast of the USA, the summer heat produces plants with a vigour and "burnish" unequalled in Europe or England, and a lavish display of flowers in the spring.

As in the other azalea groups, there are almost too many varieties to choose from, and any listing will be fiercely assailed because some local favourite is not on it. The list below includes clones which have withstood the test of time and are deservedly popular. They may be supplanted in future years, but the challengers will have an uphill struggle. Because of the great difference in climate between the New England States and Alabama, the list is divided into three parts according to cold-hardiness, with the middle group also being the best for the west coast.

A special note is in order about the huge group called the Glenn Dale hybrids, produced by B. Y. Morrison at the National Arboretum in Washington, DC. It is the supreme cautionary lesson about the dangers of profligacy in introducing new clones. Over 600 varieties were named and offered for distribution and almost none ever made it into commerce! There must be at least a dozen real gems in this horde but nobody has had the space, time and temerity to grow them all and sort them out. In contrast, the one and only variety ever introduced by an exacting New Jersey hybridist ('Delaware Valley White') is the standard for its colour, grown and planted by the million each year, and still always "sold out".

COLD CLIMATES. The following are suitable for Zones 5–6.

'Blaauw's Pink. Hose-in-hose, rich pink.

'Delaware Valley White'. Pure white with large and abundant flowers and fine foliage. Low and dense.

'Fedora'. Large salmon-pink flowers, abundantly borne. Vigorous, open growth.

'Herbert'. Deep magenta-purple, hose-in-hose.

'Hino-crimson'. Brilliant red, hardy and prolific. A seedling of 'Hino-degiri', but hardier and a clearer red.

'Karens'. Medium lavender flowers. Lavish bloomer. Hardy even in Chicago, Illinois!

'Mothers' Day'. See European List.

'Poukhanensis'. From Korea, unsurpassed for hardiness. Large, fragrant, lavender flowers. A major genetic resource in breeding cold-hardy azaleas. Dense and low.

'Rosebud'. See European list.

'Stewartsoniae'. Fiery orange-red. Tall, rapid grower. Leaves turn maroon in winter.

TEMPERATE CLIMATES. The following are reliable in Zones 7–8.

'Addy Wery'. See European list.

'Balsaminiflora'. Low, widely spreading. Profuse, double salmon-pink flowers. Fine ground-cover.

'Coral Bells' ('Kirin'). Very dense plant with small, hose-in-hose flowers of a luminous shell-pink.

'Glacier'. Large white flowers on a robust plant. Glossy, leathery foliage.

'Gumpo'. Very dwarf and spreading. Large, frilled, white flowers. Blooms late and long. There is also a fine pink clone.

'Hino-degiri'. See European list.

'Hino-mayo'. See European list.

'Macrantha'. Dense, spreading clone with lovely salmon flowers continuing after all others have faded. There is also a double form.

'Martha Hitchcock'. See European list.

'Pink Pearl' ('Azuma-kagami'). Hose-in-hose flowers of a marvellous shrimp-pink.

'Sherwood Orchid'. Large rose-purple flowers with a dark patch.

'Snow'. White hose-in-hose flowers on a dense, spreading plant. Flowers tend to hang on too long after fading.

WARM CLIMATES. The following need the conditions of Zones 9–10.

'Albert Elizabeth'. Large, white semi-double, frilled flowers, with orange edges.

'Dogwood'. Very large, pure white.

'Fielder's White'. The standard warm-climate white. Large, frilled flowers with pale chartreuse patch.

'Formosa'. Large magenta-purple. Robust growth.

'George Lindley Taber'. White flushed purple.

'Mission Bells'. Very showy, double, cerise flowers. Low, spreading growth.

'Pride of Mobile' ('Elegans Superba'). Deep pink, profuse, very vigorous.

'Red Wings'. Large hose-in-hose flowers of a glowing red.

'Shinyo-no-Tsuki'. Large white flowers with crimson patch and margin. Dwarf.

'Sweetheart Supreme'. Rich, rose-pink hose-in-hose.

'Vervaeneana'. Very large, double, purple-red with white margin.

RHODOTYPOS
Jethead

The jethead or makino, *R. scandens* (also sold as *R. kerrioides*), is a very nice, easy-going, general-purposes, deciduous shrub. It has a very erect carriage, 6ft high and displays its flowers, which are four-petalled, white, papery and 2in

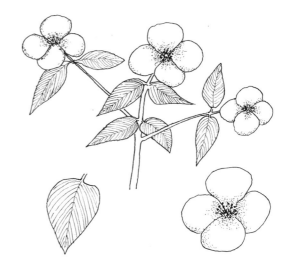

74.   Rhodotypos scandens

wide, on short lateral twigs throughout May and June, with some scattering for another month, followed by small, shining, black fruits. These flowering laterals grow from canes thrown up in the previous season and, as the canes sprout readily from the base, you can cut them back right to the ground or to promising new growth near it. Do this immediately after blossom-fall, forgoing the berries. For sun or half-shade. z5.

RHUS
Sumach

The sumachs or sumacs are a curious breed of many mixed qualities, some of them vicious. The average gardener knows only the stag's-horn sumach (*Rhus typhina*), but there is a great deal more to them than that popular species. They range from 30ft giants to mere ground-lings. The wood is pithy and brittle. A few have economic value, such as R. coriaria, used for tanning and dyeing. To some people (not all) many are poisonous to the touch, such as R. radicans (the "poison ivy"), R. toxicodend-ron ("the poison oak"), R. vernix and R. verniciflua (the varnish tree, used in Japan for lacquering), which can cause extremely painful and long-persistent eruptions. R. trichocarpa is less seriously poisonous and R. michauxii is a subject of divided opinions. So obviously these are best avoided in gardens and parks. Should they be there already handle them with rubber gloves.

The name *Rhus* is the ancient Greek one and sumach is the Middle English spelling of the Arabic name *summaq*.

For the rest, the sumachs are easily grown in any reasonable soil and they are of particular value in sandy ones. Their leaves are nearly always pinnate and often large. They have little floral attraction, the blossoms, displayed usually in pyramids, being green, yellowish or off-white and tiny, and usually unisexual. Small, red berries (drupes) follow in the females if pollinated. We think of them primarily for the richness of their autumnal fireworks, but they can be good summer foliage plants also, especially the cut-leaf varieties of the smooth and the stag's-horn species, if pruned as we suggest. We omit the very large tree-like species.

In popular esteem the dominant species is **R. typhina**, the stag's-horn sumach, so called because of the clustered twigs at the tips of the main branches which, when leafless, resemble the antlers of a stag and are picturesque against the open sky in winter. This is a big, many-stemmed, flat-topped, wide-flung shrub which, in favourable circumstances, can stretch up to 30ft, but does not often do so, and never when cut back. The branches, when young, are thickly covered with brown hairs and the large, pinnate leaves become robed in a Joseph's coat of brilliant dyes in autumn, especially when in full sun. Large pyramids of green flowers are carried on male plants, smaller clusters on the female, which, if pollinated, provide very showy bunches of red, hairy fruits in the fall. The female plants are the more handsome, but only larger gardens have the space for both sexes. The plant may throw up suckers, which can be either chopped off or used for propagation.

Grown naturally, the stag's-horn sumach suffers from the defect that it becomes a lanky creature, with several naked legs and tufts of leaves on top. The way to overcome this defect is to chop it nearly down to the ground, as for the cotinus, about 1st March, then to thin out the resultant new shoots to one or two and feed the plant richly. The effect will be an erect shrub of only about 6ft, with huge leaves. This kind of treatment is particularly effective in the splendid cut-leaf variety 'Dissecta', in which each leaf appears to have been shredded or snipped with scissors. Cutting back results in huge, fern-like leaves. Grown naturally 'Dissecta' is not as big as the species. Avoid the form 'Laciniata', which often becomes grotesque and do not confuse it with the fine 'Laciniata' of R. glabra. z3.

The thick, yellow cream exuded from a cut stem is a mild irritant to some people, so wear rubber gloves and coat the cut stem of the shrub with a wound-healing wax.

In the smaller gardens **R. glabra**, the smooth sumach, is more easily accommodated, averaging 8ft in Britain but up to 15ft in its native North America. This we may regard as a junior version of the stag's-horn sumach, except for its smooth bark, and every bit as good, especially in its cut-leaf variety 'Laciniata', which can be equated with the 'Dissecta' of its bigger brother and which can be cut very hard back and richly fed in the same way to provide big, sumptuous, feathery leaves, 3ft long. z2.

R. aromatica, as you would expect, has aromatic leaves. They are trifoliate, on a low bush of 3ft, which spreads rapidly underground. A cloud of small yellow florets, quite conspicuous, appears in late April, followed by small, bright red berries that gleam among brilliant autumnal foliage. Good for covering banks. z3. *R. trilobata* is related but it smells offensive and is subject to mildew in damp climates.

R. copallina is only 4ft in Britain but up to 30ft in its homeland, which is eastern North America. Polished pinnate leaves with winged midrib. Fine autumn colours. The big *R. chinensis* is similarly winged and bears showy, ivory panicles in late summer. z4.

R. coriaria. Of no garden value, but

interesting as being the original Arabic *summaq*, used for tanning and dyeing leather. Once common in England.

R. cotinus. Now in a separate genus. See *Cotinus*.

RIBES

Flowering Currants and *Gooseberries*

For the most part these are easy-going cottager's plants, usually of erect growth, deciduous, with saw-edged leaves shaped into three or five lobes, with dangling (or sometimes erect) spikes of very small flowers, though the gooseberries behave a little differently. A few are evergreen. The great majority of this very large breed are of little garden value, having too often insipid, greeny-yellow florets and their foliage, though pleasant enough, being too commonplace. Nearly all are unisexual. All form stools just below ground level and so willingly throw up new canes from the base, inviting the gardener to get rid of the old stems to encourage the new for next season's display.

Botanists divide the ribes into a number of sub-genera. One of these (Grossularioides) is of the gooseberry breed, which is prickly. Virtually all others are smooth of stem. All produce their flowers on canes that have grown up in the previous summer, the most ornamental blooming all along the stem, so, in general terms, what you aim for in pruning is to get rid of the old stems as soon as they have done their job. Thus you can cut the currant types right down to the ground or to a promising new growth low down on the old, but some people like to keep a few of the old to maintain a balance. The gooseberry types do not behave in quite the same way and you prune less severely, with the general idea of getting rid of all stems more than five years old. Old and neglected specimens of all types are best cut back very hard all over. Replacement pruning is very necessary when *R. speciosum* and its like are fanned out against a wall, but perhaps it is advisable to wait until the new shoots have grown out strongly.

The ribes of the fruit garden, from which delicious pies and jams are made, are improved forms of *R. uva-crispi* (the gooseberry), *R. nigrum* (the blackcurrant) and *R. rubrum* or *sativum* (the redcurrant).

If any of the plants are attacked by aphis, use a systemic insecticide. Caterpillars of the gooseberry saw-fly can devastate a shrub; spray with fenitrothion. In large areas of North America the law forbids the planting of several species of ribes which act as carriers of the white-pine blister rust disease.

In the following list we give (out of 150 species) only those that have some distinctive character. Heading all opinion polls is R. sanguineum, but speciosum and odoratum are good runners-up.

R. alpinum, the extremely hardy Alpine currant of Europe, including Britain. Dense, close-knit growth to 7ft. Poor, greenish flowers. Scarlet fruits of both sexes present. A very good hedger and very good in the cold prairies of North America. The variety 'Aureum' has yellow leaves when young and grows broader than high. 'Pumilum' is an excellent, low mound of 3ft, which needs no routine pruning. z2.

R. americanum, the American blackcurrant. 6ft. Worth growing only for its gorgeous autumn colours. 'Variegatum' has a cream mottling in the leaf. z2.

R. gayanum. Evergreen, thornless, often hairy. A nice shrub of 5ft, with soft, velvety hairs, worth growing for its small, sweetly scented, pale yellow bells in tight, erect spikes in early June. Fruits black and hairy. z7–8.

R. × gordonianum. Dangling clusters of many florets, coppery-red on the outside, yellow within, in April. An English hybrid, *odoratum × sanguineum*. z6–7.

R. lacustre. Thorny, gooseberry-style but attractive shrub of 4ft, the bristles chestnut. Hanging clusters of pale flowers spotted pink from May to July. Naturally a swamp-dweller. z4.

R. laurifolium. A 4ft, thornless evergreen with little clusters of greeny-yellow flowers in

February–March and drooping leaves, laurel-shaped but toothed. A very good, early-flowering shrub for small gardens. z7–8.

R. lobbii. Thorny, gooseberry-type shrub of 5ft, with tiny leaves and pretty flowers with red, re-curved sepals and white mini-skirts and protruding tufts of stamens, like a miniature version of Abutilon megapotamicum. Chestnut-coloured fruits. z7–8.

R. maximowiczii. Remarkable for its vivid red flowers (Bean says "dull, lurid red") borne in small, erect racemes in May. Deciduous, thornless, with blackcurrant leaves. 8ft.

R. menziesii. Very like lobbii, but with bristly shoots as well as the spines and a little taller. z7.

R. odoratum is the favourite old clove currant, so called because of the aromatic, golden flowers that smother the shrub in early May to a height of 6ft. Distinguished by its loose, supple, open bearing. The shining leaves become a vivid red in autumn. One of the best currants, sometimes sold as *R. aureum*. z4.

R. roezlii. Gooseberry-type. One of the more colourful, with hanging, fuchsia-like little flowers, with purple calyx and pink skirt, followed by very bristly, purple berries. About $4\frac{1}{2}$ft. z6–7.

R. sanguineum. Most popular of all the flowering currants, forming a strong and rigid framework about 8ft high or more. A typical cottage plant with showy, rose-red, hanging racemes in April. Some people find the odour disagreeable. Prune as for deutzia and philadelphus. Almost a dozen named varieties are to our hand, of which the outstanding one is the deep crimson 'King Edward VII'. Others of a high order are:

Album. White.

'Atrorubens'. Blood-red.

'Brocklebankii'. A very distinctive, small shrub, with butter-yellow leaves and pink flowers; partial shade.

'Carneum'. Flesh-pink.

'Lombartsii'. Large rose, with white centre.

'Pulborough Scarlet'. Deep crimson flowers in profusion.

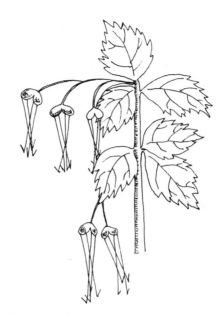

75. Ribes speciosum

'Splendens'. Extra-long racemes of rosy-crimson.

All these sanguineums must be hard-pruned to the ground after flowering. Easily propagated by ripe wood cuttings in autumn in sandy, shaded soil, without cover. z5.

R. speciosum. Perhaps the best of the gooseberry type and half-evergreen. Very small, shining leaves from bristly, chestnut stems. Hanging clusters of red, slender, fuchsia-like florets with exceptionally long and elegant stamens from March till May in great profusion. In cold areas a very good wall plant. About 9ft. z7–8.

RICHEA

Rather tender evergreens, mainly from Tasmania, needing a moist, acid soil. Small, rigid, spiky leaves crowd the stems, which are topped with clusters of small flowers. In *R. scoparia*, the one usually grown, the flowers are in tight, spike-like racemes, usually red, pink or white, abundantly carried. About 10ft. z8–9. *R. dracophylla* is more tender, bulkier and has much longer leaves.

ROBINIA

The big robinias, often falsely called acacias and, even more falsely, locust-trees, have a few shrubby brethren. For a very short period in June they produce hanging bunches of pea-flowers in the manner of the wisteria, with pinnate leaves of a like resemblance. Their wood is brittle and easily damaged by rough weather, so they are best planted in a "lean and hungry" soil, to deter sappy growth, and in full sun to harden the wood. Many are sharply barbed and some throw up thickets of suckers. Prone to bleeding, any pruning that may be needed must be done as soon as summer is over. Named after Jean Robin, herbalist to Henri IV of France. All z5 except *elliottii*.

The one that gets the best press is **R. hispida**, known as the rose-acacia, a gaunt shrub of 6ft (less in America) with big, handsome, wisteria-like bunches of rose-pink, but it is fiercely thorny and is a devil for suckering; thus it is good for preventing erosion on a steep bank and is widely so used in the USA. Its clone Macrophylla excels it and is nearly thornless.

Much more beautiful, but still rather prickly, is **R. kelseyi**, which grows to 10ft and bears a profusion of small bunches of bright rose florets, maybe eight in each cluster, in June, followed by bright red pea-pods. z6–7.

R. hartwigii is a 12ft wisteria-like, bristly beauty, with flowers varying from white to purple at midsummer. *R. elliottii* is the smallest of its kind, rarely 6ft high, with erect stems, branching only near the tips, with a grey overtone in its foliage, and rose-purple flowers in bunches (z6–7). *R. boyntonii* is very like hispida, but reaches 10ft and is not so bristly.

ROCK ROSE. See *Cistus*

ROMNEYA
Tree poppy

Like some others in this book, the Californian tree-poppies are sub-shrubs, losing their upper parts in cold climates and really looking at their best in an herbaceous border. They give us very large, lovely, white, sweetly scented, crinkly, poppy-like flowers enlivened by brushes of golden stamens, rising to about 6ft from July to October above deeply cut, blue-green leaves. For full sun and preferably a light, sandy soil. They throw up suckers, more so in a rich soil than in a lean one. You must start with small plants, which may sulk the first year. Afterwards cut them nearly to the ground every March. Propagate by root cuttings.

Perhaps the one most often grown is *R. coulteri*, but *R. trichocalyx* is almost the same, differing only in having more slender stems and bristly flower buds. 'White Cloud' is a hybrid between the two. z8.

Romneya coulteri

ROSA
Rose

What can we say of the rose? Poets for many centuries have sung its praises, but none has ever found words to define its essential spirit, its secret heart or the peculiar quality of its charm. Perhaps it is enough to say, as Gertrude Stein did, that it is simply a rose and that no more need be said. Yet roses vary immensely in their outward images and lineaments, from the tiny, five-petalled cupids of the wild, to the big, full-bosomed Junos of the modern hybrid teas. One may well, borrowing from Kipling, demand: "What do they know of roses who only the HTs know?"

In this vast and amorous company, as in that of the rhododendrons, we are obliged to avoid many beguiling sirens and to seek converse with only one of the choicest and most engaging coteries — the shrub roses. In a general sense, all roses are shrubs, as we have defined that term, but to the rosarian it has a special meaning, that is to say what we might call a shrubby shrub, different in character from the bedding roses and usually larger. So there will be no hybrid teas, no floribundas, no climbers, no miniatures. For, although such HTs as 'Peace' and such floribundas as 'Queen Elizabeth' can become shrubs if pruned to that end, and such climbers as 'Danse du Feu' may be allowed to become big, sprawling shrubs, they do not properly qualify for our pages. Even here, as in the rhododendrons, we are forced to be selective and not so comprehensive as in other genera, but we have included one or two for special reasons, such as extreme hardiness. Gardeners who are keen to dig more deeply should acquire Mr Graham Thomas's *The Old Shrub Roses* and *Shrub Roses of Today*.

Roses have a wide tolerance of soils but, in general, they are at their finest in a rich, fat, loamy soil which is slightly acid. They do well enough in a limy soil, some even in a chalky one, but are hard-pressed in very light, sandy ones unless fattened up with bulky organic matter. There are, of course, exceptions. Thus the handsome rugosa roses are happy in almost pure sand, even down to the seashore, and *R. palustris* grows naturally in swamps. Extra-acid, peaty, wet soils will not do at all. Sun is another almost essential condition, though a little shade is tolerated and one or two, such as *R. arvensis*, are natural woodlanders.

Dig the soil two spits deep. In the bottom spit incorporate well-rotted manure or good compost liberally. If the soil is very light and sandy add plenty of turf, chopped up small.

Into the top spit mix some peat, very generously if the soil is a heavy clay or if it is thin and sandy. Add a good all-purposes fertilizer and some spent hops if you can get them. Stir all well together; do not make sandwiches.

The precepts for planting are few and simple. If the soil is either heavy clay or thin sand, make a planting mixture of peat and bonemeal and plant the roots in this, filling all cavities. Plant to the depth of the union of stock and scion as nearly as possible. Tread firmly if the soil is not soggy. Nowadays roses often come from the nursery with their roots all lying in one direction. If so, spread the roots out fanwise, not attempting a round hole, but see that the root tips are pointed in the direction of the prevailing wind.

Let us face the fact that, of all the plants in this book, roses need the most attention. The shrub roses need less than the hybrid teas and floribundas, but they still have to be protected against various diseases and insect pests, they have to be watched for suckers from the root-stock, they have to be dead-headed (as a rule) when the blossoms fall and need a certain amount of pruning.

A systemic insecticide will go a long way to controlling aphids and other insects that suck leaf and stalk. Fenitrothion kills caterpillars. Black spot, mildew and rust are debilitating or even killing fungus diseases, for which various proprietary concoctions are available and new ones are constantly being brewed by the ingenious chemist.

Pruning is a fairly simple matter for the shrub roses. In general terms (having observed the primary canons of Chapter 4), snip two or three inches off the tips of the stems in the first two

76.   Contrasts in rose leaves. *Above*, Rosa
primula. *Below*, Rosa rugosa

years and thereafter cleave to the general
concept of getting rid, in winter dormancy, of
old stems, in whole or in part, in proportion as
new ones develop low down. Where the
flowers are produced mainly on lateral twigs,
shorten these laterals to about 6in. Always
behead spent flowers back to a node, unless the
rose is one that fructifies in handsome hips in the
autumn, as in *R. moyesii* and some of the
rugosas, but even there you should dead-head
until the plant is well established. These simple
guiding lights serve well enough for garden
purposes, but we shall note a few special cases,
such as the albas and the centifolias, as we go.
Several roses can be pruned to become informal
hedges, but their wide spread must be taken
into account.

In the following list we have collected from
three main groups — the wild species, the
shrubbier versions of the "old" or "old garden"
roses prevailing before the hybrid perpetuals
and then hybrid teas thrust themselves forward,
and the "modern shrub" roses. In the first two
groups, with rare exceptions, we must expect
them to flower once only in the season, but
their display is generally longer than that of
rhododendrons, peonies, lilies and other treasures of the garden. It is therefore important
that we should pay some attention to their
foliage after flowering. Several, having shed
their petals, show nothing but their "long,
loathly legs", as John Skelton put it, poorly
clothed with leaves; *R. moyesii*, for example,
has nothing to offer us between its beautiful
flowering and fruiting. But *R. primula*, by any
standards, is one of the most beautiful of foliage
shrubs all the summer. Likewise, the "old
roses", which have been the subject of many
rhapsodies and many of which are indeed of
rare beauty when in flower, are of little attraction to people indoctrinated with the notion of
the modern, high-pointed, spirally coiled roses,
especially as so many have a floppy and even
slovenly habit. Thus many of the shrub roses
need the companionship of other plants, which
may be herbaceous or shrubby. Hydrangeas
and hypericums will carry on the season for
them very well. Rosemaries complement them
very well. The hardy, ground-covering geraniums, especially blue-flowered, are often
recommended. Not so well known is the small
Hyssopus aristatus, blue in flower from July to
September. We may also begin to consider the
beautiful *Clematis durandii*, which scrambles but
does not cling and is much better for this
purpose than the popular large-flowered clematis. Prune it knee-high in winter.

For everyone's convenience we have in this
case assembled all those cultivars and hybrids
which are closely associated with a species or
group. Thus 'Céleste' will be found under the
albas and 'Cornelia' under "Musks, Hybrid".
Thus we do not here follow the strictly botanical method of Bean. In cases of doubt the index
will give the clue.

Several of the wild species throw up thickets

of suckers if grown on their own roots, but these may be useful for stabilizing banks or other rough ground.

The classification of roses has recently been revised by international agreement, but the old names (such as "HT" and "floribunda") continue to be used and our chosen types here remain unaffected.

R. acicularis. The Arctic rose. Native of the extremely northerly parts of the world, yet classed by Rehder as only z4. 4ft, with weak prickles and smooth laterals. Flowers bright rose, 2in wide. May–June. Suckers madly.

R. × alba 'Semi–plena' is the White Rose of York, the Jacobite Rose, etc, full of historical association. Cried Plantagenet, as the Wars of the Roses loomed: "From off this brier pluck a white rose with me". And Vernon, following him, exclaimed: "I pick this pale and maiden blossom here", foretelling the later name of 'Maiden's Blush'. Pliny, the Roman soldier and naturalist, tells us that England was called Albion as much for the white roses that grew in quantities as for the white cliffs that the Romans knew.

The White Rose, a wild hybrid of conjectural origin, but very closely related to the dog-rose of our native hedgerows and wild places (*R. canina*), has given our gardens some of the loveliest and most sweetly scented roses in the world, though they flower once only. The parentage suggested is *corymbifera × gallica*. The growth is vigorous, erect, the leaves tinted grey and usually resistant to disease. Prune by shortening the main stem by one-third, spurring back last year's laterals to an inch or two. z4. The following suit us best.

'Céleste' ('Celestial'). Pink buds of exquisite moulding, unfurling to pink of a paler hue, semi-double, sweetly scented, enriched by a coronet of golden stamens. The nonpareil of the old roses. 6ft.

'Mme Legras de St Germain'. Glistening ivory, flushed yellow at the centre, opening flat from a cupped bud. A superb, almost thornless shrub of 6ft.

'Maiden's Blush'. An old, old favourite, particularly in the form 'Great Maiden's Blush', which the French (without blushing) call 'Cuisse de Nymph'. It takes slightly different forms and has many nicknames and is supreme among all roses for its delicious savour. The flower is of informal design, warm pink with reflexed petals. The 'Small Maiden's Blush' is only 4ft but almost as good.

'Königin von Dänemark' ('Queen of Denmark') gives us a marvellous flower of multitudinous, tightly packed petals in warm pink, gloriously scented, but the shrub is a lanky 6ft.

'Aloha'. Pillar rose of rather narrow, erect growth to 9ft, with densely petalled, scented flowers of deep coral-pink. Very useful for filling gaps and planting between windows.

R. amblyotis. Extremely hardy, from chilly Kamtchatka, and of value only for that reason. 5ft, single red flowers, 2in, in early June. Hips deep red. z2.

'Andersonii'. A glamorised edition of the dog-rose (*R. canina*), 5-petalled, with larger (3in) flowers of richer pink, with a sweet scent. 6ft, arching, midsummer only, good hips.

'Ballerina'. Charming small shrub of informal character, breaking out into large mops of small pink florets, white-eyed. A country-girl rose, to be kept away from anything large and rumbustious. Flowers again in autumn. About 3ft. Origin unknown. 'Belinda' is a slightly taller version.

R. blanda. Another exceptionally hardy American species. A 6ft shrub with large, single pink flowers in May–June. z2.

R. × borboniana. These are the celebrated Bourbon roses, traditionally accepted as having originated in the Ile de Bourbon (now Réunion) in 1817. Diverse in form, they are characterised by their sweet odour, their prolonged flowering, their informal charm, their abundant petallage and their usually elegant deportment. Most are prone to mildew and mostly need a little support. Full sun, z7–8. The best-known is the non-stop, almost thornless 'Zéphirine Drouhin', but this is usually treated as a short climber. Other suitable ones are:

'La Reine Victoria'. Large, globular flowers of lilac-pink which are continuously borne on erect, 6ft stems.

'Louise Odier'. Soft pink, nearly always in bloom, on rather lax, spreading 6ft stems.

'Mme Isaac Pereire'. Enormous purple-crimson flowers, voluptuously scented, of loose formation. Very vigorous and best used as a pillar rose.

'Mme Ernst Calvat'. A pink sport from the above, otherwise similar.

'Mme Pierre Oger'. A very distinctive plant of great beauty, with globular blooms in pink and cream of shell-like delicacy in great quantity on a very slim, erect shrub.

'Souvenir de la Malmaison'. A beautiful white, delicately flushed pink, large and continuous in flowering. Smaller than the others — only 4–5ft.

R. californica is seen best in its splendid semi-double form 'Plena'. This is a big, wide-spreading shrub, 8ft high, displaying itself in corymbs which form cascades of pink, scented flowers in midsummer only. z5.

'Canary Bird'. One of the most spectacular of roses, alive with quantities of fresh, clear, spring-like yellow flowers, of the shade that one associates with most daffodils. They are small and single and begin to open in late May. It can grow 6ft high and wide, its brown stems swooping out and down and luxuriantly clad with small, pinnate, fern-like foliage, that clothes the plant down to the ground. Believed to be the progeny of *xanthina* and *hugonis*, 'Canary Bird' is much superior to both, but seems to prefer a rather dry soil to a wet, heavy one, when it may suffer from die-back.

R. × cantabrigiensis. Offspring of *hugonis × sericea*, forming a tall shrub liberally dressed with single, pale yellow, 2in, scented flowers in late spring only, accompanied by elegant, scented leaves of up to 11 small leaflets. Raised at the Cambridge Botanic Gardens.

R. carolina. Prickly, 3ft shrub with rose-pink flowers in June, followed by red hips. Suckers madly, so useful for stabilising banks. z4.

R. caudata. A thrustful, erect shrub of maybe 10ft, sparsely thorned. Bright pink flowers in corymbs in June, followed by dazzling red, pear-shaped hips. z5.

R. × centifolia. Another of the classic groups of old garden roses, known by numerous nicknames, such as the Rose of a Hundred Leaves (our ancestors having used "leaves" for "petals"), the Painter's Rose (beloved of the old Dutch flower artists), the Rose of Provence and, unfortunately, the Cabbage Rose, because of its usually globular shape. Centifolia itself is a rare bird but from its nest many fledgelings have fluttered and matured. They produce beautiful flowers but on the whole are not good garden shrubs, their whole aspect being droopy as well as very spiny. The droopiness suits them well enough when in flower, but afterwards they have little to interest us. The long-leggity 'Tour de Malakoff' (named after an engagement in the Crimean War) and the smaller 'Robert le Diable' are indolent ground-floppers. 'Petite de Hollande' and 'Rose de Meaux' are small, pretty and appealing. Of the larger sorts the best is 'Fantin Latour'.

The moss roses, *R. centifolia muscosa*, also come in rightly here. They are interesting but of little value as garden shrubs.

The centifolias need a richer soil than the other veterans and are pruned in the same way as the albas. z5.

'Chinatown'. A modern shrub, flowering more or less continuously, with HT-style blossoms of bright yellow. 5ft.

R. chinensis. The China or India or Bengal rose has had an immense influence on modern rose-breeding, especially for its continuity of flowering. z7.

We shall mention only two. One is the 'Old Blush' or 'Monthly' rose, valuable for its compactness and for flowering intermittently right up to Christmas in favourable climates. The flowers are pink and scented of sweet-peas. Normally about shoulder-high, it is a splendid hedger of 3ft.

The other is the remarkable 'Mutabilis', a tall, slender shrub with flowers that are orange in the bud, opening pale yellow, changing to coppery-pink and finally purple-red, all within four days, but flowering from June till autumn.

Known also as 'Tipo Ideale'. It needs a warm situation and in a cool one may not grow more than 3ft.

'Complicata'. Complicated only in its origins, otherwise a very simple, delightful, singly petalled rose of rich, clear pink with a white centre, like a sublimated dog-rose. Normally about 6ft, spreading broadly, but can climb into a tree.

'Constance Spry'. A beautiful rose of modern production but of distinctly "old rose" character. A big, 7ft, arching, spreading, well-clothed shrub, bearing very large, globular, sweetly scented, rose-pink blooms in summer only. It needs what Shakespeare's gardener called "some supportance". Parentage: the gallica 'Belle Isis' and the floribunda 'Dainty Maid'.

R. × damascena. The Damask Rose, another of the basic old roses and another of the rose's many mysteries, for no such plant as *damascena*, whether species or hybrid, is known beyond doubt to exist. Yet it has given its name to several siblings of diverse character, including one used for concocting attar of roses. z4.

The only one for us, however, is the tall, queenly 'Madame Hardy', a rose of superb quality, which, at midsummer only, is dressed in a lovely gown of white, scented flowers, which open flat with overlapping petals, revealing, when mature, its green carpels at its heart.

R. davidii. A strapping shrub of loose, spreading habit reaching to 10ft, throwing out many-flowered clusters (corymbs) of the subtle shade known as mallow-pink, and leaves composed of about 9 leaflets. Valuable for flowering in June–July, followed by showers of bottle-shaped hips. z5.

R. ecae. Slim, elegant, whippy stems of 5ft, chestnut-hued, swinging in the wind and glittering in late May and early June with small, golden sovereigns among leaves with up to 11 small leaflets. A lively little shrub found in Afghanistan by the British army doctor Aitchison and named rather awkwardly from the initials of his wife and pronounced Ekee. Full sun. z7.

Aitchison's rose has produced one or two brilliant offspring by marriage with other roses. One of these, of very recent introduction, is 'Helen Knight', a superlative rose of small, glittering golden flowers, magnificent on a wall at Wisley, where it grows at least 10ft high. Its male parent is not categorically certain. It arose in the garden of Mr Frank Knight, when Director of Wisley. Rather scarce so far. *Cf.* 'Golden Chersonese', which it resembles florally.

R. eglanteria (*rubiginosa*) is the old sweet briar or eglantine of Shakespeare, but of value as a garden shrub only for the marvellous perfume exuded by its leaves, especially after rain. z4.

'Erfurt'. A charming, modern, but country-girl rose with large, semi-double flowers made up of a broad zone of cherry-red surrounding a creamy centre with golden anthers. Blooms all summer on wide-flung, thorny arms 6ft high by 8ft wide in a loose and open manner.

'Fountain'. Large, blood-red scented, HT-style roses are borne singly or in small clusters on 5 to 6ft stems by this modern shrub. It has a proud look and breaks freely from the base, making the pruner's job easy. Best protected from keen winds.

'Fred Loads'. A big, upright, modern shrub of 7ft or more with glossy foliage and large, single, scented blossoms of brilliant vermilion, borne with frequent succession.

'Fritz Nobis'. One of the most beautiful of all modern roses, giving us semi-double, elegantly moulded flowers in two tones of soft, melting pink, scented of cloves. A Cupid among roses, flowering at midsummer only on 6ft canes.

'Frühlingsgold'. When at its best this modern rose is one of the loveliest, producing, in June only, richly golden single blossoms, amorously scented. Only for this reason does it scrape into these pages, for its foliage is thin, its 7ft legs haggard and its flowers fade to cream in hot sun. Plant it behind something lush and leafy.

'Frühlingsmorgen'. We think this even

more beautiful than its half-sister, which it resembles in habit. The blossoms are broadly rimmed with rich pink around a centre of pale lemon, from which issues a brush of chestnut stamens. There is often a second blossoming in September.

R. gallica. This is the historic "French" rose, of ancient lineage. Among its many progeny, totally different from the moderns, are several of great beauty in flower and not drooping like the centifolias but looking you straight in the face. When their time is past, however, about mid-July, they are of little value as shrubs, their leaves being very dull, slack and very prone to mildew. If we had to choose only one, it would be the tall 'Tuscany' or 'Tuscany Superb', for the sheer luxury of their red, velvety blossoms, packed with petals and for their more erect carriage.

We should also hanker after 'Cardinal de Richelieu', which is of the essence of the old French roses, with its mass of tightly packed, maroon-purple petals folding back upon themselves and refreshingly scented. We should also like to find room for 'Charles de Mills', which grows only 3ft high and produces an alluring blend of purple, claret and lilac, the petals tightly packed in a flower that is at first flat-topped and then rolls over into a ball. All z5.

'Golden Chersonese'. This new star in the rose firmament was raised by Mr E. F. Allen, formerly President of the Royal National Rose Society. It is the gifted child of *R. ecae* and the hybrid 'Canary Bird' and, like its parents and grandparents, is a glittering gold, and scented to boot. Its bearing is erect and its stems brown, as in *ecae*, and its flowers large and abundant. A stunning rose of maybe 8ft with a good scent, for May–June only, but afterwards still a desirable shrub in its small, pinnate, frond-like leaves, which clothe it to the ground.

'Golden Showers'. A slim, erect pillar rose with scented flowers of soft yellow and HT style that never stops blooming. Hardy for many uses, like 'Aloha'. 6–8ft, according to pruning.

'Golden Wings'. Single or semi-single blooms of soft, pale yellow, beautiful in their clarity and their open countenance, scented, with mahogany stamens, are borne more or less all the summer on a tidy shrub 5ft high and wide, according to pruning, with thorny canes and seven leaflets to the leaf.

'R. 'Harisonii'. Large, semi-double, pale yellow, cup-shaped flowers borne for several weeks in June, with multiple leaflets, on a rather gaunt 6ft shrub. Popular in America, though not choice as a shrub. Believed to be a cross between *spinosissima* and *foetida*, found in the garden of a New York lawyer named Harison. z4.

R. hugonis. First-rate as a shrub, luxuriantly robed in fern-like multiple leaflets from brown stems, reaching commonly to about 7ft and spreading broadly. The elegant, simple flowers are pale yellow, 2in wide, on short, lateral twigs in May. Subject to canker in some parts of America. z5.

'Marguerite Hilling'. A lovely sport from 'Nevada', with the same ostrich-plume aspect, but enriched by large, single flowers of a subtle and engaging pink, displayed in quantities at midsummer and again later.

'Marjorie Fair'. Of the same behaviour as 'Ballerina', one of its parents. Big trusses of massed florets, crimson with a white eye, flowering repeatedly. About 4ft.

R. × micrugosa 'Alba'. A nice, little, erect 5ft shrub, densely bushy in the manner of rugosa, very prickly, with a succession of white, single, scented flowers. Parents: *roxburghii* × *rugosa*.

R. moyesii. A "lean and haggard" creature that is adorned in June with the loveliest single flowers of blood-red, followed in autumn by a shower of brilliant hips in the shape of a chianti flask. The leaves are pretty but sparse. Hide its naked legs with something seemly. An edition with the ridiculous name 'Geranium' is scarlet. Succeeds in chalk. z5.

'Mozart'. A charming small shrub very like 'Ballerina', but of a deeper pink, flowering profusely for most of the season.

R. multibracteata. Another good foliage shrub, the small leaves divided into 5 to 9 tiny, dark green, shining leaflets, carried on grace-

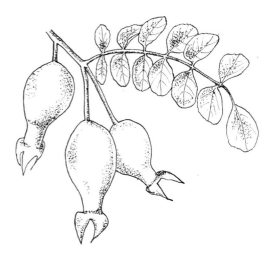

77. The scarlet hips of Rosa moyesii

fully bending stems up to 8ft long, and forming a rounded outline. Small (1in), bright pink, single flowers for a long spell in July, some in terminal clusters, some solitary, thrusting out from a nest of leaf-like bracts which give the plant its name and form a ready means of recognition. z6.

Musks, Hybrid. "Hybrid Musk" is the name of doubtful validity given to a trugful of delightful, cluster-flowered shrubs evolved by a parson named Pemberton and of high standing among all flowering shrubs. They have a loose, open structure, and beat the modern floribundas hollow for prodigality of bloom, throwing out great sprays and cascades of small, pastel-tinted blossoms of informal design, heavily drenched with scent on long parabolas that may reach 7ft, though normally a little less. They bloom at least twice in the season and their autumnal sprays are often better than their summer ones. 'Cornelia' is a coppery-apricot, fading to a creamy-pink. 'Penelope' is salmon, likewise fading, splendid in autumn.

These are probably the two favourites. 'Buff Beauty' is delicious until it pales. 'Danae' is similar but only 4ft. 'Felicia' is a charming warm pink, becoming silver-tinted, 5ft high but much broader. 'Francesca' is a soft apricot. 'Prosperity' is white. 'Pax' is also white and of languid growth. 'Nur Mahal' is a soft mauve, only 4ft.

'Vanity' is cherry, a thruster of 8ft, shooting out rigid branches at rather awkward angles.

Decapitate the flower trusses after blossom-fall. In February reduce the long basal canes by about a third and cut back the side-shoots.

Others besides Pemberton have produced roses that are loosely grouped under Hybrid Musks, but they are totally different from the Pembertons and lack their grace and their sweet breath. 'Wilhelm' ('Skyrocket' in America) is a big, assertive crimson 8ft high and wide, but a good, leafy shrub. 'Will Scarlet', a sport from it, is scarlet and less massive. Both flower continuously.

'Nevada', mother of the aforesaid 'Marguerite Hilling', is in the very front rank of flowering shrubs, forming a crown of ostrich plumes, 6ft high and more in spread, crowded with big, single or semi-double, white flowers, crested with yellow stamens. A magnificent spectacle in June and quite a good one in August also, with a few scattered blossoms at other times. In very hot weather, especially in the second display, the blossoms are dyed pink.

R. nitida. A very pretty, small American native, extremely hardy. Large, single, bright pink blossoms are borne in June only on 2ft stems, with lustrous green leaves divided into 7 or 9 leaflets that become brilliantly ensanguined before they fall. If on its own roots it throws up a lot of suckers. z3.

R. × paulii. See Chapter 5

R. pendulina, the Alpine rose. A pretty and uncommon rose of 4ft with few thorns, multiple leaflets and red-purple flowers on bending stems in early summer, followed by a brilliant display of red, elongated hips. There is a double form. z5.

R. pomifera (or **villosa**) the "apple rose", so called because of the shape of its big hips, but, being hairy, they are really much more like red gooseberries. Otherwise, it is a stiff, erect shrub of about 5ft with much-divided leaves covered with soft hairs and resinously scented, and pretty flowers of a fuchsine pink in June, their stalks covered with glandular bristles. A semi-double form with pale purple flowers is familiarly known as "Wolley-Dod's rose". z5.

R. primula, the "incense rose", ultimately of 8ft, is in the very front rank of ornamental shrubs. Its young stems are chestnut, their thorns red. Its foliar robe, flowing to the ground, is woven of a mass of small, finely divided, richly aromatic leaves, swaying gracefully to the impulses of the wind. Its cup-shaped flowers, also scented, of the colour of primroses, crowd the branches in May. This is a rose that succeeds in chalky soil. z5.

'Raubritter'. A 3ft mound, spreading widely, of thorny, interlacing stems. Pretty, pale pink, semi-double, cup-shaped flowers with a refreshing scent, break out in clusters throughout July and August. Use it to cover old tree-stumps or to hang down a terrace wall, but it is a brute if you have to do any weeding.

R. rubrifolia. Essentially a rose for the "flower arranger", its appeal being in its violet-flushed stems when young and grey-mauve leaves, when grown in the sun. Otherwise, it is simply an open, rangy, extremely hardy shrub, reaching 8ft, with few thorns. Flowers small, red with a white eye; small chestnut hips. z2.

R. rugosa. These are among the very best of shrubs for any sort of garden. They make dense, rounded plants of clean outline, shrouded to the ground in very dark, wrinkled leaves, beneath the canopy of which few weeds can survive. Their long stems are furred with innumerable small prickles. Their flowers have a clove bouquet, usually bloom on and off throughout summer and often develop handsome, tomato-like hips. They dislike lime but perform extremely well in sand, even down to the sea-shore, have a sub-arctic hardiness and are the most resistant to disease of all roses. In a sandy situation a scattering of seed will produce a plantation. z2, but some of the hybrids may not be quite so hardy.

alba. Beautiful natural variety with single, white blossoms enlivened by a brush of golden stamens.

'Blanc Double de Coubert'. As the name implies, the flowers are white and double. Very nice but the petals do not fall as they fade. Very fine *qua* shrub.

'F. J. Grootendorst'. Avoid this dull red hybrid, but accept its pink sport 'Pink Grootendorst'. The petals are frilled.

'Frau Dagmar Hartopp' (or 'Hastrup'). A rose of exceptional beauty, producing exquisite, delicately chiselled, single blooms of peaches and honey, which develop into spectacular little "tomatoes". Not much second blooming as a rule. 4–5ft.

'Roseraie de l'Haÿ'. The most sumptuous of all, producing large double, loosely constructed blooms of rich burgundy. Gives a constant succession of flowers, but, being double, no hips. Maybe 7ft high and of impenetrable density. Originated in the famous Parisian garden of l'Haÿ.

rubra. A variable natural form, which at its best is a vinous red.

'Sarah Van Fleet'. Robust, erect hybrid with rigid stems, viciously armed, producing a constant succession of large, semi-double, scented blossoms of soft appealing pink, prettily wrought.

'Scabrosa'. Of all roses this (excepting 'Golden Showers') is the most positively "continuous" in its flowering if dead-headed and the most regrettable in its name. Its very large, single flowers, up to 5in wide, are, let us say, a rosy-purple and warmly scented, followed by brilliant hips, which, if allowed, will smother the later bloom. In some opinions this is the finest of all the rugosas. It makes a magnificent hedge, as may be seen at the gardens of the Royal National Rose Society near St Albans.

'Schneezwerg' ('Snow Dwarf'). Despite its name, grows nearly 5ft high, continuously displaying its pretty, semi-double, white flowers. Leaves a paler green than in a typical rugosa.

'Scharlachglut' ('Scarlet Fire'). A dramatic plant, bearing large, single flowers of brilliant and deep, velvety scarlet, carried on arching stems 7ft high and wide in midsummer. Large, red, pear-shaped hips.

R. spinosissima (or **pimpinellifolia**) called the Scotch or Burnet rose, though it ranges far round the northerly parts of the globe. Usually rather small, spiny shrubs, which sucker rapidly if on their own roots, forming prickly thickets.

The leaves, copiously borne, are small and much divided, making good leafy plants. The flowers are small, with a wide range of colours, rather fleeting, blooming early, usually scented, followed by small, black hips. Successful in poor soils, especially sandy, seaside ones. z4.

There are several natural varieties and hybrids of the Scotch roses, from which the following are chosen. Some of its more famous hybrids — 'Golden Wings', 'Frühlingsmorgen', 'Frühlingsgold' — we have listed separately, as they have quite different garden characters. Undoubtedly the best all-rounder is the hybrid 'Stanwell Perpetual', which, unlike other Scotch roses, produces its pretty, small, scented pink flowers all summer. 3ft. Some others are:

altaica. From the Altai Mountains, Siberia. Large, single ivory flowers, freshly scented, with leaflets usually in nines. 5ft.

'Mrs Colville'. Purple, single. Hips red. $2\frac{1}{2}$ft.

'William III'. Double, purple, scented. Leaves grey-green. Close habit. 2ft.

'Williams' Double Yellow'. The best of the various Scotch yellows that have come and gone over the centuries. Good scent, but the dead petals hang on. 2ft.

R. sweginzowii. Very like *moyesii* but with pink flowers. To 12ft. z5.

R. virginiana. We cannot do better than quote Mr Jack Harkness in his book *Roses*: "One of the most handsome wild roses in the world; everything about it is right." It might also have been designed by the Creator for a cultivated garden, forming itself into a fair round shrub of graceful carriage, comely proportions, up to 6ft high, well-clad with glossy leaves of 7 or 9 leaflets, and producing very lively single flowers of bright rose-pink in June and July. Later comes a fine crop of bright red hips to enhance the splendour of the autumnal colouring of its leaves. When necessary, it responds well to the pruner's knife and makes a splendid hedge of up to 4ft. On its own roots it thrusts up colonies of suckers. z3.

R. webbiana. A very graceful foliage shrub formed of slender, drooping, plum-coloured branches, thickly clothed with small feathery leaves right down to the ground and richly spangled in June with single, lilac-pink flowers of $2\frac{1}{2}$in, which fructify as small, brilliant red, bottle-shaped hips. A very elegant shrub of 6ft. Thorns yellow. z6.

R. willmottiae. Another beautiful foliage shrub, akin in style to *hugonis* and *primula*. It averages 7ft with purplish stems and delightful, 1in flowers of pale rose-purple in immense quantities in May–June, followed by small, red hips. A very decorative shrub, full of grace. z6.

R. xanthina. We mention this double yellow wilding for the record only. A fine shrub indeed, but 'Canary Bird' excels it. *R. x. spontanea* is a single-flowered form. z5.

ROSE OF SHARON. Of USA is *Hibiscus syriacus*; of Britain and elsewhere is *Hypericum calycinum*.

ROSMARINUS
Rosemary

We shall not attempt to compete with the poets, the cooks and the old herbalists in our observations on this shrub of ancient usage, beyond reminding ourselves that both Ophelia and Perdita tell us that rosemary stands for "remembrance". In fact, rosemaries can be awkward creatures in the garden unless you plant them with full knowledge that they will develop a "middle-age spread" and that they rarely prosper in damp soils or shade-afflicted ones. But their thick clothing of small, dark, grey-green leaves, which are white on the underside and are richly aromatic, earn them a place in most gardens. They are meet companions of the old alba roses, among others, and look well near broad steps or a gate. They are drought-hardy and windproof and are splendid in dry soils near the sea.

The usual one is *R. officinalis*, which produces small, pale blue, open-mouthed flowers in May or earlier along branches of the previous year's growth. There are several forms, of which 'Alba' is white and 'Rosea' pale pink. Others of value are:

'Benenden Blue'. Beautiful, smaller than most, with flowers of bright blue. Rather tender, it is a selected form of var. *angustifolius* brought to England by Captain Collingwood Ingram from Corsica.

'Fastigiatus', often called "Miss Jessop's Upright". More erect than most, but still a plump matron.

'Majorca'. A charming shade of blue.

'Primley Blue'. Compact, spreading tidily.

'Severn Sea'. A dwarf, arching shrub with brilliant flowers.

'Tuscan Blue'. Beautiful, rather small, decidedly tender. Flowers bright blue. Leaves bright green, not grey-tinted, larger than in others and pungently aromatic, as of nutmeg. In Tuscany it is used for hedging.

In general, the common rosemary may be rated z7, if in full sun and a dry soil. Most people leave it unpruned, but it responds to the knife much better than is generally reported. Pruning after flowering results in good new shoots. Cut back hard any straggling, misshapen specimens in spring.

We bypass the prostrate sorts. Propagate by cuttings, in the same way as for lavender.

RUBUS

Bramble

A visitor to a well-tended garden might very likely suppose that brambles are the last thing that he would expect to see. Yet raspberries and blackberries are brambles (R. idaeus and R. fruticosus respectively), and there are also some highly ornamental ones, valued for their flowers, their pretty stems and their fruits. They are not perhaps quite the thing for the formal garden and are seen best in open, freehand pictures, in light woodland, in larger spaces and in parks.

In general, the brambles are marked by long canes, usually thorny, and decorated with simple, five-petalled flowers, like those of the dog-rose, though a few are doubled. The best are clothed in elegant leaves, which vary a great deal in form. Bramble-like fruits come in summer, some decorative, some edible.

Cultivation is easy if you plant them in a good, loamy soil. All but a few are deciduous and they produce their flowers on canes that have grown in the previous year, readily throwing up new shoots from the base and thus clearly showing the gardener how they expect to be pruned.

Ignoring, as is our wont, the scrambling climber and the ground-creepers, we are left with two different styles of rubus. One group is grown for its brilliant white stems that enliven the winter scene and the other for the attraction of its dog-rose flowers in May, followed very often in July or August by decorative fruits which are usually edible, though lacking the savour of the cultivated raspberries and blackberries.

Those that are grown for the sparkling beauty of their stems include cockburnianus, biflorus and thibetanus. All are very good indeed of their kind, but the first-named is the star. One's aim is to ensure a constant succession of their icing-sugar stems in winter, which occurs only on the young shoots. After their first winter they begin to mature and flower and lose the waxy coating, so you cut them down then right to the ground, as soon as the new shoots begin to show their noses. Their flowers are of no account, but their ferny, cut leaves are very attractive. Try to place all these in front of an evergreen background.

Similar very hard pruning has to be done to most of the second group, which are valued for the excellence of their flowers and perhaps their berries, such as R. odoratus. Cut these also to the ground after blossom-fall or after fruiting if the fruits are attractive. New shoots will readily break from the ground. Others which we shall note, such as 'Benenden', the king of all brambles, do not throw from the base so readily, but in all cases remember the general precept of removing old stems and twigs in proportion as new ones appear.

R. amabilis. A graceful, slender-stemmed shrub of 5ft with prettily cut, pinnate leaves and white, 2in, solitary flowers at the tips of short, leafy twigs in June–July and edible, red fruit.

Prune after fruiting. z7.

R. biflorus. One of the finest icing-sugar raspberries, branching at the tips, beautiful in winter. Large, pinnate leaves, the undersides coated with a white felt. Flowers trivial, except in the variety *quinqueflorus*. Fruits yellow, edible. Cut right back after fruiting. z7.

R. cockburnianus (or *giraldianus*). Perhaps the finest of the "whitewashed" brambles, much branched and pendulous at the tips, with pretty, fern-like leaves. Lovely in its winter nakedness. The small, purple flowers and black berries are of no account. Prune down to the ground as soon as the whiteness goes off. 8ft × 8ft, suckering sometimes. z5.

R. deliciosus. A deep purple raspberry. The fruits are poor and not "delicious", but the plant as a whole is to be numbered among the most beautiful of shrubs, its graceful, thornless stems reaching to 8ft, clothed with broad, currant-like leaves and ornamented prodigiously with large, white flowers like dog-roses in May–June. It is excelled among its like only by 'Benenden'. This is a rubus that does not send up new basal shoots as readily as others, so, after cutting off the spent flowered parts, keep a certain amount of the old stem to form a good framework, in proportion as new shoots appear. z5.

R. laciniatus is the rambling cut-leaf or fern-leaf blackberry, sometimes grown for the elegance of its leaves alone, but it also yields exceptionally fine fruits. It seeds too freely, scattered by birds. About 9ft.

R. leucodermis, averaging 6ft, is rather like biflorus, but the stems are blue-white and the fruit is dark purple, sweet and of an agreeable flavour. z5.

R. lineatus. A rangy, rather tender 10ft shrub, remarkable for its handsome leaves, which are formed just like those of the horse-chestnut, the five leaflets radiating from a common point, but brilliantly silvered beneath. The middle leaflet may be anything up to 9in long. White flowers, small red or yellow fruits.

R. mesogaeus. A raspberry with velvety stems up to 12ft and large, trifoliate, grey-tinted leaves. Flowers pale pink in June–July.

Rubus tridel

Fruits black. z6.

R. × nobilis. Very like R. odoratus, but not so big and lacking fragrance. A handsome shrub, flowering June–July. Parentage: odoratus × idaeus.

R. odoratus. One of the stars of the rubus, but much addicted to suckering and so best suited to open woodland or other places, rather moist, where such behaviour is allowable. It has thornless, peeling stems up to 8ft high, covered with glandular hairs, very large, velvety, lobed, vine-like leaves, large, purple, scented flowers from June to September, followed by red, flat raspberries in a favourable season (rarely in Britain). Cut the old stems to the ground immediately the main display is over. z3.

R. parviflorus. Again very like odoratus, but the flowers are a trifle smaller and lack scent, and the stems are less glandular. z3.

R. phoenicolasius, the wineberry, so called

because of its heavy crop of bright red berries which are sweet and juicy but of insipid flavour. The 8ft stems are covered with red, glandular bristles. Large, trifoliate leaves, white-felted beneath. Small, pale pink flowers grouped in terminal spikes, rare in brambles, not opening until July and remarkable for their large, star-shaped, hairy calyces. z8.

R. spectabilis. A suckering shrub for the wild garden, with 5ft stems, trifoliate leaves, magenta flowers in April and large, orange, edible fruits. z5.

R. thibetanus. Purple 6ft stems, prettily dusted with a blue-white, waxy bloom in winter. Handsome pinnate leaves with multiple leaflets, covered with silky hairs. Small purple flowers and black berries. z7.

R. × tridel 'Benenden'. Finest of all the brambles, raised in England by Captain Collingwood Ingram in 1950, the selected clone being named after his celebrated garden in Kent. Its erect, thornless, peeling stems may reach to 10ft and as much wide and are crowded in April with large (2in) pure white flowers of virginal beauty displaying a tuft of golden stamens. Prune as for deliciosus. Parentage: deliciosus × trilobus.

R. trilobus. A lovely, thornless, 5ft shrub with very large, deeply lobed, currant-like leaves on arching stems and flowers very like those of 'Benenden' from May to July.

RUE. See *Ruta*

RUSCUS

These small, darkly evergreen sub-shrubs are among nature's curiosities. What looks like a leaf is really a flattened branch, known as a cladode, and it is from the middle of this cladode that the tiny flowers appear. They are unisexual, male and female flowers on separate plants, so that both sexes are needed to produce their bright berries. They are scarcely orna-mental plants unless in fruit, but have the great merit of being able to prosper under the densest

78. Butcher's broom (Ruscus aculeatus)

shade of big trees, as they will also in full, hot sun. In fact, they seem to grow anywhere and they spread by underground stems, forming thickets.

No need to prune, beyond the removal of withered growth. Some people believe in chopping them right down to the ground to induce close growth, but this is of doubtful value in poor, dry soils. Propagate by division. z7.

The best-known ruscus is *R. aculeatus*, known as "butcher's broom" because, we are credibly told, butchers used its bristly foliage to scrub those huge slabs of tree-trunks upon which, older readers may remember, the but-cher cut up his meat. The plant averages about 2ft. There are a few varieties, such as *angusti-folius*, with narrow leaves and 'Sparkler', both at Wisley.

R. hypoglossum is a smaller plant with larger, leafier, spineless cladodes, and tiny, green flowers in the middle. *R. colchicus* oddly pro-duces its wee, white flowers on the underside of the cladode.

R. × microglossus, is a suckering shrublet, with elegantly poised cladodes.

RUTA
Rue

Ruta graveolens is the "herb of grace" of Shakespeare's day, its value to the old herbalist lying mainly in the volatile oil that permeates its small, blue-tinted, pinnate leaves. Today 'Jackman's Blue' stands out almost alone as the one for the gardener, its blue-washed mound standing in bright contrast to other plants, notably heathers and the old roses. Give it, if you can, a rather dry place in full sun, shear off the paltry, mustardy little spikes of flower at leaf-top level and cut it hard back in April, removing also any weak shoots, in order to keep the plant compact, for rue otherwise has a tendency to sprawl. It should form a neat dome, possibly 3ft high. Rue is a sub-shrub, its stems not wholly woody. It likes lime. Propagate by summer cuttings of side-shoots.

An alternative to 'Jackman's Blue' is 'Variegata', in which the leaflets have a white border.

SALIX
Willow

A few of the small, shrubby willows deserve mention. Their main attraction is their catkins, of which males and females are nearly always borne on separate plants, the male being usually the more handsome. They are short, plump, stubby, cone-shaped and tightly packed, not long, loose and dangling like those of the garrya, hazel and others. The tiny flowers in the catkins are in the axils of bud-scales, which may themselves be colourful, and consist in male flowers merely of one or two stamens, without petals. The pollen is wind-borne.

In general, the catkins are at their best in middle spring, usually on naked branches before the leaves, and when their flowering is over the shrubby species are not of great ornamental value in the smaller garden but suit well the mixed company of a larger one. A good way of prolonging their usefulness is to use them as hosts for the beautiful, non-clinging Clematis durandii.

Propagation of willows is as easy as pie; merely stick a twig — or an 8ft branch for that matter — into the ground in a shady spot.

Willows always look well near water and to a few a moist foothold is very important, but the majority are quite happy in any good, loamy soil. The golden Goat Willow or Great Sallow or Palm, S. caprea, which becomes the old "pussy willow" in its silvered male, is unfortunately beyond our reach here, exceeding 25ft. Challenging it in size are S. lucida, the Shining Willow, of glossy leaves, and S. aegyptica, both of which can become tree-like. The following offer us more shrub-like choices.

S. × balfourii, a fine and very hardy hybrid of 10ft or so, combining the woolly young foliage of the small S. lanata and something of the bright catkins of the big Goat Willow, which appear on naked branches in April. Said to have been born in Scotland and to favour damp places. z4.

S. bockii. A low, spreading shrub, usually not more than 4ft high. The only cultivated willow to flower in late summer and early autumn, the shoots having developed in the current year. Bright green leaf clusters in spring. z5.

S. fargesii. 6–8ft. Erect and slender and of open habit. Glossy leaves 6in or more long. Conspicuous, chestnut-brown buds in winter. Large, erect catkins developing about the same time as the leaves. Nuseries often supply the closely related *moupinensis* instead. z6.

S. gracilistyla. A charming willow averaging 7ft. Young leaves silky-grey before turning green. Catkins develop early spring. The males a silky-grey, flushed red by the unopened anthers, which later sparkle as goldenly as you please. z5. The hybrid S. 'The Hague', which appears to be its child after marriage with the goat willow, is a wide-spreading female with woolly limbs.

S. hastata 'Wehrhahnii', the "snow pussy", grows slowly in purple-tinted stems to about 5ft, spreading widely, and sparkling with quantities of upright, silvery male catkins with yellow anthers. A lovely picture in April. Known also sometimes as the "halberd-leaved willow" but the reason is not apparent, the leaves, though varied, being more or less oval. z5.

S. irrorata. A 10ft shrub remarkable, especially in winter, for its stems, which are purple overlaid with a chalk-white powder, like the "whitewashed" brambles. The anthers of the male catkins are mahogany before maturing yellow. z4.

S. lanata, the woolly willow. A little chap of barely 4ft, with silvery-grey leaves and erect, woolly-grey catkins flushed yellow. 'Stuartii' is a beautiful dwarf form, very colourful in winter with its yellow shoots and orange buds, followed by larger catkins. z3.

S. 'Melanostachys', known also as 'Kurome' and by other names, stands 6ft with decorative catkins, which have nearly black scales and brick-red anthers maturing yellow.

S. purpurea, the "purple osier". A large shrub of 10ft or more which has slender, purple-stained, arching stems, bearing its slender catkins all along them, followed by leaves that are a vivid ice-blue beneath. It will thrive in fairly dry soils as well as in the wet ones typical of osiers. Its supple stems are used for weaving baskets.

The variety 'Lambertiana' has large leaves. 'Pendula', the "weeping purple willow", which is often grafted high on a "leg", may be used where there is not room for the big weeping willows, but too often it becomes only a wide-spreading tangle. z4.

SALVIA

Sage

We are interested only, of course, in the shrubby salvias, not the annual, biennial or herbaceous species. All are labiates, characterised by flowers formed of two lips, sometimes widely agape.

The shrubby sages are generally spreading evergreens, beautiful in leaf and flower and an adornment to any garden, but the majority are too tender for those of us who live in climates that are subject to the bite of frost. The flowers are in whorls, often formed into spikes.

The hardiest (z5) and most wooable are a few forms of the "common" sage, **S. officinalis**, as used by the cook. This itself is a nice, grey-leaved, aromatic shrublet, soft to the touch and mauve in flower, except for the white form 'Albiflora'; but for the ornamental garden one wants some of the varieties with coloured leaves. They keep low and spread very widely if in a hot spot and good soil, suppressing weeds, but seem to be a little less hardy than the original. They include:

'Purpurascens'. Leaves deeply dyed a dusky purple.

'Tricolor'. A subtle blend of grey, cream, pink and purple.

'Icterina'. A combination of green and gold. Perhaps the choicest but not the hardiest.

All the varieties on the theme of the "common" sage are apt to become bare and woody as they age. To prevent this tendency, trim them back after flowering in late summer. Neglected specimens can be rejuvenated by hard cutting back in spring.

The more tender salvias, most of which come from Mexico, reach an average height of about 3ft in good conditions, are drought-hardy and are valued more for their flowers than their foliage, and bloom for long periods. You must plant them only in full sun. Pruning is important, for, left alone, they become weak and uncouth. So cut back to the older growth just as the new shoots are about to break in spring. Winter's knife may do it for you.

The species usually preferred is **S. microphylla** (**S. grahamii**), the blackcurrant sage, so called for the odour of its crushed leaves. It has ovate, dull green leaves and red-purple flowers in terminal racemes from June onwards. z8 if in a warm spot. Often cut to the ground in that climate but rarely killed. Plants at Wisley are thirty years old.

S. greggii has narrowly oblong leaves on slender, drooping stems, flowering continuously from June onwards. The upper lip of the flower is rosy, the lower carmine. Rated z7 by Rehder, but more like z9 in Britain.

Graham's and Gregg's sages are the best-known of the tender species, but the following are also meritorious and add a touch of distinction to the scene. All had best be regarded as z9 and not all are easy to come by.

S. coerulea. Soft, heart-shaped leaves and long spikes (racemes) of deep sky-blue from July to autumn.

S. fulgens, the Mexican red sage. Heart-shaped leaves and long racemes of scarlet, hairy flowers in late summer.

S. gesneriiflora. Like the above but of even more brilliant scarlet.

S. interrupta, from Morocco. A sub-shrub with diverse foliage and tall, loose panicles, sometimes 4ft long, of blue-violet, white-throated, throughout May and June.

S. involucrata. Long pointed leaves, hairy beneath, and spikes of rosy-purple flowers, sticky to the touch, in late summer. At the bases of the whorls are groups of pink leaves which fall off as the flowers open. The clone 'Bethellii' is of stronger growth, heart-shaped leaves, flowering from midsummer onwards.

S. lavandulifolia, from Spain, resembles the common sage but has narrow leaves.

S. microphylla neurepia has soft, aromatic leaves and long racemes of red-magenta flowers in July and onwards. Like *microphylla*, but has wider leaves.

S. rutilans. Soft, heart-shaped leaves scented of pineapple and loose panicles of crimson-purple flowers all summer.

SAMBUCUS
Elder

The elders give us one of the most beautiful of all deciduous golden-leaved shrubs and several others which can also provide decorative foliage if properly pruned. Otherwise they tend to be rather commonplace vagrants of our woodlands and hedgerows. Their leaves are pinnate, their flowers usually off-white, crowded into thick clusters, which may be flat-topped or conical, and their small berries are of various colours. Home-brewed wines can be made from both the flowers and the fruits of some species, especially S. nigra and S. canadensis. We are not here concerned with the elderberry's qualities as a fruit, but may note that only the black ones are edible.

Elders do best in a moist, loamy soil. They tend to be rather short-lived, but are very easily propagated by simply sticking leafless shoots into the open ground in early winter.

As in so many other deciduous shrubs, direct your pruning to cutting out old stems in winter in proportion as new ones develop. In plants grown for their foliage you may cut right to the ground every winter, but you will get a better-furnished effect if you sever the one-year stems down half-way and cut the older ones down to the ground. Feed well after pruning.

Undoubtedly the sovereign choice among elders is to be found in the ranks of the red-berried elder, **S. racemosa**, a shrub of multiple leaflets, large, conical trusses of dirty-white flowers in great profusion in April, fructifying in summer in dense clusters of scarlet berries, though the fruiting is uncertain and capricious. The parent is, however, eclipsed by its golden child 'Plumosa Aurea', which, standing at 5ft or more, has deeply cut, almost tattered-looking leaves of most decorative appearance and is aptly described by Hilliers as "one of the élite of golden foliaged shrubs". It is grown for its foliage alone, but, as we have noted of similar shrubs, it looks shabby in very hot, dry, continental summers.

Another pretty member of this species is the dwarf 'Tenuifolia' which forms a low mound of leaves as finely divided as those of the cut-leaf Japanese maple. 'Flavescens' has yellow-mottled berries. z4.

Other elders of merit are:

S. canadensis, the American elder, is accustomed to very wet soils but is also at home in fairly dry ones. A big, rather coarse-leaved plant of 10ft to 12ft, with white flowers in flat or convex clusters in June–July, followed by blue-black berries, but only if two or more shrubs are planted together, for it is not self-compatible. There are several variants, notably 'Maxima', which has leaves more than a foot long and massive flower-heads a foot wide, on persistent purple stalks. Prune this one right to the ground every winter. Other variants of the American elder are 'Aurea', which has yellow foliage and red berries, 'Rubra', another with red fruits, and the grey-tinted *submollis*. z3.

S. nigra is the "common" elder of Britain, Northern Europe and elsewhere. It has flat clusters of off-white flowers of heady scent in June, followed by glistening black berries in September. It thrives in chalk and is a first-class defence against sea winds. Not a choice plant, it can reach tree proportions, but a few selected forms are certainly decorative in informal settings. Thus 'Aurea', the golden elder, though not as ornamental as S. racemosa 'Plumosa Aurea', is excellent and very hardy. 'Laciniata', the fern-leaf or parsley-leaf elder, has attractively dissected leaves. 'Albo-variegata' has leaves prettily bordered white. 'Aureo-marginata' has a bright yellow edge. 'Fructuluteo' has yellow berries. 'Pulverulenta' has white-marbled leaves and 'Purpurea' is flushed purple. In addition, several selections, such as 'Sambu' and 'Korser' are grown, commercially or otherwise, for their fruits in continental Europe and in America, but rarely in Britain. z5.

S. pubens is the scarlet elder of America. A big shrub that may exceed 20ft, with its off-white flowers in pyramids in May, then scarlet berries. The variety 'Dissecta' closely resembles racemosa. Vancouver Island, where pubens does particularly well, produced a handsome variety with golden berries called xanthocarpa. z4.

SANTOLINA

Cotton-lavender

The cotton-lavenders (or lavender-cottons) are fine, aromatic, evergreen little shrubs, especially in poor, dry, stony soils, but often degenerate through lack of pruning. The most popular are those that have very small, tightly packed leaves, toothed along their edges and dressed as it were in white, fleecy lamb's-wool. You must keep them tight and compact. To this end, trim them over lightly in autumn,

removing entirely any long, straggling stems, and cut them very hard back, almost to the ground, every two or three years in April; they regenerate very quickly. They are sub-shrubs. Cuttings taken in July root readily in a sandy soil with a little heat. All z7.

The most favoured cotton-lavender is one for which you need to take a long breath and address as **S. chamaecyparissus** (formerly and more conveniently *S. incana*), which you expect to grow into a mound about 2ft high, but for most purposes it is more charming in its dwarf form *corsica*, more often called 'Nana'. The thread-like leaves are accompanied in July by small, yellow, globular flowers, quite agreeable but of no distinction.

A bird of very similar feathers, believed by some botanists to come from the same nest, is **S. neapolitana**, a slightly larger shrub, with slightly larger, segmented leaves of rather looser growth. It is useful for breaking outlines, for growing near to steps or on the tops of terraces. In its 'Sulphurea' the foliage is grey-green and in 'Edward Bowles' more so, with flowers of creamy-yellow.

S. rosmarinifolia (better known as *virens* or *viridis*) is rather like *chamaecyparissus*, but a bright, vivid green, very effective where such a colour is wanted. The flowers are lemon, except in the self-explanatory 'Primrose Gem'.

SARCOCOCCA

Sweet or Christmas Box

These are neat evergreens with polished leaves like those of the box, which, together with their berries in winter, explain their nickname. They are of special value for flourishing in deep shade and for their appreciation of chalk. Their tiny flowers, which are unisexual but have both sexes side by side on the same branch, usually have a delicious scent and a single spray will sweeten a whole room. They usually spread by suckers, forming low thickets. The name is a verbal hybrid between the Greek *sarkos*, flesh, and *kokkos*, a berry.

All have a strong family likeness and we need cite only the following among the confusion of names.

S. ruscifolia chinensis grows to about 6ft, with long, slender, dark green leaves. Berries dark red. z7–8.

S. hookeriana digyna is usually not quite so tall and has bright green leaves and black fruits. 'Purple Stem' is a selection that explains itself. z7–8.

These two are possibly the best, but *S. confusa* is also very good, resembling the first-named but spreading widely. Berries black.

S. humilis does not exceed 4ft and is excellent cover in dry areas. Berries black. z5–6.

S. saligna is smaller still, less hardy, scentless and has purple berries. z8.

SASA. See Bamboos

SEA BUCKTHORN. See *Hippophae*

SCHINUS

Big, tender, ornamental evergreen from South America, not needing a rich soil. The most dependable seems to be *S. polygamus* (or *dependens*), a somewhat spiny 15ft shrub with rather slender leaves. Flowers greeny-yellow, tiny, but in impressive masses. The sap is scented of turpentine. *S. latifolius* is similar but spineless. *S. molle*, one of those called "pepper tree", is a very graceful creature, with pinnate leaves, very popular in southern Europe, but decidedly tender. The fruits of all are pea-size. Do not confuse this with the tree-like Schima.

SECURINEGA

These are mostly tropical or sub-tropical deciduous shrubs of botanical rather than garden interest, but *S. suffruticosa* is hardy enough for z5. It reaches to about 5ft, with slender, graceful branches, small, pale green leaves and tiny creamy-green flowers, often unisexual, in July and August. No routine pruning is needed, but it can at will be chopped down to the ground in part or in whole in early spring. The name of the genus is hybrid Latin for hard wood. z5.

SEDUM

We know sedums mainly as fleshy-leaved plants for the herbaceous border or the rock-garden, but *S. populifolium* is quite a pretty, erect sub shrub about a foot high, with small, oval, toothed leaves and small terminal clusters (corymbose cymes) in white or pink, with purple anthers, scented of hawthorn, in July and August. z5.

SENECIO

The features by which most of us recognize the shrubby senecios is the white or grey down that clothes their stems and leaves, in whole or in part, and their brazen, daisy-form flowers.

They form but a very small part of a huge mixed army of senecios, including some weeds and that plant with brilliantly silvered filigree leaves that most nurseries wrongly call Cineraria maritima. The name of the genus was used by Pliny himself, who took it from *sennex*, Latin for an old man, because of the tuft of grey hairs formed by the seed.

The shrubby senecios, which are evergreen, come chiefly from New Zealand and so are not quite as hardy as we should like. Apart from their aesthetic value in the garden picture, they are first-class seaside shrubs, resisting the ferocity of ocean gales and shielding other plants that cannot stand such hardship alone. They seem, indeed, to be hardier when breathing the sea breezes than inland.

Otherwise, you can use senecios any way you like to diversify the scene, remembering to give them full sun and that most of them can cover quite a large area of ground and are therefore highly skilled at the suppression of weeds, their branches growing out close to the ground before turning erect. Several succeed in chalk. To keep them compact and bushy, cut them hard back every three or four years in the spring or trim them lightly every spring. If a shrub has been neglected and gone woody in the centre or been damaged by snow, chop it back to the bare bones.

Propagate by late summer cuttings in a sandy soil, preferably with some bottom heat.

The most popular, because the most hardy, species is the victim of arguments about its name, being called either **greyi** or **laxifolius**. All such plants grown in gardens, however, are now regarded as Dunedin Hybrids, of which the clone 'Sunshine' is nearly always the one grown. It is doubtful if the true species exist outside specialist's collections. These Dunedin

Hybrids are recognised by chalk-white flower stems, a white fur on the reverse of the leaf and loosely pyramidal clusters of brassy, daisy-form flowers. z7–8.

Another much favoured senecio is the tough **S. monroi**, easily recognized by the wavy edge of its leaf. The obverse is green and the reverse has the typical fleecy coating, as has the rest of the plant. It makes a dense mound of 6ft and is a first-class shelter plant for coastal gardens.

Probably the most wind-hardy of the lot is the big **S. reinoldii** or rotundifolius, which has tough, leathery, rounded leaves, glossy green above, shiny white below, a beautiful sight when tossed by a strong wind. It can reach 20ft if allowed and, even when blasted by the Atlantic gales, presents to the world a round, well-tailored shape. The flowers, which lack ray florets, are of little worth. z7.

Senecis Dunedin hybrid 'Sunshine' ("S. laxifolius" etc)

Also lacking ray florets in its flowers is **S. elaeagnifolius**, a 10ft shrub, broader than high, the large leaf (up to 5in long) dark green, with a buff reverse, as in Elaeagnus pungens. The closely related and deservedly popular natural dwarf, *S. buchananii*, is a fine little shrub, easily accommodated, with its flowers in a raceme. z8.

One of the most beautiful but least hardy is **S. compactus**, which, growing to perhaps 4ft, but twice as broad, is almost completely chalk-white, its leaves prettily crinkled, its flowers bright yellow. z9.

S. leucostachys. A lax, silvery-white sub-shrub with elegantly cut leaves and white flowers. Hardy enough to grow at Wisley. z8–9. The following are too tender for anything cooler than z9.

S. hectori. A gaunt shrub with white flowers and toothed leaves.

S. huntii. A big, almost tree-like shrub with stalkless, pale green leaves and a massive display of flowers in pyramidal clusters.

S. kirkii. A 10ft, all-green shrub with white flowers in vast quantities.

S. perdicioides. A 6ft, all-green shrub, with finely toothed leaves. Flowers funnel-shaped, with few ray florets.

SHEPHERDIA
Buffalo-berry

These deciduous, unisexual North American shrubs are of no great distinction but are useful for very cold climates (z2) and for very dry and limy soils. The small flowers, borne in late winter on leafless twigs, are a grey-yellow, without petals, and are of no account, but, if fertilized by a male, the female displays very showy berries in summer. Named after John Shepherd, one-time curator at Liverpool Botanic Garden.

S. argentea, slightly thorny, can become a big, 20ft shrub, with slim, faintly silvered leaves, like pewter, and scarlet berries, edible but sour. It looks best if trained on a single stem,

when it makes quite an elegant miniature tree. Sometimes confused with Elaeagnus argentea, a much more ornamental shrub with broader leaves. The buffalo-berry is a good hedger.

S. canadensis is a much smaller (8ft) and more spreading shrub, without prickles. The leaves are green on the upper surface, faintly silvered below, with brown speckles; these and the brown scales on the stems result in the nickname Russet Buffalo-berry. The berries are bright orange and make a fine display.

SIBIRAEA

Entered for the record only, S. laevigata is an erect, deciduous shrub, up to 6ft high, with blue-tinted, slightly spiny leaves and plumes of off-white flowers at the tips of the shoots in May–June. Formerly labelled a spiraea. z4. In *angustata* the leaves are narrow and in *croatica* obtuse and stalkless.

SINOJACKIA

Though usually classed as "trees", the sino-jackias, which resemble the elegant styrax, may also be regarded as large shrubs, with many crossing branches. They are deciduous and need a rich lime-free soil. Named after J. G. Jack, of the Arnold Arboretum, whose special study was Chinese plants. **S. rehderiana** grows to 16ft, with small, pointed leaves with white flowers on slender stalks in June. z7.

S. xylocarpa reaches perhaps 20ft, with rather larger leaves and a curiously beaked fruit. z7–8.

SINOWILSONIA

Named after E. H. ("Chinese") Wilson, the English plant-hunter, S. henryi is a very large, deciduous shrub with linden-like leaves and green, dangling catkins. For acid soils. z5.

SKIMMIA

Skimmias are fairly well-known, evergreen shrubs, forming low, neat mounds, accoutred with closely set, half-glossy leaves of slim ovals. When a group has grown together they are among the best of all guardians against weeds. They prosper in any well-fed soil, are happy in moderate shade and will indeed endure the gloomiest corner and shadiest courtyard. They prosper also at the seaside and in industrial areas. Their flowers are a fuzz of small, off-white florets in spring, but, except in Reeves's species, they are unisexual and one male to about every five females is needed for the female to produce the bright red berries that are so much desired. The males, however, are much more shapely shrubs, have a superior flower display and make a very good show on their own.

No regular pruning is needed, but straggly stems can be amputated and ancient plants cut to the ground. Propagate by simply sticking hard-wooded stems into the open ground in shade in early winter, but they are slow developers.

The name is a Latinized version of the Japanese *skimmi*. All z7.

There is some argument about the classification of skimmias but, as is our wont when in doubt, we follow Bean.

The dominant species is the remarkable **S. japonica**, which abounds in named varieties, but many of which are not at all easy to find. This will flourish in full sun as in part-shade and is one of the finest evergreen shrubs for towns and industrial sites, thriving in smoky areas. In time it forms a 3ft dome, with fragrant flowers and leaves scented of bay when crushed. For sheer exuberance of berrying the best female variety is 'Nymans', a plant of uncertain lineage, with small leaves and a slender, open growth. 'Veitchii' is also very good and much bigger.

Among the males, the 4ft 'Rubella' stands out for the beauty of its flowers, which are red in the bud all winter on coppery stalks, richly scented when open. It is sometimes reported, however, to be illiberal in its pollen, and for this the smaller 'Fragrans' may be better. Others of each sex are available.

S. x foremanii, a hybrid between japonica and the handsome, bi-sexual reevesiana, is also much in vogue, but of dubious background, Foreman's name having been given to several skimmias. Those in general cultivation seem to be predominantly female, but there seem to be some males and even some hermaphrodites. The flowers of all are excellent and scented and the berries on females abundant.

Skimmias described as '**Rogersii**' are similar to Foreman's, but not uniform. They are smaller and several clones are dwarfs, of which 'Nana Femina' can be quite spectacular in both flower and berry. Given the right conditions, **S. reevesiana** is perhaps the best bet of all. Growing to only about 2ft, it is almost invariably bi-sexual and produces handsome crimson berries, which over-winter and are still there when the plant comes into flower again next spring. But it must have a rich, moist, acid soil and a certain amount of shade.

S. laureola is a very variable woodlander, usually spreading. The leaves are pungent when crushed and the flowers very sweetly scented, but a dull ochre. Only male plants are known in cultivation, but they make good ground-cover in shady places.

S. anquetilia is no show-piece. The flowers are drab and the leaves rank when crushed.

SLOE. See *Prunus spinosa*

SMOKE TREE. See *Cotinus coggygria*

SNOWBALL TREE. See *Viburnum*

SNOWBERRY. See *Symphoricarpos*

SNOWY MESPILUS. See *Amelanchier*

SIPHONOSMANTHUS. See Osmanthus delavayi

SORBARIA

False Spiraea

Handsome, deciduous shrubs which lend enchantment to a distant view and which, when in leaf, provide the "rich, harmonious masses" of green of which William Chambers spoke. They are big or fairly big shrubs with long, ornamental, pinnate leaves, the leaflets toothed, and tiny, white flowers massed in plumes or panicles that resemble those of some spiraeas. They are best used in massed plantings in large gardens or open landscapes and some of them run to suckers, which often provide the strongest growths. All are easy to grow in any reasonable soil in sun.

Flowering is mainly in July and August. Behead the trusses after blossom-fall. To preserve a disciplined behaviour, prune hard in late winter almost back to the old wood. Propagate by suckers or seed.

S. aitchisonii, 9ft, has red stems, bright green leaves and pyramidal panicles a foot long. Perhaps the best. Suckers. z6.

S. arborea is also very fine, but rather too big, unless you want a bush of 20ft. Suckers. z5.

S. assurgens, 10ft, has an erect deportment and flowers in slender pyramids. z5.

S. sorbifolia is an extremely hardy 6ft, suckering madly. z2.

S. tomentosa is another big fellow, growing gracefully up to 18ft, with long, doubly-toothed leaves and nodding flower panicles sometimes 18in tall. z7.

X SORBARONIA

Deciduous hybrids between various species of sorbus (mountain-ash and whitebeam) and aronias (chokeberries). Hardly as good as their parents but quite effective in the garden if trained as small trees by restricting them to a single "leg" until the desired height is reached. All have white flowers in spring and purple berries. All z5.

× *S. alpina*, 10ft, has the oval leaves of a whitebeam.

× *S. dippelii* has narrower leaves, colouring well in autumn.

× *S. hybrida* is a big, wide-spreading shrub with irregularly divided leaves and of little value.

× *S. sorbifolia*. Another sorbus-aronia hybrid, of little merit.

X SORBOCOTONEASTER

A very rare natural hybrid by the forests of Eastern Siberia, hard as nails. The genesis is obvious. It is said that there are two forms, but the only one within our ken has a name, to which we do not dare to give tongue. This is × *S. pozdnjakovii*, a 8ft shrub with ovate (pointed oval) leaves deeply cut into three lobes. Flowers in white trusses, fruit red. (*S. sibirica* × *C. melanocarpus*).

SORBUS

A few small brethren of the whitebeam and rowan (or mountain ash) are useful for gardens and landscapes that are not too stylistic, especially where the soil is alkaline. Possibly the best is *S. anglica*, which is endemic to the British Isles, is not known to us as more than 8ft high and might be regarded as a junior version of the whitebeam, having downy, pale-grey leaves, white flowers and scarlet fruits.

More specifically endemic to England is *S. minima*, a 10ft shrub likewise of whitebeam style, with rounded clusters of white florets and abundant scarlet fruits.

S. chamaemespilus is a pretty, 5ft European of shrubby habit, with trusses of pink flowers and red fruits. z5.

S. × hostii is a variable hybrid of about 12ft, with lobed leaves, grey-haired beneath, pink flowers and erect trusses of shining red berries. z5.

S. reducta is a suckering dwarf of not more

than 2ft, with the pinnate leaves of the rowan and pale pink berries. z7.

S. sitchensis is a very tough Alaskan that is reported as reaching 15ft. z2.

SOUTHERNWOOD. See *Artemisia*

SPARTIUM. Included in Brooms

SPHAERALCEA

The tender *S. monroana* is a pleasant, deciduous little Mexican of about 18in with small, lobed leaves, its stems strung with small, orange-tinted pink bugles, rather like penstemons, from July till autumn. z9.

S. fendleri is a little sub-shrub, with wide open, orange flowers in small clusters for a long season. Cut hard back to developing shoots in spring.

SPINDLE. See *Euonymus*

SPIRAEA

There is a horde of spiraeas, many of which are not fit to be paraded and others that too closely resemble one another. Several herbaceous plants, such as aruncus and filipendula, still linger in the popular mind as spiraeas, but they have been driven out to form colonies of their own. The plume-flowered astilbes are also often mistaken for spiraeas.

The true spiraeas take their name from the ancient Greek *speiraia*, a plant used for garlands. All have small flowers but their floral habits, or inflorescences, are very diverse. Some form plumes or plume-like racemes, some are distributed in tight little bunches or rosettes all along the branches, usually on twiggy side-shoots from the main stems, others (in the later half of the year), deploy their tiny flowers in flat trusses, like plates. All those of the first half of the year are white, those of the latter part are usually pink or red. All are deciduous. Their seasons range from early March to September and in size they vary from the diminutive *S. decumbens* to the big *S. veitchii*. They flourish in any reasonable soil, in sun or light shade, but a few dislike chalk. Several, such as the species, *salicifolia*, *oxyodon*, *latifolia* and *tomentosa*, form dense thickets of suckers, and these we exclude.

For the practising gardener spiraeas arrange themselves fairly conveniently into two compartments: (a) those that flower in spring or early summer on stems that have developed in the previous year and (b) those that flower late on shoots that have developed in the spring of the same year. These habits help one in the design and display of the garden and, more positively, point to the right methods of pruning, which are very important in spiraeas.

Broadly speaking, those that flower in the first half of the year have their heads cut off after blossom-fall and have a few of the older shoots cut hard back to a point where new growth shows itself. Of such are thunbergii, prunifolia and the hybrid arguta. Those that flower late are reduced by one-half or more in the first spring and afterwards each year's new shoots are taken back to within a few inches of their starting point on the older wood — the normal hard pruning of late performers. Here are japonica and bumalda. Many spiraeas make very good hedges, such as thunbergii, and these you prune just after flowering. Propagation is usually very easy. Just stick an unflowered twig in sandy soil in a shady place.

There has recently been a very thorough reshuffling of the spiraea pack by the botanist, to which probably no nursery catalogue yet conforms, so that the old gardener will find it difficult at times to pick out the right cards. We had better review them alphabetically, rather curtly, but to introduce them, may note that the species most generally favoured are:

S. × arguta
S. thunbergii
S. × vanhouttei
S. japonica and its varieties
S. nipponica and its varieties
S. prunifolia

Spiraea arguta

With special emphasis on the first three.

S. albiflora. See under *S. japonica*.

S. arcuata. 6ft. White flowers in small posies all along the arching branches in May. 77–8.

S. × arguta, the bridal-wreath of Britain or garland-wreath of America. 5–6ft. A glorious sight in April and May, when its long, slender, much-branched stems are bowed down all along with its rich treasure of small, pure white, round-petalled flowers, arranged in tight little bunches, looking rather like a fall of snow. The variety 'Compacta' measures only 4ft. z4.

S. bella. 4 to 5ft. Pink flowers in small clusters in June. Not for chalk. z6–7.

S. betulifolia corymbosa. A handsome little shrub of 3ft, decked with white snowballs from midsummer onwards. Renews itself annually by new stems from the ground, so cut the old ones back very hard.

S. × brachybotrys. 8ft. June–July. Small, pink plumes at tips of leafy twigs springing copiously from the previous year's stems, forming sheaves of bright, pink blossom. One of the best for summer. Not for chalk. (canescens × douglasii). z4.

S. bumalda. See under *S. japonica*.

S. calcicola. 3–4ft, of graceful carriage, with very small, lobed leaves. Pink buds, opening white, in small posies all along the stem.

S. canescens. A handsome shrub averaging 9ft, arching, with whippy, down-coated branches and grey-tinted leaves. White flowers in 2in clusters on twiggy laterals from last year's stems in July. 'Myrtifolia' has leaves dark green above, blue-tinted below. The double-flowered form is preferred. z7.

S. cantoniensis. 3–5ft, spreading densely and arching in every direction. Rounded clusters of white in June. Rated z6, but really needs a warmer climate to luxuriate.

S. chamaedryfolia. 5ft. Small bunches of white in May. Variable. Sends up strong suckers every year which bear flowers the next on short twigs. More handsome in its natural variety *ulmifolia* having narrower leaves and elongated flower trusses. z7.

S. densiflora. A hardy and pretty shrub of no more than 2ft from western N. America, massed in June with rose-pink flowers. No pruning needed.

S. douglasii, a suckering shrub of erect bearing, 6ft high, crowned with tossing magenta plumes after midsummer and looking very well near water. Prune hard in early spring and cut antique stems right out. Its natural variety, *menziesii*, formerly treated as a separate species, is extra-hardy, and its cultivars 'Triumphans' and 'Eximia' excel their parent.

S. gemmata. 6ft. Slender, bending stems, slender leaves, slender buds opening to form 1in bunches all along the stems in May. z4.

S. henryi. 8ft, of lax growth, spreading widely. Flowers packed in 2in bunches on twiggy laterals in June. A fast-growing shrub of the first order readily producing new shoots, but needing plenty of elbow-room.

S. hypericifolia. 4–5ft. Dense, swaying

branches, clustered all along with small, white balls in May. An European naturalized in parts of America. Not choice. z4.

S. japonica, formerly a small but distinguished clan has recently been expanded by botanists to a considerable empire, exercising dominion over several spiraeas hitherto of independent status, including some that old gardeners would never have associated with japonica, such as the hybrid bumalda. Thus japonica is now presented to us as a "variable species" (Bean). *S. japonica* itself is an erect, 5ft shrub, bearing, after midsummer, large, flat, terminal pink plates, often supplemented by smaller ones. I shall take its main cultivars alphabetically, as now designated.

'Albiflora'. A pretty shrub of only 2ft, with rather weak growth, with white, flat plate-like trusses.

'Alpina'. See 'Nana'.

'Anthony Waterer'. Dull crimson sport from 'Bumalda', common and very overrated, 4ft. Prune very hard in March.

'Atrosanguinea'. Flowers deep rose-pink.

'Bullata'. A pretty dwarf, little more than 1ft high. Leaves rusty and puckered. Flowers rose-red in profusion in late July.

'Bumalda'. Long known as *S. × bumalda*, but now demoted. A small shrub of little value, except perhaps in the rock-garden.

'Fortunei'. 5ft, deep pink. Leaves deeply cut.

'Froebelei'. Large leaves, flowers bright crimson in compound trusses. Neat, erect carriage.

'Glabrata'. Huge, compound, rose-pink trusses.

'Goldflame'. A pretty foliage shrub, with leaves of orange and lemon, later pale green. Flowers dull, pale crimson. Excellent for garden design. Previously described as originating from 'Bumalda'. Cut to 5in of the ground every March.

'Leucantha'. A large edition of 'Albiflora'.

'Nana' ('Alpina'). Low, wide-spreading. Flowers lilac-pink, early. Neat habit. Prune lightly.

'Ruberrima'. A dark red selection from 'Fortunei'.

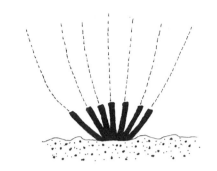

79.   Spiraea japonica 'Anthony Waterer' and 'Goldflame' pruned to within 4in of the ground every spring

Spiraea japonica 'Anthony Waterer'

S. lowndesii. A pretty shrub of about 4ft, with tiny leaves and small, white rosettes all along the branches in summer.

S. × 'Margaritae'. One of the nicest summer spiraeas. A 4ft shrub with big, rose-pink plates from early July onwards. In winter cut the old stems right out and in spring shorten the new ones to 1ft. A sheet of blossom results. Remove flowers as they fade (japonica × 'Superba'). z4.

S. media. Long, slender plumes of white in April–May. Of merely botanical interest. z6.

S. menziesii. See under *S. douglasii*.

S. mollifolia. Arching shrub of 4–5ft with tiny, silky leaves and small bunches of creamy flowers in June–July, on leafy laterals from the previous season's stems. z5.

S. nipponica. A beautiful 7ft shrub with all too short a display in May and June. Seen at its best in the variety 'Rotundifolia'. The leaves are nearly round and the tiny, white flowers are packed in small snowballs on short lateral twigs which crowd the upper sides of the branches. The American 'Snowmound' is noted for its larger and more abundant flowers. The Japanese natural variety *tosaensis* becomes a low, dense dome, with slender leaves, but sparse in flowers. Pruning is important to all these nipponicas. Old shrubs that produce nothing but a mass of twigs should be cut right down and the shrub well fed. z4.

S. prunifolia plena. A dense, arching 8ft shrub with white, double flowers in tight, stalkless bunches in April and May. The saw-edged leaves, resembling those of cherries, have a high polish and become brilliantly coloured in autumn. The single-flowered form is of no merit. z4.

S. rosthornii. 6ft. A handsome shrub with bright green, doubly saw-edged leaves, flowers in rather flat clusters, 3in wide, in June on arching stems. z5.

S. × sanssouciana. Named after the old German palace of Sans Souci. The clone 'Nobleana' is an erect, 5ft shrub crowded in July with broad clusters of bright rose.

S. sargentiana. 6ft. Of graceful deportment. Narrow, toothed leaves. Cream clusters

80.   Spiraea nipponica

in June on short twigs growing from stems developed in the previous year. z5–6.

S. × semperflorens. The selected clone 'Syringiflora' is a 4ft spreading shrub, with pink, lilac-form trusses in late summer.

S. thunbergii. Myriads of tiny, white stars dispersed at random all along the wiry twigs throughout March and April (later in USA). One of the real "joys of spring", giving one a lift of the heart as one passes by. Plant it where you can see it from the house or in your daily comings and goings. Small, narrow tapering leaves of pale green. Cut the flowered stems back, in whole or in part, in proportion as new shoots develop from the base or near it.

Thunberg's spiraea grows normally to 5ft, but it also makes a stunning, dense hedge. Clip after flowering. z4.

S. trichocarpa. 5–6ft. Rigid growth, apple-green oblong leaves and choicely ornamented in June with virginally white rosettes all along its bending terminals.

S. trilobata. A neat, many-stemmed shrub, maybe 8ft by 10ft ultimately, with coarsely toothed leaves and white flowers in crowded clusters on short twigs from the previous year's stems. z4.

S. × vanhouttei. The standard by which all white, bunched-flowered spiraeas should be judged, challenged only by arguta. It grows 5–6ft high, its stems at first erect, then bending, soon to become weighed down by the extraordinary profusion of its clusters on the upper sides of its stems in June. Leaves coarsely

Spiraea thunbergii

Spiraea vanhouttei

toothed rhomboids. Prune as for thunbergii, (cantoniensis × trilobata). z4.

S. veitchii. A big shrub of maybe 12ft, useful for the back of a border; its long arms strung with crowded white clusters, 2in wide, in June–July, on twiggy laterals on stems grown the previous year. The new shoots may grow 8ft long in a single season. z5.

S. × watsoniana. 5–6ft. Rose-pink platters in June–July. (douglasii × densiflora splendens).

S. wilsonii. Differs from *S. henryi* only in botanical detail.

STACHYURUS

These are fairly big, usually deciduous, wide-spreading shrubs that are attractive in late winter and early spring, but of no great ornamental value thereafter. The leaves are broadly based but drawn out to fine, rat-tail points. The flowers are borne in dangling spikes, like catkins, the buds forming in the autumn but not opening until early next year, when they form small cups, usually yellow. For sun or part shade and any reasonable soil, but a moist, humusy or peaty one is preferred.

81. Stachyurus praecox

Systematic annual pruning is not needed, but the plants form stools, freely producing new stems from the ground, so cut down all old and weak wood to the ground after flowering.

The one usually grown is **S. praecox**, which begins to open its tassels of 2–3in in February in mild conditions, but otherwise waits until March. z6.

S. chinensis is similar but rather bigger, has longer tassels and flowers a fortnight later. The leaves of its variety 'Magpie' are a mingling of grey-green, cream and rose. z7.

Much more tender and not flowering until April are the species *himalaicus*, which has *vin rosé* flowers and *lancifolius*, yellow. z9 or fanned out on a warm wall in z8.

STAPHYLEA
Bladder-nut

Large, deciduous shrubs with excellent bright green foliage, usually trifoliate (having three leaflets), sometimes pinnate, but known better still for the inflated bladders that enclose their seed in early autumn. The flowers are white (occasionally flushed pink) and very small and arrange themselves at the tips of the branches either in spikes (racemes) or in small, lilac-form panicles. A few, such as holocarpa and elegans, are too big for us, becoming trees. The name comes from the Greek *staphyle*, a cluster.

S. pinnata, perhaps the first choice, is an upright shrub of about 12ft, with pinnate leaves and hanging clusters 3–6in in length in May–June. z5.

S. colchica. A fine, upright shrub of 12ft, with leaflets in threes or fives and massed trusses, 7in long in May of small, elegant, white bells, with pale lemon stamens protruding. Its hybrid offspring 'Coulombieri' is more robust, but smaller. z5.

S. bumalda. A slender, branching shrub of 5–6ft. Short flower clusters. May–June.

S. emodi. Averages 10ft but can be twice as high. Trifoliate, serrated leaves. Flowers in drooping clusters about 3in long in May. z7.

S. trifolia. Upright shrub to 15ft, of value only for its hardiness. Off-white flowers in nodding clusters in May. z3.

STEPHANANDRA

Graceful, deciduous shrubs appreciated for their slender, widespread branches and their bright green, deeply fretted leaves. The tiny flowers, massed in small, loose clusters, are of no account. Plant in a moist, loamy soil. Good as specimen shrubs or as backgrounds for more colourful plants. Good autumn colour and colourful winter branches.

After flowering cut the old stems either to the ground or to healthy side branches low down, in order to encourage young growth, which springs up from the ground readily.

S. incisa averages 5ft, has wiry, zigzag branches and 2–3in leaves, deeply cleft into lobes and toothed along the margins. Flowers greenish. z5. Rather better is *S. tanakae*, a twiggy 6ft, with much larger, vine-like, jaggedly toothed leaves that colour brilliantly in autumn. z5.

STEWARTIA

We have reviewed the larger specimens of this handsome aristocratic race in our book on trees and there remains little to add. They com-

82.   The vine-like leaf of Stephanandra tanakae

memorate the eighteenth-century Earl of Bute, John Stuart or Stewart, who was a keen patron of botany and was chief adviser to Princess Augusta when she founded what is now world-famous as the Royal Botanical Gardens at Kew in 1759–60. Bean now spells the name Stuartia. They are of the first order among trees and shrubs, adorning themselves with flowers that resemble white camellias, bearing in their centres coloured ringlets, like little haloes.

Their requirements are a moist, leafy, acid or neutral soil in a setting of light, open woodland. They must not be crowded by other trees, but do need some shade at their roots, and a grass sward sweeping up to them creates an idyllic picture. Their flowering season begins in July and is extended in Britain into August, when any flowering shrub of distinction is welcome. The individual flowers, which occur in the leaf axils, are not of long duration but break out in constant succession. The leaves are small and neat and colour beautifully in autumn. You must plant them when very young and pruning is strictly prohibited.

The most accommodating is **S. ovata**, a 15ft shrub, in which the big, cup-like flowers have orange anthers, but its variety *grandiflora* is superior, having purple anthers. z5.

S. malacodendron reaches 15ft and is a great splendour, its white flowers similarly purple-eyed. z7.

STRANVAESIA

Lusty, evergreen, rather gaunt shrubs which are rather too big and too wide for us, but they make good shelters or screens and are tolerant of most conditions. The red berries are bird-proof. The usual species is **S. davidiana**, especially its variety *salicifolia*. *S. d. undulata* is less vigorous and 'Fructu Luteo' has yellow berries and slim, pale leaves. z7. *S. nussia* is a small tree with shining, leathery leaves for mild places. z9.

Named for the nineteenth Earl of Ilchester, whose family name was Strangways.

STYRAX

Most of these are small to middle-sized, deciduous trees, and very beautiful they are in June, when their white flowers droop from the branches, at first somewhat like bells or snow-drops but later opening out more in the manner of fuchsias, with the petals reflexed. Some American journalists unnecessarily call them "snowbells". They need a moist, loamy, lime-free soil. If possible plant them on ground which is (like Rosalind) "just as high as my heart", lest the dangling flowers be obscured by the leaves.

The generic name is straight Greek for the species *Styrax officinalis*, which is the source of the fragrant resin storax. A difficult plant outside its own environment.

Of those that behave as shrubs, the most accommodating is *S. wilsonii*, a delightful 9ft shrub of dense, twiggy growth, which, unlike most styrax, blooms when quite young. z7.

S. americana averages about 7ft and is a pretty shrub but not always an easy one. z6.

SUAEDA
Shrubby Goosefoot

S. vera (or *fruticosa*) is a 3ft sub-shrub with blue-washed, close-set foliage, of no ornamental value, but useful for enduring sea-spray and for planting in brackish situations and in sand. Small, green flowers and black berries. z6.

SUMACH. See *Rhus* for the stag's-horn and *Cotinus* for the Venetian

SUN ROSE. See *Helianthemum*

SWEET BRIER. See *Rosa rubiginosa*

SWEET GALE. See *Myrica*

SWEET PEPPER. See *Clethra*

SYCOPSIS

S. sinensis is a very big, stalwart, evergreen shrub with oval leaves. The curious little flowers, borne in quantities close to the stems, have no petals and consist of small clusters of yellow stamens, topped by red anthers, the whole inflorescence enclosed by chocolate bracts, which open in February or March. z7.

SYMPHORICARPOS

Snowberry, coral-berry, etc

Usually misspelt, the symphoricarpos are deciduous, undistinguished shrubs, but useful in very cold climates and in poor soils. They are grown for their berries. Several sucker rampantly and are unacceptable among plants of ornamental value.

The commonest is **S. albus laevigatus**, or **S. rivularis**, the snowberry or more appropriately the moth-ball bush, which exactly describes its large berries. It suckers with abandon. Maybe 6ft. z3.

S. orbiculatus, the coral-berry or Indian-currant of America, another suckerer, usually grows to 6ft with red-purple berries, borne all along the slender stems. In 'Variegatus' the leaves are bordered yellow. z2.

S. × chenaultii, the Chenault coral-berry, is a neat 3ft and has close, terminal clusters of berries, red on the sunny side, white on the other. (microphyllus × orbiculatus). Its Canadian cultivar 'Hancock' is a ground-creeper, 2ft high, excellent for dry, poor soil.

S. × doorenbosii. Dutch hybrids with various clonal names, but the only one of value is 'Mother-of-pearl', which speaks for itself.

S. occidentalis, the wolf-berry, is 3–4ft, dense, erect, producing white moth-balls. z2.

SYMPLOCOS

Sweetleaf

Brilliant blue berries sparkle on the bare boughs of this big shrub (**S. paniculata**) in October

The blue-berried Symplocos paniculata

and November and well into winter, preceded in May and June by small, hanging clusters of little white, scented florets thronged with stamens. An elegant, twiggy bush that can become tree-like and needs a long, hot summer to show up well. Known colloquially as the Asiatic Sweetleaf, it is a plant for large estates and parks, and two or more plants together are needed to produce the berries. z5.

S. tinctoria, the American horse-sugar, has sweet leaves eagerly chewed by horses and cattle. Not very hardy.

271

SYRINGA
Lilac

You should know by now, Reader, that by "syringa" the instructed world today does not mean the philadelphus (or mock-orange), but the lilac. By all means call the syringa by its vernacular name of lilac, but for heaven's sake do not call the philadelphus a syringa.

The lilacs form a considerable plantation of species, hybrids and garden varieties, through which we shall do our best to clear a path. Do look a little further from the popular, named varieties of the "common" lilac (*S. vulgaris*). Look, for example, at the Persian lilac, at the Canadian hybrids, at the so-called dwarfs and at *S. villosa*.

Culturally, there is not a great deal to say. Lilacs prosper in most reasonably fertile soils, but have a partiality for lime, including chalk; the popular varieties of *S. vulgaris*, however, profit from generous feeding. Full sun and ample spacing are important to ensure strong and compact growth. The clones of the common lilac and of others that do not wear small, close-packed leaves are of no ornamental value after flowering, the foliage being common-place, so site them where this weakness will not be noticed and hide their feet in low, summer-flowering plants, or plant at their feet a *Clematis × durandii* or some annual climber, such as *Thunbergia alata* or a morning-glory, to scramble up their poorly clad legs.

Pruning is important but easy. The floral design, or inflorescence, of the lilac is typical of a "panicle", being a branched floral mass, bearing quantities of small, closely packed, open-mouthed tubes or tiny trumpets. Sometimes several panicles are clustered together. These panicles you must behead immediately after blossom-fall at the base of their foot-stalks. This is a positive command, though you may perhaps be in part excused when a small-leaved species grows so large as to bear its trusses in hundreds.

Beyond this, in most species, the thing of most importance is to control suckers. Plants that have been grafted or budded on an under-stock of the common lilac throw out a thicket of suckers. Others grafted on to a stock of privet (an old stratagem of nurserymen) can also create difficulties, unless the young shrub is planted with the union, or crown, well below ground level, so as to encourage root growth by the scion itself.

When necessary, lilacs can quite safely be severely amputated. If you inherit a neglected old specimen, chop it down to within 6in of the ground in November. Left until spring, the plant may bleed.

A few of the larger species, sometimes called "tree lilacs" such as *reticulata* and *pekinensis*, grow to 20ft or more, are florally inferior to most others and are difficult to place, but they can be made decorative specimens in the larger scene by pruning away their lower limbs so as to form a trunk with quite attractive bark. They are considered by some botanists as a sub-genus intermediate between the syringa and the ligustrum (privet) and are called Ligustrina.

In the following review assume all to be scented, unless noted otherwise. The colours can be given no more than approximately, for they change almost daily and we fight shy of such fancy terms as "Argylle pink", "lobelia purple" and "Tourmation pink".

S. afghanica. A dubious name often mis-applied to *S. laciniata*.

S. × chinensis, the Rouen lilac. A big shrub up to 15ft, with fairly dense foliage and panicles of soft lavender in pairs towards the end of each stem in May. Said to have been the first hybrid lilac, originating at Rouen in 1777 (× *persica* × *vulgaris*).

The variety 'Alba' is almost white, 'Metensis' is flushed pink and 'Saugeana' almost red. z5.

The term + correlata is often used for what is here labelled 'Alba'. It is a chimera, joining vulgaris and chinensis.

S. × diversifolia. Some leaves pinnate, others not. Available only in the clone 'William H. Judd'. About 10ft (oblata giraldii × pinnatifolia).

S. emodi, the big Himalayan lilac of possibly 15ft, with leaves up to 8in long. Pale flowers fading to white, not pleasantly scented, in June. Sends up young shoots freely, allowing some older ones to be cut out, after flowering. Similar to *S. villosa* but inferior to it. In 'Aurea' the leaves are suffused yellow and in 'Aureomarginata' they are edged yellow. z6.

S. × henryi. A collective name for some good, extremely hardy French hybrids, which have yielded some good clones of about 10ft, of which the favourite is 'Lutèce', a fine shrub giving us in June large violet panicles that fade graciously. 'Alba' is a lax white. z2.

S. × hyacinthiflora. Hybrids raised first in France and then in California, from which several selections have been made. Their special feature is their early flowering, usually in late April. Cut the flowered stems back by one-third after blossom-fall, for their habit of growth is different from others. Today, perhaps the most favoured is 'Esther Staley', with red buds opening pink. 'Clarke's Giant' has panicles up to a foot long, rose opening lavender. Others are:

'Alice Eastwood'. Claret opening pink. Double.

'Blue Hyacinth'. Mauve-blue.

'Buffoon'. Soft pink.

'Lamartine'. Large blue lilac.

'Purple Heart'. Deep purple.

Parents: vulgaris crossed with oblata or oblata giraldii. z3.

S. × josiflexa. One of the handsome and ultra-hardy group raised in Ottawa by Miss Isabella Preston, from which several selections have been made. 'Bellicent' is a magnificent 10ft or more with enormous plumes of a charming rose-pink in May–June. 'Guinevere', nearly as big, has orchid-purple flowers in large, loose clusters. (josikaea × reflexa) z3. See also *S. × prestoniae*.

S. josikaea. The ultra-hardy Hungarian lilac, of 12ft, giving us glossy leaves and lilac-violet flowers in June. Named in compliment of Baroness von Josika. Resembles the splendid *S. villosa* when not in flower, but known by its glossy leaves. z2.

S. julianae. A spreading, small-leaved shrub of about 6ft, slightly furry in parts, with small, profuse panicles in clusters in May. Florets violet, opening nearly white. No scent. When young has a resemblance to persica. z5.

S. komarowii. 15ft with large leaves and nodding, densely packed panicles about 5in long, usually rose-pink, in June. z5.

S. laciniata. A delightful small shrub with divided leaves and clusters of violet flowers, hitherto often classed as a variety of the Persian lilac.

S. meyeri. Grows slowly but densely to 6ft with small leaves and violet panicles 4in long. A distinct and pretty shrub but known best for its delightful small offspring, which, according to the latest botanical thinking, should be known as the cultivar 'Palibin'. Hitherto it has commonly been labelled *S. palibinana*, the name still used by most nuserymen, or sometimes as *S. velutina*. Though often classed as a dwarf, 'Palabin' is quite capable of reaching 5ft and is comparable with *S. microphylla* in general growth, but it has slightly larger, 2in leaves, rather variable, and the flowers are of flesh pink, without the rosy tint of its competitor. On the whole, *microphylla* just wins on points. z5.

S. microphylla. One of the most charming of "dwarf" lilacs, reaching 6ft in time. Robed in small, close packed leaves, averaging $1\frac{1}{4}$in and never more than 2in. Flowers in small rosy-lilac panicles in pairs in June and often again in September. The slender stems bend under their floral burden and normally the plant forms a pyramid with the lowest branches sweeping the ground. Delicious scent. Compare with its rival "Palibin". z5.

The variety 'Superba' grows twice as broad as high, but may become straggly unless disciplined.

S. × nanceiana. Named for the town of Nancy. Offspring of henryi × sweginzowii, from which has emerged the good clone 'Floréal', with lavender flowers in May.

S. oblata. 12ft. Heart-shaped or kidney-shaped leaves. Pale lilac panicles in pairs in late April. Vulnerable to spring frosts after a mild winter, as often in Britain. After flowering cut back to upright growth any weak branches that have bent over. There are a few variants. *Alba* is white; *dilatata* is violet with good leaf colour in the fall; *giraldii* is tall and open with loose, violet panicles, believed by Lemoine and others to be a separate genus; 'Nana' is obviously dwarf. z3.

S. palibiniana. See S. meyeri 'Palibin'.

S. × persica, the "Persian" lilac. A syringa of elegant bearing, slenderly branched and forming a dome, ultimately perhaps of 8ft, tightly packed with small, slender leaves and smothered in May with 2in panicles of soft lilac strung out in little clusters all along the branches. In time some of the branches may trail along the ground, so you must occasionally shape them to upright shoots. As usual, there is a white form (very nice). Averaging 5ft, the Persian lilac is one of the most beautiful of the smaller specimens. See also *S. laciniata*. z5.

S. pinnatifolia. Of interest only for having truly pinnate, feather-like leaves. Flowers dull lavender. 10ft. z4.

S. potaninii. A 9ft shrub of graceful carriage with rose or white panicles, loosely pyramidal and 4 to 8in long, in June. z5.

S. × prestoniae. Another fine breed of hybrids raised by Miss Preston at Ottawa, using this time the large-leaved villosa and the drooping reflexa. These are sometimes called the "stenographer" lilacs, several of them having been named after members of that genus. Other breeders followed. They produce huge and fascinating plumes in May–June on stems of the current year's growth. Sturdy, hardy and richly colourful, the outside of the petal often contrasting with the inner. Average height 9ft. Not much scent.

The following are cited, with 'Isabella' and 'Elinor' as perhaps the best. All about 9ft. z2.

'Audrey'. Deep pink.

'Donald Wyman'. Very deep pink.

'Elinor'. Red-purple bud opening lavender.

'Ethel M. Webster'. Flesh-pink in lax panicles.

'Hiawatha'. Red-purple opening pink.

'Isabella'. Huge pyramid of warm pink.

'Juliet'. Lilac-pink.

'Kim'. Very large trusses of mallow-pink.

'Royalty'. Violet-purple.

'Virgilia'. Rosy-lilac opening paler.

A cultivar of Syringa × prestoniae 'Virgilia'

'W. T. Macoun'. Lilac-pink, large.

S. reflexa. A distinctive and picturesque shrub of 12ft, with large, dark green, slightly hairy leaves and purple-pink flowers in June in a drooping inflorescence so slim as to look like a spike or raceme, lacking the broad shoulders of most lilacs. No scent. z5.

S. × swegiflexa. Deep red buds opening pink on an accommodating 9ft shrub in May–June. (sweginzowii × reflexa). z5. The clone 'Fountain' has pale pink, drooping clusters.

S. sweginzowii. Flesh-pink panicles, sometimes in groups, in June. 12ft. z5.

S. tomentella. 15ft, spreading widely. Leaves corrugated. Flowers pale lilac in erect 8in panicles. z5.

S. velutina. See *S. meyeri* 'Palibin'.

S. villosa. Of almost Arctic hardiness, this excellent species does not flower until early June, after the common lilacs have faded, when it breaks out in an abundance of rosy-lilac panicles that may be a foot long, but lacking scent. Robust, erect, handsome of bearing and well-clothed, it can reach to 10ft, with some of its leaves 6in long. z2.

S. vulgaris, the "common" lilac of Europe, in its natural state can grow to 20ft, usually in a crowd of erect stems, suckering freely, flowering in May in true "lilac" (or white), delightfully scented. Today we are presented with a whole host, in many colours, single-flowered or with the florets doubled. For the great majority of these we are indebted to the great French house of Lemoine. In parts of America the common lilac of Europe has almost "gone native" and the Arnold Arboretum, in Massachusetts, has probably the largest collection of cultivars in the world.

If you can, always get these named varieties on their own roots, not grafted. Treat the ground generously with organic matter and dress the soil with manure or a substitute every other year. Be careful to decapitate the spent panicles as soon as possible to the point from which new side-shoots are appearing, and keep suckers under control. Take measures of some sort to counteract their somewhat dowdy appearance after blossom-fall. We give a straightforward alphabetical review of those not too difficult to find.

'Ambassador'. Azure-toned, white eye, single.

'Ami Schott'. Deep blue tone, double.

'Belle de Nancy'. Purple, opening pink, double.

'Capitaine Baltet'. Blue bud, opening carmine, single.

'Charles Joly'. Fine purple-red, double, first-class.

'Charles X'. The like, single, apt to fade.

'Congo'. Deep lilac-red. single.

'Edith Cavell'. Cream bud, opening white, double. Named after the heroic British nurse of the 1914–18 war.

'Ellen Willmott'. Similar, but looser trusses.

'Firmament'. Straight lilac, early, single.

'Glory of Horstenstein'. Rich red tone, changing to deep lilac.

'Jan van Tol'. White, single, drooping.

'Katherine Havemeyer'. Of the first order, popular everywhere. Big, double lavender panicles, passing to lilac-pink.

'Masséna'. Splendid, colourful, deep purple-red, single, in broad trusses. Late.

'Mme Antoine Buchner'. Rosy-mauve, double, richly scented. Tall, open growth.

'Mme Casimir Perier'. Cream bud, opening white, double.

'Mme Florent Stepman'. The like, single.

'Mme Francisque Morel'. Huge mauve panicles on an erect shrub.

'Mme Lemoine'. Very fine white, double, well-proven old friend.

'Maud Notcutt'. White, single. Trusses up to a foot long.

'Mont Blanc'. Buds tinted green, opening white, in long panicles, single.

'Mrs Edward Harding'. Superb claret, double. Late.

'Paul Thirion'. Claret, turning rosy-lilac, densely packed, double, late.

'President Grévy'. Lilac-blue, massive trusses, double.

'President Lincoln'. Purple bud, opening pale violet, single.

'President Poincaré'. Claret, heavenly scent, very large, double flowers. First-class.

'Primrose'. Almost true yellow, single.

'Réaumur'. Violet flushed carmine, single.

'Sensation'. Florets red-purple, margined white. Very picturesque, but may revert.

'Souvenir de Louis Spaeth'. Exceptionally fine vinous red, single. Almost 100 years old at the time of writing, but still of the first order.

'Vestale'. A very fine single white.

S. wolfii. A big fellow of up to 20ft with ample foliage and flowers of pale purple in June. z4.

S. yunnanensis. Loose, open habit and pink flowers on slender trusses. Of no great distinction. z5.

TAMARIX
Tamarisk

Most of us think of tamarisks as dwellers on the sea-coast, throwing up light and airy plumes of tiny, pink flowers from slender wands and tossing excitedly in the wind. These are, indeed, their natural loci and behaviour, with their roots in saline soil, but they will grow elsewhere if the soil is damp. Their failing is that, their leaves being minute, they do not form a barrier or screen, but are of great value as a filter. All are deciduous.

Because of their lack of density, pruning is important. Some of them flower early in the year on stems grown in the previous season and others in the later months on stems that had begun growth in the spring. On the former you cut back the expended stem fairly hard immediately after blossom-fall. On the latter, cut back harder still (by one-half) in early spring.

Propagation is simple; merely stick a twig or longer stem in the open ground in shade. Their name is the ancient Roman one.

The species usually considered to be the best are *T. pentandra* (or *ramosissima*) and *T. tetrandra*, but we will note the following also.

T. gallica (curiously known also or separately as **T. anglica**, the Englishman being probably a slight local variant of the Frenchman) grows along both coasts of the English Channel. It is a spreading shrub of 12ft or more, flowering in late summer on spring-grown stems. z5–6.

T. hispida. A decorative and distinctive shrub of only 4ft, the leaves and twigs coated with white hair. Flowers in late summer. Comes from the desert east of the Caspian Sea, so is accustomed to dry soil. Needs the hot summer of a continental climate and is not a success in Britain. z6.

T. chinensis (or **juniperina**). In this variable breed the dominant variety is 'Plumosa', a shrub of about 15ft set with pencil-slim and even thread-like branchlets, plume-like in appearance. Needs hard cutting to prevent it from becoming gaunt. Spring-flowering, but very shy in Britain. z5.

T. parviflora. Rather like tetrandra, flowering in May, but growing to a good 15ft. z4.

T. ramosissima (better known as **pentandra**). Extremely hardy and anything up to 15ft if allowed. Flowers in summer and autumn, when it becomes a foaming cloud of feathery pink on long, slender, rose-tinted branches. The most beautiful tamarisk. Prune hard, almost back to the base of last year's growth. z2. The special selection 'Rubra' has flowers of a beautiful rose-red.

T. tetranda. May be thought of as an early-flowering version of pentandra, lavishly decorated with lace-like plumes, composed of slender racemes, in May. Perhaps the most widely grown in Europe under various fancy names. Cut the flowered stems back by two-thirds. Not for saline soil. z4.

TELOPEA
Waratah

Rather tender Australasians of brilliant flowering. The Australian waratah is too tender for us, but **T. truncata**, the Tasmanian, is at home in Zone 9 and, indeed, grows in parts of Britain in Zone 8, making a very large shrub.

In June the Tasmanian waratah is a dazzling crimson with dense trusses of honey-filled flowers that resemble those of the embothrium. The slender, curved petals (perianth), about an inch long, split to expose the female style, crowned with a knob, which is the stigma. The leaves are tough and leathery, broadly lance-shaped as a rule.

The waratah needs rather moist, acid soil, as for rhododendrons. In its native pastures it is often associated with the blue-rinsed leaves of the eucalyptus.

TEUCRIUM
Germander

The flowers of the germander have open lips, like those of the sage, but the upper lip is split down the middle. Most of them are rock-garden dwarfs or else herbaceous plants, but **T. fruticans**, the shrubby germander, is a pretty, evergreen and rather tender shrub of 7ft, distinguished by the white felt that clothes its stems and the reverse of its leaves. Pale blue spikes decorate its white clothing all summer. Full sun and preferably a light soil. z8 on a warm wall, otherwise z9.

TRICUSPIDARIA. See *Crinodendron*

TRIPETALEIA

T. paniculata is a deciduous shrub, averaging 5ft, needing an acid, moist soil. The flowers have three, rather ragged, pink petals in erect trusses, up to 6in tall, from July to September. z6.

T. bracteata is a slender shrub, producing erect spikes on leafy twigs, each flower growing from small bracts. z6.

T. paniculata bears its flowers in erect plumes, 6in tall. z5.

ULEX

Gorse or *Whin* or *Furze*

The dazzling golden splashes of the gorse are a common picture of the moorlands, hillsides and coastal regions of Britain, so common indeed, that we take the gorse for granted, not realizing that, properly employed, it is also a first-class garden plant, outdoing in its splendour many a guest from overseas. If the gorse came from China or Japan, we should rave over it. Often growing in association with heathers, it flourishes in poor, dry, sandy, stony or gravelly soils, but in average garden soils, if not too rich, and if in full sun, it luxuriates even more and is a splendid clothing for banks. We have never seen it in a prim, formal garden, but we see no reason why the skilful designer should not use it there also, if the soil were right.

The gorse, whin or furze (names which are to a large extent local ones, the "whin" being favoured in Scotland) belongs to the pea family

and has the keeled and winged flowers typical of its kind, but the calyx (sometimes slightly hairy) is yellow as well as the petals. All are densely spiny shrubs, the foliage consisting of a mass of small, attenuated leaves tipped with sharp prickles. Their peculiarity is that they stubbornly resist transplanting and, except as we shall note, must be raised in pots and planted out when very small.

Pruning is not needed but, if a specimen becomes straggly and bare, it can with confidence be cut down almost to the ground. When there is a bush fire it is one of the first to burst into flames, but usually regenerates well.

A few species are too tender for our uses and the most familiar one is **U. europaeus**, the "common" gorse, which can stand 6ft high and wide and which flowers goldenly from March to May and intermittently throughout the year. It is as splendid as any golden barberry and looks very like one. It joined the ranks of the American colonists quite early and has gone native in Vancouver and parts of the USA. Propagate by sowing seed where the plant is to grow, without any disturbance. However, the double-flowered 'Plenus' is much superior to the single and has a longer season. Unfortunately it does not set seed, so that propagation has to be by cuttings of young, newly grown shoots, about 3in long, taken in August and put into very sandy soil in a cold frame or propagating box and kept moist. They should root next spring. When the roots are one inch long move them carefully into 3in pots and plant out in their permanent places in early winter. The erect Irish form 'Stricta' is of no decorative value but makes a good, thorny hedge. z6.

U. gallii is just as good but grows only 2ft high, if that, flourishing from August to October. Usually it is less spiny than the common gorse. Propagate by seed sown singly in small pots and plant out the seedlings when very small. z7.

U. minor (or **nanus**) rarely exceeds 18in and is sometimes prostrate. Glittering in autumn, it must have a starvation diet and is the least spiny. Propagate in the same way as gallii. z7.

VACCINIUM
Blueberry, bilberry etc.

Vacciniums, which may be evergreen or deciduous, are plants that are grown mainly for their juicy fruits or for their vivid autumnal foliage. The small flowers, which open in May or June, are seldom conspicuous or decorative, taking the form of dolls' bells, often nipped in at the mouth, like many heathers; they are usually white, but may be tinted pink. The berries are usually suffused with a blue "bloom" and in many species are sweet and toothsome.

As natural denizens of moorland and mountains, most vacciniums are accustomed to poor, worn-out soils, usually damp or even boggy ones. Thus they are seldom ornamental if grown solo and are best seen *en masse*. An acid soil is essential, peat or old leaf-mould being preferred. In the wild they are found scattered over large areas of the world, so they vary considerably. The name is an ancient Roman one of obscure derivation.

In chapter 5 we have already mentioned the excellent little ground-creeper, **V. vitis-idaea**, the cowberry, where the summers are not excessively hot.

No pruning is normally needed, but, when the old stems of deciduous sorts cease to be productive, cut them right out.

The most widely favoured and the most decorative species is the deciduous **V. corymbosum**, the highbush or swamp blueberry, which is specially important in America for its sweet, grape-like fruits. The wilding itself is a fine shrub, but the US Department of Agriculture has vastly improved its fruiting qualities and even improved it as a shrub. The fruit is delicious and grown commercially on a large scale. 'Earliblue' is the best for early fruiting, 'Bluecap' tops the mid-season varieties and 'Coville', which has exceptionally large fruits, is excellent for late picking. The heaviest crops are provided if "two or three are gathered together".

As a shrub, the highbush blueberry is of erect deportment but much branched, can reach 12ft if allowed and in autumn the 3in, slim, pointed

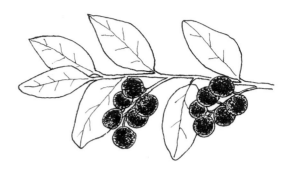

83. The blueberry, Vaccineum corymbosum, in fruit

leaves blaze with scarlet before falling, while the twigs remain red all winter. The small flowers appear in clusters at and near the ends of the twigs in May and the fruiting season is spread over two months, according to the particular variety or clone. z3.

If one wants particularly to encourage fruit production, some pruning must be done. The fruit buds form on twigs of the previous year's growth, so pruning should be done in early spring. It is the vigorous shoots from the base of the plant or strong laterals that produce the best berries. Remove also very old branches with lots of short twigs.

We pass by the big, tree-like farkleberry, V. arboreum, and, apart from the aforesaid cowberry, must also step over the many miniatures and ground-crawlers, such as deliciosum, caespitosum and the red-berried praestans, several of which yield tasty fruits for public gathering in wild places but which have no place in the ornamental garden. This means passing over also the sharp-flavoured cranberries (V. macrocarpum and V. oxycoccus), which are wiry or thread-like creepers for boggy places.

Exceptionally, two extra-hardy species are accustomed to dry soils. One is the low-bush blueberry, **V. angustifolium**, which is stoloniferous and which, in America, is often grown in abandoned and acid pastures, where it is periodically burned and fertilized to stimulate fruit production. z2. The other, known specifically in the vernacular as the dry-land blue-berry, is **V. pallidum**, a quite decorative shrub of 3ft with arching branches and sweet fruits and is one of the best all-rounders, particularly in sandy, acid soil where little else will grow. z3.

Returning to those accustomed to wet feet, we find the following that are within our range.

V. arctostaphylos, the Caucasian whortle-berry, a deciduous shrub of normally about 8ft and open growth, has the largest leaves of any vaccinium (up to 4in). They turn a red-purple in the fall and (we read) are used in Caucasia as an infusion known as "Broussa tea". Florets tinted purple. It may bloom twice, in June and September. Berries purple-black. z5.

V. atrococcum, the black huckleberry, averages about 8ft, resembles corymbosum in general looks, but the berries are black, and shining without any bloom.

V. bracteatum is an attractive evergreen from the Far East, of 5ft. Each little, white flower is cupped in a leafy bract and the berries are red. z7.

V. canadense, the Canadian blueberry, sour-top or velvet-leaf. A dwarf of about 10in, is the wet-ground version of V. angustifolium, with excellent wild fruit, ripening late. Flourishes even in Labrador. z2.

V. delavayi. A very nice evergreen of about 4ft from China. Small, leathery, box-like, crowded leaves and pink-tinted florets at the tips of last year's shoots. Fruits purple. z7.

V. erythrocarpum. Quite a pretty de-ciduous shrub, averaging 5ft and spreading. The flowers are nearly red, the petals curling back to display the anthers. Berries red turning purple, acid. z5.

V. floribundum (or **mortinia**). A beautiful evergreen of 4ft from the mountains of Equador, but hardy enough for the southern counties of Britain and similar climates. The leafage is dense, purple when young and then dark green. The pink flowers tend to be hidden by the foliage. Red, edible berries. z8.

V. glauco-album. A 4ft, rather tender Himalayan evergreen of special character. The bristly leaves are grey-green above but vividly blue-white beneath. The bracts of the pink-tinted florets are also blue-white and the fruits conform to the generally blue impression by the bloom that suffuses them. z9.

V. hirsutum is the "hairy huckleberry". It is a small, suckering shrub developing thickets of slender, 3ft, hairy stems, flower-stalks and calyces and giving us hairy berries also, sweet to the tooth, though not highly flavoured. For the wild garden. z5.

V. moupinense. A 2ft evergreen, notable for its tiny, nodding chestnut-coloured, or sometimes pink, florets. Berries dark purple. z7.

V. myrsinites is the "evergreen blueberry" of 2ft or less and of spreading and variable habit. Berries typically blue-black. z7.

V. myrtillus, the bilberry, whortleberry, whinberry or blueberry of Britain and Europe. A suckering shrub a foot or more high. Of no value as an ornament but useful in the wild and yielding good fruits for pies and so on. It is a mountaineer and seems seldom at ease in lush lowlands. z4.

V. ovatum. At its best, the "box blueberry" is a stalwart 12ft evergreen, densely arrayed with leaves which are brilliant copper on emergence before turning a polished dark green; much used for foliage by florists in N. America (where it thrives on the west coast but not on the east). Berries black. z7.

V. padifolium, the deciduous Madeira whortleberry, is hardier than its origin suggests. It is a shrub of erect, rather stiff growth. The little, nodding flowers are clustered in a short raceme in June. Berries blue. Looks rather like the Caucasian whortleberry, but has a denser growth, rather smaller leaves and is less hardy.

V. stamineum, the deerberry, is a very twiggy, deciduous shrub averaging 3ft, notable among vacciniums for its pretty flowers, which are relatively large bells, with protruding stamens of bright yellow, freely borne in May and June in small racemes, each cupped in a leafy bract and appearing in the axils of last year's stems. Fruits inferior. z5.

V. uliginosum, the very hardy bog bil-berry. A deciduous native of Britain and elsewhere, up to 2ft high, bushy and rounded, with pink flowers and blue-tinted leaves. Not garden-worthy, but its fruits, suffused with a blue bloom, are sweet. z2.

V. urceolatum. An evergreen, averaging 5ft high, with thick, leathery, handsome leaves. Flowers pink in June. Berries black. z7–8.

V. vacillans. An excellent, deciduous, stiffly-branched shrub, averaging 5ft, with tough leaves and decorative clusters of flowers of various tones of pink, displayed in May on the leafless tips of shoots of the previous year. Sweet, blue-black fruits. From the eastern USA.

VELLA

V. pseudocytisus, the "cross rocket", is a low evergreen with bristly leaves, carrying spikes of small, yellow, claw-tipped flowers at the tips of the stems throughout June and July. For hot, dry soils near the sea. Precariously z8. *V. spinosa* proclaims its nature and is smaller. z7.

VERBENA

We think of verbenas as herbaceous perennials or as annuals, but *V. tridens*, the "mata negra", is an interesting shrub from Patagonia of about 5ft. Of stiff deportment, thickly coated with very small leaves, rather like a heather's, it changes its behaviour after the first year, the leaves on the new stems crossing each other at right angles ("decussate") and forming in time a contorted mass of foliage. Its crowded, tubular flowers, white or lilac-pink, exhale a very sweet and pervasive scent. z7–8.

VERONICA. See Hebe

VESTIA

V. lycioides (or *foetida*) is a small, tender, evergreen, erect shrub, with plenty of small, yellow, tubular, nodding flowers in the leaf-axils from April till July. Not very exciting.

VIBURNUM

Viburnums are performers of remarkable versatility, showing many faces to the world and varying in almost every particular. Taken as a whole, their performances run the whole cycle of the Zodiac, from January to December. They may be evergreen or deciduous. They display their flowers in several contrasting shapes. Some earn renown for their resplendent fruits, often edible. A great many earn no less renown for their sweet scents. Leaf shapes vary also, some being maple-like, most others more or less slim ovals and several are foliage shrubs of high merit. In deportment the shrubs vary from the erect to the rounded, and, perhaps most spectacularly, to the absolutely horizontal.

What interests most gardeners, however, are the inflorescences or floral arrangements. All are made up of very small florets, which may be tubular, opening at the mouth, or flat and circular ("rotate") or bell-like. These are compressed, sometimes tightly and sometimes loosely, in various ways. They may form complete orbs, which we call "snowballs", they may be prominently domed or shallowly domed and nearly flat. Occasionally they form small pyramidal panicles, in the fashion of the lilac. Some very important ones congregate in the manner which Mr Haworth-Booth, speaking of hydrangeas, calls "lacecaps", a term which, to avoid constant repetition, we shall apply here also to those which have a flat or slightly domed inflorescence consisting of a central mass of very small, fertile florets, escorted by a ring or large, sterile ones to attract the bee.

The one thing that all viburnums have in common is that the flowers of virtually all are white or off-white, though often pink in the bud and, very rarely, palely flushed with pink when they open. The fruits are technically drupes, but we shall often call them berries.

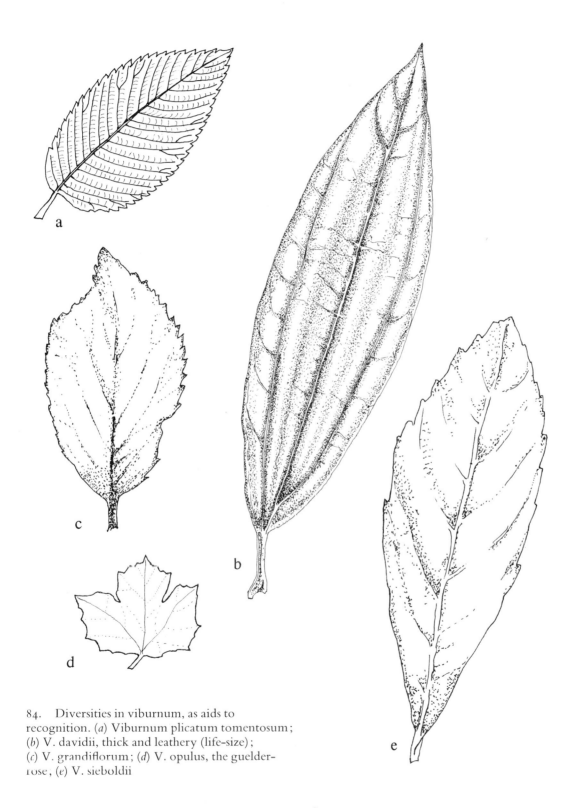

84. Diversities in viburnum, as aids to recognition. (*a*) Viburnum plicatum tomentosum; (*b*) V. davidii, thick and leathery (life-size); (*c*) V. grandiflorum; (*d*) V. opulus, the guelder-rose, (*e*) V. sieboldii

A weakness of some viburnums is that, when out of season, they are not of great value in the garden picture, notable exceptions (among others) being David's and Siebold's viburnums and those that are horizontally branched, as in *V. plicati m*. The winter-flowering, deciduous ones also, even when in flower, are gaunt, leafless for the most of their limbs, and the gardener must do something to overcome this aesthetic defect.

Viburnums as a whole do well in any reasonably good soil, generally preferring a rather moist one. One or two are not conditioned to lime. Systematic pruning is not necessary, but old, spent stems can be cut to the ground or near it, for viburnums are stool-forming. Avoid snipping off branch tips. For viburnums of horizontal growth, see *V. plicati m*.

There are well over 100 species of viburnum, many of which closely resemble each other, except for botanical detail. We list nearly half of them, denying admission to those of tree-like stature, such as *V. cylinc ricum* and *lentago*, and those of no garden merit. Disregarding the botanist's method, there are several ways in which one can group viburnums, such as their seasons of flower and their types of inflorescence, but we think it best here to give a straightforward alphabetical list and let the gardener sort them out as he wishes. The viburnums that have the most ornamental berries (drupes) tend usually to be self-incompatible and if you want to be certain of the fruits you must plant two or more together. These include the species *davidii*, *betulifolium* and *dilatatum*, but the guelder rose (*V. opulus*) can stand alone.

V. acerifolium, the "dockmackie". A 6ft shrub with maple-like leaves, which turn a pretty lavender colour in the fall. Florally of no importance, but useful in shade. z3.

V. 'Anne Russell'. A charming Burkwood hybrid, evergreen, bearing sweet-smelling orbs, richly tinted pink in the bud. At Wisley it measures 8ft by 5ft.

V. betulifolium. A very big, rather gaunt shrub which, when mature, can provide quantities of glistening fruits, like redcurrants, on long, swaying branches, weighed down by the massed fruits. Bunches (corymbs) of white flowers in June. Give the shrub a clear foreground so that the berries are not obscured. z5.

V. × bodnantense. One of the great beauties of the harsher months, producing, on naked, rather sparse branches, tight clusters of white, tubular flowers that are not quite "snowballs". They are pink-tinted and deliciously scented from October onwards and, according to the weather, open all winter. The original hybrid was raised at Bodnant, North Wales, from *farreri × grandiflorum*, and grows to 10ft or so. Two lovely clones are the rose-tinted 'Dawn' and 'Deben', the latter raised in Notcutt's nursery in Suffolk. z8.

V. × burkwoodii is the very happy issue of *carlesii* out of *utile*, born at Kingston upon Thames. The floral results are loose, sweetly scented, incomplete snowballs from February to May, supported by burnished evergreen foliage, coated underneath with a fawn down. The shrub grows to 6ft and is of no ornamental value after flowering. Quite easily reproduced by cuttings. z5.

Other products related to Burkwood's viburnum are some good clones described as of the "burkwoodii group", all rather alike and very good of their kinds. We have already noted 'Anne Russell' and others are 'Chenaultii', 'Fulbrook' and 'Park Farm', a strong and spreading shrub with large flowers. 'Mohawk', a fine new hybrid from the US National Arboretum, has extra-large snowballs, red in the bud.

V. calvum. A well-clothed evergreen shrub of 8ft or more, resembling the laurustinus but flowering in June and July. z7–8.

V. × carlcephalum. Obviously *carlesii* comes into the lineage here, together with *macrocephalum*. The result is a splendid shrub of about 7ft with very large, moderately scented snowballs, pink in the bud, in May. The deciduous foliage often turns claret-colour in autumn. z5.

V. carlesii. A popular shrub of moderate size and slow growth from Korea with spicily scented snowballs in May, but not as good as some of its offspring. See, e.g., *V. × juddii*. There are however some selected forms that are superior to the original. They include 'Aurora', red in the bud opening pink, 'Charis', wide-spreading and red in the bud, and 'Diana', pink. z4.

V. cassinoides, the "withe-rod", is an extremely hardy and pretty shrub of 6ft bearing slightly domed clusters frothing with cream florets in June to a height of 6ft, followed in autumn by small berries that change from green to yellow to red and finally to black. The young leaves emerge bronze before turning dark green and in autumn blaze with vivid reds. For acid soils in partial shade or in the open. The popular nickname derives from the use of its pliant branches as withies to tie up fences in Canada. z2. The dwarf 'Nanum' has wavy leaves.

V. cinnamomifolium. Big evergreen, of 15ft or more. Leaves glossy and deeply veined, rather like those of the more famous *V. davidii*. Big, loose clusters (cymes) of dull white flowers in June. Blue-black berries. z7–8.

V. cotinifolium. A deciduous shrub of 8 to 10ft, densely hairy on the young shoots and the reverse of the leaf and small, rounded trusses of white, pink-tinted, funnels in May. Fruits red turning black. z6.

V. davidii. One of the most distinctive and valuable of evergreen shrubs. Its oval, leathery leaves are a very dark green and deeply veined longitudinally, giving the appearance of being corrugated or pleated. They crowd together in an ornate mass, and the shrub builds up to a rather low, wide-spreading dome, which, over the years, may become 5ft high and 8ft wide, utterly suppressing weeds. The small white flowers are of no account but they fructify in autumn, rather sparingly, as small, sparkling amethysts if "two or more are gathered to-gether". Though not classed by the botanist as being "dioeceous", some plants seem to be dominantly male and others female.

David's viburnum is often recommended as a shrub to be grown in shade, but it is finer still in full sun, a splendid dome of green at all seasons. In America it thrives in the north-west, but languishes in the east. z7.

V. dentatum, the arrow-wood, so called because the strong, straight basal stems are said to have been used by some American Indians for arrows, is another exceptionally hardy shrub. It is of little floral value, but its leaves turn a fiery orange in autumn and it does well in dry soils, provided that they are free of lime. z2.

V. dilatatum is a fine, densely leaved shrub averaging 8ft (sometimes very much more) and distinctly hairy. Creamy-white flowers are nicely arranged in flat clusters in June in great quantity, followed by bunches of vivid red fruits which last well into the winter. Better fruiting occurs if several are planted as a group, for the same reason as given for *V. davidii*. Its form xanthocarpum has yellow berries of equal excellence. z5.

V. erosum. White flowers in loose trusses in May on a deciduous, slender-stemmed, erect shrub of up to 6ft. Leaves sharply toothed, of variable shapes. Fruits red. z5.

V. erubescens gracilipes. The species itself, *V. erubescens*, is not very hardy but is rare among viburnums for displaying its flowers in pendulous clusters (panicles). Its variety *gracilipes* is notable for being much hardier and for having longer clusters, which measure 4in and which are white, tinted pink, and fragrant, and delay their display until July. z6.

V. farreri (better known as **fragrans**). An old winter-flowering favourite, seen in many a cottage garden as well as in baronial acres. From November onwards in Britain (but not until spring in the colder zones of N. America) its white, pink-tinted snowballs open to exhale an odour like that of the heliotrope, on naked branches, at their tips and on laterals. When young the shrub is gaunt and stiff but later it becomes a broad and expansive outline, reaching about 9ft. 'Candidissimum' is an all-white variety. Our old friend is now surpassed, it must be admitted, by its Bodnant hybrid offspring. z5.

V. foetens. Another great joy of winter, similar in general character to Farrer's, but semi-evergreen and of 8ft, with white, sweetly scented snowballs from January to March. Is most at home in a rather moist, loamy soil in some shade.

V. foetidum is also semi-evergreen, giving white, rounded clusters that are not quite snowballs in July. About 10ft. Brilliant red autumnal fruits, but two or more should be planted in proximity. Dried specimens have a bad breath. z7–8.

V. grandiflorum is another old favourite, resembling Farrer's, but the flowers are rather larger, deep red in the bud, opening pink in February and March and scented. Unlike many viburnums, the leaves are all of a kind, being narrowly oval but pointed, regularly toothed, of a dull green but firm of texture, hairy on the reverse.

V. harryanum. An evergreen shrub distinguished by having privet-like leaves. Pure white flowers forming small domes. z7.

V. henryi. Evergreen, stiffly handsome, tree-like with long, narrow leaves and white flowers arranged conically in loose panicles at midsummer. Handsome also in its berries, which are red, turning black. About 10ft. z7.

V. × hillieri 'Winton'. A good hybrid of about 10ft that occurred in Hillier's nursery from *erubescens × henryi*. It is a semi-evergreen, with cream panicles in June. The young leaves emerge copper-tinted and all colour fairly well in autumn.

Also colouring well in autumn, with red fruits, is **V. hupehensis**, an 8ft, deciduous shrub with broad, hairy, coarsely toothed leaves and loose trusses (corymbs) of flowers in May–June. z5.

V. japonicum (*macrophyllum*) is a sturdy, handsome evergreen with broad, burnished leaves 6in long. The white, very sweet flowers are in 4in domes in June, followed by a lovely

Viburnum × juddii

display of red berries. About 6ft. z7.

V. 'Jermyn's Globe', a dense, rounded evergreen with narrow, leathery leaves and flat clusters (cymes) of white flowers, opening sporadically in winter, with the main effort in spring. Few fruits (*calvum* × *davidii*).

V. × juddii. This is a hybrid often mistaken for its parent *V. carlesii*, but decidedly superior to it all round — bushier, more leafy, taller (to 8ft) and displaying larger snowballs, though not of quite so sweet a breath. Named after one of the staff of the Arnold Arboretum (*bitchiuense* × *carlesii*) z5.

V. lantana, the deciduous wayfaring tree of Britain and Europe and the original *viburnum* of the Romans. Common in the hedgerows of chalky counties, where it may be recognised by the velvety surface of its broad leaves and of its young shoots and buds. The white flowers appear in flat, 3in clusters (cymes) in May and June. It can grow to 15ft if given a chance and, although not of the first quality in flower, is distinctly ornamental and is, like *V. dentatum*, one of the few viburnums that do well in dry soils. Good autumn colour. The variety *discolor* is a Balkan variation with smaller leaves and *rugosum* has wrinkled leaves. z3.

V. lantanoides (or **alnifolium**), the "hobble-bush", so called because you are liable to trip over its lowest, ground-hugging branches. Also called the American wayfaring tree. It can be a strapping 12ft in America (less in Britain) and spreads by suckers with large, heart-shaped leaves, colouring quite well in autumn, and white lacecaps in May, followed by red berries, turning black. Of value only in acid soil in moist woodland. z3.

V. lobophyllum differs from betulifolium only in minor details. z5.

V. macrocephalum, the Chinese snowball, is one of the splendid snowballs, which may be anything up to 8in in diameter if in a rich soil, produced in May. It is sterile, can grow to 12ft, is deciduous in the cooler counties, maybe evergreen in warm ones. z6. The wild form is quite different, having a flat, lacecap inflorescence. This is generally known as forma *keteleeri*, though it seems to us that this is the wrong way round. In America it is much more logically called *V. macrocephalum* 'Sterile'. See also what is said under *V. plicatum*.

V. nudum, the "smooth withe-rod" of 12ft, erect in habit, is often described as a more southerly (i.e. less hardy) and thinner version of *cassinoides*. Leaves, dark, glossy green, flowers off-white in 4in clusters (cymes) in June. Good autumnal display of leaves and red fruits, turning black. Acid soil. z6.

V. odoratissimum is an exceptionally fine, very large evergreen that, in deep, moist soil, may in time reach to 15ft or more, in pyramidal form. The leaves are more or less oval, burnished, leathery and may be 6in long. The white-scented florets are arranged in pyramidal clusters (panicles) up to 6in high in late summer when the shrub has become well established.

V. 'Oneida'. An American hybrid. About 10ft, the branches in tiers, leaves of variable shape. Creamy flower trusses in May and intermittently all summer. Fruits dark red, lasting well into winter. (*dilatatum* × *lobophyllum*).

When alphabetically we reach **V. opulus** we are among the *crème de la crème* of viburnum society. This is our much-loved guelder rose or, sometimes, water-elder, of Britain, but native to other parts of Europe also. The wilding is an easy-going shrub of perhaps 12ft, spreading broadly, equipped with 3-lobed leaves (sometimes 5-lobed). The flowers, opening in early June, are of the lacecap type and afterwards comes a copious harvest of red, glistening, translucent berries, when the leaves also colour brilliantly. The autumn is, indeed, its finest hour. The guelder rose shows at its best in wet, even boggy, soils. z3.

The wilding is, however, surpassed or at least equalled by some of its selected offspring. Thus 'Aureum' is golden-leaved if not exposed to too hot a sun, 'Compactum', a splendid shrub, speaks for itself and is massed with brilliant berries, and 'Notcutt's Variety' has extra-large flowers and fruits and '*americanum*' has sweeter, edible fruits.

Two guelder roses have yellow fruits. 'Fructu-luteo' starts pink and turns yellow.

'Xanthocarpum' (in its best form) starts apricot and finishes a glistening gold.

The variety that wins the most applause, however, is 'Sterile' (or 'Roseum'). This is the European snowball, which discards the lacecaps of its sisters. Disillusioning the bee, the all-sterile flowers pack themselves together in tight orbs of white or off-white. No fruits, of course, but it is one of the most decorative of shrubs, grown in England for 500 years or more. In most parts of N. America it is victimized by plant lice, so that, in such conditions, the Japanese snowball (*V. plicatum*) is to be preferred in the colder states and the Chinese (*V. macrocephalum* 'Sterile') in the milder ones.

Originally the popular term Guelder Rose was applied only to the sterile snowball, but now it is used for the whole species of Viburnum opulus. "Guelder" is said credibly to derive from Guelderland, in Holland, whence the variety appears to have originated; while "rose" has simply the connotation popularly attached to many other plants called "rose", "lily", "daisy" and so on. The sterile snowball was also called the Rose Elder by our forefathers, who considered it to be not a viburnum but an elder (*Sambucus*).

V. phlebotrichum ("hairy veined"). An awkward mouthful for quite a nice 7ft shrub, of slender, erect habit and slim leaves, spiny when adult. Fruits crimson. Brilliant autumn colours. z8.

We are again in very aristocratic society when we meet **V. plicatum**, the Japanese snowball, a creature that has suffered several changes of name by the botanical lawyers, and known for long as *tomentosum*, with or without suffixes. Like the Chinese snowball (*macrocephalum*) it is sterile and not a true species in the wild, but the botanists for their own reasons have sanctioned its usurpation over its apparent parent, which is *V. tomentosum*. Rather silly, it seems to us. Although the snowball garden form was found and introduced to Europe before the wild species, it seems curious to treat the wilding as a "variety" of a sterile plant and is a reversal of the order of nature. However, the Japanese snowball is a superlative, de-

Viburnum plicatum, the Japanese Snowball

ciduous shrub of about 9ft, displaying its snowballs in a double row all along the length of its arching branches. This it does from late May until well into June in the most dramatic fashion, especially in the large-flowered form 'Grandiflorum'.

No less dramatic but totally different in character are those that take after the parental wild *V. tomentosum*. Their character is to throw out, to no great height, tier upon tier, wide-flung arms that are more or less horizontal, displaying, all the way along their length, large, white lacecaps, looking straight up at you, so that the shrub looks as though covered in snow. This very distinctive and unusual kind of tabulated structure has a very marked effect on the architecture of the garden.

The most generally favoured of these splendid creatures is 'Mariesii', a marvellous shrub, having branches that are quite horizontal, upon which the beautiful white plates sit firmly balanced.

'Lanarth' resembles it, but the arms are not quite horizontal and the growth is much stronger, and it may in time be 15ft by 15ft.

'Rowallane' is usually rather smaller and is a real beauty with large ray florets. Unlike them, it often produces a good crop of fruits.

In the charming 'Pink Beauty' the ray florets flush to a pretty pink as they age.

And so to *V. p. tomentosum*, the usurped founder of the breed. This is normally a 9ft shrub with its arms not quite horizontal. The oval leaves are pleated and the flowers surrounded by white sterile ones, strung out in double rows all along the upper edge of the branches.

These horizontally tiered viburnums may sometimes disconcert the gardener by throwing up erect shoots from the ground through the horizontals. You may cut these off at an early stage of their growth or use them as replacements if the shrub is old, but if the mature branch system is healthy there is no point in cutting it out simply to encourage the new, which may be used to extend the stature of the shrub.

V. 'Pragense'. Raised in Prague. About 12ft, spreading. Dark green, corrugated leaves, white-felted beneath. Flower clusters dull cream from pink buds in May (*rhytidophyllum × utile*).

V. propinquum. Bushy, evergreen, with 3in dark, polished, deeply veined leaves and loose clusters (cymes) of greenish flowers in May. Berries blue-black. 77.

V. prunifolium, the very hardy black haw.

Viburnum plicatum (formerly tomentosum) 'Mariesii'

Rather too big for a viburnum, often exceeding 20ft, especially when trained on a "leg". The flowers are in small, white clusters, but the shrub is known particularly for its large, dark blue, sweet berries, which make an excellent preserve. It thrives in even dry, sterile soils. z3.

V. rhytidophyllum. A big, fast-growing, evergreen shrub considered by some gardenwriters as "handsome". In our view, however, it is a coarse-leaved creature with dull buff flowers and looks the picture of dejection in winter, unless, perhaps, in a warm climate. It has some value for doing well in shade and its variety 'Roseum' is quite pretty in the bud stage, when it is pink. z5.

This species has been married to others with equally difficult names, including the very big *V. × rhytidophylloides*, the result of a partnership with the English wayfaring tree, of which 'Willow Wood Seedling' is a good clone, and *V. × rhytidocarpum*, in which we see no virtue.

V. sargentii is a strong, 12ft deciduous, somewhat coarse version of *V. opulus* with the same lacecap inflorescence, but the maple-like leaves are larger on red stalks and the anthers are purple. It is a splendid fruiter, with dangling bunches of red, glistening berries. Its form 'Flavum' has golden fruits and 'Onondaga' is a fine variation with leaves that open bronze and retain a bronze tint all summer. z4.

V. setigerum is engaging for the changing colours of its slender leaves, which end up orange before falling, accompanied by large, brilliant fruits. In the variety 'Aurantiacum' the fruits are a glowing orange, making a wonderful autumnal show with the leaves. The shrub grows to 12ft with slender branches in a loose and open manner. Flowers in flat clusters in July. The leaves, we are told, were used by Chinese monks for making a tea and the plant was accordingly called *V. theiferum* by Rehder. z5.

V. sieboldii is a strong, tree-like structure, spreading widely and of the most handsome appearance, densely clothed to the ground with dark green, wrinkled leaves up to 6in long. Its growth is most attractively patterned with areas of light and shade and it is decorated with

loose clusters of cream flowers in May–June. The fruits, in grape-like clusters, are bright red before turning black in the fall, but are liable to be pillaged by birds before showing any colour except in the new American selection 'Seneca', which for some reason is unmolested. It may grow 30ft high in America, but it wants a continental climate and is not seen at its best in Britain. z4.

V. suspensum. A rather tender evergreen, averaging 9ft in height with oval, leathery, glossy-green leaves. The flowers are fragrant and are unusual for being rose-tinted panicles in spring. Fruits red, if the climate is warm enough. z9.

A very old friend of 500 years' acquaintance greets us in **V. tinus**, the laurustinus. Common? Yes. Unexciting? No doubt. But a very good, dense, reliable evergreen, clothed to the ground, admirable for screening, accustomed to neglect, submitting to being chopped back hard at need, good in sun or shade and of the easiest cultivation where the soil is not excessively wet. The small flowers are in loose, semi-snowballs, one may say, pale pink in the bud opening white. Not of the first order of beauty but borne in succession throughout autumn, winter and early spring, followed by small lapis lazuli berries. There are several varieties and cultivars, of which the best is 'Eve Price' in which the buds are carmine, opening pale pink. 'Lucidum' is larger in all its parts. 'French White' is all-white. 'Pyramidale' and 'Variegatum' speak for themselves.

Europeans who consider the laurustinus to be one of the hardiest of shrubs are surprised to learn that in America it is rated only z7–8. The hairy *hirsutum* is still less hardy.

V. tomentosum. See *V. plicatum*.

V. trilobum. See **V. opulus americanum**.

V. utile is an elegant evergreen of about 7ft with slender branches clad with polished, dark green leaves, coated white beneath, accompanied in May with spherical trusses of white, sweet-scented flowers. z6.

V. veitchii. A 5ft shrub, much coated with down and of rather straggly habit. Flowers in flat, white clusters in June. Berries red, then black. Chinese relative of *V. lantana*. z5.

Last but certainly not least, **V. wrightii**. This is a 9ft shrub, the greatest value of which is its brilliant display of red, glistening berries. They are preceded by flat flower-clusters above leaves that are a metallic green, turning chestnut-red in autumn. Its cultivar 'Hessei' is a splendid, compact 3ft, with pretty leaves and no less fruitful. z5.

VITEX

Most vitex are too tender or too big for our pages, but there are a couple of accommodating and very distinctive shrubs that ornament the autumn. Both grow to 10ft or so and are readily recognised by their grey, compound leaves, in which the slender, finger-like leaflets all fan out from one point on the tips of their stalks ("digitately compound"). From the axils of the leaf stalks spring small spikes of numerous, flat-faced florets. They seem to like a continental climate, with hot summers, rather than a maritime one, to harden their stems and, although rated for cold-hardiness in America as low as z5-7 do not favour the climates of Britain and western Europe, where they are regarded as wall-shrubs. They are deciduous and the whole plant has a pungently aromatic odour.

In the open not much pruning is needed until the older stems degenerate, when they should be cut right out in late winter. So should frost-damaged shoots, for the vitex sprouts readily from the base. Indeed, in the coldest counties it can be cut back to a stump every year, like David's buddleia. On walls, fan out the main stems and prune the spent side-shoots back to about 2in from their point of origin to form spurs, as in the wisteria.

The usual species is **V. agnus-castus**, the "chaste tree', the name of the species being a slightly Latinized version of the name used in ancient Greece, where the shrub was regarded as holy and a symbol of virginity. The dense flower-spikes are pale violet and fragrant in

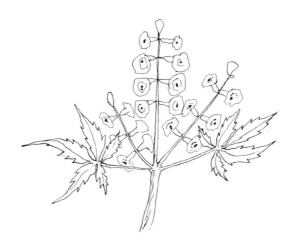

85.   Vitex negundo 'Heterophylla'

August and September. The shrub is spreading and the leaflets toothless, 2 to 4in long. 'Rosea' is pink, *alba* white and *latifolia* has broad leaflets. Rated z7 in USA.

V. negundo *heterophylla* is a rather larger shrub of loose, open character, with elegantly cut, toothed leaves and lilac flowers more loosely arranged. z5 in USA.

WAYFARING TREE. See *Viburnum lantana*; of America, *V. lantanoides*.

WEIGELA

The weigelas used to be numbered with the diervillas until recently, but there are important differences. The diervilla, besides being a less attractive creature, produces flowers rather like those of the honeysuckle on stems that have grown out earlier in the same year, whereas the weigela flowers on laterals from stems developed in the previous year. Its name commemorates the old German professor Weigel of Georgian days.

Weigelas are among the easiest and most decorative shrubs for late spring and early summer enjoyment. They are deciduous, with trim leaves, and become as a rule neat, rounded, well-behaved shrubs of about 6ft or more. The little flowers are funnels or trumpets and are displayed for a considerable length along the stems. The most popular and showy are a troupe of large-flowered garden hybrids, but some of the species have a charm of their own.

Pruning is simply a matter of cutting back the stems after flowering, a process of special importance for the hybrids.

In our estimation the most beautiful of all weigelas is **W. florida 'Variegata'**, in which the small flowers have rosy mouths and pale pink lips among leaves narrowly rimmed cream. At its best in June, it is one of the most charming of variegated shrubs, growing to about 6ft. It is a beautiful companion for the golden elder or the golden philadelphus, where golden shrubs can be grown. There is also a slow-moving dwarf form, 'Variegata Nana', of pretty foliage.

The straightforward *W. florida* is itself excel-

lent and so are its other variations. Thus 'Foliis Purpureis' is a slow-moving dwarf form with purple-flushed leaves that makes an even better companion for golden-leaved shrubs. *Venusta* is larger than its parent with flowers of a richer rose-pink.

All these florida weigelas will take to some shade as well as to sun, but 'Foliis Purpureis' is rather sombre in shade. z5.

Other species are as follows.

W. coraeensis, an elegant shrub of 12ft or more with small pale bells that become carmine in June. z5.

W. hortensis 'Nivea' (or 'Albiflora'). About 9ft. Pretty white flowers in May and June among leaves that are thickly felted beneath. z6.

W. japonica. About 10ft with pale pink or white funnels in May, maturing carmine z5.

Weigela middendorffiana

The Chinese form *sinica* is much larger. z6.

W. maximowiczii. A small, spreading shrub (4–5ft) with pale yellow, green-tinted flowers in May. z5.

More decorative than any of these, and with a very distinct character of its own, is **W. middendorffiana**, a 4ft shrub with 1in trumpets of pale yellow, touched orange, grouped in 2in clusters in April and May. The bark peels off. A shrub of good class. z4.

W. praecox 'Variegata' is also distinctive, being a 6ft shrub with conspicuous flowers of rose, yellow in the throat and sweetly scented, in May, the leaves edged cream. The earliest weigela to bloom. Probably a hybrid of *W. amabilis*. So also may be the variegated *florida* above. z5.

GARDEN HYBRIDS
Many hands in several countries have been at work to present to the world weigelas with large, bell-like flowers. In good conditions they average about 8ft, flowering in May and June. Cut back the flowered stems immediately after blossom-fall as far back as promising new growth.

There are a great many of these hybrids and it is difficult to give a complete list, because each country has its own specialities. Many are of French raising. The one that receives most acclaim today, however, is 'Bristol Ruby', a fine, vigorous shrub, with large, deep red bells of a sparkling quality. It really displaces its parent 'Eva Rathke', an excellent weigela that was formerly itself a leader in popularity and is still very good indeed for small spaces, as 'Bristol Ruby' is much bigger. The following are also very good, but the colours of the flowers can be given only approximately, as they are often blends. All flower in May, and most can be rated z5.

'Abel Carrière'. Rose-carmine, speckled gold.

'Avalanche'. White.

'Ballet'. Large, deep rose, the stems drooping.

'Bristol Snowflake'. Blush.

'Buisson Fleuri'. Rose, speckled gold, fragrant, early.

'Candida'. Pure white.

'Conquérant'. Rose, 12ft.

'Dame Blanche'. White.

'Espérance'. Salmon, white within, early.

'Eva Supreme'. Bright red, 8ft.

'Floréal'. Purple.

'Gracieux'. Salmon and yellow, 12ft.

'Ideal'. Two-tone red. Very free.

'Looymansii Aurea'. An outstanding and charming choice with pale pink flowers among gold-tinted leaves. It sometimes blooms again in September. For partial shade.

'Mont Blanc'. Perhaps the best white, scented.

'Newport Red' ('Vanicek'). A very fine, upstanding shrub with large flowers of bright red.

'Styriaca'. Rose buds, opening purple on bending stems.

WINTER'S BARK. See *Drimys*

WINTERSWEET. See *Chimonanthus*

WITCH HAZEL. See *Hamamelis*

XANTHOCERAS

X. sorbifolium is a strapping, deciduous shrub of up to 20ft, clothed with prettily pinnate leaves and quantities of erect, torch-like flower-trusses made up in wide-lipped, crimson-mouthed bells in May. The fruits are mini-chestnuts, spilling out from a large capsule. The lustrous leaves, however, are feather-like, more like those of a sorbus or mountain-ash.

This is a handsome fellow, worthy of some better nickname than "silver-leaf yellow-horn". It is happy in any fertile soil, including chalk, but is liable to winter damage in both its pithy branchlets and its flowers, yet formally rated z5. There is a good specimen on a wall at the Cambridge Botanic Garden. The name is fabricated from the Greek *xanthos*, yellow, and *keras*, a horn.

Xanthoceras sorbifolium

86. The pinnate leaf of Xanthoriza simplicissima ("Aunt Eliza"), the leaflets sessile

XANTHORRHIZA

Familiarly known to old English gardeners as "Aunt Eliza", less picturesquely in America as the "yellow root", *X. simplicissima* is a 2ft deciduous shrub, spreading by underground stolons and making a level mass of most attractive foliage. The leaves are pinnate, stalkless and delicately chiselled in a freehand manner, and they turn a clear yellow in autumn. The tiny purple-brown flowers droop in little clusters as the leaves begin to unfurl in March or April. The name is coined from the Greek *xanthos*, yellow, and *rhyza*, a root. z4.

YUCCA

Outside their native pastures, which are mainly the southern United States and Mexico, the yuccas look decidedly tropical, like the aloe and the agave, but several of them are surprisingly resistant to a frosty breath. In general the leaves are stiff and sharply pointed, looking like a dense circle of bayonets as seen in old baronial halls and museums and suggestive to imaginative minds of an old-time chevaux-de-frise, once used to deter cavalry charges. The leaves of a few species also have bristly edges from which dangle thread-like filaments.

From these prickly fortifications arise erect steeples, profusely hung with carillons of creamy or ivory bells, often tinted pink. Some species, however, form a thick trunk before bursting into leaf and flower.

In the average garden yuccas are not easy to place. Aesthetically, they look antagonistic to

Yucca filamentosa

soft lush growths, but agree quite well with such small shrubs as helianthemums, and the dwarfer cistuses and brooms, which will precede their flowering season of July and August. Some herbaceous plants are also good company for them, such as sea-holly (Eryngium) and the classic acanthus. Too often one sees yuccas dotted about singly, whereas they are assuredly most telling when in bold, close-set, isolated groups in hot, dry, stony ground, with some rocks thrusting out. They are splendid plants for parks, but are best kept out of the reach of children. Surprisingly, they are also very good tub-plants, if the less fiercely armed species are chosen.

The most generally popular species are *filamentosa*, *flaccida* and *gloriosa*. The name is of Caribbean origin, mis-applied by Gerard.

Y. filamentosa. A cluster of long, slender bayonets, margined with curly, white threads, with flowering steeples up to 6ft high, or 10ft in hot climates, flowering when quite young. It spreads by stolons and is the best one for wet climates. 'Variegata' is a nice form with cream streaks and margins on the leaves. z4. In the United States (where it is called "Adam's Needle") plants catalogued as *filamentosa* are really *Y. smalliana*.

Y. flaccida. Unlike most yuccas, the leaves of this small and attractive species bend down at their tips, giving a less spiky effect. Curly, white threads clothe the margins. It spreads by basal side-shoots. To 4ft in cooler climates. 'Ivory' is a fine clone described by its name, with flowers that face outwards instead of hanging down. z4.

Y. glauca. A compact plant with grey-tinted leaves, margined white and thrown out nearly horizontally to form a spiky rosette, 4ft wide. Flowers milky-green, seldom borne on young plants, but in 'Rosea' they are tinted pink. Not happy in wet climates. About 5ft. z4. There are several related species, less hardy and often dwarf.

Y. gloriosa. "Adam's Needle" in Britain, "Spanish Dagger" in USA. Well named but fiercely armed, the leaf-points as sharp as stilettos. Of tree-like form, it shoots up a stout

Yucca gloriosa 'Variegata'

Y. recurvifolia. The name explains the shape of most of the long, spiky leaves, at the head of a spiky trunk, which usually has several branches.' An easy one and good for town gardens. z6.

Y. rupicola. From a dense rosette of sea-green, slender, toothed leaves arises a branched panicle, averaging 5ft high, of milk-white bells. z6.

Y. smalliana. Closely resembles *filamentosa*, but the leaves are narrower, flatter and thinner.

Y. whipplei. A splendid Californian with a dense, globular cluster of long, sharp-pointed and saw-edged dragon's teeth and a tall plume of large, milky-green, scented bells that may be 3in wide and edged purple. It can be anything up to 15ft high and is one of the finest yuccas, but for dry places only. Sometimes called "Our Lord's Candle". z9.

ZANTHOXYLUM

Spiny, pungent trees and shrubs, not of the highest ornamental merit, but often excellent for foliage effects. All listed here are deciduous, with pinnate leaves. The flowers are of no consequence. They like a good, deep soil. Those just within reach of our pages include the following.

Z. americanum, the "prickly ash" or "toothache tree". A very large, upright shrub. Its acrid, black fruits, we are told, used to be chewed by the American Indians to relieve toothache. z3.

Z. piperitum, the "Japanese pepper". A graceful shrub, sometimes tree-like, with trim, bushy foliage, having up to 21 leaflets. The slender thorns are in pairs. The black seeds from the red fruits are ground into pepper in Japan. z7.

Z. planispermum. A 12ft, spreading shrub, clothed to the ground. The stalks of the leaves are boldly winged and the few leaflets are broad. Many of the spines are nearly an inch broad at the base. z6.

Z. schinifolium. A very large but graceful

trunk, at the summit of which its dense bundle of daggers breaks out, crowned in due course with a superb plume of creamy bells from July to September. Sometimes it branches at the summit, and it can grow to 15ft. There is a variety striped and margined cream and 'Nobilis' is a very good form with short, forking trunk with arching, glaucous leaves. z7–8.

Y. × karlsruhensis. This hybrid resembles *glauca*, but the flowers are cream and the leaf margins more generously threaded. z4.

Y. parviflora engelmanii. A distinctive and beautiful Texan with bright green leaves, margined with white threads. The bells are tomato-red outside, golden inside. About 4ft. Now included in the genus *Hesperaloe* but kept here for convenience. z8–9.

Zenobia pulverulenta

shrub, with fern-like foliage, having anything up to 21 fine leaflets, ruffling in the wind. z5.

Z. simulans. A handsome shrub of 12ft or more, spreading gracefully with lustrous leaves and very bold prickles like those of planispermum. z5.

ZENOBIA

We finish our Register of broad-leaved shrubs with one of the most endearing shrubs at our command if we have a lime-free soil rich in old leaf-mould or peat. This is **Z. pulverulenta**, which will reach 5ft or possibly more in the best conditions; and in warm places it may be evergreen, forming a rather loose, open and airy structure. Everything about it is gracious and delicate and of good breeding. The leaves are slender and, until they age, are suffused with a blue-grey bloom. The lovely flowers, looking like enlarged lilies-of-the-valley, hang down in thronged clusters of pure white, scented of aniseed, in June and July from the upper reaches of the stems.

It likes an acid soil, a little passing or lightly dappled shade and must not get its feet too dry. There is a form called *nuda*, which lacks the blue-grey bloom on the leaf.

Prune back the flowered portions of the stems after blossom-fall. If necessary, cut out ancient stems right to the ground, for the plant breaks readily from the base as from elsewhere. z5.

SOME CONIFERS

ONIFERS IN ALL THEIR wonderful diversity of form, colour and texture have a special significance in the design of the garden picture and of a large countryside panorama. One is tempted to say that no garden is complete without them, but one can say the same about so many other plants. Their special value, of course, is in winter, when they keep the garden alive, especially those that are painted in gold or washed with blue or stippled with silver. In our book on trees we surveyed the larger conifers at some length and we would have liked here to inspect the multitude of the smaller ones. Our ground is too small, however, and all we can do is to pick out a very small collection to diversify the "splendour" of the broad leaf shrubs that we have been reviewing. All are well known, readily obtainable, easy to grow in most conditions, but unfortunately conifers are of all plants perhaps the most cursed with jaw-cracking names, often of very confusing similarity.

We start with a caveat about what are often called "dwarf" conifers. So enticing are these pygmy darlings when seen a few inches high in a nursery, but such awkward customers may they prove when they run up to 12ft or more and fat in proportion.

87.   Some space-saving, erect conifers, popular and easy. *From left to right*: the blue-tinted Chamaecyparis lawsoniana 'Columnaris', best of all; Juniperus virginiana 'Skyrocket'; Juniperus communis 'Hibernica', the Irish juniper; Taxus baccata 'Fastigiata', the columnar Irish yew, of which there are golden-leaved forms

CHAMAECYPARIS
Neo-cypress

This genus offers us the widest of all choices. Its mongrel name is an ill-considered one for a tree that has the general appearance and habit of a cypress (*Cupressus*) and is usually interpreted as "dwarf cypress" but is often transcribed also as "false cypress". Its primary species, however, are by no means dwarf and there is certainly nothing "false" about them. One is repeatedly asked: what is the difference between the two? Most obviously it is in the arrangement of the leaflets. In the chamaecyparis these and the sprays that they form are flattened and fan-like, whereas in the cupressus the leaflets spring radially around the parent twig, giving a faintly bristly appearance to the plant, compared with the usually smoother, more flattened aspect of the others. All seem to be very easily propagated by cuttings.

The celebrated "Lawson's cypress", **Chamaecyparis lawsoniana**, provides an interesting horticultural analogy to the affirmation of Holy Writ that "a prophet is not without honour save in his own country"; for Lawson's cypress is a native of the fog belt of California and Oregon, but no one took much notice of it until a nurseryman of Edinburgh named Lawson saw its value as a garden plant, nurtured it and put it forth to the public in 1854. It was an instant success in Britain and it was not long before some of its extraordinarily versatile progeny found their way to the land of their forefathers in new forms and colours. Today its varieties number about 100, in diverse shades of green, in gold, in blue and in silvery tints and varying in size from pygmies to stalwart trees of 75ft, as in the blue-grey 'Triomf von Boskoop'. Many seem to be still unknown in America, where, in the wild state, Lawson's cypress may reach 200ft.

We have no hesitation in saying that the most beautiful variety of Lawson's cypress is 'Columnaris', sometimes incorrectly called 'Columnaris Glauca'. This is a slim, pointed, tightly compacted tree with distinctly blue-rinsed foliage. Its ultimate height is not yet known, but my own specimens have grown to 20ft by about 3ft after $20\frac{1}{2}$ years, which is rather faster than usual. In some years it blushes bright red as the tiny flowers ("strobili") open before fructifying in very small, round cones (another feature of the neo-cypress).

Similar in silhouette, but much smaller, is 'Ellwoodii', a very slim creature of rarely more than about 15ft. 'Fletcheri', also often sold as a "dwarf", is rather like it but can on occasions grow twice as high.

Other very fine lawsons are the dark green 'Kilmacurragh' and the beautiful 'Pembury Blue', which is broader in the beam. Some golden lawsons are also very fine, 'Lutea' being perhaps the most favoured one, but all these are prone to sunburn in very hot climates.

All of these grow to about 25ft or a bit more in time. Very much smaller, but of the highest quality, very tightly packed and very stylish in its smooth outline, is the really dwarf *C. l.* 'Minima Aurea'. This is a very choice blend of dark green and gold, which, with me, has in all specimens grown about $2\frac{1}{2}$ft in 20 years. A splendid consort for heathers, as are many other conifers.

Chamaecyparis obtusa, the "Hinoki Cypress", 120ft high in its native Japan, yields some great treasures, of which we pick first the elegant 'Crippsii', a gold-and-green tree which fulfils the artist's idea of contrasts of light and shade. It grows slowly and broadly, with horizontal branches and a blunt summit, and with me grows to about 15ft by 5ft in some 20 years, but in 60 years it may go to 50ft.

There are also some delightful dwarf or half-dwarf obtusas of the most picturesque patterns, but cursed with confusing names. The most attractive of them are characterized by small, neat, concave, shell-like or fan-like sprays, tightly packed together. Among them, 'Nana' is really too slow and small for anything but the rock garden, but its sparkling green-and-gold form, 'Nana Aurea', is more fleet of foot and perhaps the most aristocratic of all dwarf golden conifers. 'Nana Gracilis', all green, is bigger still, in time becoming a dense mass of convoluted sprays. 'Nana Pyramidalis', very slow, explains itself and 'Spiralis' is an elegant and lively spire of twisted branches. All these are charmingly ornamental in a "Japanesey" sort of way and in time make distinguished solo specimens or are elegant contrasts among plants of very low stature.

C. o. 'Tetragona Aurea' is a bird of a different feather, with a branching, spreading character, glittering with golden sprays. It becomes a fairly strapping shrub in time, growing about 10in a year until, in favoured places, it reaches about 30ft, but is rarely more than 2ft wide.

C. pisifera ("with pea-like fruits") is the "Sawara cypress", a lofty tree in origin but providing us also with some engaging and distinctive trees or shrubs of accommodating size and picturesque appearance. These develop diverse shapes and habits and fall into three main groups.

'Squarrosa' has billowing sprays of soft, grey-tinted leaves and in time becomes quite a sizeable and handsome tree. Removal of its lower branches discloses a chestnut-coloured trunk. 'Squarrosa Aurea Nana' is a dwarf with yellow leaves. 'Snow' is a very likeable dwarf dome in pale, blue-grey foliage which is white at the tips; it is sun-shy and must be grown in oblique shade.

Most popular of all the squarrosas is the clone 'Boulevard', which Francis Bacon would have called a "pretty pyramid" of steely blue (*C. p. squarrosa cyano-viridis*). It is certainly a little charmer until it begins to exceed about 3ft, when it begins to deteriorate, becoming gappy and ragged. However, it is easily renewable by cuttings.

'Plumosa', which heads the second of our pisifera groups, has feathery, plume-like foliage, which looks soft to the touch but is not so. It shows itself in several forms, of which the most favoured is 'Plumosa Aurea Compacta', a most attractive, small, yellow pyramid, but after several years it degenerates in form, losing its compactness. Full sun.

'Filifera' ("thread-like"), the third group, is the very opposite of the plume-like pisiferas, being formed of drooping, whip-like branches, tightly clasped by tiny leaves, so that each stem

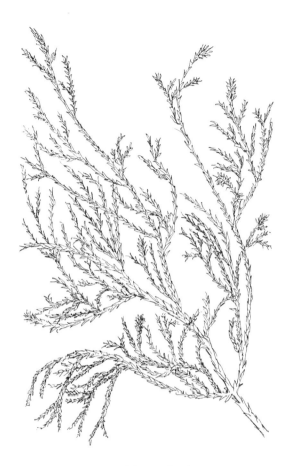

88.   Foliage of the gold-wire bush, Chamaecyparis pisifera 'Filifera Aurea'

looks like a cord, all the cords congested to form a mound. Easily the most favoured is the "gold wire shrub", 'Filifera Aurea', a dense broad mound of golden, drooping cords. When you site it bear in mind that it will in time grow 10ft high, perhaps more. 'Golden Spangle' is a very good sport from it.

Other good species of chamaecyparis, all lofty trees, are the curious *C. formosensis*, which has an enormously obese trunk, the handsome *C. nootkatensis*, rather like Lawson's species, and *C. thyoides*, a dweller of swamps.

JUNIPERUS
Juniper

Junipers are numbered in legions. We have mentioned a few of the ground-crawlers in Chapter 5 and for the rest must be selective, choosing only a few of those best suited to our purpose. All those we mention make splendid garden plants and most are as happy in chalky soils as in slightly acid ones.

Junipers have two types of leaves. The tiny juvenile foliage is usually described in books as "awl-like", but it is in fact much more like drawing-pins. Later these may metamorphose and become tiny scales, clinging closely to the stem. In some specimens, however, the adult foliage never materialises.

First we shall look at the Chinese juniper, **J. chinensis**, which, apart from its own lofty self, embraces some splendid smaller offspring that are the subject of much botanical debate. Those that we have in mind have fairly recently been marshalled by a controversial botanist named Van Melle under the banner of *J. × media*, but we have said from the beginning that we shall follow Bean, so follow him we will by grouping them as variations of the Chinese juniper. To the gardener such debates are of little import; what concerns him is the clonal name. z4.

Best-known of all these is 'Pfitzerana', often familiarly called "Pfitzer". This is a shrub of high "architectural" value in the garden, its many stems shooting out at angles of 45°, drooping at the tips and heavily clothed in dark green foliage, mainly of the adult kind and of soft texture. In time it will grow shoulder-high and spread its wing-like limbs a good 12ft. 'Aurea' is the "golden Pfitzer", in which the terminal shoots are suffused with yellow in summer. Several other variations are to be had.

The Pfitzer is one of the king-pins of garden design. Plant it in isolation or to break an outline, to mark a change from one kind of scene to another. Never allow it to be cluttered around by perennials or by plants of competitive intention. Consider it also as a bulwark against weeds. It does surprisingly well in deep shade.

Very like the Pfitzer, and just as good, is 'Hetzii'. Its leaves, which are of the adult form, have a silver-grey tint and are soft to the touch, and the branches have a slightly more erect stance, easily reaching head-high in a few years and often going on to twice that height. In time the whole plant looks like a huge vase.

'Blaauw' is another good shrub often labelled among the *media* hybrids, but it does not normally exceed 5ft. It is a pretty conifer with feathery sprays of grey-blue of adult form on ascending stems with short laterals.

J. communis, the "common" juniper, widespread throughout the northern hemisphere, is a legion in itself. Its leaves are always of the juvenile type and some varieties produce a "berry" which is used to flavour gin or, in Norway, a brew like beer. A great many of the common junipers are ground-creepers, but overtopping them all is the so-called Irish juniper, *J. c.* 'Hibernica'. This is as slim as a pencil, standing out in the garden like an exclamation mark. It has silvery-grey foliage and can grow to 10ft. Similar to it, but plumper, is the form *suecica*, the Swedish juniper, for which the correct name is 'Pyramidalis'. z2.

J. × media. See *J. chinensis*.

J. sabina is the savin, nearly always dwarf or semi-dwarf and very familiar in the low, tabulated *tamariscifolia*. But there is special ornamental value in the stronger 'Hicksii', which is only semi-prostrate and rather like a Pfitzer in wood-smoke blue. It grows about 4ft and throws out 10ft branches with prickly, juvenile leaves. z4.

J. squamata is a very variable species, ranging from ground-creepers to tree-like bushes, the leaves always of the juvenile type. The most generally valued is 'Meyeri', an elegant shrub when young, with leaves that have the general appearance of steely-blue, for they point forwards along the stem, so revealing their glaucus undersides. The stems arch outwards, giving what is usually called a "vase-like" outline. In time, however, the shrub may grow anything up to 20ft long, when it is less attractive. Its sport 'Blue Star' is a particularly beautiful silvery-blue and is the one you should try to get. z4.

J. virginiana, oddly known in popular speech as the "pencil cedar", is the prolific and hardy parent (z2) of many versatile offspring. Itself it is a very large tree of up to 100ft with both kinds of foliage and it has made marriages with other species. From these we give here two entirely different clones, both of which have special merit in designing the garden picture.

The first, which perhaps ought to have a separate entry, is the hybrid 'Grey Owl', a very elegant shrub of silvery-grey, behaving in the manner of the Pfitzer but not exceeding 4ft.

The other is the remarkable wilding 'Skyrocket', which you might suppose to have undergone a slimming diet, so lean and skinny is it. The foliage is blue-grey. When 16ft high its diameter is still only 1ft. Use it for the same purposes as you would the Irish juniper or the columnar yew and take advantage of its blue tint for contrasts.

PICEA
Spruce

Big, impressive forest trees, with rough bark and sharply pointed leaves. The only one that qualifies for our pages is the dwarf form of the white spruce, **P. glauca albertiana 'Conica'**. This is a neat, compacted pyramid of bright green, just the thing to put among little plants of contrasting behaviour. It is a slow-coach, taking 20 years to reach 6ft, though it usually starts off quite smartly. Found by Professor Rehder and Dr J. C. Jack in the Canadian Rockies and distributed by the Arnold Arboretum. z2.

TAXUS
Yew

In Britain and in northern Europe generally the yew is a tree of immemorial associations. Though it is often associated with churchyards,

it used, in fact, even long before Christianity arrived, to be regarded as a symbol of everlasting life, for it was one of the very few native evergreens and branches of it were strewn on graves. Hence its customary planting in churchyards in olden days. It is a tree that grows to a great age, many in Britain being more than 1,000 years old and one in Scotland being professionally assessed at 1,500 years. Many are older than the churchyards over which they keep watch.

> *Old yew, which graspest at the stones*
> *That name the underlying dead,*
> *Thy fibres net the dreamless head,*
> *Thy roots are wrapt about the bones.*

So Tennyson, mourning at the graveside of a lost friend.

No churchyard thoughts, however, need affect the gardener, for the yew presents him with some splendid ornamental plants. Their foliage resembles a double-sided comb and the leaves are not needles, but are small, narrow, flat leaves. Their "berries" consist of a red, fleshy aril, within which is embedded a poisonous seed, but these are borne only on the female, for yews (usually) are trees of separate sexes. Birds eat the fleshy coating, but discard the pip, this explaining why yew seedlings are found where no yews grow.

The dominant species is **T. baccata**, the "English" yew, though very far from being confined to England. Primarily it is a fairly big, pyramidal tree and, conversely to Lawson's cypress, is more honoured in America than in its native lands and prospers as far north as New York. Of its many forms the one that is generally of greatest value to the gardener is the Irish yew, *T. b.* 'Fastigiata', particularly its gold-flecked version 'Fastigiata Aureomarginata'. Both make perfect, close-knit pillars, though the former may bulge with age if many-stemmed. The golden one is somewhat slow-paced. Oddly, the all-green one is female and the golden male. Both are splendid as specimens on a lawn, collected in little groves or, most impressive of all, when planted as avenues.

Other good versions of the English yew are:

'Dovastoniana', found by John Dovaston, of Westfelton, Shropshire. Very distinctive, gracefully lusty, wide-spreading, with foliage falling curtain-like from its long, horizontal branches, it is usually female. 'Dovastoniana Aurea' is a glowing, golden version of it. Male. If these lose their leaders, by design or accident, they become wide-spreading, shrubby thickets.

'Elegantissima' is a popular, vigorous, wide-spreading yew in which the young leaves are yellow, fading to straw, but retaining the full yellow on the rims.

89. Yews. *Above*, splayed-out foliage of the English yew. *Below*, the upswept leaves of the Japanese yew

'Lutea' has yellow fruits, often spectacular.

'Semperaurea' is a slothful male in which the leaves begin old gold and turn to burnt-orange. All z6.

T. cuspidata, the hardy Japanese yew, is recognisable by having its leaves upswept from the twigs, and yellow on the under-surface. There are several variants, some becoming quite big trees, others dwarfs and others broader than high. Not quite meet for our pages, but 'Aurescens' is an attractive small specimen, shaping itself in the form of a vase, with deep yellow leaves that turn pale green next year. z4.

T. × media, the result of a mating between the English and the Japanese yews, deserves a brief mention, having several good clones, most of which are distinctly adipose. They combine the hardiness of the Japanese and the ornamental quality of the English. 'Hatfieldii', a male, is a favourite, growing 12ft high by 9ft wide in 20 years. 'Hickii' is more definitely erect, like the Irish yew, a plant of great merit, usually female. 'Browniss', by contrast, is a rotund male, wider than high. 'Stoveken', a male, is broadly and densely columnar, 12ft × 6ft after 20 years. z4.

THUJA

Often misspelt Thuya, but correctly so pronounced, the thujas are also called "arbor-vitae" in books from the sixteenth century onwards, but almost never so spoken of in popular speech. They are magnificent, very hardy forest trees, particularly the species *occidentalis*, *orientalis* and *plicata* (the "western red cedar", so called). For our uses chief honour is given to 'Rheingold', very deservedly popular. This is a clone of *T. occidentalis*. An alluring pygmy pyramid of gingery-gold when seen in the nursery, grows very stylishly to 10ft in 20 years, keeping (if properly reared) its finely pointed tip, but swelling broadly at the base. A shrub with a distinguished air that should not be cluttered up, it is altogether a happy note on which to end our pages. z2.

APPENDIX A

Selected Shrubs For Special Purposes

THESE LISTS ARE PUT together as quick reference for the gardener or landscape designer who may have particular problems of soil, situation and climate or one who may seek some special quality in foliage, scent, berry and the like. The lists are not exhaustive and they do not necessarily imply that a shrub recommended for one purpose or set of conditions may not be equally good in another, so that very often one shrub may be found in more than one list. Of course, all in the lists are subject to other conditions being right, such as climate, acidity and humidity. Refer to the Register in all cases.

Starting at ground level, we take soil conditions first.

For Clay
The following are good selections where the soil is heavy.

Abelias, in mild zones

Aralia elata, the Japanese angelica tree

Aucuba japonica, the common "laurel", for really stiff soils

Various bamboos, in damp clay

All barberries

Brooms (*Cytisus* and *Genista*), good in limy clay

Bay (*Laurus nobilis*)

Box (*Buxus*)

Chamaecyparis (neo-cypress)

Chokeberries (*Aronia*) in damp clay

Choisya ternata

Cotoneasters

Flowering currants (*Ribes*)

Deutzias

Dogwoods (*Cornus*)

Escallonias

Forsythias

Hibiscus syriacus

Hypericums. Sun or shade

Junipers

Mahonias, sun or shade

Osmanthus species

Philadelphus

Potentillas, anywhere

Pyracantha ("Firethorn")

Roses

Skimmias, acid soil

Thujas (arbor-vitae)

Viburnums

Weigelas

Witch hazel, acid soil

Yews (*Taxus*)

Damp Soils

This is a wide-ranging term which can include anything from "moist" to "bog". Refer to Register.

Bamboos, most
Calycanthus floridus
Chokeberry (*Aronia*)
Clethras
Cornus alba and *stolonifera*
Elders (*Sambucus*)
Hollies (*Ilex*) several. *I. verticillata* and *glabra* grow in swamps. *I. cassine* in very wet ones
Hydrangeas. Merely moist
Kalmias
Ledum groenlandicum, in cold, peaty, acid bogs
Lindera benzoin, the spice-bush, merely moist
Myrica gale, the bog myrtle
Photinia villosa
Rhododendrons, of variable demands
Sea Buckthorn (*Hippophae rhamnoides*)
Spiraeas, several, merely damp
Willows (*Salix*). Several
Vacciniums, acid soil, but see next list
Viburnum alnifolium, *V. opulus* and others
Zenobia pulverulenta, moist

Dry and Sandy Soils

All plants need a certain amount of water but, of garden plants, the following are the best fitted for standing up to long periods of dryness. Most shrubs with "silvered" leaves are good.

Amorpha canescens (Z2)
Artemisias
Atriplex, for salty sand
Barberries, but not too dry
Bayberries (*Myrica*) other than *M. gale*
Brooms (*Cytisus*, *Genista*, *Spartium*)
Buddleia alternifolia
Callistemons (Australian bottle-brushes)
Caraganas
Ceanothus americanus, but not choice
Cistus species and cvs
Colutea arborescens (bladder senna)
Cotton-lavender (*Santolina chamaecyparissus*)
Elaeagnus angustifolia
Garrya elliptica
Gorse (*Ulex*)
Hamamelis virginiana

Hebes
Ilex crenata, the Japanese holly
Indigofera species
Junipers, most
Kolkwitzia amabilis
Lavenders
Lyciums, very good but not choice
Myrtles
Pernettyas, acid soil
Privets (*Ligustrum*)
Roses: rugosa (very good), *spinosissima* (very good); also *caroliniana* and *virginiana*, both thicket-forming
Rosemary
Sumachs (*Rhus* and *Cotinus*)
Tamarisks, for seashore
Vaccinium pallidum and *V. stamineum*, acid soil
Vitex agnus-castus, the chaste tree
Yuccas, prime choices for very dry places

Acid Soils

As we have seen earlier, almost any shrub will prosper in a soil that is short on lime. Those that must positively have an acid soil and no other are themselves very numerous and we can only enumerate them generally (though very often a neutral soil does just as well). They include:

Rhododendrons, witch hazel, pieris, pernettya, desfontainia, embothrium, zenobia, clethra, kalmias, enkianthus, eucryphia, fothergillas, leucothoë, vaccineums and most heathers other than the ericas carnea and mediterranean and the hybrid darleyensis. Camellias also enjoy acid soils but are quite at home in neutral ones. In many genera there are some species that demand acid soil but their brethren do not, such as *Viburnum lantanoides*, the "hobble bush", and *V. cassonoides*, both acid-lovers.

Virtually all roses succeed well in acid soil, though they do not positively demand it.

For the Seaside

Of course, a great many plants of all sorts are happy in a seaside air, which is usually moist, and relatively balmy, but only a limited number of shrubs actually enjoy or tolerate the salty taste of sea-spray and the rude winds that bring it. The following will do so in greater or lesser degree:

Atriplex species, for salt spray
Baccharis halimifolia, the same
Bayberries (*Myrica*), especially *M. pensylavanica*
Buckthorns (*Rhamnus*), especially *R. alaterna*
Cotoneasters, most
Cytisus, most
Elaeagnus species
Escallonias, in mild zones
Gorse (*Ulex*), very good
Griselinia littoralis, in warm zones, spray-proof
Halimodendron halodendron, spray-proof
Hippophae rhamnoides, spray-proof
Hydrangea macrophylla varieties
Lavatera olbia (Mallow)
Lavenders
Lyciums, excellent
Olearias (daisy bushes), in mild climates
Pittosporums, in mild climates
Prunus maritima, the beach plum
Roses, many, including *rugosa* (on the seashore), *spinosissima* (the Scotch rose, in sand), *virginiana* (thicket-forming)
Rosemary
Spiraeas, most
Suaeda vera (*fruticosa*), in brackish spots
Tamarisks (*Tamarix*), spray-proof
Viburnums, most
Willows (*Salix*), most, especially *S. caprea*
Yuccas

In Cities

The following are among those shrubs that have been found to be the most resistant to the pollution of the air in cities.

Aesculus parviflora (dwarf chestnut)
Bayberry (*Myrica pennsylvanica*)
Buckthorns (*Rhamnus*)
Chokeberry (*Aronia arbutifolia*)
Elaeagnus angustifolia
Fatsia japonica
Forsythias
Fringe-tree (*Chionanthus virginicus*)
Hawthorns (*Crataegus*)
Hibicus syriacus
Hypericums
Kerria japonica
Lilacs (*Syringa*)

Lindera benzoin (Spice-tree)
Lyciums, but not choice
Philadelphus
Pittosporum tobira
Potentillas
Privet (*Ligusttrum*)
Japanese quinces
Sorbarias
Spiraeas, most
Sumachs
Viburnums
Xanthorhiza
Yuccas, but place with care

In Shade

We have noticed in Chapter 3 that "shade" may mean anything from a gentle dappling to a deep sepulchral gloom. The following shrubs will flourish or exist in deep or fairly deep shade, in addition to the "ground cover" creepers of Chapter 5. We omit also the obvious rhododendron, because the multitudinous species and hybrids differ widely in their adaptability to shade. All will do in a certain amount of shade, but the "ironclads" prosper in full sun.

Box (*Buxus*)
Butcher's broom (*Ruscus aculeatus*) in Stygian gloom
Daphne laureola and *D. pontica*
Elaeagnus pungens
Euonymus fortunei
Fatsia japonica
Hollies (*Ilex*), all tolerate a good deal of shade, but *I. aquifolium* (the "common" holly) and the hybrid *altaclarensis* accept quite deep shade
Hypericums
Laurels of common speech (*Aucuba*)
Mahonias
Paeonia delavayi
Paxistima canbyi, moist shade, dwarf
Photinias, fairly deep shade
Privet (*Ligustrum*)
Ribes alpinum, deep shade
Rubus (bramble) *odoratus*, *spectabilis* and *tricolor*, dense shade beneath trees
Skimmias

Vacciniums, acid soil
Viburnums, many, especially *V. acerifolium* and
   V. davidii
Yews (*Taxus*)

Silver and grey

The following short selection may help gardeners when looking for some sparkle in his picture. We omit those, many in number, that have merely a pewter-like patina and choose only those that are more positively silver or soft dove-grey or chalk-white. All but one need full sun and most of them like a dry soil.

Artemisias, silvery-grey, warm spots
Buddleia alternifolia 'Argentea'
Buddleia fallowiana
Calluna vulgaris 'Silver Queen' and 'Anthony
   Davis' (see under Heathers), dove-grey
Cotton-lavender (*Santolina chamaecyparissus*),
   dwarf
Caryopteris incana
Elaeagnus angustifolia, the oleaster, and *E. commutata*, the "silver berry"
Euryops acraeus, perhaps the most brilliantly
   silver of all.
Fejoia sellowiana, rather tender
Helichrysums, white-felted, tender
Olearia mollis and *O. moschata*
Perovskias, very effective
Phlomis fruticosa (Jerusalem sage, pale grey
   felted)
Potentilla 'Beesii'
Senecios, especially *S. compactus* (chalk-white)

S. 'Sunshine' (lamb's wool, see Register) and
   S. leucostachys
Chamaecyparis pisifera 'Snow', whitens only in
   shade.

For degenerate soils

The following tough customers are resistant to the most unpropitious soils, though not all are of great beauty. You will vastly improve their chances by digging in organic matter — compost, manure, old leaf-soil, old turf of any sort and imported fresh soil. By these means (and by hard work) even an old coal slag-heap in England has been converted into a most attractive garden. Surprisingly many barberries flourish, including *B. thunbergii* and its variants, *B.* × *ottawensis* and *B. dictophylla*.
   Others are:
Gorse (*Ulex*)
Elders, including the golden *Sambucus racemosa*
   'Plumosa Aurea'
Spiraea japonica 'Bumalda'
Box-thorn (*Lycium*)
Buckthorn (*Rhamnus*)
Bladder senna (*Colutea*)
Bupleurums
Hawthorns (*Crataegus*)
Symphoricarpos
Ligustrum obtusifolium and *L. regelianum* (the
   regel privet)
Genista tinctoria (dyer's greenweed)
Myrica pensylvanica
Vaccinium angustifolium

APPENDIX B

Glossary

THIS SHORT LIST OF definitions is confined to the terms that are used in this book, plus one or two others that may be useful.

Acid soil. One with a low lime content.

Alkaline soil. The opposite to acid.

Alternate. Of leaves, not opposite to one another on their stem.

Anther. The pollen-bearing part, usually coloured, of the male organ (the stamen) of the flower.

Axil. The angle between two branches or between a stem and a leaf-stalk.

Bipinnate. Doubly pinnate. See pinnate.

Bloom (on a fruit or leaf). A fine, powder-like, waxy deposit.

Bract. A modified leaf at the base of a flower or cluster of flowers, sometimes very colourful, as in a poinsettia.

Breastwood (on shrubs trained close to a wall). Shoots that sprout outwards.

Bud. There are flower buds and growth buds. Horticulturally, means not only an obvious bud but also any incipient swelling, often axillary. Important to distinguish.

Calcareous, of soil. Chalky or limy.

Calcifuge. A plant that fails in limy soil.

Calyx (pl. calyces). The circlet or whorl of sepals that encloses the petals of a flower before it opens.

Capsule. A dry seed-pod of several cells.

Carpel. A simple pistil or a member of a compound pistil.

Chlorosis. Loss of green pigment in a leaf.

Clone. A fixed, unvarying individual plant, perpetuated by cuttings, layers or other "vegetative" means, not by seed. Thus Rose 'Peace' is a clone, but *Rosa canina* is not. Virtually any plant name printed in Roman type within inverted commas is a clone. See also "cultivar" and "variety".

Compound, applied usually to leaves, being a leaf divided into several leaflets, whether pinnate, palmate, trifoliate etc. See under each and in the drawings.

Corolla. Collective term for the whole assembly of petals in a flower.

Corymb. A flat-topped or domed flower head, with the outer petals flowering first and their foot-stalk springing from separate points in the stem. Compare with umbel and cyme.

Cultivar (abbreviated to cv). Botanist's technical jargon for a plant originating under cultivation or sometimes a variant occurring in the wild and maintained in gardens as a clone. Much the same thing as a clone and printed in the same way.

Cyme. In its simplest form consists of a single

flower terminating a stem and a flowered stalk below it. More often there are two flower stalks below the terminal one and each one branches twice again and so on; this is a "dichotomous" cyme.

Digitate. A form of compound leaf, with finger-like leaves arising from a common point. See illustration of Vitex.

Dioecious. Having male and female flowers on separate plants, as in most hollies, etc.

Double. Of flowers, having more than one ring or circlet of petals.

Downy. Softly hairy.

Fastigiate. Erect, with the branches pressed close together, like a bundle of rods.

Fibrous. Of roots, thin but dense.

Filament. The stalk, usually very slender, of the male stamen, with the anther at its tip.

Florets. The small, individual flowers in a dense inflorescence.

Glabrous. Smooth, hairless.

Glaucous. Covered with a bluish or blue-grey bloom.

Indumentum. Dense, hairy coating.

Inflorescence. The method by which a plant arranges its whole floral display, whether "solitary", in "spikes", in "panicles", etc.

Involucre. A ring or whorl of bracts surrounding the base of a flower or cluster of flowers.

Leaflet. One of the members of a compound leaf.

Lobe. Any protruding segment of a leaf, whether pointed, as in most maples, or rounded, as in the currant, or sinuous, as in most oaks; applied also to flowers.

Monoecious. Having separate male and female flowers but borne on the same plant.

Mulch. A covering of the soil with decaying leaves, manure, grass-mowings etc, to provide natural food for the plant, preserve moisture, protect it against winter cold, deter weeds and finally to rot down into plant food.

"New Wood". A stem, branch or twig that has sprouted and grown in the current season.

Node. A joint where a leaf-stem joins its parent stem.

Obovate. Used mostly of leaf shapes. Having the outline of an egg, more or less oval, but broadest below the middle.

"Old Wood". A shoot that grew last year or earlier.

Palmate. Of leaves. Having lobes or sections radiating like fingers from the palm of a hand.

Panicle. The usual definition of "a branched raceme" evades the issue. It is a spike or raceme with several little branches, themselves branching again, as in a lilac.

Pedicel. The stalk of an individual flower.

Peduncle. The stalk of a flower cluster, or the stalk of a "solitary" flower.

Perianth. A floral structure in which the calyx and the corolla are more or less fused together, as in many bulbs.

Petiole. The stalk of a leaf.

Pinnate. A compound leaf having leaflets on both sides of a central rib, as in the ash, the rose, the robinia and many other plants.

Pistil. The female organ of a flower, comprising stigma (usually protruding), style (supporting the stigma) and ovary (within which the seed forms).

Plicate. Folded into plaits.

Raceme. A spike of flowers on which each floret has a short stalk.

Rotate. Of a corolla, having a flat, circular limb, perhaps with a very short tube.

Scale. Minute leaf or bract or gland clinging closely to a stem, giving it a rough appearance, sometimes applied to a leaf or flower.

Scion. A cultivated variety of a tree or shrub that is grafted or budded on a different rootstock, usually of a wild species.

Sepal. One of the leaf-like members that collectively form the calyx surrounding a flower-bud.

Serrate. Saw-edged.

Sessile. Stalkless.

Single. Of flower, having only one ring or circlet of petals, as in the dog-rose and common buttercup.

Solitary. An inflorescence consisting of only one flower, as in magnolias.

Spike. An inflorescence having stalkless flowers on a central axis, as in the lavender.

Spit. The depth of one spade in digging (10in).

Sport. A shoot occurring by chance that differs from its parent in flower or leaf or other feature. Often the origin of very good cultivars when propagated, but sometimes, as in variegated shrubs, apt to "revert" to its parent.

Spur. A short, woody projection on a branch on which a cluster of flowers or fruits may form, as in the apple and pear. Also a narrow, tubular extension of a flower, usually posterior and secreting the honey, as in the delphinium and columbine.

Stamen. The male organ of a flower, consisting of a pollen-bearing anther supported by a filament.

Stigma. The sticky tip of the pistil, the female organ in a flower; it receives the male pollen.

Stock. The rooted growth, often of a wild species, on which the cultivated scion is grafted or budded.

Stolon. An underground shoot that produces a new plant at its tips.

Stoma (pl. stomata). Minute orifices on leaves which constitute breathing pores.

Sucker. Shoots that spring up from underground buds on the roots of a plant. Usually undesirable, especially if from the root-stock on which a desired scion has been grafted or budded.

Umbel. A flat or slightly domed inflorescence of many florets, the stalks of which all spring from the same point (like the spokes of an umbrella). Compare with corymb.

Variety. Strict professional botanists nowadays use this term to specify natural variants (other than individuals) found in the wild and print it in italics, e.g. *Erica arborea* var *alpina* (maybe without the "var"). The International Code governing plant names, however, specifically permits "variety" to be used for a cultivar also, and this is its use by the common man (who has no means of distinguishing) and also often our own use for the sake of simplicity.

Vegetative propagation. The raising of

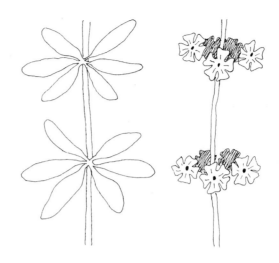

90.   Whorls. *Left*, of leaves. *Right*, of flowers.

plants by cuttings, budding, division etc, not by seed, ensuring that the progeny are exactly like their parents.

Whorl (whirl). Several leaves, petals or other members springing from the same point and arranged in a ring.

Some Latin and Greek Terms

Below is a sprinkling of some of the Latin and Greek words, suffixes and prefixes more commonly used in plant names. They may help one to understand the character of the plant and overcome the feelings of rage of gardeners who have forgotten or have never learnt the ancient classics. Many are obvious as in *rosea, alpina, suspensus* and so on. Several denote the countries of their origin, as in *japonicus, americanus,* etc.

Others are named after persons, as in *davidii, mariesii, fortunei* or, in the feminine, *wilsonae.* Where the terms are adjectival we give the masculine.

acantho- Spiny, as in *triacanthos,* 3-thorned.
acaulis. Stemless.
alatus. Winged.
albus. White.
-anus, -eanus and *-ianus.* Pertaining to; usually of a person, as in *davidianus.*
angusti-. Narrow.
-anthus. Flower, as in polyanthus.
arboreus. Tree-like.
argenteus. Silvery.
argutus. Sharply notched.
atro-. Deep in colour, as in *atropurpureus.*
aureus. (and *aureo-* in compound words). Golden.
baccatus. Berry-like, pulpy.
bi- Two or twice (Latin).
brevi- Short.
carneus. Flesh-coloured.
-cephalus. Head, as in *macrocephalus,* large-headed.

chamae- ("ch" pronounced "K"). Close to the ground.
cinereus. Ashen.
coccineus ("koksineus"). Scarlet.
coeruleus or *caeruleus* ("serrooleus"). Blue.
cordi- Heart-shaped, as in *cordifolius,* heart-shaped leaf.
crenatus. Having rounded teeth.
cyanus. Dark blue.
-dendron. Tree.
dentatus. Toothed; *denticulatus,* fine-toothed.
di- or *dis-.* Two or twice (Greek), as in *discolor,* two-coloured.
dissectus. Appearing to have been cut into many narrow strips.
elatus. Tall.
-ense or *-ensis.* Denotes a place, usually of origin, as in *kewensis* and *canadensis.*
eximius. Beautiful.
flore pleno, (often abreviated to *fl. pl.* or *f. p.*). Double-flowered.
-folius. Leaved, as in *longifolius.*
fruticosus or *frutescens.* Shrubby, often used to distinguish between a shrubby species and an herbaceous one, as in potentillas.

graveolens. Of unpleasant smell.

-ianthus. Purplish.

hetero- Diverse, as in *heterophyllus*, having leaves of different shapes.

hispidus. Bristly.

hirsutus. Hairy.

hortensis. Of gardens.

incanus. Hoary, white.

integerrimus. Of leaves, toothless.

lacti- Milk-coloured.

lati- Broad, as in *latifolius*, broad-leaved.

leavigatus and *laevis*. Smooth.

leuco- White.

littoralis. Of the seashore.

luteus. Yellow.

macro- Large, as in *macrocephalus*, large-headed.

maculatus. Spotted, splashed.

micro- Small.

mollis (*molle* in compound words). Soft.

mono- One or once.

nanus. Dwarf.

nitidus. Shining.

nutans. Nodding.

officinalis. Of commercial or medicinal use.

oides. Resembling, as in *jasminoides*.

oxy- Sharp, as in *oxyacanthos*, sharp-spined.

-phyllus. Leaved, as in *microphyllus*, small-leaved.

platy-. Broad.

plicatus. Folded, pleated.

poly- Many, as in *polyanthus*.

praecox. Early, precocious.

procumbens. Procumbent, lying on the ground.

pubescens. Covered with short, soft hairs.

pulverulentus. As though dusted with powder.

pumilus. Dwarf.

racemosus. With flowers in racemes.

radicans. Having rooting stems, of prostrate creepers.

repens and *reptans*. Creeping.

reticulatus. With net-like veins.

ruber (*rubri-* and *rubro-* in compound words). Red.

salicifolius. With leaves like the willow's (*salix*).

sanguineus. Blood-red.

sax- Rock-loving, saxatile. The Latin version is *saxatilis*, the neuter being *saxatile* ("saxat'illy").

scaber. Rough to the touch.

schiz- ("skys"). Split.

serratus. Saw-toothed.

serrulatus. Finely saw-toothed.

sessilis. Stalkless. The neuter is *sessile* ("sessilly").

set- Bristly.

sinensis and *sino-* Chinese.

speciosus and *spectabilis*. Showy.

spicatus. Spike-like.

stell- Star-like.

steno- Narrow, as in *stenophyllus*, narrow-leaved.

stig- marked, pitted, scarred.

strictus. Erect.

sub- partially.

sylvaticus and *sylvestris*. Of woodlands.

tenuis. Slender, thin.

tern- In threes.

tetra- In fours, as in *tetraptera*, 4-winged.

tomentosus. Thickly hairy.

trachy- Rough, as in *trachyphyllus*, rough-leaved.

tri- Three.

tricho- Hairy.

vagans. Wandering, spreading.

venustus. Beautiful.

villosus. Having shaggy hairs.

virgatus. Twiggy.

viti- Usually in *vitifolium*, having leaves like those of the grape-vine ("Vitty").

vulgaris. Common, wild.

xanth- Yellow.

APPENDIX C

Metric conversion table

1 inch	=	$2\frac{1}{2}$ centimetres (approx)
2 „	=	5 „
3 „	=	$7\frac{1}{2}$ „
4 „	=	10 „
6 „	=	15 „
1 foot	=	30 „
3 „	=	·914metres (say 90cm)
4 „	=	1·2metres (say 120cm)
5 „	=	1·5metres (say 150cm)
6 „	=	2metres
8 „	=	2·5metres
10 „	=	3metres
30 „	=	9metres

INDEX

Except for heathers, brooms, bamboos and conifers, all the genera in the Register are entered alphabetically; usually their species are also and are printed in conspicuous type. There is, therefore, no need to include them in the index, which is confined to the following classes only:

Topics in Part I

the aforesaid heathers and other groups

adventitious entries in the Register

vernacular or "popular" names of plants and their botanical identities; these occupy a disproportionate share of the index but, however fanciful, they are included for the benefit of readers who know no other.

The entry for camellias, for example, contains only those mentioned generally in Part I and the full treatment of them is to be found in their alphabetical place in the Register, and so are not recorded here. Sometimes, however, as in *Rosa*, it is desirable to enter the names of the older cultivars so that the reader will know under which species or group to find them.

The abbreviation "sp" ("spp" in the plural) means "species".